# Marketing
# Financial

ONE WEEK LOAN

## Second edition

Edited by
**Christine Ennew**
**Trevor Watkins**
**Mike Wright**

D1393093

BUTTERWORTH
HEINEMANN

For our parents

Butterworth-Heinemann
Linacre House, Jordan Hill, Oxford OX2 8DP
225 Wildwood Avenue, Woburn, MA 01801-2041
A division of Reed Educational and Professional Publishing Ltd

$\mathcal{R}$ A member of the Reed Elsevier plc group

OXFORD  AUCKLAND  BOSTON
JOHANNESBURG  MELBOURNE  NEW DELHI

First published 1990
Reprinted 1991, 1993
Second edition 1995
Reprinted 1997, 1998, 2000

**British Library Cataloguing in Publication Data**
A catalogue record for this book is available from the British Library.

ISBN 0 7506 2247 4

Typeset by Keyword Services Ltd, Wallington, Surrey
Printed and bound in Great Britain by Scotprint

FOR EVERY TITLE THAT WE PUBLISH, BUTTERWORTH-HEINEMANN
WILL PAY FOR BTCV TO PLANT AND CARE FOR A TREE.

# Contents

Preface     v

Introduction     vii

1 **The changing environment of financial services**
James F. Devlin and Mike Wright     1

2 **Understanding consumers and markets**
Sally McKechnie and Tina Harrison     33

3 **Developing marketing strategy**
Christine Ennew     60

4 **The financial services marketing mix**
Christine Ennew and Trevor Watkins     86

5 **Product strategy**
Christine Ennew     96

6 **Advertising and promotion**
Des Thwaites     113

7 **Pricing**
David Llewellyn and Leigh Drake     138

8 **Distribution channels**
Barry Howcroft and Julia Kiely     174

9 **Customer care and service quality**
Barbara R. Lewis     193

10 **Bank marketing**
Mike Wright and Barry Howcroft     212

11 **Insurance marketing**
Stephen Diacon and Trevor Watkins     236

12 **Building society marketing**
Donald W. Cowell     262

13 **The marketing of unit and investment trusts**
Paul Draper     278

14 **Credit cards**
Steve Worthington     294

15 **Case studies**     307

References     378

Index     399

# Preface

Since the publication of the first edition of *Marketing Financial Services*, interest in the topic has continued to grow as is evidenced by an increased volume of research on the subject, a growing number of courses which address financial services marketing and, perhaps most significantly, an increased number of competitors to this book. The combined effects of increased competition, rapid change within the sector and an apparent growth in demand lead us to feel justified in preparing a second edition of *Marketing Financial Services*. Once again, we have drawn on the experience of a number of established writers in different subject areas to provide specialist chapters dealing with a range of topics. All chapters have been substantially rewritten and a number of new topics have been added including chapters on the financial services marketing mix, customer care and service quality and credit cards.

As we indicated in the first edition, rapid changes in the environment in which financial services firms operated forced many organizations to develop a much more proactive approach to their marketing efforts. By the late 1980s, most had established Marketing Departments and computerized marketing information systems were extensively used. Indeed, many institutions actively sought to recruit marketers with experience outside the financial service sector in order to strengthen their marketing commitment and expertise. Nevertheless, the problems of the recession in the early 1990s have created numerous difficulties for providers of financial services. Consumers were buying less of everything – including financial services – and in many cases it was marketing which suffered heavily from job cuts designed to help organizations cope with reductions in demand. At the same time, many of the ventures undertaken during the boom conditions of the late 1980s were proving to be less than successful requiring, in many instances, large-scale divestments and product withdrawals. Increasingly, over-capacity has become a cause for concern and is likely to result in a further consolidation in the numbers of financial services retailers.

More seriously, perhaps, many commentators have begun to express doubts about the strength of the firm's commitment to marketing in the financial services sector. Increasingly, such firms came under criticism suggesting that, while they adopted many of the trappings of marketing, they failed to fully appreciate its substance. Most recently, Michael Baker expressed the view that bank marketing may have been more myth than reality, while research by David Knights, Hugh Wilmott and Glenn Morgan has suggested that much financial services marketing was merely rhetoric rather than a true commitment to marketing as an approach to business. Academic concern about the degree of commitment to marketing among financial services organizations has been reinforced by much of the recent adverse publicity concerning the mis-selling of pensions and other life insurance policies and growing concern about the adequacy of the current regulatory system.

It is our intention that this text should identify and elaborate on these and other important issues which confront those involved in the marketing of financial services and suggest ways forward for both practitioners and for academics. With this aim in mind, the book can be seen as falling into four broad sections. First there are chapters which address the changing nature of the environment confronting financial services firms. These are followed by a group of chapters dealing with the principles of marketing as they are applied in financial services and, thirdly, there is a series of sector-specific chapters that look in detail at the application of marketing techniques and marketing approaches. The final section incorporates a selection of case studies previously published in the companion text *Cases in Marketing Financial Services*.

In preparing this book, we owe debts of gratitude to a number of people. First and foremost to our authors for the speedy delivery of their various chapters. Second, to Jonathan Glasspool of Butterworth-Heinemann, who has supported the project throughout. Third, we must thank Sandra Mienczakowski and Joanne Ball for their help in the preparation of the manuscript. The editors remain solely responsible for any outstanding errors.

Christine Ennew
Trevor Watkins
Mike Wright

# Introduction

Marketing is widely recognized as being a key to success for any organization, irrespective of its size or the sector of the economy in which it operates. The concept of 'marketing' is one that is widely used and misused. At one level, it is a generic term used to describe a range of functions which organizations perform including advertising, branding, packaging, pricing, product management and distribution. At this level, marketing is essentially concerned with what people and organizations do. At a deeper level, the term is often used to describe a business philosophy which guides the organization's activities. This marketing orientation views organizational success as being driven by the provision of long-term consumer satisfaction and emphasizes the importance of ensuring an organization-wide commitment to meeting market needs. Developing marketing functions may prove relatively straightforward; developing a marketing orientation with its focus on and commitment to the market can prove considerably more complex.

The development of marketing in the financial services sector has been slow and for a long time the industry was seen as primarily product led. Until recently, marketing in most financial service organizations was largely synonymous with advertising and public relations and it was not until the 1970s that marketing departments were formed on any scale (Newman, 1984). Even then, the role of marketing tended to be more tactical than strategic and marketing tended to be seen as a relatively low status activity (Hooley and Mann, 1988; Morgan and Piercy, 1990). Despite the adverse effects of the recession, the marketing activities of financial services organizations have expanded considerably over the last five years. Companies in the sector are still among the heaviest users of direct mail and have a substantial presence in television and media advertising. Sponsorship and competitions have grown in importance as forms of promotion, salesforces have expanded and the pace of new product development has been rapid. As a function, it would appear that there can be little doubt that marketing has established itself in the UK financial services sector.

The strength of marketing as a business philosophy is perhaps more open to question. In the late 1980s, Clarke, Edward, Gardner and Molyneux (1988) suggested that the UK banks were approaching a 'marketing control' phase in which marketing would provide the guiding principles for the organization as a whole. Thwaites and Lynch (1992) were less sanguine about the speed of development of marketing as an approach to business. In a study of some seventy UK building societies, they found that around 40 per cent could be described as having marketing as a guiding philosophy while a further 40 per cent were much more concerned about marketing as a functional activity; the remaining societies had very limited or negative perspectives on marketing. More recently, it has been suggested that many financial services organizations may have been happy to adopt the trappings of marketing but have failed to acknowledge the substance (Baker, 1993) and some commentators would go further and suggest that there may be a more fundamental contradiction between the concept of customer need satisfaction and competition in financial services.

While the extent to which financial services organizations are (or can be) truly marketing oriented may be open to debate, there is little doubt that the range of marketing activities in these organizations has increased considerably. Those organizations considering dismissing marketing as either a function or an orientation may be well advised to think again; consumers and consumer groups are increasing in importance and power and potential new entrants are monitoring the financial services sector closely. The success of Marks & Spencer in retail financial services and the success of General Motors (GM) in the credit card market are both indicative of the impact which non-traditional providers can have on the market. Indeed, in a more general study, Speed and Smith (1993) provide evidence for a link between strategic marketing decisions and organizational performance in financial services.

The financial services sector has, in recent years, been among the fastest growing areas in the UK economy. Progressive deregulation, starting with the Competition and Credit Control document in 1971 and culminating in the European Community's 1992 programme, has dramatically altered the operating environment facing suppliers of financial services. These changes, in conjunction with increases in personal income and wealth, expansion in other sectors of the economy, trends towards globalization and developments in information technology, have created an increasingly competitive and demand-driven financial services sector. As a consequence of these changes, the sector has witnessed considerable innovation not only in terms of products but perhaps more importantly in terms of processes and market arrangements (Carter, Chiplin and Lewis, 1986).

Initially, the pattern of deregulation probably had its greatest impact in the corporate banking sector and was fuelled by the expanding role of multinational firms. Many banks, particularly the American and Japanese, tended to follow their corporate customers into non-domestic markets. Once a position had been established, the maintenance of that position required strategies to extend their customer base to include national, corporate and even, in some cases, personal customers. Although these developments were perhaps most noticeable during the 1970s, the EC's 1992 programme has resulted in a further wave of international expansion among financial services organizations (Wright and Ennew, 1990).

The pattern of change was more rapid in the 1980s and the impact on retail markets was much greater. The sequence of the 'Big Bang', the Building Societies Act and the Financial Services Act increased competition, particularly in retail markets, and forced many suppliers to move away from the supply-orientated approach which they had traditionally adopted in those markets. The barriers which had delineated retail and corporate markets and which had separated large and small-scale investors were slowly being eroded. Similarly, the distinctions between institutions such as banks and building societies were breaking down as organizations sought to supply an increasingly broad range of products. Despite the expansion in demand for financial products, the battle for market share has increased in importance and with many organizations offering a much broader range of products the strategy of cross-selling to an existing consumer base has become a key component of marketing.

The growing importance of marketing and its strategic function in the financial services sector provides part of the rationale for the present book. However, we should consider whether this need for a greater understanding of marketing issues in the financial services sector warrants separate treatment. A variety of texts deal with general marketing issues and a separate treatment for service products in the literature is justified on the basis of certain distinctive characteristics (Cowell, 1984). These include, first, the fact that services are intangible; the consumer has nothing physical to show for the purchase, the service cannot be displayed or tested prior to use. Second, services are typically inseparable which means that they are produced and consumed simultaneously and production requires the presence of the consumer. Accordingly, services are also perishable and cannot be stored for future sale. Third, as a consequence of inseparability services are heterogeneous; quality control is difficult and the quality of the service itself is often highly dependent on the quality of the service provider. These particular characteristics of services mean that the application of marketing principles and the emphasis placed on specific areas can be quite different from the case of product marketing.

Furthermore, in the case of financial services the complexity of many products, particularly on the investment side, creates problems for the presentation of such products to the consumer. This adds to the dimension of intangibility in that not only are financial services impalpable in the sense that they have no physical form, they are also intangible from a mental point of view in that they are not easily defined and may be difficult to understand (Donnelly et al., 1985). A further, and related complication, from the marketing perspective, is the implicit responsibility which financial services organizations have in relation to the management of funds and the financial advice they supply to their customers. This element has been incorporated into notions of 'best advice' as a component of the recent regulatory changes. Despite these formal requirements, any organization involved in the provision of financial services must retain an awareness of the magnitude of the impact which their marketing and selling activities can have on the lifestyle of an individual or the prosperity of a company.

As marketing has increased in importance as a management function in financial services, a growing literature appeared on the application of marketing techniques, both at a strategic and at a tactical level. Initially, much of the literature focused attention on the banking sector (Donnelly et al., 1985; McIver and Naylor, 1986; Marsh, 1988), in part at least because of the requirements of professional examinations. More recently, other texts have focused on corporate financial services (Stevenson, 1989), insurance (Dyer and Watkins, 1988) and retailing (McGoldrick and Greenland, 1994).

In this text, we seek to provide a thorough coverage of the key issues which surround the marketing of financial services. It is anticipated that the reader will have some familiarity with basic marketing concepts and, accordingly, the authors concentrate on illustrating the application of these concepts in the financial services sector. The diversity of the financial services industry seemed to warrant an approach which brought together experts in the various sectors. Indeed, while the boundaries between the activities of the different financial institutions have become increasingly blurred, most organizations can still identify a core business and as a consequence still face a number of distinct marketing issues. Indeed, although it is common to talk about financial services products and institutions it would be rare to encounter a financial services marketing manager.

The book is organized into four broad sections. The first section focuses on the financial services environment and the development of marketing strategy. In Chapter 1, James Devlin and Mike Wright examine supply side developments in some depth, paying particular attention to regulation, globalization and technology. Chapter 2 by Sally McKechnie and Tina Harrison focuses on demand side developments and considers consumer buying behaviour and market segmentation as well as examining trends in the purchase of financial services. Finally in this section, Christine Ennew examines the development of marketing strategies for financial services organizations in Chapter 3.

The second section of the book deals with the more tactical aspects of marketing. In Chapter 4, Christine Ennew and Trevor Watkins examine the general concept of the marketing mix and its applicability in the financial services sector. In Chapter 5 Christine Ennew then deals with the issues surrounding the management of the product component of the mix. Advertising and promotion are discussed in Chapter 6 by Des Thwaites, and the issues surrounding pricing are reviewed by David Llewellyn and Leigh Drake in Chapter 7. In Chapter 8 Barry Howcroft and Julia Kiely address direct and indirect distribution systems and examine the factors driving change in delivery systems. The last chapter in this section, Chapter 9 by Barbara Lewis, deals with the increasingly important issues of service quality and customer care.

The third section of the book consists of sector-specific case studies which seek to highlight the particular marketing problems which confront different organizations. Rather than conforming to a standard approach, each of these chapters employs different analytical frameworks in order to reinforce the practical application of concepts discussed in earlier chapters. In Chapter 10, Mike Wright and Barry Howcroft examine the development of bank marketing and provide a useful example of the application of the Ansoff matrix. Chapter 11 by Steve Diacon and Trevor Watkins examines the marketing of insurance using both the market mix framework and the product life cycle. Porter's generic strategies are illustrated in the context of the building society sector in Chapter 12 by Don Cowell. In Chapter 13, Paul Draper analyses the marketing of unit

and investment trusts, paying particular attention to the impact of regulatory changes on the marketing activities of organizations in this sector.
In Chapter 14, Steve Worthington examines the development of credit
cards and their marketing implications.

The final section, comprising Chapter 15, contains a range of case studies previously published in the companion text *Cases in Marketing
Financial Services* (Ennew, Watkins and Wright, 1993), which support
the material presented in the preceding chapters.

# 1 The changing environment of financial services

## James F. Devlin and Mike Wright

## 1.1  Introduction

The structure of the UK financial services sector has changed markedly over the past twenty-five years. Prior to this the market was characterized by functional demarcation and regulatory restrictions, the result being limited competition both domestically and internationally. The forces of deregulation, advancing technology and a general trend towards globalization have vastly increased the competitive pressures within the financial services market which has in turn affected both the structure and operation of firms within the industry. Two examples help illustrate such developments.

In 1968, at the time of its creation by the merger of three smaller banks, the National Westminster, the UK's largest clearing bank, provided few services beyond traditional retail banking. Two decades later its interests have spread worldwide and include venture capital, a substantial network of automatic teller machines and a wide range of corporate financial services. In the late 1980s the bank's strategy continued to evolve with the divestment of certain activities, most notably its unit trust management company following the decision to register as an independent intermediary under the Financial Services Act. This decision has now been reversed and National Westminster is entering into a joint venture with Clerical Medical and staff at NatWest branches will be tied agents for the new subsidiary.

Up to 1986, the Abbey National, as the UK's second largest building society, was restricted to the provision of housing finance, various retail savings products and the introduction of insurance policies associated with house purchase. In 1989, the Abbey National became the first building society to convert to a public quoted company and had developed an extensive range of new products including a substantial estate agency network and an office in Spain.

These two illustrations of developments in products and markets reflect major environmental changes which began in the late 1960s and which continue to influence the behaviour of financial services firms. In any market economy, change is a continuous, dynamic process. Competition between firms is an important factor in effecting change but is itself influenced by the degree to which profitable opportunities are perceived to be available, the regulatory framework and changes in information technology which may reduce costs and introduce new methods of distribution. Environmental change may also encourage organizations to alter their structure (internally and externally) in order to enhance their ability to exploit new market opportunities. All these factors provide the context in which the marketing effort of financial services firms will be developed. The changing environment for financial services is examined in this chapter under the following headings: changes in the nature of personal assets and liabilities, changes in the regulatory framework, the trend towards globalization, the effects of fundamental changes in information technology, and the redrawing of the boundaries of financial services firms.

## 1.2 Personal assets and liabilities in the UK

Financial assets of the personal sector in the UK increased almost eightfold in current price terms from 1978 (Table 1.1). Financial liabilities, such as loans and consumer credit rose by a similar amount in the same period (Table 1.2). The last fifteen years have also witnessed considerable shifts in the composition of personal sector assets and liabilities in the UK. These changes have been closely associated with a continuing emphasis on individual home ownership, reinforced by a fundamental change in attitudes towards share ownership ushered in by the election of the first Thatcher government in 1979.

In broad terms, there has been a shift towards investment in equities, either directly or indirectly (Table 1.1). The importance of equity in insurance and pension funds has become particularly dominant over this period, as personal pensions have been promoted by the government and sold (or oversold) zealously by financial institutions. Direct investment in equities forms a higher proportion of wealth than in 1984, this form of investment having recovered from the setback of the stockmarket crash of 1987. The proportion of personal sector assets held in unit trusts almost doubled in the fifteen years from 1978, but still accounted for only 2 per cent of the total. Even so, unit trusts form an important part of the product

**Table 1.1** *Financial assets of the UK personal sector (percentages)*

|                                        | 1978    | 1984    | 1992      | 1993      |
|----------------------------------------|---------|---------|-----------|-----------|
| Notes and coin                         | 15.0    | 12.3    | 13.1      | 11.2      |
| Building society deposits              | 17.3    | 16.3    | 13.2      | 11.6      |
| UK shares and loan stocks              | 14.2    | 10.9    | 12.3      | 14.0      |
| Unit trusts                            | 1.2     | 1.4     | 1.6       | 2.0       |
| Equity in insurance and pension funds  | 31.7    | 42.1    | 49.4      | 52.5      |
| Other                                  | 20.6    | 17.0    | 10.4      | 8.7       |
| Total (%)                              | 100.0   | 100.0   | 100.0     | 100.0     |
| Total (£m)                             | 211,508 | 555,857 | 1,408,200 | 1,677,400 |

*Source*: Financial Statistics

**Table 1.2** *Financial liabilities of the UK personal sector (percentages)*

|  | 1978 | 1984 | 1992 | 1993 |
|---|---|---|---|---|
| Bank loans | 13.6 | 19.4 | 17.1 | 15.8 |
| Loans by credit companies and retailers | 4.8 | 2.4 | 0.8 | 0.7 |
| Housing: Banks | 2.8 | 9.7 | 19.8 | 21.4 |
| Housing: Building societies and insurance companies | 51.5 | 49.2 | 44.0 | 44.6 |
| Other | 27.3 | 19.3 | 18.3 | 17.5 |
| Total (%) | 100.0 | 100.0 | 100.0 | 100.0 |
| Total (£m) | 64,659 | 174,498 | 486,600 | 501,500 |

*Source*: Financial Statistics

range of banks and life insurance companies. Moreover, the changes in the regulatory framework discussed below have paid considerable attention to dealing with the satisfactory marketing of, amongst other things, unit trusts. On the liabilities side, the past decade has witnessed the maintenance of the building societies as the main source of borrowing for housing finance, but with the banks and other forms of institution substantially increasing their market share (Table 1.2).

Against this background of increasing personal wealth financial services firms have sought to introduce a myriad of new products. Moreover, non-traditional suppliers have also entered the market. For example, a securitized mortgage product has been introduced by new institutions aimed particularly at the higher income end of the market and the traditional credit card companies face increasing competition from several high street retailers, such as Marks & Spencer, Burton and Debenhams, who have introduced their own store cards as well as co-branded cards such as the GM card (Robbie and Wright, 1988; Worthington, 1988; Worthington, 1994).

## 1.3 Regulatory changes

The financial services market in the UK has been subject to radical transformation since the Bank of England initiated a period of regulatory change by dissolving the clearing banks' interest rate cartel and actively encouraging competition between institutions in the early 1970s. Until this time the financial arena had been highly structured, based on specialist institutions with clear functional demarcation taking place (Llewellyn, 1990). Initially diversification was essentially limited to merchant banking, Eurocurrency lending, unit trust management, leasing, credit finance, trade finance and trustee services, with credit cards just beginning. Many of the changes in regulation which have occurred subsequently have had the objective of liberalizing markets to increase competitive pressures and hence efficiency. As a result, over the last twenty years the range of activities of the four main UK clearing banks have developed to include securities dealing, insurance broking, insurance underwriting, venture capital, personal financial planning, estate agency, cash management and services for high net worth customers. With the abolition of the Supplementary Special Deposit Scheme or the 'Corset' in 1979, banks and other institutions also entered the mortgage market, greatly increasing competition in an area which was previously almost exclusively the domain of building societies. Building societies in turn campaigned for greater freedom to compete and the Building Societies Act 1986 provided them with scope, albeit limited, to enter new markets. This also helped increase competition in markets such as that for personal loans. The process of deregulation and reregulation continued with the publication of a White Paper concerning the regulation of financial services and the subsequent implementation of the Financial Services Act 1986 (FSA). In introducing this Act the government's objectives included a reference to promoting efficiency and competitiveness in the financial services industry both domestically and internationally (Rider, Abrams and Ferran, 1989). The implementation of the FSA signalled an important move from institution-based to market-based regulation recognizing the similarity of service provision in those areas of overlap between traditionally separate institutions.

The aims of fostering competitiveness and ensuring that the City of London remains an important financial centre were central to the motives for introducing reforms to the Stock Exchange rulebook in 1986, known as 'Big Bang'. Prior to this, Stock Exchange rules placed limits on the investment of outside capital in member firms and maintained the single capacity dealing system whereby brokers conducted all their business through jobbers who did not deal directly with customers. Relaxation of Stock Exchange restrictive practices allowed banks and other financial institutions ownership of member firms and the strict separation of principle and agent was ended. Many large national and international financial institutions took advantage of the opportunities presented by the changes and purchased member firms. The resulting financial conglomerates further reduced the level of demarcation within the financial services marketplace.

Each of the major forms of regulation will be examined in turn. The next section examines the developments in the UK regulatory framework which have caused the most fundamental changes, namely the Financial Services Act (FSA) and the Building Societies Act. Problems in the implementation of the FSA and subsequent developments will also be discussed.

### 1.3.1 The Financial Services Act 1986

The Financial Services Act 1986 (FSA) embraces all types of financial securities and collective investments, and all types of investment activity including the management of, giving advice regarding, and arranging deals in, investments. The twofold purpose of the FSA remains to define and regulate so-called 'investment' business (thus affording greater protection to investors) and to promote competition in the savings industry. Two key features are the consistency of treatment between competing types of financial service, and the degree of reliance placed on self-regulation within a statutory framework. The FSA only applies to 'investment' business, and so excludes general insurance, short-term deposits, mortgages and loans, deposit-based pensions and Personal Equity Plans, all of which are covered by other legislation. Thus, the Banking Act 1987 provides for the Bank of England to supervise the deposit-taking functions of banks and to monitor their capital adequacy, rules for which have important implications for the ability of banks to effect growth strategies with the goal of ensuring prudent behaviour. Where banks conduct investment as well as other types of business and there is thus supervisory overlap, the Bank of England, under the 'lead regulator' approach, coordinates the supervision exercised by itself and other supervisory bodies. According to the Memorandum of Understanding between the Bank of England and the Securities and Investment Board (SIB, see below), the former monitors capital adequacy and the SIB, together with the relevant Self-Regulating Organization (SRO, see below) monitors compliance with conduct of business rules (Hall, 1989).

Under the FSA, an individual or company transacting investment business is authorized by the appropriate Self-Regulating Organization (SRO), a Recognised Professional Body (RPB), or directly by the SIB, it being a criminal offence not to do so. The emphasis on self-regulation arose from a belief that regulation would be best undertaken by people with practical experience of the business in question; the costs of the SROs also fall directly on the investors whose interests they are designed to protect. More recently the appropriateness of self-regulation has been questioned by both consumer groups and some industry professionals as evidence has arisen of malpractice and mis-selling, as discussed below. Further concerns over issues such as commission disclosure have also developed, leading to a number of investigations and recommendations for changes to the FSA. The regulatory framework introduced by the FSA will now be detailed, before an investigation of subsequent developments is undertaken.

### The Securities and Investment Board

The FSA established the Securities and Investment Board as the designated agency required by the Act, responsible for overseeing the working of the legislation and the operation of the SROs (see Figure 1.1). In particular the responsibilities of the SIB include: the initial and continuing recognition of the SROs and RPBs, the maintenance of a rulebook to be used for firms choosing to be regulated by the SIB and to act as a minimum standard for SRO rulebooks, the exercise of powers of enforcement, authorization of collective investment schemes, the maintenance of a central register of authorized firms and acting as regulator to those firms that prefer direct regulation (Large, 1993). The right of firms to be regulated directly by the SIB rather than a particular SRO was granted to firms under the initial terms of the FSA. It was hoped and envisaged that the amount of direct regulation undertaken by SIB would be kept to a minimum; however over 130 firms, including many large banking groups, applied to be regulated directly. It remains the case that a number of firms are regulated directly by the SIB, which has given rise to concerns over possible conflicts of interest between SIB's role as direct regulator and that of monitoring of SROs. There is also a suspicion that needless duplication of tasks is occurring. The problems surrounding the creation of the Personal Investment Authority (see below) have further added to the weight of argument suggesting that direct regulation should be reserved as very much a last resort option, such as when an SRO is derecognized.

## *The self-regulating organizations (SROs)*

The place of the SROs is shown in Figure 1.1. Initially there were five main SROs: The Securities Association (TSA), the Investment Management Regulatory Organization (IMRO), the Association of Futures Brokers

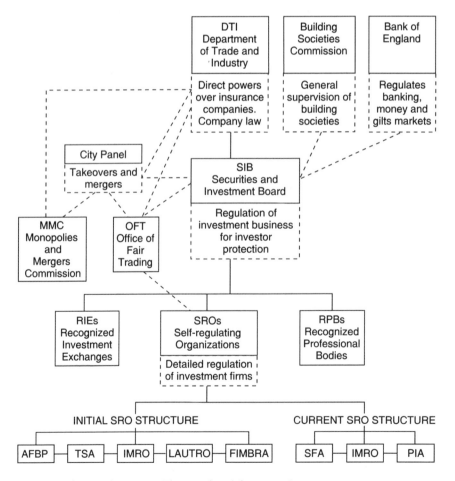

**Figure 1.1**  Personal financial services: The regulated framework

and Dealers (AFBD), the Life Assurance and Unit Trust Regulatory Organization (LAUTRO), and the Financial Intermediaries, Managers and Brokers Regulatory Association (FIMBRA). Subsequent developments in the number and coverage of the SROs are highlighted later in this section.

*LAUTRO* Initially LAUTRO's main function was to deal with the process of marketing investment-related life insurance and unit trust units. The authorization and prudential supervision of life insurance companies continues to be undertaken by the Department of Trade and Industry and the provisions of the Insurance Companies Act 1982. However, authorization could be withdrawn by the DTI for serious infringement of the FSA rules. The authorization and regulation of unit trusts was formerly undertaken by the DTI but since July 1988 unit trust management companies have been regulated by the Securities and Investments Board.

The LAUTRO rules covered the registration of sales representatives and the behaviour to be expected of the employees of life offices and unit trust management companies. Sales representatives were expected to offer 'best advice' in the light of their customers' circumstances, and were required to sell the type of product most suitable for the client (rather than the one which might produce greatest remuneration for themselves). In the absence of any suitable product from within their company's range, the sales representatives must refrain from making a recommendation.

The LAUTRO rules required very detailed information (on benefits, premiums payable, surrender values for the first five years, expenses and commissions paid to independent intermediaries) to be provided to the client at the point of sales or as soon as possible thereafter. Companies were required to issue a cancellation notice (which applied to almost all types of long-term insurance, personal pensions and unit trusts) and to give clients time to change their minds about the purchase. LAUTRO also controlled the projections of future benefits from investment products. The most contentious issues relating to marketing undoubtedly concerned the fixing of maximum commission rates paid to independent intermediaries, and the disclosure to the client of such commissions and of the expenses levied by the life office. These important issues are returned to below.

*FIMBRA* FIMBRA's role was in regulating the provision of services by independent investment intermediaries to their retail customers. In order to qualify for membership, applicants had to demonstrate that they were fit to carry on investment business of the specified category, and would conduct that business in a prudent manner. FIMBRA members were required to observe high standards of commercial honour, just and equitable principles of trade and to give paramount importance to the client's interest where conflicts of interest arose.

In their dealings with clients, FIMBRA members were required to maintain an independent status, were required to take steps to discover the relevant personal and financial circumstances of their clients ('know your client'), to use reasonable care in arranging and effecting investment transactions which were most suitable for their clients (i.e. 'best advice'), and were to effect the transaction upon terms which are no less advantageous than the best currently available in the market paying regard to the performance, charges and reputation of the institution concerned ('best execution'). In addition, members were to give clients written details of their professional standing and the service to be provided. The conduct of business rules also regulated the advertising standards to be observed by members, the records that they should keep, the standards of staff supervision and the way in which complaints should be dealt with.

In March 1992 Sir Kenneth Clucas recommended that the aforementioned SROs be superseded by a single regulatory authority to be responsible for the regulation of all retail financial services business in the UK. Thus plans for the creation of the Personal Investment Authority (PIA) came into being with the formation of a committee to oversee the proposed changes. The rationale for the proposed change along with subsequent problems are returned to below.

*IMRO*   IMRO continues to be concerned with the authorization of investment managers in respect of the conduct of business and financial requirements and the authorization of trustees. Managers must continually know and demonstrate that they have adequate financial resources. Regular financial statements have to be filed, together with statements on compliance and representation. IMRO has to be notified if rules are breached at any time. Managers also have to keep records where they deal for their own account. Separate accounting records for each product line (e.g. each trust) have to be maintained. Similar financial regulation applies to trustees. A small proportion of the business at present regulated by IMRO, that concerned primarily with the private investor, will be transferred to the PIA (see below).

*TSA*   The TSA replaced the Stock Exchange as the monitor of several hundred firms ranging from provincial stockbrokers and licensed securities dealers to large international investment banks. Monitoring activities of the TSA extended beyond the stockbroking and jobbing firms covered by the former Stock Exchange. The change in the means of operation of firms on the Stock Exchange itself contributed to the need to make a more detailed set of rules which gave investors legal rights. The SIB laid down that functions should be separated as between SRO functions and those which come under the Act's Recognised Investment Exchange (RIE) provisions. Concern also arose in respect of TSA's proposal to deal with the investment management and futures dealing activities of its members, which would have obviated the need to join SROs such as IMRO and AFBD in addition to TSA.

*AFBD*   Any firm that wished to carry out futures and options dealing, or management of portfolios in options and futures as a primary business had originally to be a member of the AFBD, whether or not it was a member of an exchange. TSA, however, authorized firms for futures and options trading where this was ancillary to their main activities.

*The recognized professional bodies* Under Sections 15 to 21 of the Financial Services Act 1986, members of professions whose business does not consist wholly or mainly of investment business may become authorized to undertake investment business provided they hold a certificate issued for that purpose by a recognized professional body (RPB), reporting directly to the Securities and Investment Board.

Included amongst the professional bodies accepted by the Secretary of State for Trade and Industry as 'recognized professional bodies' are the three main Institutes of Chartered Accountants, the Insurance Brokers' Registration Council and the Law Society. In registering with a RPB, members have to comply with regulations which are approved by SIB, and which are broadly similar to those of the self-regulating organizations.

## Developments in the regulatory structure

In 1991 the TSA and the AFBD amalgamated to form the Securities and Futures Authority (SFA). Hence all exchange related activities were bought under the auspices of a single SRO in order to economize on costs and to avoid duplication of regulation for professional investors. This reduced the number of SROs to four. Concerns regarding the functioning of the SROs which covered retail investment business precipitated a wide-ranging review of the system of self-regulation by Sir Kenneth Clucas, who published a report on such matters in March 1992 (Clucas, 1992) . The report highlighted concern regarding the consistency of regulatory standards across the SROs and RPBs as well as the costs of regulation and compensation. The main recommendation in the report was the formulation of a single SRO to regulate investment business conducted primarily with the private investor. The committee set up to facilitate the formulation of the new SRO, to be named the Personal Investment Authority (PIA), stated that the creation of the new body would be in the interests of both consumers and the industry. For consumers the PIA would provide consistency in standards of competence across the sector as well as cost effectiveness due to less duplication of effort by regulators. It was argued that the development of the PIA would be in the investment industry's interest as a single body would, over time, be beneficial in terms of compliance and compensation costs. It would also enable more firms to register with a single regulator rather than seeking recognition from two or more SROs. It was envisaged that the PIA would replace both LAUTRO and FIMBRA, and also regulate firms providing fund management for private investors previously regulated by IMRO.

The formulation and recognition of the PIA has not been a straightforward task. The fact that different types of institutions such as banks, building societies and insurance companies are to be regulated by a single regulator as well as the fact that both product providers, their representatives and independent financial advisers also fall under the PIA's remit has resulted in much debate regarding the influence of particular groups, especially with respect to board representation and voting powers. As the debate intensified, some of those opposed to self-regulation cited the fact that each group seemed concerned with establishing a position of influence within the PIA as clear evidence that self-regulation is characterized by self-interest rather than public interest and should therefore be abandoned. The majority of practitioners within the financial services industry continue to espouse the merits of self-regulation; however, there is some debate as to whether the PIA and the composition of its board amounts to self-regulation. The prospectus of the PIA states that the maximum number of board members is to be twenty-one, including the Chief Executive, with the remaining places being split equally between practitioner representatives and public interest representatives with the Chairman being designated a public interest member. Some large life assurance companies, such as the Prudential and Standard Life, expressed concern that as the practitioner members are not in the majority then the legal approach can no longer be classified as one of self-regulation. The decisions taken by the PIA are understandable as it had to be seen to be heeding the requests of the SIB for a 'step change in standards and practices' in regulation (Financial Times, 1994a).

Initially the four main clearing banks were also reluctant to apply to join the PIA as they were concerned that their contributions to the Investors Compensation Scheme would be increased substantially to cover defaults from small independent advisers. These fears were eased with the publication of the PIA prospectus and detailed rules designed to limit the amount of cross-subsidy of compensation claims.

The majority of financial services firms eligible to join the PIA have applied to do so, including the main clearing banks and many building societies and insurance companies, albeit reluctantly in some cases. The SIB has completed the process of formally recognizing the PIA as a suitable regulator and the PIA began operating in mid-July 1994. Perhaps the biggest remaining problem for the authorities is the Prudential Insurance Company which remains adamant that it wishes to be regulated directly by SIB, which it is entitled to do under the terms of the FSA. However, it is envisaged that the government will in due course ask SIB to subcontract any direct responsibility for regulation back to the PIA. This will eradicate any remaining duplication of regulatory effort and clarify SIB's role as a regulator of regulators, rather than being involved in front-line regulation itself.

The number of SROs subsequent to the changes in regulatory structure therefore stands at three. The Securities and Futures Association regulates professional investors involved in exchange related activities, the Investment Managers Regulatory Organization regulates firms which provide fund management services to professional investors and the Personal Investment Authority regulates retail financial services markets. The rationalization process has been a painful one. However, it is hoped that increased investor protection along with increased cost efficiency will be the ultimate result. Should such benefits fail to materialize then the introduction of a statutory body and the end of self-regulation cannot be ruled out.

## Other issues arising from the implementation of the FSA

Development in the structure of the SROs has perhaps been the major issue to arise from the implementation of the FSA, although a number of other significant points have also emerged and these matters are now discussed.

### Polarization

A key feature of the FSA is polarization; intermediaries who advise on investments have to conform to one of two categories: fully independent intermediary ('independent') or representative of just one company ('tied'). The polarization rule applies to financial conglomerates (such as banks) although separately incorporated parts of a group can polarize in different ways. Independent intermediaries are required to recommend the most suitable product, if any, from all those on offer in the market-place. Tied representatives are restricted to selling the investment products of one company only, and have to so inform their clients. Tied agents are still required to offer 'best advice' by recommending investments which are appropriate to the circumstances of their clients. The employer, rather than a SRO, is responsible for the behaviour of its sales representatives. Companies operating a tied salesforce have to take considerably more care in the training and licensing of their employees. The remuneration of company representatives must not be structured such that it influences the representatives unduly to recommend particular trusts or, say, life policies in preference to trusts.

Much attention in the polarization debate has been focused on the initial decisions of the various banks and building societies and the subsequent alterations in status from independent adviser to tied agent by many institutions. Of the major clearing banks, Barclays, Lloyds, Midland and TSB opted for 'tied' status for their branches immediately; originally the Midland did not have a life office subsidiary and in late 1987 it formed a new company jointly with the Commercial Union. Lloyds Bank supplemented the range of products available to it from its in-house life assurance company, Black Horse Life, by acquiring a majority stake in Abbey Life. These banks also own insurance broking subsidiaries which operate independently of the branches. The other clearing banks – National Westminster and the three Scottish banks – initially chose to polarize the other way by pledging to offer independent advice through their branches (and hence committing themselves to massive staff-training programmes). Consequently NatWest sold County Unit Trust, its unit trust management company. However, these Banks have all now reversed their initial decision and have become tied agents as the expected competitive benefit of being an independent financial adviser did not materialize.

The main building societies have, perhaps not surprisingly, been through a similar process. According to information provided by the Building Societies Association, a minority of societies (23 per cent) adopted independent intermediary status under the polarization rules. Most of these societies were the larger ones who had the resources to provide independent advice. Initially, the main exceptions amongst the larger societies were the Abbey National, which has a tied relationship with Friends' Provident, and the Cheltenham and Gloucester which has changed from independent to tied status. Subsequently however, many other societies altered their plans in this respect and opted for tied status, including the Halifax, the Woolwich, the Alliance and Leicester, and the Leeds Permanent. The impetus for this change came first from the realization that many customers did not appreciate the significance of 'independent financial advice' (see Ennew, 1992) and second that there were considerable efficiency gains to be made from dealing with only a single supplier together with high commission rates being offered to encourage societies to switch to tied status (Ennew and Wright, 1990a). It is also important to note that societies may adopt a dual approach, with the society itself being 'tied' and a separate subsidiary offering 'independent' advice (e.g. Halifax, Northern Rock, Lancastrian, Principality and Skipton) a similar strategy to the main clearing banks. This allows for segmentation of the marketplace and ensures that the institution concerned is also able to meet the requirements of those customers who prefer independent advice. Such customers tend to be more knowledgable regarding financial matters and are often high net worth individuals, meaning they are potentially very profitable to the institution. More recently there has been a trend towards building societies setting up their own life offices, often by way of a joint venture with an established life company, the main motivation being that of greater long-term profitability.

Polarization has produced increased concentration at the retailing stage and some concern has been expressed as to the continued availability of Independent Financial Advice. The shift from IFA to tied agency status is a function of supply and demand characteristics. Tied agency provides the opportunities for greater efficiency and profitability whilst it would appear also that although financial services consumers are in general becoming more sophisticated they do not particularly value independent financial advice (Ennew, 1992).

*Best advice and the concern over mis-selling*
All sales representatives of investment products, be they tied employees or independent intermediaries, are required to give clients 'best advice' on the type of investment which is best suited to his or her needs and circumstances. Independent intermediaries may have regard to non-financial considerations such as the quality and assurance of performance. Where precise comparisons between products are impossible independent intermediaries will be expected to survey the market regularly and make a judgement on which of the top group of products it would be reasonable

to recommend. Differential pricing or price discrimination, the practice of offering products at different prices to different sellers, has implications for the giving of best advice. The LAUTRO rulebook initially prevented differential pricing, but in November 1987 SIB announced relaxations to this rule. The requirement to offer best advice on the type of investment may involve intermediaries having to expand the range of their advice beyond unit trusts and investment products.

In practice, the regulatory framework has been less than successful in producing the intended degree of investor protection. A recent Consumer Association report highlighted the persistence of problems relating to both disclosure of status and the provision of best advice. Similarly, a report by the Office of Fair Trading (1992) noted that in 1991 there were more than 4300 complaints to the Insurance Ombudsman Bureau, which represented an increase of over 60 per cent on the previous year. Further figures from the Life Assurance and Unit Trust Regulatory Organization (LAUTRO) show an increase in complaints of 77 per cent to 4069 in the year 1990–1. A proportion of these rises could be explained by increased awareness of complaint and redress channels although further statistics suggest that this is not a particularly significant factor. The level of early surrender or lapse of long-term insurance policies, mainly in the form of life linked products such as Unit Linked and With Profits policies, is widely recognized as a reliable indicator of the amount of overselling taking place. It is inevitable that a small proportion of individuals buying such policies will experience a marked, unforeseen change in circumstances leading to forced surrender. However, in the vast majority of cases it is likely that such policies are not suitable and that customers do not understand the nature of the commitment they are undertaking. A further proportion of these early surrenders may also be attributable to the practice of 'churning' which involves an intermediary or a member of a direct salesforce cancelling existing policies and writing new ones. A survey commissioned by the Securities and Investment Board (quoted in OFT, 1993) found that 22.3 per cent of Unit Linked life policies and 13.8 per cent of With Profits policies are surrendered within one year. The figures rise to 37 per cent and 23 per cent respectively for policies surrendered within two years. Policies surrendered this early in their life are likely to be almost worthless since the bulk of the premiums paid will have been absorbed by commission payments. In addition many large financial services organizations have been fined significant amounts by the regulators as they continue to fail to comply with the procedures laid down in the FSA (Devlin and Ennew, 1993).

The most recent controversy has concerned the 'overselling' of personal pensions and especially poor advice regarding pension transfers from occupational schemes to personal pension plans. A study conducted for the SIB published in December 1993 showed that in 80 per cent of cases where a pension transfer from an employer's scheme to a private pension was recommended, insufficient information was gathered to enable agents properly and competently to advise the customer concerned (Financial Times, 1993). As many of the individuals who subsequently chose to transfer their pensions may well be worse off in retirement as a result, a review committee was set up by SIB to ensure compensation is forthcoming for the victims of mis-selling. Many large life assurance firms have set aside reserves to meet future potential claims with the total cost of compensation being estimated at between 100 million and 1 billion (Financial Times, 1994b). The SIB has subsequently tightened guidelines on the selling of pension transfers.

SIB implicitly recognized that the system of self-regulation was not providing sufficient investor protection when in October 1991 it appointed Sir Kenneth Clucas to undertake a study of the regulation of retail financial services in order to achieve a more satisfactory regulatory environment. As detailed above the main result of this review was the formulation of the PIA, which hopes to tackle such problems by introducing high quality training programmes to increase professionalism and to improve monitoring procedures (PIA, 1994). The industry itself realizes it has an image problem and some innovative solutions are emerging. Allied Dunbar is offering its sales managers £3000 for every new recruit who measures up to specific standards in terms of previous experience and age etc. In this way it is hoped that the quality of advice offered will improve and the amount of mis-selling will diminish (Financial Times, 1994d). It is perhaps not an exaggeration to state that the advent of the PIA provides the industry with one last chance to prove that self regulation can offer the desired amount of investor protection by controlling less than scrupulous sales agents. Should the PIA fail in this respect then the calls for statutory regulation will undoubtedly increase.

*Commission disclosure*
The original LAUTRO proposals set maximum commission rates along with a 'soft disclosure' rule that clients need not be told what commission the independent intermediary earned on the transaction so long as the client did not ask directly and the commission did not exceed the maximum payable under the maximum commissions agreement. The commission agreement was justified on the grounds that it protected the consumer from the possibility of receiving biased advice (even though it was at that time contrary to the FIMBRA rules for an intermediary to be influenced by commission) and that it prevented a commission war which would be detrimental to the interests of clients. However, the Office of Fair Trading objected that the agreement was an illegal price/commission-fixing cartel (since the maximum level for commission would probably also act as a minimum), that it limited an independent intermediary's ability to compete with direct salesforces (since the payments these sales agents received were not controlled and there was no obligation for them to reveal their commission earnings), that it kept client's in the dark on the amounts their advisers earned from dealing with the client's business, and that, in any case, clients were entitled to negotiate with their advisers for a share in the commission.
Furthermore the Office of Fair Trading recognized that insisting on 'hard disclosure' (the compulsory full disclosure by intermediaries of their commission earnings) would not by itself help the cause of the independent

intermediary. Consequently, the Office of Fair Trading recommended that the commission agreement be erased from the LAUTRO rulebook, and that intermediaries be obliged to make a 'hard disclosure' as a first step towards a fully fee-based system; competition between intermediaries should then ensure that commission rates are maintained at a low level. In addition, following the recommendations of a report commissioned by the SIB, the OFT also requested that all life offices be required to reveal the expenses to be charged under their contracts. However, commission and expense disclosure was not required in monetary terms, but rather was to be expressed as a percentage of the appropriate base. The ending of the Maximum Commissions Agreement in May 1989 led to commission rates being increased by some 30 per cent above the LAUTRO rules.

The OFT has continued in its role of principal proponent of greater commission disclosure. After much consultation by SIB, the rules on commission disclosure were changed in favour of greater disclosure in May 1992. The Director General of the OFT in a report to the Chancellor in March 1993 (Office of Fair Trading, 1993) stated that he was still concerned that the SIB rules were significantly anticompetitive in a number of respects. In particular the report stated that rules regarding illustrations of surrender values were unsatisfactory, as were rules regarding illustrations of cost using industry standard levels rather than life office specific information. More generally, this lack of transparency in pricing has been criticized on ethical grounds (Ennew, MacGregor and Diacon, 1994). Finally the fact that IFAs were not bound to disclose commission in cash term early in the selling process was tantamount to withholding the price of independent financial advice and was therefore anticompetitive. As a result the Treasury directed SIB further to consider its disclosure rules which resulted in the publication of SIB Consultative Paper 77 in January 1994. Notwithstanding the fact that attempting to put an actual cash figure on 'commissions' paid to tied agents is a difficult process, the document detailed proposals for disclosure in cash terms, prior to the signing of contracts for both IFAs and company representatives. Details regarding penalties for early surrender are also included. Further discussion continues as to exactly how cash figures are to be calculated and as to the most appropriate and easily understood form of disclosure.

The life assurance industry has vigorously resisted full disclosure throughout the debate, claiming that other factors such as fund performance and the level of charges are more important in the decision-making process. The OFT has recognized the importance of such factors by campaigning also for disclosure of the effects of early surrender and charges and expenses. As a result these were also incorporated into SIB's rules detailing the full disclosure of commissions, effects of early surrender and expenses and charges which came into effect in January 1995 and companies have until August 1995 to operationalize the proposals. It is hoped that the increased transparency of information in these areas will increase competition and result ultimately in a better deal for customers.

*Costs*

The regulatory framework has been consistently criticized as involving excessive costs. The regulatory environment initially imposed increased costs because of the need for compliance in marketing and administration: the introduction of new systems; increased emphasis on investment performance in order to win business on best advice recommendations from independent advisers; effects on commissions; pressure on profits. The direct costs of the SIB and SROs may well be in excess of identified losses suffered by investors in public scandals. The simplification of the regulatory structure and the formulation of the PIA was motivated in part by a desire to reduce the costs of compliance in the longer term, although in the short term costs are estimated to increase (Personal Investment Authority, 1994). To these more obvious costs may be added the potential costs involved in the financing of compensation funds, the diversion of business overseas, the restriction of competition and the possible stifling of financial innovation.

Compensation funds could encourage the taking of excessive risks as firms know that losses will be borne by the funds. This problem may be reduced by the introduction of a generous depositor insurance scheme plus strong capital adequacy requirements. The PIA prospectus also contains provisions to limit the amount of cross-subsidy between product providers and independent practitioner firms, in an attempt to further reduce the degree of moral hazard. Tougher penalties for transgressions and greater requirements for public disclosure of information may also have an important role to play. The possibility of regulatory capture remains, although the composition of the board of the PIA with a balance between industry practitioners and public interest members, reduces this risk.

*Advertising*

The SIB rules on advertising cover all media and extend to direct mail. Three types of advertisements are identified: image advertisements – to promote awareness of a company and its products; short form advertisements – which include listings of fund prices in publications and computer networks; and advertisements relating to a particular product. Advertisements are required to be legal, decent, honest and truthful, clear and precise, in no way false or tendentious and must conform to the principles of fair competition. Section 57 of the Financial Services Act 1986 stipulates that no person other than one authorized under the Act shall issue an investment advertisement.

The SIB rules governing the above types of advertising cover a wide range of issues. Clearer guidelines for practitioners are provided in SRO rulebooks. Information to be disclosed in investment advertisements includes the basis of forecast performance and the level of future benefits, the risks involved in acquiring or holding the investment, and the penalties which may be incurred from liquidating the investment. This has obvious implications for the marketing actions of financial services firms.

The implementation of the Financial Services Act 1986 has been far from straightforward with many complex and contentious issues emerging, as detailed above. The system has been radically simplified and rationalized and the fundamental level of investor protection increased since the Act's inception. The industry will continue to find itself under the scrutiny of the media, regulators and the Government and must therefore pay particular attention to: integrity; skill; observation of standards; fairness; provision of sufficient information by the customer; provision of information for the customer; avoidance of conflicts of interest; customer assets; financial resources; and internal organization.

## 1.3.2 The Building Societies Act 1986

The Building Societies Act 1962 closely constrained the activities of societies. Competition between societies was also restricted by the interest rate cartel which ensured that prices moved closely in the same direction. The formal ending of the cartel in the early 1980s reflected growing competitive pressures but societies' ability to compete with banks and other financial institutions, many of whom were increasingly encroaching on societies' traditional markets, remained tightly controlled. Concerted effort to establish a strong presence in the mortgage market by the banks, together with the introduction of securitization of mortgages by new market entrants (Robbie and Wright, 1988) contributed to the fall in societies' share of new advances to its lowest level of 50.3 per cent in 1987. In addition, the introduction of interest-bearing cheque accounts by the banks put pressure on societies' traditional retail sources of funds and correspondingly on their profit margins. The existing regime placed tight controls on societies' access to the lower cost wholesale markets.

Changes to the legislative framework contained in the Building Societies Act 1986 allows societies, particularly the larger ones, to provide a much wider range of services under the supervision of a newly created body, the Building Societies Commission. The main powers concerned the ability to extend unsecured lending, the provision of housing, the provision of an integrated house-buying package (including the provision of estate agency services), the provision of agency services, enhancements to the provision of insurance broking services, the provision of full personal banking and money transmission services, and an extension to the range of financial services societies could provide. Organizationally, societies were permitted to create subsidiaries to carry out certain of the riskier new activities as a means of protecting the central function of housing finance provision. Certain other services were permitted through joint ventures. Societies' abilities to raise funds from sources other than individual members were to be increased to a level of 20 per cent of all funds.

Although the Act essentially embodied the Green Paper's proposals, certain important caveats were imposed. First, unsecured lending was to be limited to £5000 per individual. Three classes of societies' assets were created. Class 1 assets, comprising advances secured on a mortgage of residential property were to remain the main form of activity. At least 90 per cent of commercial advances would need to be of this kind. Class 2 assets comprise other forms of secured lending, which may comprise no more than 10 per cent of commercial assets. Class 3 assets relate to unsecured lending and housing provision and were limited to 5 per cent of commercial assets within the 10 per cent Class 2 limit. It is clear that the ability to introduce new forms of lending was heavily restricted, being allowable only for about sixty societies who at the time of the passing of the Act had total assets in excess of £100 million. However, smaller societies were to some extent to deal with the problem of restrictions imposed by the new regulations by engaging in a variety of joint arrangements (Ennew and Wright, 1990a).

The changes to the regulatory framework include powers for societies to convert from mutual to public limited company status. Any society so doing would become subject to banking regulation and cease to be subject to the Building Societies Act. In order to protect members' interests, high levels of participation in a vote to become a public limited company have been set by the legislation. Protection from a hostile takeover following conversion is also built into the legislation in the form of super-majority requirements for shareholders to vote in favour of such an acquisition. Societies may wish to convert to the status of the bank to reduce the restrictions on obtaining funds and on the product areas into which diversification may take place. To date only the Abbey National has converted to public limited company status; the Halifax and Leeds building societies recently announced an intention to merge their operations and a desire to convert to PLC status subsequently. If successful, the merger will create the third largest UK high street bank and will represent a major development in the restructuring of the UK personal financial services industry. However, the trend towards conversion by societies, expected after Abbey National's demutualization, has not materialized. A recent article provided some arguments as to why this may be the case (Llewellyn and Holmes, 1991). It challenged the conventional wisdom that PLC status was preferable in all cases, arguing that the discipline of competition is an adequate substitute for the discipline of the capital market for mutual societies. The study also argued that mutual societies do not suffer unduly from capital constraints and are able to grow and diversify in a similar fashion to PLCs.

The speed of increased competition taking place in the UK personal financial services sector in the late 1980s meant that, despite the regulatory relaxation contained in the Building Societies Act, societies still considered themselves to be at a competitive disadvantage in relation to the banks. In late 1987 a major review of the 1986 Act was completed. The recommendations resulting from the review were to allow societies to increase their unsecured lending limits from £5000 to £10 000 per individual and to offer a wider range of banking and housing related services. Societies were also permitted to undertake unit trust fund management and are allowed to hold a minority stake in stockbrokers. Most crucially, societies are now allowed to become directly involved in the operation of life and general insurance companies. Initially the degree of involvement in non-life insurance companies was limited to an equity stake of no more than 15 per cent of an existing or new insurer, although this restriction is to be relaxed as detailed below.

The building societies continued to campaign for wider powers of diversification and a further Treasury review of building societies legislation resulted in 1994. Considerations as to how to promote change in the sector are continuing and some proposals have been published (Financial Times, 1994c). Building societies will be able to raise up to 50 per cent of their funds from the wholesale market, the figure having been raised to 40 per cent in the interim period. The 15 per cent limit on societies' stakes in general insurance companies will be abolished, allowing complete ownership, and societies will be able to form subsidiaries to make substantial loans not secured on land. It is hoped that the latter measure will introduce a further source of funds for small businesses and provide competition in this area for the high street banks. Consideration continues to be given to governance issues as well as how to best transfer the benefits of mutuality to societies' members.

The relaxation of powers to provide insurance broking services has been seen as of particular importance by societies. Schedule 8 of the Act also permitted societies to offer estate agency services, and to the end of 1988, twenty-three societies had established estate agency subsidiaries. Estate agents occupy a key place at the front of the house-purchase process providing opportunities to cross sell mortgages and general insurance in particular. Subsequently, the crash in the housing market and the failure to realize expected benefits led many societies to withdraw from this market, often having sustained considerable losses. Involvement by societies in the provision of Unit Trusts, Personal Equity Plans and share-dealing services has been limited except among some of the larger societies. This may well be due to the fact that the typical building society customer may not be particularly interested in such services.

The trend towards greater concentration has continued in the building societies sector, with an interesting recent development being the attempted merger between Lloyds Bank and the Cheltenham and Gloucester Building Society. This is the first attempted takeover of a building society by a bank. The regulations regarding the takeover of building societies by other institutions as enshrined in the Building Societies Act are quite stringent and the Government has made it clear that it will continue protect societies in a similar manner (Financial Times, 1994d). However, Lloyds' bid for Cheltenham and Gloucester was an agreed one with both parties convinced of the potential benefits. The rules regarding the takeover of a building society require a super majority vote in favour by members of 75 per cent. There are also restrictions on payments from third parties, such as Lloyds Bank, that can be made. These restrictions were upheld in the High Court and make it difficult for the required majority to be achieved. Lloyds Bank and Cheltenham and Gloucester are considering their options and it is clear that if they do find a feasible route to a merger then more mergers may follow between building societies and other financial institutions as building societies' large relatively untapped customer bases and low cost income ratios prove an attractive proposition. Many such mergers may be between building societies, but a number of banks are also considering following the Lloyds strategy.

### 1.3.3 Competition legislation

Whilst mergers have come within the powers of the Office of Fair Trading and the Monopolies and Mergers Commission, there has traditionally been less attention addressed to other anticompetitive practices (Chiplin and Wright, 1987). For example, the building societies' interest rate cartel which existed formally until 1983 was exempt from the restrictive trade practices legislation. Subsequent changes have attempted to strengthen the role of the Office of Fair Trading. Reference has already been made to the role of the competition authorities in ensuring that the Financial Services Act's provisions have the desired effect of protecting consumers and enhancing competition. The Building Societies Act prohibits societies from offering mortgages conditional upon customers taking a range of other products offered by the society. The threat of a reference of the Stock Exchange dealing arrangements to the Restrictive Trade Practices Court was also seen to have been a crucial factor in changing long-standing practices.

A further issue to have received the attention of the Monopolies and Mergers Commission (MMC) was the behaviour of credit card companies and in particular the rate of interest charged to customers and the restrictions placed on retailers in respect of charging credit card customers different prices from those wishing to pay in cash. The initial Monopolies Commission investigation in 1980 was critical of credit card companies' actions and the subsequent report published in 1989 had further grounds for taking an adverse view (Monopolies and Mergers Commission, 1989). The MMC found that a monopoly situation existed in credit card services and that agreements between Visa International and MasterCard/Eurocard and their UK members should not prevent their acting as merchant acquirers as well as card issuers. In respect of the first finding, the MMC considered that increased competition would reduce credit card profitability and charges paid by retailers. The result of the second finding has been to quicken the pace of duality, the process by which card issuers can be members of both Access and Visa and can issue both these cards under the brand name of their institution. Competition, which includes the growing availability of in-house credit cards offered by retailers (Worthington, 1988), should decide whether fees for credit cards, discounts for cash payments or shorter interest-free periods should be introduced. However, the MMC did take the view that retailers' ability to set their own prices was adversely affected by the rule that goods and services had to be offered at the same price irrespective of the method payment. At the end of 1989, in an effort to enhance competition, this no-discrimination rule was brought to an end and a requirement was introduced for credit card companies to provide the Director General of Fair Trading with information on their charges to retailers.

The MMC has also been instrumental in restricting the amount of concentration in retail and small business lending. The proposed bid by Lloyds Bank for Midland Bank in 1993 caught the attention of the MMC and as a result was dropped allowing the Hong Kong and Shanghai Banking Corporation to acquire Midland and as a result a major branch network in the UK market. Lloyds has now turned its attention to the Cheltenham and Gloucester Building Society as a possible route for expansion and has encountered further regulatory problems as detailed above.

## 1.3.4 Other legislation

Whilst not directly influencing the regulatory framework, other legislation may be relevant to the behaviour of financial services firms. In particular, legislation may introduce new products. The conditions attached to these products, for example in terms of the tax benefits to be gained and the scope of their applicability, will influence the manner in which financial services firms market the products to consumers. In the UK important legislative changes which have given rise to new products have been associated with a government philosophy in the 1980s which emphasized individual share ownership and personal provision for the future.

The annual Finance Acts may be particularly important in introducing new investment products. One of the most important developments in recent years has been the establishment in the 1986 Finance Act of a scheme for Personal Equity Plans (PEPs) aimed at direct investment in UK companies by individuals and specifically targeted at the first-time investor. PEPs have established themselves in a relatively short time as an element in the marketing strategy of most financial services groups. PEPs are run by approved plan managers who are professional investment advisers, authorized to deal in stocks and shares. The managers design individual plan contracts for the investor subject to the statutory limitations. Under the scheme, shares in UK companies can be bought without liability to income tax or capital gains tax. Shares must be ordinary shares of UK companies listed on the Stock Exchange, of USM companies, or of unit trusts or investment trusts.

Tax relief is available on three aspects of the scheme: dividends are free from income tax if reinvested in the plan; gains from selling shares within a PEP and withdrawals of capital are free of capital gains tax; and interest from cash held in a PEP is free of income tax if reinvested in the plan. While PEPs are now an established part of a financial service company's range of products, take-up rates following their introduction were low. A survey in early 1987 commissioned jointly by the Stock Exchange and the Treasury found that only 1 per cent of a sample of 7008 persons had backed the scheme, whilst a further 2 per cent said that they intended to do so. Initially, clearing banks took a leading role in the introduction of PEPs, ahead of insurance groups.

In subsequent Finance Acts the limits on the amounts of money that individuals can invest in a PEP linked to an investment trust or unit trust

have risen, which may mean an increase in the number of unit trusts
providing a PEP route to investing in their UK equity-oriented range of
unit trusts. Under the new rules, investments in PEPs in unit or investment trusts are no longer restricted to 50 per cent of the total. PEPs may
also be used as a means of repaying a mortgage and as such may provide
competition for the more traditional endowment mortgage. There has
been some debate as to whether PEPs provide any significant benefits
for basic rate tax payers who have insufficient wealth to suffer capital
gains tax. In such cases the tax advantages may be all but cancelled out
by the fees payable and as a result PEPs have attracted mainly higher rate
tax payers who already own shares rather than widening significantly the
amount of shareholders.

A second influential piece of legislation has been the Social Security Act
1986, which set out wide-ranging changes to the operation of the State
Earnings Related Pension Scheme (SERPS) and to the individual pensions
market. The income of occupational pension schemes rose from £16.5
billion in 1981 to £19.1 billion in 1987. The personal pension market has
experienced greater growth in the 1980s and 1990s. Between 1981 and
1992, annual premium income increased tenfold from £0.45 billion to
£4.55 billion and the number of policies in force increased from
2 195 000 to 17 417 000 in the same period (Table 1.3). Further growth is
expected through the 1990s, although recent negative publicity regarding
the mis-selling of personal pension plans may curtail expansion of the
market somewhat. Under the provisions of the legislation, members are
to be encouraged to contract-out of SERPS either by taking up their own
'portable' personal pensions or by forming new contracted-out occupational pension schemes under simplified rules. The Act also widened the
choice of providers of pension arrangements. Banks, building societies
and unit trust management companies, as well as life offices, are now
able to design and offer their own personal pension plans and occupational pension schemes.

**Table 1.3** *Personal (self-employed) pensions in the UK, 1981–92*

|      | No of policies in force (000s) | Increase (%) | Yearly premiums (£m) | Increase (%) |
|------|------|------|------|------|
| 1981 | 2,195 | – | 450.2 | – |
| 1982 | 2,571 | 17.1 | 555.3 | 23.3 |
| 1983 | 2,971 | 15.6 | 668.9 | 20.5 |
| 1984 | 3,560 | 19.8 | 888.8 | 32.9 |
| 1985 | 4,460 | 25.3 | 1,228.4 | 38.2 |
| 1986 | 4,936 | 10.7 | 1,370.3 | 11.6 |
| 1987 | 5,697 | 15.4 | 1,614.2 | 17.8 |
| 1988 | 7,908 | 38.8 | 2,364.0 | 46.4 |
| 1989 | 11,640 | 47.2 | 3,124.0 | 32.1 |
| 1990 | 13,995 | 20.2 | 3,786.0 | 21.2 |
| 1991 | 15,212 | 8.7 | 4,212.0 | 11.2 |
| 1992 | 17,417 | 14.5 | 4,552.0 | 8.1 |

*Source*: Association of British Insurers

The regulations controlling the selling of deposit-based personal pensions, issued by the Department of Social Security and DHSS, are designed to be complementary with those rules governing the investment-based personal pensions of life offices and unit trusts. However, they are more relaxed on several counts. The major differences between the DHSS rules and those resulting from the FSA include: no obligation on building societies to reveal charges, no requirement to make illustrations in 'real terms', and no cancellation period.

### 1.3.5 European Union regulation of financial services

The 1992 programme, the main aim of which continues to be to create a single internal market in goods and services, includes financial services. The fact that financial services markets throughout Europe have been subject for some time to differing national regulatory regimes has made the task of achieving meaningful integration in financial services a difficult one. Price differences in financial services products are also significant. The price reductions from the establishment of an integrated market are difficult to determine precisely, partly because of the simultaneous effects of other restructuring, but they are expected to be substantial. Estimates suggest a central indicative price reduction for the eight main Community economies of 10 per cent. However, the price reductions are expected to vary substantially from country to country and from sector to sector. Spain is expected to experience the largest price falls, with Luxembourg, the UK and The Netherlands providing the lowest decreases. France, Germany and the UK were found to have relatively high prices in respect of consumer credit. Existing prices in respect of commercial banking products were found to be highest in Spain and Italy and lowest in Germany. The traditionally more competitive insurance markets in the UK and The Netherlands were found to have significantly lower prices than in Belgium, Luxembourg, France, Spain and Italy. In Belgium the insurance markets have traditionally been protected from competition, and are highly concentrated with associated high overhead cost and profit levels. In France, high regulatory costs are coupled with an under-developed retail distribution system. In Italy, the insurance markets are generally less well-developed.

The creation of a free flow of capital and free trade in financial service and financial service firms are key in the establishment of the Single Market. In respect of the first, exchange controls have been abolished for some time by the UK, West Germany and Denmark. Other EU member states were required by the Capital Movements Directive, 88/361/EEC, to allow the free flow of capital by July 1990, except Greece, Ireland, Portugal and Spain who were given until the end of 1992 to comply.

The principle of free trade in financial services calls for neutrality between buying a service from a domestic institution, importing from another country or buying domestically from a local branch of a foreign institution. Once a provider of a financial service has been authorized in one country, it would be allowed to operate in all other EU countries. If these moves become effective, benefits may be derived from economies of scale and scope, improvement of service provision by entry of the best providers into currently protected markets, and increased competition in markets currently tightly regulated or dominated by cartels.

In respect of banking services, the second Banking Directive, the Own Funds Directive and the Solvency Ratio Directive are together concerned with requiring countries to recognize any financial institution authorized or licensed in another EU country on condition that it respects local regulations – the so-called 'passport principle'. Insurance companies already have freedom of establishment although national regulations vary significantly from one country to another. However, in respect of cross-border trade in general insurance services it has been unusual for member states to permit foreign insurers to solicit business directly. Rather, insurance contracts have been required to be provided by established or authorized insurers. The Non-Life Insurance Services Directive, which became effective in 1992, provided the basis for a wholesale market in 'large risk' insurance, where policy holders are companies with a turnover of 12.8 million ECU or other equivalent criteria. The Third Life Assurance Directive has been adopted and is now in force in all member states. As a result a single authorization for life assurance is now valid throughout the European Union with branches and agencies being authorized and supervised by the insurer's home state, making entry into other EU markets more straightforward.

Changes have also been introduced to the regulatory regime concerning open-ended mutual funds (unit trusts). From October 1989, the introduction of the UCITS (Undertakings for Collective Investments in Transferable Securities) directive meant that a unit trust operated in other EU countries was allowed to be marketed in the UK. The UCITS directive aimed to harmonize the structure of collective investment schemes throughout the EU. UCITS covers open-ended investment schemes in transferable securities, but will not cover new unit trust types such as money market, property or futures and options funds. Investment trusts are also not covered by the directive. UCITS defines common procedures for the authorization of UCITS schemes, the supervision of schemes by EU governments and the investment and borrowing powers of UCITS schemes. As long as a scheme meets the requirements of UCITS, it can be marketed in other EU member states and be subject to whatever marketing rules and regulations apply to financial services in each country.

The effects of UCITS may vary from country to country, depending upon the relative restrictiveness of the marketing regime from one state to another. Whilst the UK has a large number of independent intermediaries charged with giving best advice, in France and Germany, for example, UCITS products are predominantly distributed through bank branches who seem unlikely to recommend foreign-based products unless forced to do so. Hence, UK firms may need to engage in recruiting high cost direct sales forces if they want to enter the continental European market, whilst European firms may gain entry through recommendation by independent intermediaries.

A number of problems are raised by the developing regulatory framework for the establishment of a single EU market. First is the problem of harmonizing the standards required for the different types of financial intermediaries and the difficulties such moves pose for designing regulatory compromises which are politically acceptable to all EU members. A second difficulty concerns the distinction between licensing rules and operating rules. Hence an institution may be licensed to enter other EU member states' markets outside its own but face difficulties in using the same techniques as it does in its home market. For example, UK building societies lend money for house purchase at variable rates of interest. In Belgium, it has traditionally been illegal to offer housing loans on these terms. The Mortgage Credit Directive which implicitly required mutual recognition of techniques between member states, was superseded by the Banking Directive. Whilst covering mortgage lending the Banking Directive does not implicitly allow for mutual recognition of techniques. Rather institutions were to be allowed to undertake any activity within a list of recognized banking activities on condition that this was possible in their home markets. However, as Davis and Smales (1989) point out, the manner in which the list is presented does not appear to give clear guidance and protection for institutions wishing to use techniques which are acceptable in the home market in other member states' markets. A third problem emerges in that despite the intention of the directives, individual governments may still erect barriers to entry through various forms of bureaucratic procedures which firms have to follow if they are actually to operate in other countries. Fourth, long-standing and rational differences in national preferences and circumstances may inhibit the extent of change and the acceptance of new entrants. Finally, the actual extent and method of entry may be problematical.

These problems have led some institutions to question whether EU retail financial services markets are in fact contestable, the main barriers to entry being the cost of acquiring distribution networks and the cultural differences outlined above. A recent study (Bank of England, 1993) shows that banks in the EU have forged a number of cross-border alliances (247), with French banks being the most active. Of these only twenty-two included links with insurance companies, the majority being concerned with retail banking. Institutions continue to plan for acquisitions and establish joint ventures, although it is recognized that this process may take longer than initially anticipated.

## 1.4 Globalization

The spread of financial services' firms interests into global markets has been influenced by two main factors, regulatory constraints and developments in information technology. Regulatory constraints in domestic markets may push firms to seek international markets as a means of achieving growth. For example, restrictions on inter-state or even inter-county banking in the US meant that branch networks were limited to a small geographical area. Consequently, growth opportunities were often dependent on the banks' ability to expand into overseas markets, most usually by following corporate customers as they expanded internationally. Development of these banks as cross-border institutions was in part to extend the range of services offered to the corporate sector but also to escape regulatory constraints. This development was particularly true of the more restricted New York banks and less so for those in California where state-wide branching was permissible (Lewis, 1986).

The ability to extend into foreign markets was severely constrained by regulations in individual countries which limited cross-border activities. As well as the barriers within Europe (discussed earlier), similar barriers to entry existed elsewhere such as in Japan, Canada and Australia. In Japan the brokerage market had been regulated so as to prevent entry by US firms and in Canada and Australia entry by foreign banks was not permitted until the early 1980s (Channon, 1988). The development of international and global markets was slowly made possible by the ability of firms to exploit differences between national regulations and the lack of coordination between regulatory regimes. The different rate at which deregulation occurred between countries gave a further impetus to this process.

Where regulatory barriers persisted, innovations in delivery systems provided an increasingly effective means of entering international markets and introducing new types of product particularly by new types of competitor. The evolution of the global securities and capital markets has been facilitated by electronically based dealing systems. Worldwide branch networks began to be developed in the 1970s but by the 1980s many firms were experiencing problems in generating sufficient profitability and were seeking either to rationalize or add new services. By the late 1980s a number of retail services had been developed on a European or even global scale such as travel and entertainment cards, automatic teller machine (ATM) networks, travellers' cheques and private banking. For corporate clients, global cash management, foreign exchange and other products were introduced. Other products were developed which were to be sold across the globe but targeted at the more attractive country niches.

## 1.5   Information technology

Developments in information technology (IT) in the financial services sector introduce major changes in respect of the link between consumers and firms, links between financial services firms, internal information systems and the generation of new products. Information technology links between consumers and financial services firms in the distribution of products may be categorized into electronic funds transfer at place of banking (EFTPOB, i.e. automatic teller machines, ATMs), electronic funds transfer at place of living (EFTPOL, i.e. home banking) and electronic funds transfer at point of sale (EFTPOS).

Automatic teller machine networks are now well-established in the UK with new generations of machines being introduced which provide a broader range of services. The substantial system costs, which have been shared between institutions, need to be balanced against the cost savings from using fewer bank staff to deal with routine transactions. ATMs may pose a problem in that individuals make less use of the inside of the bank branch so that marketing opportunities may be lost. EFTPOL and EFTPOS have been slow to develop in the UK although many of the initial problems are now being overcome. A more recent development is the Mondex card, which is a 'smart card' providing electronic currency to replace cash. The system is being pilot tested on up to 40 000 people in Swindon. Funds can be transferred to the card, which contains a microchip, by using an ATM or the telephone. The funds can then be spent like cash in outlets with Mondex terminals, or alternatively transferred to other Mondex cards. If the test is successful then the card and system could be available nationwide in 1996. It is highly likely that this development will, in time, accelerate the rate of increase of cashless transactions, which have been rising as a result of debit cards etc.

Links between financial services firms may involve shared networks to provide certain products in order to minimize costs. A key point about such joint ventures is that they may be highly pro-competitive as they keep in business firms who may otherwise disappear and it also makes entry easier if exclusionary and other non-competitive factors are prohibited (Chiplin, 1986). Links have also developed between different types of financial services firms. For example, building society, bank and independent broker branches may use a terminal link to obtain the best insurance policy quotation for a potential purchaser.

Internal uses of information technology which are of particular relevance for this book are the development of marketing information systems. Databases may be constructed from information contained in, for example, insurance policy proposal forms, mortgage applications, and savings account details. The information so collected, when suitably organized to relate to individuals, may be integrated for marketing purposes. For example, individuals with the characteristics of purchasers of a certain range of products may be selected to receive a direct mail shot of a new related product. However, in order to achieve such uses of information technology great effort is required in obtaining information of sufficient detail and reliability. Some financial institutions have faced major problems in converting computer systems developed on an account rather than an individual basis and also in training personnel to use information for marketing purposes at local levels (Watkins and Wright, 1986), and many millions of pounds have been invested in more marketing-orientated systems.

## 1.6 The changing boundaries of financial services firms

The changes in the general competitive and regulatory environment that have been analysed in the previous sections have had direct implications for the boundaries of financial services firms. The changing boundaries which occur may be both internal and external as firms seek to restructure themselves so as to be better able to compete. Internally, there may be a need to shift from a functional based organization structure to a flexible one which focuses on products (Johne and Harborne, 1985). In retail banking, the traditional head office–branch relationship has come under increased pressure which reflects the need to market different products in different ways. The hierarchical structure and related attitudes apparent in the branch network have become increasingly inappropriate to the new requirements of retail banking, such as relationship banking and the increased need for specialists to assist in the cross-selling process. Major training and recruitment programmes have been introduced to develop a body of staff with the requisite skills. Also many older staff have been offered early retirement to avoid the need for retraining. In addition improved management accounting systems have been introduced to enable product profitability and cost control to be effected. Internal cohesion may need to be increased in order that opportunities for cross-selling in diversified groups can be fully exploited. This has also precipitated further investment in information technology to help ensure that all opportunities are pursued. For example, in a typical small management buy-out proposal received by a bank branch there will be a need to introduce equity capital, key person insurance, industrial mortgage, leasing, factoring etc. Traditionally, it would not be uncommon for these product opportunities to be offered to local outside providers even thought they were available within another part of the group. Internal marketing and communication may be required to increase awareness, reduce cross-activity jealousies and to enable cross-selling to occur. Increased competition places particular emphasis on the need to make these changes. A survey by the Nottingham Institute of Financial Studies undertaken as firms were implementing their strategic development plans showed that the main internal organizational problems were as shown in Table 1.4.

**Table 1.4** *Major management difficulties in the introduction of new products (%)*

|  | Very important | | Important | | Not important | | Not relevant | |
|---|---|---|---|---|---|---|---|---|
|  | B. Soc. | Bank | B. Soc. | Bank | B. Soc. | Bank | B. Soc. | Bank |
| (a) | | | | | | | | |
| Products introduced by acquisition | | | | | | | | |
| Difficulties in combining management styles | 31.7 | 36 | 29.3 | 36 | 9.8 | 5 | 29.5 | 23 |
| Difficulties in combining computer systems | 34.1 | 50 | 29.3 | 18 | 9.8 | 9 | 26.8 | 23 |
| (b) | | | | | | | | |
| For products introduced by internal product development | | | | | | | | |
| Difficulties in recruiting specialist staff | 41.5 | 32 | 41.5 | 68 | 17.1 | – | – | – |
| Difficulties in dealing with change in the organization | 43.9 | 36 | 46.3 | 50 | 9.8 | 9 | – | 5 |

*Source*: Ennew and Wright (1990b).

Recruitment of specialist staff was seen to be a major difficulty, together with the need to develop an appropriate organization structure. The techniques of strategy assessment were also found to be limited and to be in the process of development so as to permit financial services firms to better analyse their market positions (Ennew and Wright, 1990b).

External changes to a firm's boundaries relate to increased or occasionally decreased size and may be undertaken to better enable the firm to compete in existing markets or to enter new ones. These markets may be in the home country or increasingly of a cross-border nature, either within Europe or globally. As firms seek to implement these strategic developments, three essential choices are available: the establishment of new outlets ('greenfield sites' or branch conversions), joint ventures and links with other service providers, or acquisition. The second half of the 1980s saw a sharply increased trend towards joint ventures and acquisitions carried out to enable diversification to occur. More recently some large building societies have decided to cease acting as a tied agent to a particular insurance company and to form their own life assurance subsidiary instead. Those societies feel that the profits from administering such business themselves will outweigh the commission payments received from the life company concerned. In addition, takeovers and mergers within institutional types have continued as will be seen in detail later on in this book. For example, the number of building societies fell from 273 in 1980 to 115 in 1989 and the trend has continued unabated. Mergers occurred both amongst the smaller regional societies and between some of the very large ones – the former seeking to strengthen their niche market positions, the latter aiming to have sufficient resources to enable a broader range of services to be provided (Ennew and Wright, 1990b). Such mergers raise a number of well-known problems concerning the integration of management styles and computer systems, and rationalization of personnel and branches. In addition, where societies are tied agents for the distribution of the products of different insurance companies under the provisions of the Financial Services Act, a choice has to be made as to which tie will be maintained. The direct acquisition cost has also begun to arise as an issue in the building society sector. Hitherto, account holders in societies had not been compensated as would happen with shareholders in a business whose ownership was transferred. The acquisition by the Cheltenham and Gloucester Building Society of the Guardian Building Society in 1989 was the first case in which account holders were compensated. The attempt by Lloyds Bank to take over the Cheltenham and Gloucester Building Society has invoked much debate regarding the legality of a third party offering compensation to certain types of members and borrowers. The Lloyds–Cheltenham and Gloucester merger and the proposed merger between Halifax and Leeds are indicative of a long-term trend towards greater concentration in branch-based retailing of financial services.

Such issues arise, perhaps to an even greater extent, in diversifying market entry and are, for example, reflected in the different routes chosen by financial services firms entering estate agency (Ennew and Wright, 1990b). Acquisition, franchising, joint ventures, partial acquisitions and new start-ups have all been used, often by the same firm as it seeks to build market share quickly. A recent study of diversification by building societies (Ingham and Thompson, 1994) concluded that larger firms which had sufficient capital and other resources preferred wholly owned ventures rather than collaborative ones due to the control costs associated with joint ventures.

This pattern in the UK market is being reproduced across Europe as financial services firms seek to reconfigure their size and span of activities either as a proactive move to take advantage of new opportunities or as a defensive move in the light of increased competition. There has been a substantial increase in the level of acquisition activity involving banks in the same country which reflects the need for rationalization of large numbers of regional banks in some countries (see for example, Mottura and Munari, 1990 for the case of Italy). Also in the banking sector, the French savings banks have pioneered a framework of cooperation agreements with other Community savings banks as a cost-effective alternative to establishing new branch networks or acquisitions.

Cross-border entry may further magnify the problems of entry and diversification found in domestic markets. For example, 'greenfield site' cross-border entry in banking may be unattractive in markets with existing branching capacity and entry into retail insurance may only be feasible on a large scale with a tied salesforce. Entry by merger also is not without its problems. Community merger policy has been notoriously problematical to establish and national restrictions on takeovers may still pose problems of entry. Moreover, the attainment of economies of scale and scope from merger are by no means unambiguously clear, varying as they do, between retail and wholesale sectors. In the wholesale (and corporate) sector cross-border provision of services is less problematical as there is no need for extensive local branch networks. In the retail sectors, economies of scale and scope may be outweighed by economies of specialization. The key financial service attributes of trust, security, confidence, branding, and consumer protection (Carter et al., 1986) may be perceived by individuals as coming from those financial institutions established in their country with a local, familiar name. As a result, the structure of the European financial services industry may be more heavily influenced by the extent to which intermediation by retailers – between wholesalers and customers – is profitable. Intermediaries fulfil the role of monitoring a large number of providers of services which would be beyond the ability of individuals. If economies of scale and scope are limited, organizational forms other than those produced by merger may also be important for service provision. In particular, various forms of horizontal or vertical quasi-internal or managed market relationships may be more effective (Thompson and Wright, 1988).

Where there is experimentation in the nature and extent of market entry, some failures may be expected with a consequent need to undo arrangements which initially seemed correct (Ennew, Wong and Wright, 1992). In the UK, divestments by some building societies of at least part of the estate agency networks they have established by acquisition reflect the difficulties of integration. These problems are magnified where very high acquisition prices have been paid. The perceived need to build market share quickly in competition with other entrants contributed to this problem. However, where rates of growth in the sector could not be sustained, prices may have been paid which more than discount future benefits. Problems may also arise with joint ventures and other similar arrangements. Different managerial approaches may be difficult enough to resolve in straightforward acquisitions, where it is usually clear that the acquirer is the dominant partner (Jones, 1985). In joint ventures there may be no such clarity. One party may want dominance but be resisted forcefully by the other. Hence, great care and caution are required in selecting the appropriate partner and in defining the scope of the joint venture. Clear evidence of an increased rate of divestment by financial services firms towards the end of the 1980s and early 1990 is provided by a study which showed the annual amount of divestments doubling at this time (Ennew et al., 1992). This increase is a function of both an increase in efforts by financial firms to rectify unsuccessful diversification and also continuing organizational experimentation.

Many cross-border relationships were established in advance of the regulations to facilitate the EU single market. Evidence from the UK's financial services firms indicated that they generally felt well-placed to benefit from the increased opportunities which were available (Bank of England, 1989). However, it should be noted that there has not been a headlong rush into pan-European diversification with institutions taking so far a more measured approach.

## 1.7 Conclusion

This chapter has reviewed the changing environment affecting financial services firms in the UK and Europe and sets the scene for the development of marketing activity which is addressed in the chapters that follow. It has been shown that the environmental changes have several dimensions and that the full implications of regulatory changes in the UK and Europe continue to be worked out. The appropriate actions to be taken by firms in the light of these environmental developments will vary according to circumstances but many changes have occurred and indeed continue to occur in both their internal and external boundaries.

Such changes allow for the introduction of new management styles and skills and the provision of new products either within the firm, following acquisition, or outside in some form of joint arrangement with other institutions. Different market strategies require a variety of entry methods. The market strategies adopted are influenced not only by different managers' perceptions of future prospects, but also the capital base available to individual firms to enable prudent growth policies to be introduced. It is also clear that with the high degree of uncertainty in financial service firms' environments, caution and experimentation have been exercised. By its nature, experimentation is likely to produce the need to undo failed actions. Many companies have reasserted their initial decisions and have as a result embarked on a major change of course. Hence, in considering entry strategies firms also need to weigh the costs and barriers to exit, as divestment becomes a more common phenomenon in financial services markets.

# 2 Understanding consumers and markets

## Sally McKechnie and Tina Harrison

## 2.1 Introduction

Marketing is concerned with supplying consumers with products or services which they want. In order for an organization to be able to do this successfully, marketers need to be able to understand the needs and motivations of existing and potential consumers, as well as how they go about making buying decisions. This knowledge is crucial to the development of suitable marketing strategies, whereby a competitive advantage for an organization in its chosen markets is identified, built and maintained. Unfortunately consumers, with their different needs, requirements and preferences, invariably do not exhibit the same behaviour across all buying situations, nor is their behaviour equally influenced by the same set of factors. Essential to the study of buyer behaviour is an understanding of market segmentation. Through the identification of fairly homogeneous consumer groupings or segments and the tailoring of specific marketing programmes for these segments rather than for the market as a whole, marketers can then engage in a closer matching of customer needs with product offerings that benefit consumer and company alike.

This chapter is concerned with examining consumer demand for financial services and aspects of consumer behaviour including both buying behaviour and market segmentation. Section 2.2 provides an overview of recent trends in the demand for financial services while section 2.3 outlines some of the distinctive characteristics of financial services and discusses their implications for buying behaviour. Sections 2.4 and 2.5 examine issues relating generally to consumer buying behaviour and specifically to financial services. Market segmentation is covered, with general issues discussed in section 2.6, personal financial services in section 2.7 and corporate markets in section 2.8. A summary and conclusions is presented in section 2.9.

## 2.2 Recent trends affecting the market for financial services

There are a number of important demographic and socio-economic trends which have influenced the patterns of demand for financial services over recent years. As Table 2.1 shows, the population of Great Britain is ageing.

**Table 2.1** *Projected population of Great Britain at mid-year by age*

|  | 1991 Base | 1995 | 2000 | 2010 | 2020 |
|---|---|---|---|---|---|
| Total (millions) | 56.1 | 56.9 | 57.9 | 59.3 | 60.1 |
| Index | 100.0 | 101.4 | 103.2 | 105.7 | 107.3 |
| 0–4 | 6.7 | 6.7 | 6.5 | 5.8 | 5.8 |
| 5–14 | 12.3 | 12.8 | 13.1 | 12.4 | 11.5 |
| 15–29 | 22.5 | 20.5 | 18.8 | 19.2 | 18.7 |
| 30–44 | 21.1 | 21.5 | 22.4 | 19.9 | 18.2 |
| 45–64 | 21.6 | 22.7 | 23.5 | 26.2 | 26.6 |
| 65+ | 15.8 | 15.8 | 15.7 | 16.5 | 19.2 |

*Source*: Advertising Association (1994a)

Between 1990 and 2020 it is projected that the number of 15–29-year-olds and 30–44-year-olds will fall by 3.8 per cent and 2.9 per cent respectively, while the number of middle-aged people is expected to rise by 5.0 per cent for 45–64-year-olds and 3.4 per cent for those over 64. Johnson (1990a; 1990b) examines the impact of demographically induced shifts on the nature of demand for goods and services, and the particular need for marketers to recognize the increasing importance of consumers over fifty in terms of their relative market power.

The number of households in Great Britain has been steadily increasing from 20.3 million in 1982 to 22.5 million in 1992 (Advertising Association, 1994b), although it is eventually likely to fall as a result of the above-mentioned demographic changes. Table 2.2 illustrates the substantial increase which has occurred over the last thirty years in the number of single-person and single-parent households as a result of postponement of marriage, high divorce rates and longer life expectancy for females.

Overall the growth in the mortgage market is due to an increase in the number of households as well as new demand from first-time buyers. When the number of owner-occupied households is compared to total housing stock, there has been a steady increase from 60.6 per cent in 1984 to 67.1 per cent in 1990 (Advertising Association, 1993). This can

**Table 2.2** *British households by type (%)*

|  | 1961 | 1971 | 1981 | 1991 | 1992 |
|---|---|---|---|---|---|
| Living alone | 3.9 | 6.3 | 8.0 | 10.7 | 11.1 |
| Married couple, no children | 17.8 | 19.3 | 19.5 | 23.0 | 23.4 |
| Married couple with dependent children | 52.2 | 51.7 | 47.4 | 41.2 | 39.9 |
| Married couple with non-dependent children only | 11.6 | 10.0 | 10.3 | 10.8 | 10.9 |
| Lone parent with dependent children | 2.5 | 3.5 | 5.8 | 10.0 | 10.1 |
| Other households | 12.0 | 9.2 | 9.0 | 4.3 | 4.6 |

*Source*: Central Statistical Office, *Social Trends, 24*, 1994

**Table 2.3**  *Weekly household expenditure on financial services*

|                              | 1981     | 1987     | 1988     | 1989     | 1990     | 1991     |
|------------------------------|----------|----------|----------|----------|----------|----------|
| Total household expenditure  | £177.40  | £269.70  | £294.80  | £330.70  | £372.50  | £383.60  |
| Savings and investments      | 1.8%     | 1.8%     | 1.2%     | 1.1%     | 1.1%     | 1.2%     |
| Loans and mortgages          | 4.1%     | 5.2%     | 5.3%     | 6.1%     | 6.8%     | 6.7%     |
| Life assurance and pensions  | 3.2%     | 3.8%     | 4.3%     | 4.2%     | 4.3%     | 4.5%     |
| General insurance            | 0.7%     | 1.2%     | 1.4%     | 1.4%     | 1.3%     | 1.5%     |

*Source*: Tillinghast (1993)

be attributed to changes in government policy and attitudes on owner occupation via mortgage interest tax relief and 'right to buy' legislation, as well as house price levels and the availability/affordability of housing finance (Hughes, 1994). The currently high levels of owner occupancy and a slower growth in the number of households has important implications for the future development of the mortgage market.

The level of consumers' income and wealth is seen as one of the most important influences on the level of financial services consumption (Vittas and Frazer, 1982). Over the past decade individual consumers have generally become better off and this has been reflected in consumption of financial services. Looking more specifically at investments, life assurance policies and pensions as a proportion of household income, there was a 7 per cent increase from 11 per cent in 1971 to 18 per cent in 1990 (Hughes, 1994).

The decline in savings and investments since 1988 shown in Table 2.3 was indicative of the exceptionally high interest rates experienced during that period. There was a marginal increase in the proportion spent on life assurance and pensions as a result of the government's launch of personal pensions.

There has been a 10 per cent shift from cash payments to non-cash payments during the period 1984 to 1992 (see Table 2.4) following the introduction of automated money transmission systems. Paying by cheque has remained popular with 68 per cent of all adults possessing a current account with a bank and 7 per cent with a building society (see Table 2.5). Surprisingly there has only been a slight increase in usage of standing order/direct debit payment facilities, yet this can perhaps be explained by research which has concluded that consumers believe such facilities result in loss of control over their accounts (Burton, 1994).

It is interesting to note that, despite the Thatcherite drive towards privatization and share ownership, there was only a 1 per cent increase in the proportion of the total number of adults owning shares over the last five years (16 per cent – National Opinion Polls Financial Research Survey, October 1988–March 1989).

**Table 2.4** *Methods of consumer payment (Great Britain)*

|                              | 1984 | 1989 | 1990 | 1991 | 1992 |
|------------------------------|------|------|------|------|------|
| *All payments*               |      |      |      |      |      |
| Cash[1]                      | 86   | 80   | 78   | 78   | 76   |
| Non-cash                     | 14   | 20   | 22   | 22   | 24   |
| *Non-cash payments*          |      |      |      |      |      |
| Cheque                       | 64   | 55   | 52   | 50   | 46   |
| Standing order/direct debit  | 22   | 23   | 23   | 24   | 25   |
| All plastic payment cards    | 13   | 18   | 20   | 23   | 25   |
| of which:                    |      |      |      |      |      |
| Credit/charge card           | 12   | 15   | 15   | 14   | 14   |
| Retailer card                | –    | 1    | 1    | 1    | 1    |
| Debit card                   | 0    | 2    | 4    | 8    | 11   |
| Other[2]                     | 1    | 4    | 4    | 3    | 4    |

[1] excludes payments under £1
[2] includes deductions direct from wages/salaries and payments made by Postal Order
*Source :* Central Statistical Office, *Social Trends 24,* 1994

## 2.3 Characteristics of services and their implications for buyer behaviour

Over the last decade there has been a growing interest in the field of services marketing in general and in the financial services sector in particular. Much of the literature to date has been concerned either with the extent to which services marketing requires a separate approach from the marketing of physical goods or with identifying specific marketing strategies to deal with the problems posed by the unique characteristics of services. Services are typically distinguished from goods on the grounds of intangibility, inseparability, heterogeneity and perishability and, while goods and services are not polar extremes, these characteristics tend to dominate in services and create problems for services marketing. Although less explicitly recognized in the literature, the characteristics of services, including those of financial services, will also have an important impact on buyer behaviour. Thus any attempt to understand the purchase decision-making process must recognize the ways in which buyer behaviour can be affected by these characteristics.

Intangibility is the main distinguishing feature, since services are processes or experiences rather than physical objects and therefore cannot be possessed (Lovelock, 1981; Shostack, 1977; Bowen and Schneider, 1988). Furthermore intangibility can be double-edged in the sense that services are not only impalpable but also difficult for consumers to grasp mentally (Bateson, 1977). Accordingly, when compared with goods, services are low in search qualities (tangible attributes which can be considered in advance) and are therefore more difficult to evaluate pre-purchase. Conversely services are high in experience qualities, which refer to attributes which can only be assessed after purchase or during consumption. Furthermore many professional or specialist services will also be high in

**Table 2.5:** *Holding of selected personal financial products (%) Social class*

| | Total | Male | Female | A | AB | C1 | C2 | DE | 16–20 | 21–24 | 25–34 | 35–44 | 45–54 | 55–64 | 65+ |
|---|---|---|---|---|---|---|---|---|---|---|---|---|---|---|---|
| Population profile | 100 | 48 | 52 | 2 | 16 | 26 | 24 | 32 | 10 | 7 | 19 | 17 | 14 | 13 | 20 |
| *Penetration* | | | | | | | | | | | | | | | |
| Bank current account | 68 | 71 | 65 | 89 | 86 | 80 | 71 | 48 | 51 | 66 | 69 | 75 | 77 | 71 | 62 |
| Building society current account | 7 | 7 | 7 | 8 | 9 | 9 | 7 | 5 | 5 | 9 | 11 | 9 | 6 | 6 | 4 |
| Bank instant access | 8 | 18 | 18 | 25 | 22 | 19 | 18 | 16 | 19 | 17 | 15 | 18 | 20 | 19 | 19 |
| Bank deposit account | 9 | 9 | 9 | 8 | 7 | 9 | 10 | 10 | 10 | 8 | 7 | 9 | 10 | 9 | 10 |
| Building society instant access | 37 | 36 | 37 | 36 | 44 | 44 | 39 | 27 | 30 | 36 | 43 | 42 | 39 | 34 | 31 |
| Building society ordinary share account | 10 | 9 | 10 | 6 | 9 | 11 | 10 | 9 | 8 | 9 | 11 | 12 | 10 | 8 | 8 |
| Bank restricted access account | 3 | 3 | 3 | 8 | 5 | 3 | 3 | 2 | 1 | 1 | 2 | 2 | 4 | 5 | 4 |
| Building society restricted access account | 14 | 14 | 13 | 24 | 23 | 17 | 14 | 7 | 5 | 7 | 9 | 13 | 17 | 22 | 18 |
| Stocks and shares | 16 | 18 | 13 | 41 | 32 | 19 | 14 | 6 | 3 | 9 | 12 | 18 | 22 | 24 | 17 |
| Bank credit card [1] | 31 | 35 | 27 | 62 | 57 | 41 | 28 | 12 | 5 | 18 | 32 | 42 | 41 | 36 | 19 |
| Bank loan [2] | 5 | 7 | 4 | 5 | 5 | 6 | 7 | 4 | 2 | 9 | 9 | 7 | 5 | 1 | * |
| Retail store account [1] | 16 | 13 | 19 | 38 | 33 | 21 | 13 | 6 | 4 | 10 | 17 | 22 | 22 | 17 | 9 |
| Life assurance [2] | 58 | 62 | 55 | 57 | 61 | 62 | 67 | 48 | 15 | 40 | 65 | 73 | 71 | 60 | 45 |

Base: 28,713 adults aged 16+ in Great Britain, October–March 1994
[1] Base: 27,451 adults aged 18+ in Great Britain, October–March 1994
[2] Base: 28,665 adults aged 18+ in Great Britain, July–December 1993
* Less than 0.5 per cent
*Source:* National Opinion Polls Financial Research Survey

credence qualities, which are attributes which cannot even be assessed after purchase and consumption (Zeithaml, 1981). Thus, for example for many consumers, any evaluation of financial advice given or product recommendations made must be based on trust in the financial adviser. As a consequence of intangibility, the ways in which services are evaluated, particularly at the pre-purchase stage, are likely to differ from goods, and this area needs further consideration in understanding buyer behaviour for services.

The second factor distinguishing services from goods is inseparability. The fact that services are processes or experiences means that typically they must be produced and consumed simultaneously. This leads to a third distinctive feature, namely perishability: services cannot be stored for some future time period, hence the need for short distribution channels so that they can be produced on demand (Bateson, 1977). The inseparability of production and consumption in services makes production and marketing interactive processes (Gronroos, 1978). The frontline service employees play an important 'boundary spanning role' in the production of services, as do the consumers themselves in their capacity as 'partial employees' (Bowen and Schneider, 1988). Therefore in understanding buyer behaviour it will be important to consider the interaction between buyer and supplier. Since services depend upon input from both service employees and consumers for their production, the quality of the service output very much depends on the nature of the personal interactions of these parties. This makes the potential for variability in the service performance high, which leads to the next distinctive characteristic of services, namely heterogeneity – the potential for greater variability in quality.

In addition to these distinguishing features of services there are two further characteristics which are particularly relevant to financial services, namely fiduciary responsibility and two-way information flows between buyer and seller. Fiduciary responsibility refers to the implicit responsibility of financial services organizations for the management of their customers' funds and the nature of the financial advice supplied to their customers. In financial services transactions what is essentially being exchanged is a set of promises between the buyer and the seller. From the buyer's point of view much depends on what exactly is being promised and the likelihood of such promises being delivered (Lewis and Chiplin, 1986). In the case of long-term savings plans, for example, it is often difficult for consumers to evaluate these promises that are given in the absence of full information. Decisions on whether or not to purchase such services are more likely to be based on experience and credence qualities as there are fewer search qualities (Zeithaml, 1981). Before any financial resources change hands consumers must have confidence and trust not only in the financial institution concerned but also in its personnel. Apart from relying more on information from personal sources, consumers are likely to consider factors such as the size, longevity and image of the financial services organization as indicators of whether or not any promises made are sound and likely to be fulfilled. The establishment of trust can also bring about a degree of inertia in buyer-seller relationships.

Since an irreversible amount of time and effort is required by an individual in order to acquire the necessary experience and information on which to assess an institution's reliability, it is usually the case that once satisfied a consumer is more likely to remain with that institution than incur the costs of searching for and vetting alternative suppliers. As far as two-way information flows are concerned, what is unique about financial services is that, rather than being concerned with one-off purchases, they involve a series of regular two-way transactions between buyer and seller usually over an extended period of time (for example through the issue of account statements or customer visits to branches or ATM usage). As a by–product of the normal operation of these transactions a great deal of up-to-date private and confidential customer information is captured, which can subsequently be used to maintain and develop relationships with existing customers as well as attracting new ones.

## 2.4  Understanding consumer buying behaviour

Understanding the nature of consumer buying behaviour has been a key component of research in marketing for some considerable time. If organizations are to be able to anticipate likely customer reactions to their marketing strategies and influence them where appropriate, it is crucial that they understand the needs and motivations of their customers and prospects. The understanding of consumer buying behaviour in the context of services is still poorly developed. Murray (1991) noted that in spite of the recent attention that had been paid to the field of services marketing, relatively less effort had been devoted to developing an understanding of consumer buying behaviour for services, particularly search behaviour in the purchase decision process. Indeed Gabbott and Hogg's (1994) literature review of consumer behaviour and services bears testimony to this fact, having sourced very little that explicitly refers to the consumption characteristics of services.

Much of the conceptual work has centred around the view of consumer buying behaviour as a decision process consisting of a number of discrete but interlinked stages. Probably the best example of this is the Engel–Kollat–Blackwell model (Engel, Blackwell and Miniard, 1991) which breaks the decision-making process into five stages: problem recognition, information search, evaluation of alternatives, purchase decision and post purchase behaviour. A similar approach was adopted by Nicosia's (1966) model of consumer decision-making and also the Howard–Sheth (1969) model. In essence these models were built around the decision-making process succinctly summarized by the mnemonic AIDA, standing for Awareness, Interest, Desire and Action. These models are part of a group of response hierarchy models, which appears in the adoption and diffusion literature. They are based on the assumption that buyers will pass through a cognitive, affective and behavioural stage when there is a high degree of involvement with a product category which is perceived to have a high degree of differentiation of products within it. There is also some evidence of similar approaches being used in organizational buying behaviour: for example, Robinson and Faris' (1967) 'Buy Grid' model which analyses buying decisions across a series of sequential 'buy phases' for different types of buying situation, as well as the models by Webster and Wind (1972), Sheth (1973) and Baker (1983).

This general type of approach has been subject to criticism. The consumer buying behaviour models mentioned above were criticized on the grounds that they could not be tested and lacked specificity (Tuck, 1976) and were all founded on a rational decision sequence which assumed too rational a consumer and did not offer any empirically testable hypotheses (Foxall, 1991). Similarly organizational buying behaviour models were criticized by Turnbull (1991) for assuming a discrete and ordered process, since there was evidence to suggest that stages in the process could occur simultaneously or out of sequence depending upon the buying situation. A further problem with these models is that they are all typically concerned with one-off purchases rather than recurrent ones.

Baker (1983) recognized that it would be unrealistic to expect any model to completely encapsulate the complexity and dynamic nature of the buying process, and stated that an additional variable was required to act as a catalyst for his composite model to work: the specialized knowledge and experience of persons familiar to the specific product–market interface being studied. The need to recognize explicitly the importance of the buyer–seller interface was more explicitly addressed by the IMP (Industrial/International Marketing and Purchasing) group of researchers, whose model of organizational buying behaviour represented a major departure from previous approaches. This model sets out to conceptualize industrial marketing and purchasing as an interactive process which takes place within the context of long-term relationships between buyers and sellers. It was because of the centrality of this relationship to the buying process that it was necessary to study the two activities jointly rather than simply look at each aspect separately. The underlying rationale of the model represents a significant shift from the more traditional view of marketing which considers a marketer actively managing a marketing mix to match the needs of passive customers in an atomistic market (Ford, 1990).

The interaction model is built on four factors: firstly, both buyer and seller are active participants in the market; secondly, the buyer–seller relationship is frequently long term, close and involves a complex pattern of interaction between and within each company; thirdly, links between both parties often become institutionalized into a set of roles that each party expects the other to perform; and, finally, close relationships are often considered in the context of continuous raw materials or component supply. In essence this framework considers the role of marketing to be the establishment, development and maintenance of relationships between buyer and seller companies (Hakansson, 1982). The constituent components of the model are the interactive process, the participants involved, the environment within which the interaction takes place and the atmosphere affecting or affected by the interaction. As a conceptual framework it enables deeper insight not only into the components of the organizational buying decision-making process, but also the ways in which these components interact with one another. However, Turnbull (1991), whilst acknowledging that this model portrayed the complex nature of the organizational buying process, pointed out that no single model adequately explained all the complexities of this process; a universal pattern of relationships had yet to be found in order to build a comprehensive model.

## 2.5   Consumer buying behaviour in financial services

Although there is a wealth of conceptual and empirical material concerned with how buyers make decisions, most of this work was developed in the context of studying purchases of physical goods rather than services. By contrast in the services marketing and financial services marketing literature the conceptual and empirical work is less well-developed. The reasons for this may be threefold: firstly, there may be problems with the conceptual models themselves in that they do not lend themselves to empirical testing (see Tuck, 1976; Foxall, 1991); secondly, it is not clear that these models are necessarily the most appropriate conceptual frameworks to use in any case; and, thirdly, there has been a lack of appropriate measures of salient dimensions for testing concepts in services marketing situations (Teas, Dorsch and McAlexander, 1988). There is little, if any, theoretical work on how consumers buy services. Zeithaml (1981) examined how consumer evaluation processes differed between goods and services: because of the intangibility, inseparability and heterogeneity of services, there are fewer tangible cues on which to base decisions prior to purchase. Therefore greater reliance is placed on experience qualities after purchase or during consumption, or on credence qualities since consumers find it extremely difficult to assess in hindsight whether they entrusted the right organization with the management of their financial resources. In contrast, Gabbott and Hogg (1994) selected stages from the general decision-making process as a means of highlighting problems consumers may have in searching for information about services, comparing them and evaluating them after consumption. Two examples are noted of models being used specifically for financial services: the adaptation of 'AIDA' by Guirdham (1987) for complex financial products such as PEPs, shares and unit trusts (see Betts 1994), and the development of a model of SME buyer behaviour as a result of differences observed between large corporations and smaller and medium-sized businesses by File and Prince (1992).

The lack of an acceptable theoretical framework has not inhibited empirical work. The results of a variety of studies of buying behaviour for both personal and corporate financial services are summarized in Tables 2.6 and 2.7. It is apparent from Table 2.6 that empirical work has tended on the whole to shy away from testing conceptual frameworks, perhaps due to the assumption that the existing ones are satisfactory or due to the difficulty of testing. Instead, the focus has been on specific issues in relation to buying behaviour such as factors affecting the choice

**Table 2.6** *Personal financial services buying behaviour*

| Author(s) | Field of study | Geographic area | Key finding(s) |
|---|---|---|---|
| Shultz II & Prince (1994) | Application of peripheral compliance-gaining techniques when selling financial services to the affluent | North America/Pacific Rim/Europe/South America | Infotainment is an important tool for relationship management |
| Boyd et al. (1994) | Consumer choice criteria in financial institution selection | USA | Reputation and interest rates (loans/savings) more important than friendliness of employees, modern facilities, drive-in service |
| Chan (1993) | Banking services for young intellectuals | Hong Kong | Financial sophistication of youth market |
| Ennew (1992) | Consumer attitudes to independent advice | UK | More importance may be attached to image and reputation of an independent financial adviser than their status |
| Joy, Kim & Laroche (1991) | Link between ethnicity and use of financial services | Canada | Ethnicity should be considered as a construct having strong potential impact on consumption |
| Leonard & Spencer (1991) | Importance of bank image as a competitive strategy for increasing customer traffic flow | USA | Preference for banks amongst students as providers of financial services; greater confidence in large–medium-sized banks; importance of courtesy of personnel, competitive deposit rates, loan availability |
| Lewis (1991) | International comparison of bank customers' expectations and perceptions of service quality | UK/USA | Very high expectations of service quality and high perceptions of service received, yet gaps did exist |
| Lewis & Bingham (1991) | Needs, attitudes and behaviours of youth market for financial services | UK | Youth market not homogeneous in terms of needs and behaviour |
| Meidan & Moutinho (1988) | Bank customer perceptions and loyalty | UK | Banks should develop ATM usage; financial institutions should review basic banking services e.g considering a service package; customer loyalty a function of more than one single variable |
| Jain, Pinson & Maholtra (1987) | Customer loyalty in retail banking | USA | Customer loyalty is a useful construct; bank non-loyal segment swayed by economic rationale, whereas greater emphasis placed on human aspects of banking by bank loyal segment |
| Furlong & Brent Ritchie (1986) | Consumer concept testing of personal financial services among corporate employees | Canada | Clear preferences on nature and delivery of financial services, sometimes at odds with professional perceptions |
| Laroche, Rosenblatt & Manning (1986) | Factors influencing choice of bank | Canada | Importance of location convenience, speed of service, competence and friendliness of bank personnel |
| Arora, Cavusgil & Nevin (1985) | Choice criteria used in financial institutions | USA | Common criteria for bank and savings/loans customers: e.g. dependability of institution, convenience and ease of transactions, variety of services and size of institution |
| Martenson (1985) | Consumer choice criteria in bank selection | Sweden | Random decisions by a third of respondents; importance of bank location, availability of loans, bank where salary paid through, and parental influences |
| Kaynak & Yucelt (1984) | Comparison of attitudinal orientations of US and Canadian credit card users | US/Canada | Similar patterns in attitudes to owning and using a credit card |
| Laroche & Manning (1984) | Information processing activity of consumer bank selection | Canada | Existence of a 'foggy set' of bank brands rather than a 'hold set' |

**Table 2.7** *Corporate financial services buying behaviour*

| Author(s) | Field of study | Geographic area | Key findings |
|---|---|---|---|
| Edwards (1992) | Current and future use of foreign banks by UK middle corporate market | UK | Very conservative approach to domestic banking with foreign banks used as secondary banks |
| File & Prince (1991) | Purchase dynamics of SME market and financial services | USA | Existence of three distinctive sociographic segments adopting innovations in bank services: return seekers, relevance seekers and relationship seekers |
| Chan & Ma (1990) | Corporate customer buying behaviour for banking services | Hong Kong | Great importance attached to banks understanding their clients' attitudes in order to serve them better |
| Yorke (1990) | Interactive perceptions of suppliers and corporate clients in marketing of professional services | UK/Canada Sweden | Need to consider atmosphere in which relationship is being conducted to build picture of mutual perceptions of parties into medium- to long-term planning activity |
| Turnbull & Gibbs (1989) | Relationship between large companies and its lead and closest substitute bank | South Africa | Predominant bank selection criteria: importance of quality of service, quality of staff and price of services; split banking common |
| Teas, Dorsch & McAlexander (1988) | Measurement of four important aspects of the long-term commercial bank and commercial customer relationship: banker's customer knowledge, personal working relationship with bank, banker's reactive and proactive behaviour | USA | Banks should take an active interest in the welfare of their commercial customers to be in a better position to develop long-term relationships with them |
| Turnbull (1983) | Relationship between banks' corporate customers and their sources of financial services | UK | Small/medium-sized companies do not always consider major UK banks as an appropriate source for all financial services |
| Turnbull (1982a) | Purchase of international financial services by medium-sized, large UK companies with European subsidiaries | UK | Greater effort required to understand the nature of customer needs and bank/customer relationships through detailed application of the Interaction theory |
| Turnbull (1982b) | Role of branch bank manager in bank services marketing | UK | Lack of customer orientation amongst bank branch managers |
| Turnbull (1982c) | Use of foreign banks by UK companies | UK | High concentration of decision-making and extent of split banking; crucial importance of development and maintenance of a company-bank relationship |

of bank and usage of financial services, customer loyalty, customer expectations and perceptions and service quality.

On the whole these empirical studies highlight the importance of factors such as confidence, trust and customer loyalty. Some of the common choice criteria in bank selection are dependability and size of the institution, location, convenience and ease of transactions, professionalism of bank personnel and availability of loans. It would appear therefore that the personal consumer is more interested in the functional quality dimension of financial services (i.e. how the service is delivered) rather than the technical quality dimension (i.e. what is actually received as the outcome of the production process) (see Gronroos, 1984b). This is not surprising given the difficulties consumers have in evaluating services (Zeithaml, 1981). The main areas of study summarized in Table 2.7 are the commercial bank/commercial customer interface in terms of the interaction process, mutual perceptions held and long-term relationships, factors affecting choice of bank and usage of international financial services and the need for customer orientation.

The application of some organizational buying behaviour models to the purchasing of international financial services was attempted by Turnbull (1982a), who concluded that no single model adequately explained all the complexities of these purchases. Nevertheless he pointed out that certain aspects of three theories seemed to lend themselves well in this respect. First of all the application of the Interaction model by the IMP group seemed to be particularly appropriate. Addressing the importance and nature of relationships between companies and banks, the interaction model examines factors which influence search and decision processes, in particular the 'atmosphere' in which these relationships are conducted. Secondly, consideration was given to the application of the stages of the purchase process put forward by Robinson and Faris (1967), which led to the conclusion that the financial purchasing process largely followed these sequences. Finally it was observed that the organizational factors in the Webster and Wind (1972) model also seemed to be appropriate. The buying centre concept from this model was also applied in another study (Turnbull, 1982c), which identified a low number of people directly involved in the decision-making process. In this same study the importance of developing and maintaining company–bank relationships was considered, and it was recognized that (although already widely accepted in US banks) customer contact employees played a key role in establishing relationships with new clients. The importance of company–bank relationships was stressed even further by Turnbull and Gibbs (1987) in their discussion of the concept of 'financially responsive relationship management' and the interactive process this entails, as well as the substantial benefits to be gained for both parties concerned. Based on more recent research it was claimed that the commercial banks which would succeed over the next decade would be those which developed systems of financial responsiveness and whose customer contact officers and senior management had a better understanding of corporate customer buying behaviour (Turnbull and Gibbs, 1989).

Yorke (1990) explicitly advocated the adaptation of the Interaction model as being appropriate for the purchase of services, particularly corporate rather than personal services; and stressed the important implications it has for professional supplier firms. Acknowledging the wide recognition of the importance of establishing long-term working relationships in services marketing, Teas et al. (1988) concluded from their empirical research that commercial customers had favourable attitudes to long-term bank relationships where the banks behaved as follows: they were responsive to these customers' requests, initiated interaction with their customers, were knowledgeable about their customers' business and business needs, and developed close informal working relationships with their customers. More recently, the topic of relationship marketing has been examined in the context of personal markets (see for example, Palmer and Bejou, 1994) and such research has typically highlighted to important role of customer contact personnel.

In summary, in services marketing where there is a complex interface between the buyer and the seller much importance needs to be given to the relationships that exist between consumers and service providers and the task of managing the total customer/firm personnel interaction process (Booms and Nyquist, 1981; Gronroos, 1990). Although Foxall (1991) criticized consumer behaviour models for implying high consumer involvement and then indicated the recent development of alternative low involvement theories, it is the case that as far as consumers of services are concerned they are indeed actively involved in shaping up a service offering due to the inseparability of production and consumption.

The relationships formed between buyers and sellers need to be built on mutual trust and commitment if they are to be developed and maintained in the long term. For services generally they can be broad or narrow in scope and continuous or discrete in nature, yet will have a great impact on the future buying behaviour of customers and on word of mouth communications about the services concerned. By their very nature financial services tend not to be one-off purchases but ones which are required on a recurring basis with the result that there is a clear need for financial services suppliers to establish initial relationships with their prospects while at the same time maintain and develop long-term relationships with existing customers. Furthermore financial services are based on customer trust and confidence not only in the organization supplying these services but also particularly in the customer contact employees themselves (Christopher, Payne and Ballantyne, 1991).

Financial services organizations operate in a high contact business where the nature of buyer–seller interactions and the establishment of long-term relationships based on confidence and trust have real implications for successful retention of customers and recruitment of prospects. A recent survey of senior financial services marketers revealed that after pricing policy they perceived the interface with customers as the second most important area of marketing activity as well as the area of second highest potential for improving company performance (Easingwood and Arnott, 1991). These findings were supported by Stephenson and Kiely (1991) who recommended that in the selling of banking services, the emphasis should shift from the promotion of an institutional image to concentration on the crucial boundary-spanning role played by customer contact personnel, since they not only sell and perform these services but are also equated by customers with the service.

## 2.6  Issues in market segmentation

In addition to understanding the factors that influence the buying behaviour of individuals, the development of an effective marketing strategy also requires an understanding of broader patterns of demand and the degree of segmentation within a marketplace. Indeed it is widely recognized that segmentation, targeting and positioning lie at the heart of modern strategic marketing. The process begins with the identification and profiling of different market segments, followed by the selection of particular target markets and finally the positioning of the offering in the mind of the customer to communicate the benefits the customer is seeking. The initial stage cannot function without an understanding of customers and their behaviour.

A number of criteria for effective market segmentation have been identified by Kotler (1994), namely measurability – there must be some way of measuring the size and purchasing power of the segment(s); accessibility – the firm must be able to reach the segment(s); substantiality – the segment(s) should be economically viable; and actionability – the degree to which effective marketing programmes can be designed and implemented to attract and serve the segment(s). Other authors have added the properties of uniqueness, in terms of the segment's response to marketing stimuli (Baker, 1992) and the stability of the segment over time (Thomas, 1980; Yuspeh and Fein, 1982).

Despite the benefits offered from a segmented approach, financial institutions have been slow to realize its full potential. Driven by changes in the regulatory environment (outlined in Chapter 1), increasing competition and pressures on product profitability, financial institutions now realize that they can no longer be all things to all customers, and many institutions are examining the constituent parts of their business to identify those customers offering the greatest potential – to whom the greatest marketing effort should be directed. The challenge lies, however, in identifying the dimensions along which customer needs vary. Since needs and motives are themselves not explicitly identifiable, behavioural scientists have turned to the use of proxy indicators viewed as having a strong correlation with behaviour, possibly even the determinants of behaviour. These variables are generally known as segmentation bases.

Segmentation bases fall broadly into two groups: 'general bases' (independent of any product or service and particular circumstances faced by the customer) and 'situation-specific' bases (related to both the customer and the product) (Frank, Massy and Wind, 1972). Situation-specific bases also appear in the literature as behavioural or product-behavioural bases (Kotler, 1994) and product instrumental bases (Wilkie and Cohen, 1977). In addition bases can be further classified according to

|              | General | Product–specific |
|--------------|---------|------------------|
| Observable   | Cultural, geographic, demographic and society economic variables | User status, usage frequency, brand loyalty, store loyalty and patronage, usage situation |
| Unobservable | Psychographics: personality and lifestyle | Psychographics, benefits, perceptions, attitudes, preferences and intentions |

**Figure 2.1**   A classification of segmentation bases

*Source:* Adapted from Frank et al. (1972)

[1] A detailed discussion of the various segmentation bases available is beyond the realms of this chapter. For further information the reader is directed to the literature reviews provided by Beane and Ennis (1987) and Tynan and Drayton (1987).

whether they can be measured objectively (observable bases) or whether they must be inferred (unobservable bases). Figure 2.1 illustrates the variables found in each category.

The vast number of bases available does not necessarily mean that they are all equally applicable to all markets. One needs to discover the best basis for dividing the particular market in question. Hisrich and Peters (1974) advocate the examination of a number of segmentation variables in order to select the correlate or correlates that are superior in explaining buyer behaviour in the particular product or market context being considered. However, a number of 'preferred' bases exist which appear to offer better segmentation outcomes for a number of marketing decisions (Wind, 1978), including benefits sought, needs and product usage patterns.

## 2.7   Personal market segmentation

Traditional market segmentation has relied strongly on conventional univariate bases, particularly demographics, to differentiate financial services consumers, primarily because demographics are easily interpretable, relatively easily gathered and easily transferable from one study to another. The abundance of demographic data from published sources has also contributed to its attractiveness as a segmentation basis. Yet demographic trends (outlined in Section 2.2) have rendered this basis less attractive in identifying and discriminating consumer segments, placing them under considerable criticism. For example, the demographic premise implies that differences in reasons for buying will be reflected in differences in age, sex, income etc. Evidence shows that demographics are, in fact, poor predictors of behaviour for a wide range of products (Haley, 1968; Frank et al., 1972) since they are descriptive rather than causal factors. Thus, people with the same demographic characteristics can have markedly different lifestyles, preferences and behaviour.

The fact is behaviour is multi-motivated and multi-determined and traditional univariate bases do not sufficiently account for this. Thus, multivariate bases and inferable consumer characteristics (e.g. attitudes and psychographics) are increasing in popularity in an attempt to discover a closer approximation to consumer needs and segment behaviour. The following section discusses some of the more widely used approaches to segmentation; further detail on the application of these techniques in financial services is provided by Speed and Smith (1992) and Gwin and Lindgren (1982).

### 2.7.1  Traditional, univariate bases

*Age and life cycle*

One of the simplest methods of segmenting a market is by the age of the consumer. Stanley, Ford and Richards (1985) show that the age of a person has discriminatory power in the usage of financial services; generally younger customers have a larger demand for loan facilities than older customers who have a greater tendency to deposit funds. Financial institutions have responded to age segments with the development of a number of different accounts. In the 1970s the major clearing banks developed student accounts aimed at school leavers going on to further education (Lewis, 1982b). The driving factor was that a vast majority of students received Local Education Authority grants paid by cheque for which a bank account was desirable. Furthermore, the future earning power of the segment also seemed attractive. Yet, the high mobility of students on graduation and the recent reduction in LEA grants has rendered this segment a somewhat less attractive proposition for many institutions. At the same time, school leavers going into full-time employment have been the focus of other institutions. The Trustee Savings Bank (TSB) is attempting to capitalize on this segment through its Youth and Independent Accounts aimed at young, single individuals in full-time employment with no dependants. This group is particularly attractive as a result of significantly larger discretionary incomes compared to young families.

At the even younger end of the scale school children are an important segment since they constitute a significant proportion of the population and have considerable discretionary purchasing power through pocket money, monetary gifts and earned income (Lewis, 1982c). Children have also been found to save extensively (Lewis, 1982a). Many financial institutions have responded to this with the introduction of young savers accounts usually backed up by gifts to act as incentives, to instil in the youngsters the importance of saving and, more importantly, saving with that particular institution.

More recently, however, demographic shifts, pointing to an ageing population (Johnson, 1990b) have focused marketing's attention on the older age groups, the so-called 'Greys' or 'Third Agers' (Kreitzman, 1994). The most significant changes are forecast to occur among those over fifty but under pensionable age. The next decade will experience an increase of 20 per cent in the number of people in their fifties in the UK (Johnson, 1990a), although this will take place within the context of a static population and a substantial decline among what have been dynamic market segments of high-spending teenagers and young adults. Important economic and lifestyle indicators also contribute to the appeal of the older segments. Silman and Poustie (1994) note that many individuals between the ages of fifty and seventy-five are income-rich (83 per cent are not solely dependent on state benefits), asset-rich (8 million own their homes outright), and the recipients of substantial windfalls largely in the form of inheritance. They also represent a particularly thrifty segment compared to younger age groups (illustrated in Table 2.8).

In addition, the attitudes of consumers change over time – different generations have different experiences and expectations. The 'Greys' of tomorrow are likely to have markedly different patterns of behaviour compared to the 'senior citizens' of the last couple of decades, with many unwilling to compromise their lifestyles. Yet, there is a tendency to treat 'the old' as a single homogeneous market. However, polarization of wealth among the older age groups is greater than among any other age group (Buck, 1990). The key is to identify the wealthy few. Silman and Poustie (1994) identify five attitudinal segments among the fifty-to seventy-five-year-olds: Astute Cosmopolitans, Thrifty Traditionals, Temperate Xenophobes, Apathetic Spenders, Outgoing Funlovers. From a financial services viewpoint the Astute Cosmopolitans are the most attractive since they are two and a half times more likely to belong to social classes A and B, are well-educated, own stocks, shares and unit trusts, have private health insurance, and have an interest in financial services which is reflected in their reading. Yet, despite the opportunities to be had from this segment many financial institutions fail to meet their needs sufficiently with a tendency to patronise the 'older' (Banks, 1990). Given the degree of financial sophistication of many over-fifties such treatment would seem unwise.

Table 2.8 *Importance of over-55s in the total savings market*

|  | % total population | % total savers |
|---|---|---|
| All savers under 55 years | 67 | 39 |
| Over 55s: |  |  |
| High savers | 11 | 50 |
| Medium savers | 11 | 10 |
| Low savers | 11 | 0 |

*Source:* Buck (1990)

While the age of a person would seem important, a financial institution should always balance its segments. If, for example, only younger customers are targeted they will be lost as they age. Thus, a life cycle approach would seem more appropriate. The classic Family Life Cycle (FLC) model presented by Wells and Gubar (1966) has received popularity in marketing. The assumptions are that family needs, income and expenditure change as the family matures. This has obvious advantages for a financial institution since if it can anticipate and provide for these changing needs it will build a solid customer base. However, the problem with the traditional FLC is that it fails to account for all sections of society. Increasingly there are a number of circumstances which do not conform to the traditional pattern (such as divorcees, childless couples, older married couples, homosexual couples). Those who do not 'fit in' are simply left out. In terms of purchasing power many of these groups offer significant potential for financial institutions.

More recently the notion of the financial life cycle has become important. Similar to the FLC it recognizes that individuals have different financial needs and objectives at various stages of life. Certain needs and objectives assume that other objectives have been or are capable of being met. Thus, a hierarchy of financial objectives is hypothesized (Kamakura, Ramaswami and Srivastava, 1991) which presupposes that basic objectives such as liquidity, cash reserves and insurance are satisfied before funds are allocated to higher-order products. This is likely to occur both later in the FLC as well as the financial life cycle. The financial sophistication and investment behaviour of the 'Greys' mentioned above bears testimony to this. The model is equally applicable to the analysis of commercial markets since companies too have life cycles – newly emerging businesses will have different financial needs to older established companies.

The life cycle and lifestages have become popular bases for financial institutions. For example, the Trustee Savings Bank talks of its customers in terms of Youth, Independent, Family, Empty Nester and Retired segments for which it recognizes there are different product requirements. The NatWest has taken the idea a step further to provide a leaflet for its customers entitled 'Life:The Map' detailing various paths through life, the general situations faced at each stage and the products which the NatWest offers to meet the needs typical of each situation. The Bank of Scotland likewise recognizes the importance of a life cycle relationship through its 'A Friend for Life' slogan. Indeed, relationship management is an important aspect of the life cycle approach. In mature markets the opportunities for gaining new-to-the-business customers are very small. Hence, customer retention is crucial. Those financial institutions which are attuned to their customers' requirements, and how they alter over time, should be in a position to provide the right product at the right time. Thus, the astute high street institutions will guide their customers from young savers accounts through school leavers, student and graduate accounts from where the full range of mortgage, loan and investment products will be made available.

## Social class and income

Social class still retains an important place in consumer behaviour models and Britain has, until recently, always had a well-defined social class structure. However, the traditional hierarchical and triangular-shaped arrangement of British society (the richest at the tip of the pyramid and the poorest occupying the majority at the base) has evolved into a mass middle-class. This development has been due partly to rising incomes and changes in the distribution of wealth outlined earlier.

The social class gradings shown in Table 2.9 provide an ever popular basis for market segmentation. Past research has indicated a strong class divide in terms of financial services behaviour with respect to credit card usage (in favour of the A, B, C1s in terms of volume of use and type of purchase) (Mathews and Slocum, 1969), save–spend behaviour (indicating that lower social classes essentially have shorter term planning horizons and opt for higher liquidity, lower risk savings items) (Meidan, 1984), and the ownership of stocks and shares and unit trusts (the upper social classes forming the significant investors) (Baker and Fletcher, 1987). This has resulted in the 'white collar' individuals being the focus of many financial institutions.

The significance in terms of banking behaviour was that these previously 'cash-paid' workers (Lewis, 1982d) were largely unbanked and while they were still being paid in cash did not perceive a need for a bank account. The incentives for employers to pay workers by other methods

**Table 2.9** *NRS social grade definitions*

| Social grade | Social status | Occupation | % of all British adults age 15+* |
|---|---|---|---|
| A | Upper middle class | Higher managerial, administrative or professional | 3.1 |
| B | Middle class | Intermediate managerial, administrative or professional | 15.7 |
| C1 | Lower middle class | Supervisory or clerical and junior managerial, administrative or professional | 25.6 |
| C2 | Skilled working class | Skilled manual workers | 26.0 |
| D | Working class | Semi- and unskilled manual workers | 17.0 |
| E | Those at lowest levels of subsistence | State pensioners or widows (no other earner), casual or lowest grade workers | 12.6 |

*Source*: Advertising Association (1994a).
* Based on grades of Chief Income Earner, NRS July 1992 – June 1993

have created opportunities for many financial institutions, providing the necessary vehicle to cross-sell other financial services to this segment. More recently, cheque payment methods have given way to electronic transfer payments direct to the employee's bank account.

Despite the historical success of social class in discriminating financial services behaviour, recent societal trends coupled with the problems arising from its theoretical underpinnings and measurement (based on the income of the Head of the Household, assumed to be male) it has been argued (Leach, 1987; Cornish and Denny, 1989) that social class is a less than optimum basis for segmentation. Even though social class may tell something about people's lifestyles, it offers insufficient guidance in terms of purchasing power. Consequently, income may be a more desirable indicator of affluence and demand for financial services. However, this is not without its pitfalls and researchers must be careful how they define income – disposable income should not be confused with discretionary income since '... high income families often have high financial commitments for housing costs, school fees and support for dependants, that they have little discretionary income to spend' (Bowles, 1985, p.38).

## Gender

Another important demographic trend having an impact on the targeting of financial services is the increase in working women. Resulting from economic necessity, the desire to increase one's standard of living or purely for personal achievement, an increasing number of women are in employment and have their own independent sources of income. Table 2.10 illustrates this rising trend against a decline in the proportions of working males. The important statistic is that over half the females in paid employment are working full time (Advertising Association, 1994).

Traditionally, financial services were targeted at men and women were of little importance in such matters. However, the above trends have resulted in working women becoming more extensive users of financial services compared with those undertaking unpaid work at home (Burton, 1994). Despite this, only a few financial institutions appear to be responding to this trend. For example, The Prudential, in its series of 'I want to be ...' commercials recognizes that women have their own ideas about their futures, even in marriage. Homogeneous though this segment may seem,

**Table 2.10** *Employees by gender*

|         | Employees | | | Self-employed | | |
|---------|-----------|------|------|-------------|------|------|
|         | 1986 | 1991 | 1993 | 1986 | 1991 | 1993 |
| Males   | 55 | 52 | 51 | 75 | 76 | 75 |
| Females | 45 | 48 | 49 | 25 | 24 | 25 |

*Source*: Adapted from Central Statistical Office, *Social Trends, 24*, 1994

Yorke and Hayes (1982) show that women as a group can be further segmented according to marital status and position in the life cycle.

## 2.7.2 Multivariate bases

### Geodemographic bases

In response to the inadequacies of single variable bases in differentiating consumer needs, wants and preferences, there have been developments over the last two decades in the area of geodemographics – multivariate systems combining geographic with demographic information, and more recently including consumption behaviour patterns. The first of such commercial systems was ACORN by CACI (A Classification of Residential Neighbourhoods) based on the 1971 Census of Population data (a collection of some forty variables on housing, demographic, social and economic factors) which classified people and households according to neighbourhood type. It was built on the premise that neighbourhoods bearing similar social and demographic characteristics will share common lifestyle features and patterns of behaviour. It simply quantifies what burglars already knew – the areas in which people live tell something about the products they buy and the things they own.

The current ACORN system classifies the population into eleven groups shown in Table 2.11. These eleven groups are an aggregation of thirty-nine ACORN types providing a very detailed level of information. Similar systems have also been developed by other companies including MOSAIC (by CCN), Superprofiles (by CDMS) and Pin (by Pinpoint Analysis). However, the most significant developments have been in the applications for specific product/market areas, particularly financial services markets. In 1986 Pinpoint launched FinPin which has been successful in highlighting the most financially active people in the country. The analysis consists of four, ten and forty level FinPin types. The four and ten

**Table 2.11** *Eleven ACORN groups*

| ACORN group | Label | % of UK population |
|:---:|:---|---:|
| A | Agricultural areas | 3.3 |
| B | Modern family housing, higher incomes | 17.8 |
| C | Older housing of intermediate status | 18.1 |
| D | Older terraced housing | 4.2 |
| E | Council estates - category I | 13.3 |
| F | Council estates - category II | 8.8 |
| G | Council estates - category III | 6.9 |
| H | Mixed inner metropolitan areas | 3.8 |
| I | High status non-family areas | 4.1 |
| J | Affluent suburban housing | 15.9 |
| K | Better-off retirement areas | 3.8 |

*Source*: CACI Ltd. Based on 1992 population statistics.

**Table 2.12** *FinPin 93: Classification summary labels (levels 4 and 10)*

| 4 level FinPin types | 10 level FinPin types | % of UK households* |
|---|---|---|
| A. Financially active | Most active | 12.2 |
| | Financially secure savers | 12.1 |
| | | 24.3 |
| B. Financially informed | Multiproduct savers and investors | 19.7 |
| | Traditional multiproduct users | 7.5 |
| | Net savers | 13.9 |
| | | 41.1 |
| C. Financially conscious | Average users | 9.7 |
| | Uncommitted investors | 1.2 |
| | Basic product | 7.9 |
| | | 18.8 |
| D. Financially passive | Inactive borrowers | 9.5 |
| | Least active | 6.3 |
| | | 15.8 |
| Total | | 100.0 |

*Source*: Pinpoint Analysis/CACI Ltd
\* Excluding Northern Ireland

level classification is illustrated in Table 2.12; level forty extends the classification by adding demographic profiles of the segments.

Since the development of FinPin the Mortgage Market Database was launched in 1992 and a prototype Savings Market Database in 1993 (by CACI). The latest development was Financial ACORN in 1994, based on a combination of census data and NOP's Financial Research Survey (FRS), i.e. on actual product usage across the full range of financial services. Similar to FinPin, Financial ACORN classifies individuals/households into four categories, twelve groups and fifty-one types (the first two levels are illustrated in Table 2.13). (CACI recently acquired FinPin and it is likely that future developments will witness a consolidation of the two systems.)

Interestingly, the 'Wealthy Equityholders', 'Comfortable Investors' and 'Prosperous Savers' consist largely of older age groups, reinforcing the importance of the 'Greys' mentioned earlier.

## Psychographic bases

Psychographics are gaining in importance since they hinge entirely on the way the consumer thinks (Wills, 1985). Yet the definition of psychographics remains a controversial one (Ziff, 1971). To some researchers psychographics refer to basic personality characteristics, whereas to others it includes attitudes, values and beliefs. Furthermore, the general concept seems to be foreign to the traditional running of financial institutions and is perhaps one of the reasons why psychographically based

**Table 2.13** *Financial ACORN 1994 (4 categories and 12 types)*

| 4 financial ACORN categories | 12 financial ACORN types | % of UK households* |
|---|---|---|
| A. Financially sophisticated | Wealthy equityholders | 7.6 |
|  | Affluent mortgage holders | 5.4 |
|  |  | 13.0 |
| B. Financially involved | Comfortable investors | 7.6 |
|  | Better-off borrowers | 11.3 |
|  | Prosperous savers | 13.6 |
|  |  | 32.5 |
| C. Financially moderate | Young spenders | 2.6 |
|  | Settled pensioners | 11.7 |
|  | Working families | 6.4 |
|  | Thrifty singles | 4.3 |
|  |  | 25.0 |
| D. Financially inactive | Middle aged assured | 4.1 |
|  | Older cash users | 16.2 |
|  | Low income unemployed | 9.2 |
|  |  | 29.5 |
| Total |  | 100.0 |

*Source*: CACI Ltd.

research has not yet reached its full potential in segmenting consumer financial services markets.

The Midland Bank was perhaps the first to make a significant attempt in this direction. Realizing the limitations of lifestyle and lifestage segmentation in providing an effective segmentation programme for its customer base they pursued attitudinal segmentation. Two 'attitudinal' dimensions were highlighted: 'confidence' and 'respect for the authority of the banking system' (Gavaghan, 1991). Generally younger people have lower confidence than older people, and there are people who have high respect for the authority of the banking system and others who have low respect for it. Four segments were identified: New Bankers, Traditionalists, Minimalists and Opportunists. New customers enter as 'New Bankers' typically exhibiting low confidence and high respect for the authority of the banking system. Over time these customers may develop into 'Traditionalists' using the bank for the full range of services. Customers whose confidence does not increase greatly over time and who maintain a low respect for authority become 'Minimalists' tending to use the banking services relatively infrequently, preferring to operate a cash-type economy. 'Opportunists' are so called since they tend to take the opportunity to avail themselves of the best deal on offer (and are willing to switch financial provider for it). The findings were used to develop and position three new multi-service accounts: Vector, Orchard and Meridian. The Vector account was targeted primarily at the 'Opportunists', younger, well-educated, aspirational and financially less committed individuals (the Yuppies of the 1980s). The Orchard account met the needs of home-owning and family formation customers comprising both 'Opportunists' and 'Traditionalists'. The Meridian account served the Empty Nester households with larger amounts of disposable income as a result of paid-up mortgages, savings and possibly inheritance. This segment showed a bias towards 'Traditionalists'.

Current research (Harrison, 1994) attempting to draw a closer link with factors important to financial services consumer behaviour considers the dimension of individual perceived knowledge of financial services. Knowledge seems important for a number of reasons. Primarily, the intangibility of financial services affects the ability of the consumer to conceptualize and formulate the service, such that it becomes difficult to grasp mentally (Bateson, 1977). The consequence of this is that the consumer is forced to seek alternative information sources (generally of a more personal nature) and possibly places greater emphasis on past experience, learning and knowledge. Perceived knowledge, compared to actual or 'real' knowledge, has been identified as this assumes the effects of confidence discussed above which appear important. Individuals who perceive their knowledge and understanding of financial services to be poor compared to others may avoid certain financial products as they feel they lack the ability to deal with them.

Segmentation along this basis produced four segments, illustrated in Figure 2.2, which differ in terms of knowledge and financial services usage. Financial services usage is measured in terms of the degree of financial maturity (Kamakura et al., 1991) exhibited by the individual which is based on the complexity of the product, the relative liquidity and the risk associated with it. The 'Financially Confused' and the 'Apathetic Minimalists' are perhaps the least interesting from the point of view of the financial institution since they do not perceive themselves to be very knowledgeable about financial services, take a rather short-term view of their futures and engage in a minimal amount of activity.

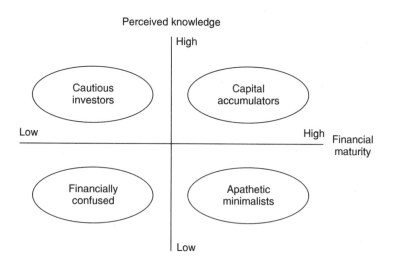

**Figure 2.2** Segmentation of financial services consumers based on perceived knowledge of the product.

*Source*: Harrison (1994)

The slightly higher financial maturity exhibited by the 'Apathetic Minimalists' would appear to be the result of successful selling by financial institutions; left on their own, research suggests that this group would adopt a minimal level of involvement. The 'Cautious Investors' and the 'Capital Accumulators' are the most sophisticated financial users, with a distinct future-orientation and longer-term financial objectives. The major difference between the two groups is that the former prefers to avoid products perceived as being high risk (such as stocks and shares, unit trusts and PEPs) and opts for 'safer' investment items (including pensions and regular savings plans).

## 2.8 Corporate market segmentation

The corporate sector differs widely from the personal sector in terms of structure and characteristics. These differences have important implications for market segmentation. Corporate customers are generally smaller in number but larger in size. Moreover, the needs of businesses and other organizations are more complex than those of personal customers, yet corporate customers have a more complete understanding of their financial requirements. Thus, in many cases financial institutions find themselves dealing with sophisticated and complex financial services users. Also important is that corporate decisions are influenced to a much greater extent by the state of the economy, and factors outside the buyer's control can take on a significant role in decision making.

Generally, many of the bases used to segment consumer markets have utility in segmenting corporate markets. Although Table 2.14 provides a list of bases more specific to corporate buyers, the most commonly used are the demographic bases which are easily obtainable from published

**Table 2.14** *Segmentation variables for corporate customers*

| Segmentation basis | Examples |
| --- | --- |
| Demographic | Industry |
| | Company size |
| | Customer location |
| Operating variables | Company technology |
| | Product and brand use status |
| | Customer capabilities |
| Purchasing approaches | Purchasing function organization |
| | Power structures |
| | Buyer–seller relationship |
| | General purchasing policies |
| | Purchasing criteria |
| Situational factors | Urgency of order fulfilment |
| | Product application |
| | Size of order |
| Buyer's personal characteristics | Age, social class, life stage, lifestyle, personality, etc. |

*Source*: Shapiro and Bonoma (1984)

sources, such as the Standard Industrial Classification, and provides information on companies operating in a particular sector. This information, together with the size of the firm, can provide a financial institution with the preliminary information necessary to understand a company's requirements. The range of approaches to segmenting corporate markets is discussed in more detail by Carey (1989) and Stevenson (1989).

With respect to the size of the firm, small and medium-sized enterprises (SMEs) have become important, due largely to the government policy decisions of the last decade. Financial institutions have responded to this with the introduction of small business sections and dedicated managers to handle their custom. Until very recently the National Westminster Bank was promoting its small business service heavily, with perhaps particular emphasis on start-ups. However, recessionary times have had a devastating effect on many smaller companies which either could not cope financially or were badly affected by poor lending decisions and bad debts. In general, approaches used to segment small business markets have been fairly simple with a particular emphasis on size. However, some institutions, such as Girobank (Roach, 1989) have attempted to develop a more sophisticated attitudinal approach to segmentation in order to distinguish the particular needs and benefits sought by different types of small business.

Chéron, McTavish and Perrien (1989) suggested that the commercial sector as a whole should be divided between corporate markets and small and medium-sized firms. The former consists of very large corporations and government accounts offering high volume sales and requiring professional account management. Such customers can feasibly be offered customized marketing programmes allowing a supplier–buyer relationship to develop. The importance of this was highlighted earlier in reference to the interaction model. Consequently, customer service, quality of service and relationship marketing are arguably more crucial for such customers than a conventional segmented approach.

The smaller end of the business market has quite different needs. Many firms in this group are newly emerging and often have limited business experience. Such customers operate smaller accounts and the customized approach is not always viable. In such cases, Chéron et al. (1989) suggest a two-stage segmented approach beginning with a breakdown of the market in terms of the observable descriptive variables such as the characteristics of the buying organization and the financial services needed followed by subsequent segmentation employing non-observable or inferred variables such as the structure of the buying unit, the degree of centralization of financial decision making and individual characteristics (as outlined in Table 2.14). Shapiro and Bonoma (1984) refer to this as the 'nested' approach recommended for segmenting industrial markets as it allows a balance of the more general but reliable demographic data with the more challengingly interpretable yet company-specific data.

## 2.9 Conclusion

In order to understand the needs and motivations of financial consumers, this chapter has considered the impact of recent significant demographic and socio-economic trends on the pattern of demand for financial services, and has reviewed the latest thinking on buying behaviour for services generally as well as specifically for financial services. Given that consumers with their different needs, requirements and preferences invariably do not exhibit the same behaviour across all buying situations, nor is their behaviour equally influenced by the same set of factors, it was then necessary to examine the important role played by market segmentation in both personal and corporate financial markets. This chapter serves as a foundation for Chapters 3 and 4 which deal with the development of marketing strategies and the formulations of the marketing mix.

# 3 Developing marketing strategy

## Christine Ennew

### 3.1 Introduction

The two previous chapters have outlined the diversity, complexity and speed of change that has occurred in the financial services sector. Deregulation and technical change have lowered the barriers between different institutional or strategic groups resulting in a redefinition of the marketplace (financial services rather than banking or insurance) and an increase in the intensity of competition (Ballarin, 1986; Ennew, Wright and Watkins, 1990). These supply-side changes have been reinforced by the impact of changing patterns of demand including rising incomes, a higher degree of financial awareness in many segments of the market (Harrison, 1994) and a growing level of consumerism. In addition to changes on the demand and supply side of the domestic market we must also recognize the importance of the process of liberalizing financial markets within the European Union (Wright and Ennew, 1990). Across Europe, many financial services organizations have had to re-examine their operating environment, both to determine whether and how to move into non-domestic markets and to consider how best to respond to increased competition from other European providers.

These changes created a range of new opportunities for actual and potential players in the financial services sector by removing many of the restrictions on both the types of product that could be offered and the markets in which they could be sold. But environmental change also presented the threat of an increase in the number and variety of competitors in various markets. In this situation, tactical marketing was no longer sufficient; no financial services organization could afford simply to continue supplying the same products to the same markets without some consideration of the longer term implications of the changing opportunities and threats which confronted them. When faced with a complex, changing and uncertain environment it becomes increasingly important for organizations to adopt a strategic approach to their markets. Such an approach will encourage careful consideration of products offered and markets served and should provide an organization with the means to allocate its resources effectively and efficiently in the pursuit of the specified objectives.

In essence, the strategic dimension of marketing focuses on the direction which an organization will take in relation to a specific market or set of markets in order to achieve a specified set of objectives. The tactical component refers to the more specific tasks and activities which have to be undertaken in order to implement the desired strategy. Both the strategic and tactical dimensions of marketing are typically embodied in a marketing plan. Developing such a planned, strategic approach ensures that the marketing efforts of any organization are consistent with organizational goals, internally coherent and tailored to the needs of identified consumer markets.

This chapter will consider the role of marketing strategy in the financial services sector; section 3.2 will deal with the key concepts of strategic marketing, prior to a consideration of the development of marketing strategies and marketing plans in section 3.3. The focus throughout will be on the strategic aspects of marketing planning, with strategies for growth, sources of competitive advantage and methods for planning the product portfolio being discussed in section 3.4. The main strategic challenges facing organizations in the financial services sector will also be reviewed in section 3.5. Subsequent chapters will confront more specific operational issues relating to the development of appropriate marketing mixes.

## 3.2 Marketing strategy

It is generally thought that organizations in the financial services sector have been slow to adopt a strategic approach to their marketing activities. For a long time, marketing as a business function tended to play a largely tactical role for most suppliers of financial services. There is increasing evidence to suggest that the strategic element of marketing has become more prominent in financial service organizations (Clarke, Edward, Gardner and Molyneux, 1988; Hooley and Mann, 1988; Ennew, Watkins and Wright, 1990; Glaister and Thwaites, 1992) although some commentators question the extent to which these changes are real (Baker, 1993; Knights, Sturdy and Morgan, 1994). What is clear is that the nature and scope of the marketing function in financial services has been enhanced in recent years and there appears to be a move towards recognizing the integral role of marketing in organizational strategy.

Within any organization, strategies develop at several levels. Corporate strategy deals with the overall development of an organization's business activities while marketing strategy focuses specifically on the organization's activities in relation to the markets served. There are many forms which strategy can take: two commonly identified forms are deliberate and emergent strategy. The concept of deliberate strategy is based on the notion of strategy as a process; strategy exists as the result of conscious planned activities. In contrast, the concept of emergent strategy is based on the notion of strategy as a pattern – that is, activities and behaviour which develop informally but which fall into some consistent pattern. In practice, it is frequently the case that most strategies, whether corporate or marketing are part deliberate and part emergent. To the extent that they are deliberate, marketing strategies are typically the outcome of some planning process.

In the context of developing a marketing plan, the notion of strategic marketing can be seen as having four key components:

- The designation of specific, desired objectives.
- The commitment of resources to these objectives.
- The evaluation of a range of environmental influences.
- The search for a match between environmental opportunities and organizational capabilities.

From the point of view of the organization, strategy is not just about being efficient; it is crucially concerned with enabling the organization to be effective. The efficiency component simply relates to doing a task well, the effectiveness component relates to doing the right task – having the right products in the right markets at the most appropriate times. Thus, for example, from the perspective of a bank, strategy goes beyond simply ensuring that money transmission activities are performed in the most cost-effective manner; it requires that the bank is supplying the right type of money transmission facility, that which best meets the needs of the bank's customers and which exploits the bank's own skills and capabilities.

The organization can only be effective if it is aware and responsive to the environment in which it operates. In a sense, it can be argued that marketing is, by definition, strategic since the ability to market a product successfully ultimately requires that the organization has the right type of product and is operating in the right markets. However, it is perhaps worth emphasizing that the concept of strategy has a dynamic component; it implies effectiveness and efficiency, but it also implies responsiveness – developing an awareness of environmental change and identifying appropriate and effective reactions to that change. The success of First Direct for example can be seen as the outcome of a strategic approach within Midland Bank which recognized the growing importance attached to convenience and flexibility within a particular segment of the market and a greater willingness among consumers in that segment to conduct business over the telephone.

## 3.3   Developing the strategic plan

Where the strategy is deliberate, it is typically the outcome of a formal planning process. Even where strategies are emergent, they are typically formalized within the framework of a plan. There are numerous variants of marketing plans, but a key feature of any particular format that is used is that it should follow a logical structure, from historical and current analyses of the organization and its markets, on to a statement of objectives and then to the identification of a strategy to approach these markets. This strategy should deal with broad issues of segmentation, targeting and positioning in order that the organization can identify which products should be offered to which markets and how those products will compete. In addition, it should identify more specific tactics

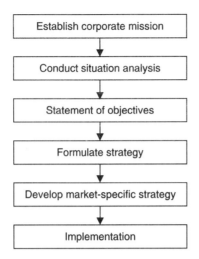

**Figure 3.1**   An illustrative marketing plan

which relate to allocation of marketing expenditure and decisions about the marketing mix. Finally, any plan should conclude with an outline of the appropriate methods for implementing the identified strategy. While offering a coherent set of clearly defined guidelines to management, the plan should remain flexible enough to adapt to changing conditions within the organization or its markets.

In principle, the methods of marketing planning which have been developed extensively in relation to products can be transferred to the marketing of financial services. However, in practice there are some features of financial services which necessarily add a further dimension to the planning problem. In particular, it is necessary to recognize the dependence of financial services on the individuals (branch employees, sales staff) who deliver them, the difficulties associated with quality control and the problems associated with presenting essentially intangible services to a consumer in a differentiated and more tangible form. While this need not alter the necessary stages associated with the planning process, it may alter the relative emphasis placed on those stages. An outline of a possible format for a marketing plan is contained in Figure 3.1.

### 3.3.1 Company mission and objectives

The mission statement essentially requires that the organization defines the area of business within which it operates and defines it in a way which will give it focus and direction. In effect, the purpose of the mission statement is to outline the goals of the organization and identify, in broad terms, the ways in which the organization will achieve those goals. For example, the mission of TSB Retail Banking and Insurance is:

To be the UK's leading financial retailer through understanding and
meeting customer needs by being more professional and innovative
than our competitors.

The nature of the corporate mission depends on a variety of factors.
Corporate history will often influence the markets and customer groups
served – thus Credit Agricole retains strong links with its farming depositors (Channon, 1986) while Coutts concentrates primarily on high income
consumers in its retail banking activities. Corporate culture may also
influence the ways in which an organization approaches its markets
and customers.

The commonest approach to determining the corporate mission is to
rely on the product/market scope. This entails defining the business in
terms of customer groups, needs served and technology employed.
Arguably, this approach is particularly beneficial from the marketing perspective since it forces managers to think of the customer groups and the
particular set of needs/wants which the firm is looking to satisfy. The
importance of this idea has its roots in the concept of marketing myopia
(Levitt, 1960). It is not sufficient for a firm to identify its mission as being
'insurance' – it would be more appropriate to identify that mission as
being 'meeting consumer needs for risk reduction and financial security'.
A mission statement of this nature can offer guidelines to management
when considering how the business should develop and in which direction. With the benefits of a clear mission statement, future growth strategies can look to rely on what are regarded as distinctive competencies and
aim for synergies by dealing with similar customer groups, similar customer needs or similar service technologies. Subsequently, within the
planning process, specific objectives must be set which are consistent
with the chosen mission.

### 3.3.2 Situation analysis

The essence of any marketing strategy is developing a 'fit' or 'match'
between an organization and its environment. Thus, the development of
strategy requires a thorough and continuous analysis and understanding
of the environment in which an organization operates. This analysis must
relate not just to the immediate market environment but also to much
broader aspects of the macro environment (Sanderson and Luffman, 1988)
and the analysis of the organization's own internal strengths and weaknesses.

The analysis of the macro environment is often described as PEST
analysis (Political, Economic, Social and Technological) and requires a
thorough consideration of economic trends, legislative developments, patterns of social and demographic change and technological developments.
As Chapter 1 illustrated there are clearly a range of political and legislative developments which have a major impact on the development of
marketing strategies; equally, economic factors such as interest rates
and income growth will affect marketing activities through their impact

on levels of demand. Other macro factors which may be relevant include the age structure of the population, changing household structures and changing social values (e.g. attitudes to debt, concern for the environment). Many of these were discussed in detail in Chapter 2.

At the market level, situation analysis requires information relating to the size of the current market, market shares and market trends, the identification of major competitors, statements of current product range, its features and its basis for competitive advantage as well as some analysis of patterns of distribution and promotion, the nature of product, market share and sales trends. One widely used approach to the analysis of the market environment is Porter's five force analysis. Porter (1980; 1985) argues that in order to develop an effective strategy it is necessary to understand the factors that determine the overall attractiveness of the industry. Industry attractiveness and profitability depends (as economic theory would suggest) on the structure of the industry and specifically on five key features:

*Bargaining power of suppliers.* Suppliers in financial services include the suppliers of essential business goods and services (computing equipment, training etc.), and to the extent that these suppliers are in a strong position they can affect the prices paid for relevant goods and thus affect costs. It could also be argued that in some instances, the term 'suppliers' could also include customers. Customers making deposits with financial institutions are effectively acting as a supplier of certain essential raw materials and again, if these suppliers are in a relatively strong position they can impact on the cost of providing certain related financial services.

*Bargaining power of consumers.* To the extent that consumers are in a relatively strong position vis-à-vis the producer, they can ensure that services are available to them on more favourable terms. Clearly, the bargaining power of buyers in financial services varies considerably. In personal markets, it seems that the bargaining power of individual consumers is relatively weak, although consumer pressure groups such as the Consumers' Association may partly counterbalance this, particularly through their evaluations of the performance of financial institutions (see Consumers' Association, 1994 for a recent example). In corporate markets, the situation may be rather different with relatively large businesses being in a rather more powerful position.

*Threat of entry.* A profitable industry will generally attract new entrants; if it appears relatively attractive for new organizations to enter a market, profitability will tend to be eroded. While there are certainly barriers to entry to the financial marketplace, not least of which are the many regulatory requirements, it is apparent that there is a real threat from new entrants. Already, retailers such as Marks & Spencer have moved into offering a range of financial services, and the decision by many grocery retailers to offer cash-back facilities constitutes a further threat to the activities of bank and building society branch networks.

*Competition from substitutes.* The existence of products which are close substitutes enhances customer choice and provides an alternative way of meeting a particular need. Thus in markets where there are close substitutes, the buying power of consumers is effectively enhanced because they have a much greater degree of choice. The extent to which there are real substitutes for financial services is perhaps limited, although in certain sections of the market, such as investment services, antiques and other collectables may be regarded as substitutes for investments in unit and investment trusts and other forms of saving.

*Rivalry between firms.* Clearly, the greater the degree of competition, the more likely it is that the industry will be less profitable and therefore less attractive. While there are few close substitutes for financial services (as indicated above), there is considerable competition within the industry, particularly as traditional institutional divisions disappear. Thus, the mortgage market which was traditionally the preserve of the building societies is now served by banks, specialist mortgage providers and various other institutions. Building societies are now competing with banks in the provision of money transmission facilities and established life offices find themselves under threat from newly established life subsidiaries of banks and building societies.

These five forces determine the attractiveness of the industry through their impact on either costs incurred or prices received or both. The development of an effective marketing strategy will depend upon a thorough examination of the market in order that the organization can identify strategic approaches to counterbalance the effects of these five forces.

Marketing research and market intelligence provide much of the information that is required for situation analysis. This information may be gathered in a variety of formal and informal means. Competitor information, for example, may often be obtained simply from personal contacts with other executives, from collecting point of sale material and from the trade press. Annual reports of competitors can also provide useful information. Trade bodies such as the British Bankers Association, the Building Societies Association, the Association of British Insurers and the British Insurance and Investment Brokers Association in the UK, are other possible sources of summarized data.

In addition much secondary information can be obtained from government publications. The Census of Population and Production data can be used to identify market potential, growth rates and macro-economic influences. In the UK, reports like *The Family Expenditure Survey, Social Trends, Economic Trends* are other easily available sources of socio-economic and demographic data. Trends in market shares are most usually obtained from syndicated research studies which carry out interviews on a regular basis on financial product purchases and/or sales and thus provide trend data on market shares. One example is National Opinion Polls Financial Research Survey (Whitmore, 1988) which carries out regular surveys of consumers and investigates their ownership of various financial products. Other surveys of insurance brokers and other financial intermediaries are available (e.g. Taylor Nelson Monitoring Service where a representative panel of 400 insurance brokers is interviewed quarterly to investigate marketing effectiveness of insurance companies, company image, advertising and promotions). Other ad hoc surveys of the sector are undertaken from time to time (e.g. Euromonitor investigates the major suppliers and can include primary research data).

Information on customer needs may often be gleaned from information provided by those customers when they purchase a particular financial service. However, such information is only partial and an understanding of customer needs often requires more extensive primary market research. The company must then decide: how to specify and interpret terms of reference and objectives for the research; what to ask – questionnaire development; who to ask – sample size and structure, sampling procedure; how to contact respondents; how to ask for information – self or interviewer completed questionnaires, dichotomous (yes–no), polychotomous (multiple-choice) or open-ended questions; short or in-depth interviews; how to analyse the resultant data – which statistical methods to use; how to interpret the results in terms of the original terms of reference; and how best to present the findings with appropriate recommendations.

Finally, to develop a suitable strategy, an organization will require some analysis of its internal environment in order to assess its capabilities and limitations in relation to a particular market/product/customer group. Information of this sort will typically be collected as a result of an internal audit of an organization's marketing activities. This process can generate a considerable volume of information which despite its importance may be of limited practical use to planners. Accordingly there is a need to organize the main points of any situation analysis in order that management may be presented with analytic summaries to guide future strategy decisions. These analytic summaries will often require that certain assumptions are made concerning the development of the marketing environment (e.g. projected growth in spending). Where such assumptions are required it is important that they are made explicit in order that the basis for subsequent strategic and tactical decisions is clearly understood.

SWOT analysis is one of the most commonly used techniques for organizing the information collected in relation to the firm's marketing environment. The process of SWOT analysis is one that is widely used by firms for organizing information relating to the marketing environment and providing guidance on strategy development. The basic principle of SWOT analysis is that any statement about the organization (derived from a marketing audit, for example) or about the environment (derived from marketing research) can be classified as a Strength, Weakness, Opportunity or Threat.

An opportunity is defined as any feature of the external environment which creates conditions which are advantageous to the firm in relation to a particular objective or set of objectives. By contrast, a threat is any environmental development which will hinder the achievement of specific objectives. What constitutes an opportunity to some firms will almost invariably constitute a threat to others. The recent disclosures about widespread mis-selling of personal pensions and the consequent consumer backlash in relation to the commission-based sales agent would be considered as a threat by many of the traditional life offices; the banks and some building societies may regard these events as an opportunity to expand their role in the sales of savings and investment products by building on an image of trust and reliability.

A strength is considered to be any particular skill or distinctive competence within the organization which will assist the organization in achieving its stated objectives. These may relate to experience in specific types of markets or specific skills possessed by employees either in relation to production, research and development, (R & D) or marketing. It may equally include aspects of corporate culture/image – for example a firm's reputation for quality and customer service may be regarded as a significant strength, as might the existence of a particularly comprehensive customer database. A weakness is simply any aspect of the company which may hinder the achievement of specific objectives and may include limited experience of certain markets/technologies, nature of reputation or extent of financial resources available. The lack of experience within building societies of money transmission facilities could be regarded as a weakness when considering the development of current accounts, while banks may consider their experience in wholesale money markets to be a strength in relation to the development of mortgage services.

These data are commonly presented as a matrix of strengths, weaknesses, opportunities and threats as shown in Figure 3.2. There are several points to note about the presentation and interpretation. First it should be recalled that effective SWOT analysis does not simply require a categorization of information, it also requires some evaluation of the relative importance of the various factors under consideration. In addition, it should be noted that these features are only of relevance if they are perceived to exist by the consumers (Piercy and Giles, 1989). Listing corporate features that internal personnel regard as strengths/weaknesses is of little relevance if they are not perceived as such by the firm's consumers. Equally, threats and opportunities are conditions presented by the external environment and they should be independent of the firm. Thus it is inappropriate to identify the potential for price cutting as an opportunity – it is not, it is a strategy which may be implemented by the firm if the opportunity exists. Thus, if the opportunity is highly price-sensitive consumers, the strategic response could then be price cutting.

In Figure 3.3 we have constructed a matrix of strengths, weaknesses, opportunities and threats for a hypothetical UK bank. The ordering of the items within the matrix reflects their relative importance. The SWOT matrix in this format can be used to provide some guidance with respect to strategy. In particular, two basic strategic options can be identified:

*Matching*. Initially, the SWOT matrix should be examined to determine the extent to which it is possible to match the particular strengths of the company to the opportunities presented by the market environment. Strengths which do not match any available opportunity are of limited

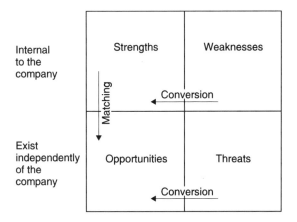

**Figure 3.2** SWOT analysis

*Source*: Adapted from Piercy and Giles (1989)

| Strengths | Weaknesses |
|---|---|
| 1 Large captive account base | 1 Staff lack selling skills |
| 2 Extensive branch network | 2 High overhead costs |
| 3 Adequate capital for expansion | 3 Inflexible technologies – account driven rather than customer based |
| 4 Considered trustworthy | 4 Historic banking culture |

| Opportunities | Threats |
|---|---|
| 1 Growing demand for personal financial services | 1 Competition from other suppliers of personal financial services |
| 2 Rising personal wealth | 2 Consumers becoming more critical |
| 3 Growth in demand from older sections of population | 3 Consumers have higher expectations of service |
| 4 Easier access to European markets | 4 Possible competition from Europe |

**Figure 3.3** SWOT analysis for a UK clearing bank in relation to the market for personal financial services

*Source*: Adapted from Thwaites (1991)

use, while opportunities which do not have any matching strengths cannot be exploited unless the organization makes fundamental internal changes. In our example, the bank may consider building on its large captive account base to cross-sell a range of financial products (to respond to growing demand), making particular use of its trustworthy image.

*Conversion*. Where there are no obvious or substantial matching opportunities, the alternative is to concentrate on converting weaknesses into strengths in order to take advantage of some particular opportunity or converting threats into opportunities which can then be matched by existing strengths. For example, the threat posed by increasingly high customer expectations could be turned into an opportunity to gain a real competitive edge through enhanced service quality. Alternatively the recognition that staff lack selling skills could be turned into a strength in the light of growing public distrust of commission-based selling.

This process should not exclude the development of completely new strategies which may occur simply as a result of SWOT analysis, encouraging a systematic approach to the analysis of the marketing environment.

### 3.3.3 Statement of objectives

Once the nature of the marketing environment has been fully analysed it is then possible to specify appropriate marketing objectives. Any plan must be guided by a coherent set of objectives which are typically indicated or determined by the nature of overall corporate strategy and the stated corporate mission. However, objectives which are identified in the overall corporate planning process must be translated into objectives which are meaningful in marketing terms. Thus, a corporate plan may specify objectives in terms of returns to shareholders; for marketing purposes, this may translate into a specified growth in numbers of accounts or assets under management. The objectives set for any marketing plan must fulfil three important criteria: they must be achievable, they must be consistent and they must be stated clearly and preferably quantitatively.

### 3.3.4 Formulation of strategy

Given the available information and the targets which have been set, planners must develop suitable strategies in order to identify which markets that the company intends to enter and the way it anticipates entering them. This process will often be conditioned by overall corporate strategy and involves making some assessment of how the organization is to develop its business in relation to its particular markets. The core of this process is often described as STP (Segmentation, Targeting and Positioning). Specifically, it is necessary to identify the nature of customer demand and the extent to which there are distinct groups of customers in the marketplace. This process of segmentation was described in detail in Chapter 2). Identified segments must then be evaluated; this requires consideration of the strengths of the organization in relation to the needs of target customers and the overall attractiveness of the market environment. Most organizations will not attempt to serve the entire market and will instead concentrate on offering products which reflect the organization's particular skills and which meet the needs of customers in the chosen target market. To do this it is essential to establish a clear competitive position in the market in order to communicate to the customer the distinctive nature of the organization's service offer.

### 3.3.5 Market specific strategy

The market specific strategy constitutes the set of policies and rules which will guide the marketing effort for a specific service or group of services in relation to a specific set of markets. There will be two key components:

*Determining the appropriate level of marketing expenditure.* The extent to which the marketing division can control this will obviously vary according to firm-specific policies and the company's financial position. However, any marketing plan would require a statement of the budget required to implement it.

*Developing the marketing mix.* This means selecting the appropriate combination of product, price, promotion and place which will ensure that the service is appropriate in terms of its features, its image, the perceived value and the availability. The nature of the financial services marketing mix is discussed in more detail in Chapter 4.

### 3.3.6 Implementation

Implementation requires an identification of the specific tasks which need to be performed, the allocation of those tasks to individuals and the establishment of a system for monitoring their implementation e.g. identifying the nature of any short-term marketing research which needs to be undertaken to determine how appropriate a product is, the nature of customer reactions etc. The implementation procedure may also include some elements of contingency planning. However well thought out the marketing plan may be, the market is always changing. Consequently, certain planned activities may turn out to be inappropriate or ineffective; it is important to be aware of these and be in a position to respond, i.e. to modify the strategy as new information becomes available.

One increasingly important dimension of implementation is internal marketing. Internal marketing deals with the way in which an organization manages the relationship between itself and its employees at all levels. As such it can play an important role in creating and maintaining a market-oriented corporate culture. The process of internal marketing is seen as particularly important in the financial services sector (Piercy and Morgan, 1991), not least because of the importance of people in the marketing process. Internal marketing helps to ensure that staff understand the product itself and believe in what the organization is trying to do. If an organization's own employees are not market oriented, if they do not support the overall corporate and marketing strategies, then the chances of successful plan implementation are minimal. Indeed, some authors (see for example Morgan, 1991) go so far as to argue that senior managers should view their strategies as products to be marketed to their employees. Further detail on internal marketing is provided in Chapter 9.

Aspects of the marketing environment facing the suppliers of financial services and the development of the marketing mix for financial services are considered in depth elsewhere. Accordingly, the focus of the rest of this chapter will be on the formulation of a broad marketing strategy.

## 3.4    Tools for strategy development

The formulation of an organization's strategic approach to its marketing activities is essentially concerned with developing some 'match' between the organization and its operating environment (Piercy and Peattie, 1988). The resulting strategy must enable the organization to meet the specific needs of its consumers and does so more effectively than its competitors. While there are a number of analytical techniques which management can employ, the role of these techniques is not to offer definitive statements on the final form that a strategy should take, but rather to provide a framework for the organization and analysis of ideas and information. No one technique can always provide the most appropriate framework and those discussed below can and should be regarded as complementary rather than competitive. Furthermore, it should be recognized that many of these techniques are relevant at different levels of the planning hierarchy; many are used explicitly for corporate-level decisions but are equally useful when considering business or market-level decisions.

The following discussion will begin with some consideration of frameworks which are used in aiding decisions regarding the management of the product portfolio. We will then move on to examine strategies for growth before examining the concept of competitive advantage.

### 3.4.1  Selecting the product portfolio

As has been indicated earlier, diversification has become an increasingly common trend in the financial services sector. In response to an increasingly competitive and deregulated environment, the major suppliers of personal financial services have been changing their product ranges, adding a range of new products and deleting others. While the nature of product strategy is discussed in greater depth in Chapter 5, this trend poses important questions which require attention at the level of market planning and strategy. In particular they raise the issue of how, in a strategic sense, the organization should manage its product portfolio. Managing the product portfolio raises broad issues such as what role should a product play, how should resources be allocated between products and what should be expected from each product. Of particular importance is the notion of maintaining some balance between well-established and new products, between cash-generating and cash-using products and between growing and declining products. Two common approaches which are used to plan product portfolios are the matrix-based approaches of the Boston Consulting Group (BCG) and the General Electric (GE) Business Screen and the concept of a product life cycle.

## Matrix-based approaches

Both the BCG and the GE matrices require a classification of products/ business units according to the attractiveness of a particular market and the strengths of the company in that market. The BCG matrix bases its classification scheme purely on market share and market growth, while the GE matrix relies on more subjective measures of market attractiveness and business strengths. In both cases, the appropriate strategy is determined by the position of a product in the matrix. A simple example of the BCG matrix is presented in Figure 3.4; the division on the horizontal axis is usually based on a market share identical to that of the firm's nearest competitor, while the precise location of the division on the vertical axis will depend on the rate of growth in the market with 10 per cent usually seen as a reasonable cut-off point. Products are positioned in the matrix as circles with a diameter proportional to their sales revenue. The BCG matrix relies on the assumption that accumulated experience and economies of scale will mean that larger market share results in lower costs and thus higher margins.

The appropriate strategy for a particular product will depend upon its position within the matrix. The Question mark (or problem child) has a small market share in a high growth industry. The generic products offered by this product are clearly popular, but customer support for the specific company versions is limited. If future market growth is anticipated and the products are viable, then the organization should consider increasing the resources available to this product to permit more active marketing of its products. Otherwise, the possibility of withdrawing the relevant products should be considered.

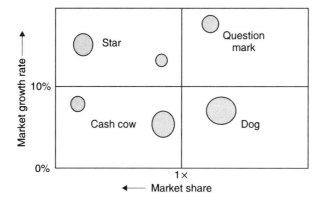

**Figure 3.4** The BCG matrix

The Star is a product with a high market share in a high growth industry. By implication, the star has the potential to generate significant earnings currently and in the future. However, at this stage it may still require substantial marketing expenditures to maintain this position, but would be regarded as a good investment for the future. By contrast, the Cash Cow has a high market share but in a slower growing market. The traditional bank current account probably falls into this category, as does the traditional building society mortgage. The products offered are typically mature and in a strong position in the market with a high degree of consumer loyalty. Product development costs are typically low and the marketing campaign is well-established, so the cash cow will usually make a reasonable contribution to overall profitability. Where market growth is reasonably strong then the most appropriate strategy may be to maintain the SBU's position. If growth and/or share are weakening, then it may be more sensible to pursue a harvesting strategy which requires that the organization cuts back on marketing expenditure and looks to maximize short-term cash flow from the product offered.

Finally, the Dog represents a product with a low market share in a low growth market. As with the cash cow, the product will typically be well-established but is losing consumer support and may have cost disadvantages. Traditional building society share accounts probably fall into this category. The usual strategy would be to consider divestment unless cash flow position is strong, in which case the recommended strategy would be to harvest.

The BCG matrix is potentially useful, but its recommendations must be interpreted with care. In particular, it is important to recognize that it focuses only on one aspect of the organization (market share) and one aspect of the market (sales growth). In addition, the BCG matrix assumes that market share is the key objective for the organization and that a large market share will mean lower per unit costs and higher profits due to either economies of scale or experience curve effects (Schnaars, 1991). Where such objectives do not hold or such relationships are not in place, the value of the specific prescriptions of the BCG matrix may be limited.

## The product life cycle

The matrix approach is not unrelated to the concept of the product life cycle as has been illustrated by Barksdale and Harris (1982) who suggest that the patterns of product development implied by the BCG matrix are consistent with those implied by the product life cycle. The idea of the product life cycle is one that is widely used as a tool for market planning, in that it can be employed both to guide an organization in the determination of the appropriate balance of products and in the development of a suitable strategy for the marketing of those products. Although a familiar concept in the marketing of products, there is no reason to believe that the basic principles are not applicable to services in general (Cowell, 1984) and to financial services in particular (McIver and Naylor, 1986; Marsh,

1988). However, there are some difficulties in considering the life cycles of certain types of financial service because the cash flow from the product can easily be confused with the product itself. For example, mortgages and other loan products require cash for their launch but will initially also be net users of cash since that is the basic feature of the product.

It is argued that a service, like a product, will pass through four basic stages, from introduction, through growth to maturity and eventually into decline. The concept is not, however, one that is universally accepted; indeed the notion of a life cycle is often seen as an exercise in attributing biological laws to inanimate objects. While the idea of a life cycle should perhaps not be taken too literally, the basic idea which underlies this model can be useful in guiding marketing decisions. The role of marketing is generally considered to be one of prolonging the growth and maturity phases, often using strategies of product modification or product improvement which are frequently regarded as less risky than new product development. While the basic life cycle pattern (see Figure 3.5) is stylized, it gives some indication of the patterns of development. In particular we should note that the life cycle is typically longer for the product class (e.g. loans) than it is for the product form (e.g. car loans) and longer for the product form than it is for the specific brand. Given the increased level of competition in the financial services sector, Watkins and Wright (1986) argue that organizations should be aware of the potential for increasingly short life cycles and be prepared to adjust their strategies accordingly. They cite the example of the variety of savings accounts which developed as a result of the competition between banks and building societies. The resulting array of products had the potential to create confusion among customers, and in response to this, a number of building

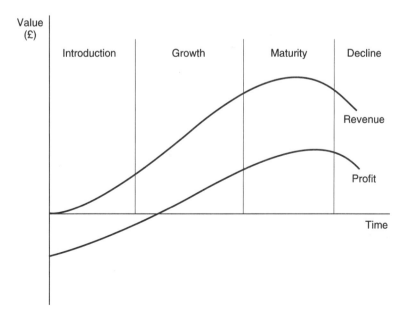

**Figure 3.5** The product life cycle

societies opted to rationalize their range of accounts to give consumers a clearer indication of the type of account and the benefits available. More recently, Harness and McKay (1994) have highlighted both the importance of the issue of product elimination and the problems associated with the process. In particular, many financial services organizations have contractual obligations which preclude the full elimination of a product. Where full elimination does occur it is typically in the context of complete withdrawal from a particular sector (e.g. estate agency).

Assessing the existing product range according to life cycle position can give some indication of the balance of the existing product portfolio. Furthermore, according to the stage in the life cycle; see below; the organization can obtain some guidance as to the appropriate marketing strategy.

*Introduction.* A period of slow growth and possibly negative profit, as efforts are being made to obtain widespread acceptance for the service. Cash flows are typically negative and the priority is to raise awareness and appreciation of the product with the result that the marketing mix will place a high degree of emphasis on promotion. In the financial services sector it is of considerable importance that new products are introduced quickly and that this phase of the life cycle is shortened, because of the ease with which new products can be copied. PEP and pension mortgages might be regarded as products which are at present in the introductory stage of their life cycle.

*Growth.* Sales volumes increase steadily and the product begins to make a significant contribution to profitability. Increase in sales can be maintained by improvements in the features, targeting at more segments or increased price competitiveness. It is at this stage that the new service product will begin to attract significant competition. Growth services currently include telephone banking, PEPs and fixed interest mortgages.

*Maturity.* Sales begin to stabilize, with replacement purchases becoming more common than new purchases. The market itself is mature and the marketing campaign and product are well-established. Competition is probably at its most intense at this stage and it may be necessary to consider modification and rejuvenation of the service to arrest future decline. Many bank current accounts are products which can be seen as having reached maturity and in many cases are being modified in attempts to prolong their life cycles. Various forms of with-profits insurance policy may also be regarded as having reached maturity.

*Decline.* Sales begin to drop away noticeably, leaving management with the option of withdrawing the product entirely, although often with long-term investment products this may not be feasible, in which case the alternative is a withdrawal of support but maintenance of the product. Alternatively, if the product is seen as one with a potential

long-term future then the appropriate strategy may be one of rejuvenation. In the financial services sector it should be noted that barriers to
product withdrawal are often high; some products such as life insurance cannot simply be withdrawn from the market because some customers will still be paying premiums. Consequently, the more
appropriate strategy may be to minimize the marketing effort rather
than formally to withdraw the product (Davison, Watkins and Wright,
1989; Harness and McKay, 1994).

The use of the product life cycle in marketing planning can provide some
guidelines for the allocation of resources among service products,
enabling the organization to attach high priority to growth products,
medium priority to mature products and consider possible withdrawal
of declining products. However, as was the case with the BCG matrix, the
recommendations should be interpreted with care and, in particular, careful consideration should be given to the idea of a market life cycle; the
marketing strategies which are appropriate for the introductory phase
when the product is launched in a mature market may be quite different
from those required if the product were launched in a growing market.

## 3.4.2  Growth strategies

A common framework for the analysis and determination of growth strategies is Ansoff's Product/Market opportunity matrix (Ansoff, 1965),
which is discussed in the context of the banking sector in Chapter 10. In
developing a strategy for growth, the organization must determine
whether to concentrate on existing or new products and existing or
new markets. This suggests four possible options which are outlined in
Figure 3.6 – market penetration, market development, product development and diversification, the first three of which are regarded as intensive
growth strategies, while diversification is regarded as a form of extensive
growth.

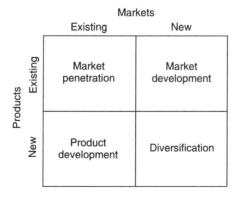

**Figure 3.6**  Ansoff's product/market matrix

*Market penetration.* With a market penetration strategy, the organization aims to sell more in its current markets by persuading existing users to use more, persuading non-users to use or attracting consumers from competitors. Increasing usage among existing customers may entail encouraging an increase the extent of life coverage, or offering higher rates of return for increased levels of savings. Barclaycard's 'Profiles' and Access' 'Air Miles' both allocate points to consumers for the use of the card, which can then be redeemed for gifts or travel; both are simple examples of how marketing tactics can be used to support a market penetration strategy. By contrast, American Express, in order to encourage non-users to use, offers free gifts to existing card holders who introduce new members. More recently, Midland have attempted to encourage switching by offering easy account transfer and compensation for any mistakes made. As a strategy for growth, market penetration will only be viable where the market is not saturated. In mature markets, such as the market for current accounts, significant market penetration can be difficult because an increased share entails attracting customers directly from competitors.

*Market development.* Market development requires that the organization looks to sell its existing products in new markets. These may be new markets geographically, new market segments or new uses for products. As a strategy, it requires effective and imaginative promotion, but it can be profitable if markets are changing rapidly. The various marketing strategies used by the clearing banks to attract student accounts, including a variety of 'special offers' provides a simple example of an exercise in market development. Movements into new markets geographically is probably the most common form of market development and the 1992 programme has presented particular opportunities for UK financial services organizations. The Woolwich, for example has expanded into the mortgage market in Italy via greenfield entry and into the mortgage market in France via acquisition. Halifax are reported to have applied for a licence to operate in Spain, and Bradford and Bingley are looking to establish a position in the German market. Additionally, the process of reform in eastern Europe has opened up a further avenue for market development. Recent proposed reforms to the Building Societies Act as described in Chapter 1 may provide the opportunity for societies to expand into non-personal markets.

*Product development and diversification.* Product development entails both developing related products and modifying existing products to appeal to current markets. The key features of a product development strategy are typically restyling service products, the addition of new features and quality changes. Recent developments in the mortgage market provide a good example of product development. The traditional standardized mortgage account is rapidly being supplemented by variants which offer lower starting rates, special terms for particular types of customer, particular mixes of fixed and flexible repayment rates etc. A strategy of this nature relies on good service design, packaging and promotion and often plays on company reputation to attract consumers to the new product. The benefits are that by tailoring the products more specifically to the needs of some existing consumers and some new consumers the organization can strengthen its competitive position.

The advantage of intensive growth strategies is that they tend to be low on risk. Diversification tends to be a more risky strategy, with the risk increasing as the organization moves into areas where it has limited experience. However, it may be the only suitable strategy if existing products and markets offer few growth opportunities. Perhaps the most common form of diversification among providers of financial services has been concentric diversification which involves developing new products which are related to existing products in terms of both markets and technology, such as the movement by the banks into mortgage provision. However, with the recent deregulation and the increase in competition there has been an increase in the levels of contiguous (horizontal) diversification which involves services which are technologically dissimilar but appeal to the same broad customer groups, for example, building societies moving into money transmission and estate agency. Such developments are not without risk and the recent and costly withdrawal of many building societies and insurers from this market indicates the extent of the risk that can characterize such strategies. Conglomerate diversification which involves both new markets and new technology is a comparatively rare phenomenon in the financial services sector because of the limited opportunities for synergy and the greater risks involved.

### 3.4.3 Developing a competitive position

The role of any marketing strategy is to enhance an organization's competitive effectiveness. In order to compete effectively, the organization must have a product or service offering that is distinct; something that gives the organization a clear competitive position. The process of positioning is essentially concerned with the identification of an appropriate competitive advantage for products or services in relation to a particular set of target markets and communicating the nature of this competitive advantage to customers. A common theme running through the alternative definitions is that positioning is essentially relative in nature, meaning that a particular product or organization cannot be viewed in isolation but merely positioned in relation to the competition using certain dimensions (Shostack, 1987). These dimensions will be a function of the main criteria used within a particular market to differentiate between organizations and services. In the motor insurance market, for instance, this may be ease of the claiming procedure and speed of payment of claim. However, perhaps the most fundamental point to be noted with respect to positioning is that, in the words of Ries and Trout (1986):

*... positioning is not what you do to a product. Positioning is what you do to the mind of the prospect. That is you position the product in the mind of the prospect.*

Effective product positioning depends upon marketers being able to identify a competitive advantage for a product or service. This competitive advantage should reflect a particular skill or competence within the organization which can be transformed into a feature or product benefit which is valued by customers in the target market. Competencies and skills define what an organization is good at, but they can only form the basis of a competitive advantage if they match with something that consumers value. Thus, identifying a competitive advantage requires a thorough understanding of organizational skills and capabilities and the needs of the target market. To qualify as a basis for competitive advantage, any set of organizational attributes must, as far as is possible, meet three criteria:

*Uniqueness.* A differential advantage must be able to create an actual or perceived uniqueness in the mind of the consumer. Unless a product can be seen as unique in some sense, the organization faces the risk of having to compete purely on price and price competition can be highly destabilizing, particularly as price changes are easily copied by competitors. A differential advantage need not be simply based on product features; other elements of the total offering may provide a basis for uniqueness. For example, Lloyds Bank have built a differential advantage through advertising and branding, particularly in the form of the Black Horse logo. Similarly, First Direct arguably have a competitive edge based on the uniqueness of their delivery system.

*Importance.* Identifying a unique differential advantage is not, by itself, sufficient to create a competitive advantage for the organization's products. This differential advantage must exist in areas which consumers regard as important. National Westminster Bank, like a number of other financial institutions, anticipated that a differential advantage could be gained by adopting the status of independent intermediary under the terms of the Financial Services Act 1986 as explained in Chapter 1. In practice, this strategy proved less than successful because independent financial advice was not an attribute that most consumers regarded as particularly important when purchasing financial products. Where a differential advantage exists in an area that consumers regard as unimportant, the organization has two options. First, it may take a reactive stance and simply seek alternative differential advantages in areas which consumers regard as important. Second, the organization may take a proactive stance and actively try to convince consumers of the importance of an aspect of the product in which they have a differential advantage. Thus, Bradford and Bingley have used promotional campaigns to attempt to convince consumers of the value of independent financial advice.

*Sustainability.* For a differential advantage to be effective, it must be sustainable; it must be something that the organization can continue to offer and it must be possible to protect the relevant features from copying by competitors. For example, a differential advantage based on price is often difficult to maintain, because competitors can easily match low prices, unless the ability to keep prices low derives from a fundamental superiority in terms of production or distribution costs that competitors cannot copy. Many organizations build competitive advantages around accumulated experience and these competitive advantages are potentially more difficult to copy and thus easier to sustain. In the service sector, products are easily copied by competitors, so a differential advantage based on product features may be difficult to sustain. Thus, Midland Bank relied on heavy branding in an attempt to maintain their differential advantage in relation to the Vector account because the basic product features could easily be copied by competitors. More recently TSB introduced its 'Family Bonus' savings scheme which provided additional rewards if several members of a family saved with the bank; this move was seen as sustainable because the bank's ability to deliver derived from certain specific features of its information systems which other banks could not match in the short term.

By identifying a differential advantage that gives the organization something to offer consumers that is unique, important and sustainable, the organization has the basis for developing an effective position in its chosen market.

Porter (1980; 1985) argues essentially that there are two basic options for developing a differential advantage, (costs and differentiation) A cost-based differential advantage requires that the organization attempts to control the market through being the low cost producer. Typically, the product is undifferentiated, although differentiation cannot be ignored, since the cost savings for the consumer must compensate for the loss of product features, while the discount offered by the organization should not be so high as to offset cost advantages associated with a highly standardized product range.

The alternative to building a competitive advantage based on cost factors is to concentrate on offering products which (can be regarded as unique in areas) highly valued by the consumer. It is the product's uniqueness and the associated customer loyalty that protects the organization from competition. However, for this strategy to be successful, the price premium received by the organization must outweigh the costs of supplying the differentiated product. At the same time, the customer must feel that the (distinctive image of the product) and (the additional features offered) more than compensate for the additional cost of acquiring the product.

On the basis of these two identified sources of competitive advantage, Porter identifies three broad strategic options. A typology of strategies is presented in Figure 3.7.

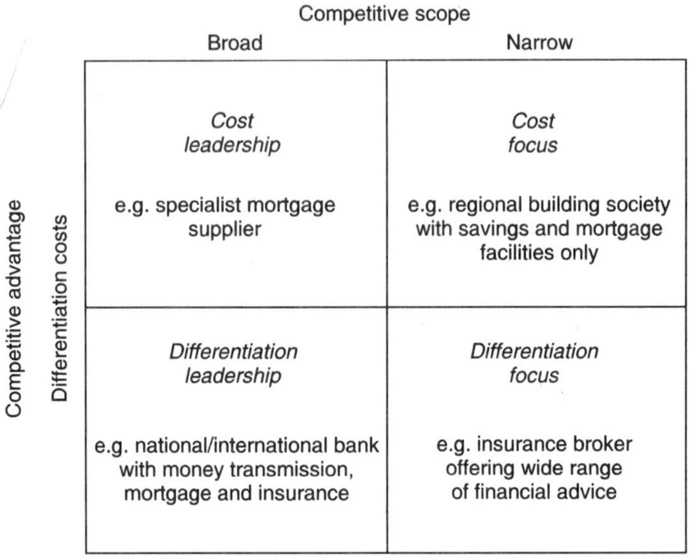

Competitive scope

Broad                                          Narrow

|  | Cost leadership | Cost focus |
|---|---|---|
| Competitive advantage — Differentiation costs | e.g. specialist mortgage supplier | e.g. regional building society with savings and mortgage facilities only |
|  | Differentiation leadership | Differentiation focus |
|  | e.g. national/international bank with money transmission, mortgage and insurance | e.g. insurance broker offering wide range of financial advice |

**Figure 3.7**   Porter's generic strategies

*Cost leadership.*  The aim of a cost leadership strategy is to control industry structure by being the low cost producer. Such a strategy typically requires up-to-date and highly efficient service delivery systems. Typically, the product is undifferentiated, but the firm cannot ignore differentiation, since the cost savings for the consumer must compensate for the loss of product features, while the discount offered by the firm should not be so high as to offset cost advantages. It can be argued that cost leadership had been a traditional strategy in many areas of financial services prior to deregulation as suppliers tended to take an institutional rather than consumer-orientated view of their markets (Ennew, Watkins and Wright, 1989).

*Differentiation leadership.*  Essentially the firm seeks to offer products which can be regarded as unique in some dimensions which are highly valued by the consumer. It is the product's uniqueness and the associated customer loyalty that protects the firm from its competitors, from the threat of entry and from substitute products. The differentiator cannot ignore costs – the costs of differentiation must be less then the premium charged for the firm to remain profitable, but at the same time the customer must feel that the extra features more than compensate for the price premium. In the light of deregulation and the opportunities it offers, many organizations are moving away from their traditional narrow product range to offer a much greater range of products, both differentiating their traditional products and expanding into new product areas. (Ennew et al., 1989; Edgett and Thwaites, 1990).

*Focus/niche*. The strategy uses either costs or differentiation but concentrates on specific segments of the market. The aim is to identify part of the market with distinctive needs which are not adequately supplied by major producers in the market. Differentiation focus is the most common form of focus strategy and implies producing highly customized products for very specific consumer groups. A number of the smaller building societies have opted for differentiation-based strategies, resulting in the appearance of specialist savings products for children (Peckham Building Society's 'Jumbo Savings Account' and Birmingham Midshires, 'SmartStart' account); other societies such as the Ecology Building Society and the Catholic Building Society specialize in the provision of mortgages to segments of the market which are deemed unattractive to the major players. Both restrict themselves to a limited range of products; the Ecology lends money for environmentally friendly housing while the Catholic Building Society has paid particular attention to the female market. However, cost focus strategies are not uncommon in the financial services sector, particularly where markets are segmented geographically. For example, many of the regional and local building societies appear to be selecting a cost focus strategy, even in the light of deregulation, concentrating specifically on the provision of a traditional service range in a narrowly defined geographical market (Ennew and Wright, 1990a).

Porter's analysis stresses the importance of avoiding a situation where the organization is 'stuck in the middle' – i.e. trying to be all things to all consumers. The firm trying to perform well on costs and on differentiation is likely to loose out to firms concentrating on either one strategy or the other. Equally, it should be recognized that in a period of rapid market change, the strategy selected as a basis for establishing competitive advantage may not be sustainable if all other organizations are reassessing their strategic position at the same time. Accordingly, there may be an element of experimentation involved in strategy selection (Ennew et al., 1992).

## 3.5 Strategic challenges

Clearly the nature and role of marketing strategy in financial services has changed considerably over the past decade. Many of the most significant developments and trends in marketing strategy are outlined by Ennew, Wright and Thwaites (1993), with particular emphasis being paid to patterns of market development and diversification. Although the pace and complexity of environmental change may now be rather less than it was in the mid-to late 1980s, it is clear that there are still a number of significant changes occurring in the industry and a number of developments within the broader operating environment which are likely to present significant challenges to those involved in the marketing of financial services. Some of the most important issues are identified below.

Clearly the process of restructuring, as illustrated by the Lloyds–Cheltenham and Gloucester and the Halifax–Leeds mergers will have a major impact on the retailing of financial services and may be one route to address the underlying problem of over-capacity in branch networks. More generally, the role of the branch network is threatened by the development of alternative and more flexible delivery systems and, while branches are unlikely to disappear, their numbers and role are certainly set to change substantially. Although delivery systems may alter, the long-term committment of the banks to the retail market is clearly in evidence with the continuing development of Allfinanz or Bancassurance, although such developments are not without problems (Morgan, 1994) and a key challenge for future marketing activities is the effective integration of insurance business and the maximization of cross-selling opportunities.

For many financial service suppliers, the 1980s were an important period for expansion and diversification. The 1990s seem to be characterized by a tendency to reassess that process of expansion and diversification. Some organizations are looking to refocus onto their core activities having found that attempting to be 'all things to all people' is both extremely difficult and very costly. Whether this is a short-term response to the recession or a more longer term change in strategic direction is still uncertain. For the majority of players though, the preferred route forward may well be some form of product or market specialization in recognition of the difficulties associated with competing head-on with the major players. Irrespective of whether organizations engage in extensive narrowing of product ranges, there will remain a need to continue to reinforce the integration of activities and to place emphasis on internal marketing in order to obtain optimum benefits from offering the chosen range of products.

Quality of service and customer care will inevitably remain as key components in the overall service offer, but subject to the constraints of remaining price competitive. Indeed the whole issue of pricing is set to return to the agenda in the form of the continuing debate over current account charges. In a period in which the popularity of the banks with business and personal customers is close to an all-time low, the issue of how to reintroduce a system of charging on current accounts will presents a major strategic challenge to the main players in this market.

Two further issues which are at present less pressing but may offer significant opportunities or pose significant threats relate to eastern Europe and environmentalism. Increasingly, major players in the financial services sector will have to consider how to respond to the pressures created by the transformation of central and eastern Europe. Early evidence of the possible strategic responses is provided by Haiss (1992) in the context of the Austrian market. Similarly, the pressure to 'go green' is currently of limited significance in the strategic marketing activities of most financial services retailers although there is evidence of some notable tactical responses (McKechnie and Ennew, 1993) and one bank, the Co-operative, has attempted to build its market position on the strength of an ethical and environmental orientation. Although the full extent of the impact of these issues on strategic marketing in financial services is uncertain, both eastern Europe and environmentalism are areas which are likely to require close monitoring in the immediate future.

Finally, there is growing evidence to suggest that issues of ethics and social responsibility may be coming to the fore in financial services. Certainly the mis-selling of pensions and the over-selling of mortgage endowments has attracted a considerable volume of adverse publicity and has raised questions about the ethical standards of the industry. The most significant problem in this context has been the heavy reliance on commission-based selling in a market in which consumers have limited information (Ennew, MacGregor and Diacon, 1994; Diacon and Ennew, 1995). More generally, there has been concern expressed about policy decisions to close bank branches in low income (and hence unprofitable) areas and about decisions by banks to foreclose on businesses, particularly small businesses. Clearly such activities generate a considerable amount of adverse publicity. At a strategic level, simply responding to such criticisms may no longer be appropriate; there is a growing need for active consideration of how best to manage strategic decisions in a way which is socially and ethically responsible.

## 3.6  Conclusion

The environment facing the suppliers of financial service has changed dramatically over the past decade. Deregulation in conjunction with developments in information technology and fluctuations in economic performance has resulted in an increasingly competitive market environment. The traditional institutional boundaries which existed between suppliers of financial services are breaking down; banks, insurance companies and building societies are all competing across the same broad markets. In such an environment, success requires a planned and strategic approach to marketing. The organization must be clear about the products and markets it serves and it must develop a thorough understanding of their various facets. It must have a clear statement of where it plans to go in the future and a clear indication of the most appropriate route to get there. That strategy itself is one that should be consistent with the distinctive competencies of the organization itself and must match the environment in which it operates. Neither of these is immutable; strategy can be used to modify the environment either internally or externally. However, in a period of environmental turbulence it is becoming increasingly important to recognize that strategies are not fixed; they can be adjusted and often need to be adjusted as the pattern of environmental change becomes clearer.

# 4 The financial services marketing mix

Christine Ennew and Trevor Watkins

## 4.1 Introduction

Traditionally, the marketing mix comprises four elements: product, price, promotion and place (the 4Ps). These elements are typically seen as encompassing the range of marketing variables which are directly controlled by the organization. In order to meet the needs of the target market, organizations seek to develop a balance between these elements which reflects the organization's desired competitive position. In many senses, the marketing mix provides a bridge between marketing strategy and marketing tactics. The aim of marketing strategy in any organization is to establish a match between the organization's skills and capabilities and the needs of the target market. Marketing tactics, by contrast, are more closely concerned with decisions about how to deliver the product or service offer which reflects this matching process. The marketing mix has both strategic and tactical dimensions. The strategic dimension of the marketing mix is primarily concerned with decisions about the relative importance of the mix elements for a particular product–market combination. For example promotion, particularly television advertising, may play an important role in the marketing mix for many retail financial services, but may be almost irrelevant for specialized corporate financial services. The tactical dimension of the marketing mix works within the framework created by decisions regarding the balance of the mix and is concerned primarily with the specification of precise details for each element in the mix. To develop an effective marketing mix requires a clear understanding of the chosen product position and of the way in which consumers are likely to respond to the individual mix elements. This chapter reviews the concept of the marketing mix as it applies to financial services. Particular attention is focused on the relevance of the traditional 4P concept and on examining the components of the various elements of the mix. Section 4.2 provides an overview of the financial services marketing mix while section 4.3 examines important themes which must be developed within the context of the traditional 4Ps framework. A summary and conclusion are presented in section 4.4.

## 4.2 The nature of the financial services marketing mix

The traditional concept of the marketing mix as comprising product, price, promotion and place was developed largely on the basis of empirical work undertaken in relation to manufacturing industry. As yet, there is no comparable empirical basis for the analysis of service marketing mixes (Cowell, 1984). Eiglier (1977) reports the result of a study of management in a variety of service sectors in France, but the focus of the study is with service characteristics and the problems they present rather than with the methods of marketing. In fact, much of the empirical work in the service area has tended to be service specific or problem oriented. As a consequence, studies of the service marketing mix have tended to concentrate attention on the conceptual development of a mix as a response to service features rather than as a result of extensive empirical observation of the practice of marketing management.

The extent to which the marketing of services differs from the marketing of goods is subject to considerable debate. The moderate position would recognize some areas of similarity and some areas of difference. In many respects, the most fundamental distinction arises because services are considered to be intangible. A service cannot be seen, touched or displayed. A customer may purchase a particular service but typically has nothing physical to display as a result of the purchase. This intangibility arises because a service is essentially a process or an experience rather than a physical object which the consumer can possess (Bateson, 1977; Eiglier and Langeard, 1977; Shostack, 1982; Bowen and Schneider, 1988). Clearly, this should not be taken to imply that products and services are polar extremes. On the contrary, there are degrees of tangibility and intangibility and service marketing deals with the 'intangible dominant' set of products (Shostack, 1977). Furthermore, it is important to remember that intangibility has essentially two meanings. At one level it is concerned with the fact that services are impalpable in the sense that they have no physical form, but it also recognizes that many services are intangible from a conceptual point of view in that they are not easily defined and may be difficult to understand (Bateson, 1977). Many services will display both aspects of intangibility and the problem is particularly acute with many professional and financial services (Donnelly, Berry and Thompson, 1985).

The fact that services are essentially acts or experiences leads to the second factor which distinguishes services from goods, namely inseparability. In general, services must be produced and consumed simultaneously. As a consequence, services are perishable, they must be produced on demand and cannot be inventoried. The presence of inseparability tends to imply the consumers themselves play a significant role in the production of services. Indeed, some commentators view customers as quasi- or partial-employees (Bowen and Schneider, 1988). For a service to be provided typically requires either the physical presence of the consumer or some contact with the consumer to provide the information required for the service to be performed. The consumer making a loan application does not have to be in the physical presence of the loan assessor, but must supply that assessor with information to evaluate the application. This interaction between consumers and employees in the provision of services leads to a third distinctive characteristic of services, namely heterogeneity. The quality of the service product is typically highly dependent on personal interactions and, as a consequence, the potential for variability is high. To a large extent, the qualities of inseparability and heterogeneity arise because of the intangible nature of services. The characterization of services as an act rather than as an object leads to an emphasis on the individuals providing the service and their interactions with the organization's customers.

In addition to these service characteristics, financial services display an additional feature which affects the marketing process. This is the issue of fiduciary responsibility which refers to the implicit responsibility which financial services organizations have in relation to the management of funds and the financial advice they supply to their customers. Although any business has a responsibility to its consumers in terms of the quality, reliability and safety of the products it supplies, this responsibility is perhaps much greater in the case of the financial service organization (Marsh, 1988). Such a situation may be explained partly by the fact that consumers of such services often find the precise details of the services difficult to comprehend and are therefore placing their trust in the organization with which they deal. Equally important of course is the fact that the 'raw materials' used to produce many financial products are consumers' deposits; thus in producing and selling a loan product the bank has a responsibility to the person taking out a loan but, at the same time, it also has a responsibility to the individuals whose deposits have made that loan possible. The importance of fiduciary responsibility has been incorporated into notions of 'best advice' as a component of the recent regulatory changes (see Chapter 1). Despite these formal requirements, any organization involved in the provision of financial services should retain an awareness of the magnitude of the impact which their marketing and selling activities can have on the lifestyle of an individual or the prosperity of a company.

While there is some suggestion that services marketing is distinctive at the strategic level (Thomas, 1978), the differences between marketing goods and marketing services become more noticeable at the tactical level. This occurs primarily because as marketing moves towards tactical issues then it also moves closer to, and so must be more tailored to, the distinguishing features of specific products and markets. In the context of the marketing mix, this suggests that in the case of services, the composition of that mix and the management of its elements can be quite distinctive. Thus, we find that the applicability of the traditional 4Ps in the case of services marketing has been extensively questioned. Gronroos (1990), for example, describes the traditional marketing mix as being over-simplistic and likely to misguide both academics and practitioners because it does not fully cover all aspects of the relationship between the consumer and the service provider. The usual textbook response is that the service marketing mix should include a fifth 'P' namely 'people' to acknowledge the important role played by individuals in the provision of services. This additional element incorporates not just personnel involved in direct communication with customers, it also includes operational personnel and the customer groups themselves (Cowell, 1984). A more radical adjustment has been suggested by Booms and Bitner (1981) and popularized by, for example, Cowell (1984) and

Magrath (1986) to the effect that the services marketing mix should be broadened to include three further 'Ps' – people, processes and physical evidence.

Although the inclusion of these additional elements in a service marketing mix is clearly a result of the intangibility, inseparability and heterogeneity of most services, there have been some questions raised concerning the need to incorporate these additional elements. Cowell (1984) raises the possibility that the use of these terms may simply be a question of semantics. In principle, each of the three additional 'Ps' can be incorporated within the existing framework of product, price, promotion and place, particularly if we recognize the importance of the augmented product, rather than the simple core or generic product. Physical evidence and the characteristics of individuals involved in the provision of the service can be encompassed within product and promotional issues, while the importance attached to processes can easily be seen as falling within the remit of service distribution. This line of thought can be developed such that people, processes and physical evidence are seen more generally as themes that should be emphasized with the services marketing mix. People, processes and physical evidence are important responses to the particular features of service products, but are relevant not as separate elements in the marketing mix but rather as themes which should be emphasized within the traditional mix. The traditional 4Ps are reviewed in the following chapters; the remainder of this chapter will examine these three themes and their role within the financial services marketing mix.

## 4.3    Themes in the financial services marketing mix

Irrespective of how the marketing mix is defined, its role is to ensure that the service offer meets the needs of the target market as closely as possible and is consistent with the identified strategy. Of course the effectiveness of any marketing mix can be reduced as a consequence of largely unpredictable and largely uncontrollable environmental variables; careful planning of the mix can reduce but not remove this threat. Each element of the mix must be consistent with the others so that a coherent message is conveyed to the target market. Indeed a coherent and coordinated marketing mix should also produce synergistic effects such that the impact of the overall mix is greater than the sum of the individual parts. Thus, individual elements of the mix should not be viewed in isolation; constant cross-referencing is essential to ensure consistency with other elements in the mix. The mix is concerned with communicating an overall offer to the target market and it is therefore essential that each element of the mix is giving the same signal to consumers. An example of this approach is the marketing campaign used by pensions specialist NPI. Given the characteristics of its target audience, NPI has developed a campaign which emphasizes British heritage, is promoted in conjunction with the *The Times* and Classic Fm and uses concessions to historic sites as a form of promotion.

The ultimate purchase decision is made by the consumer on the basis of the overall service offer. This can be decomposed into the traditional elements of product, price, promotion and place. The characteristics of service products require that marketing managers, in blending together these elements, pay particular attention to the people providing the service, the processes whereby the service is made available to the consumer and the physical evidence attached to the product. The fact that services are intangible means that the people who supply the service, the process by which it is supplied and the associated physical evidence will be key factors in creating customer satisfaction. The heterogeneity of services requires that considerable emphasis is attached to the service providers and the process of provision to ensure quality, while inseparability requires that the service provider emphasizes people and processes to ensure customer satisfaction. Thus, people, processes and physical evidence are seen as areas on which marketing should focus attention in developing the marketing mix, and therefore as inputs to the traditional components of that mix.

### 4.3.1 People

The 'people' component reflects the important role played by individuals in the provision of financial services. Consumers will often find the precise details of the product difficult to understand; they often do not see anything tangible for their expenditure and the material benefits from many products will often not be realized for some quite considerable time. As a consequence, the purchase decision is affected by the degree of trust a consumer associates with an organization and this in turn is heavily influenced by the individual who actually makes the initial contact with the consumer and carries out the sale. Indeed, the people component of a services marketing mix is most commonly associated with personal selling, although we should recall that this overlaps with both promotion and distribution.

For many financial services, the essence of the delivery system is based on people. The use of direct sales forces has traditionally been an important component of the distribution strategies of insurance companies, but it is now becoming important for all types of financial service providers, although often in the case of banks and building societies the responsibility for personal selling falls to branch staff rather than specialist sales personnel. There is some evidence to suggest that many banks are developing specialist sales teams to meet the more specific needs of corporate clients. Other direct distribution methods are increasing in importance, as will be outlined in Chapter 8 but, in most instances, direct mail and direct response advertising provide only the preliminary contacts, and it is through the personal selling medium that the majority of sales are negotiated and sealed. Despite the increased cost of salesforces and the problems associated with commission-based remunerations, the importance of personal selling is likely to increase as competition within the financial services sector intensifies and product ranges both expand and become more complex (Ennew et al., 1989). Personal selling is a two-way process and the opportunity to adapt presentations to the needs and nature of the individual customer and the specific selling situation means that personal contact and personal selling is likely to remain a central component of any distribution system, whether face to face in the consumer's home, in the branch network or over the telephone.

While the principles of personal selling are similar whether a salesforce is dealing with goods or services, there is some evidence to suggest that the selling of financial service may pose some particular problems. The ethical problems associated with the use of commission-based selling in financial services have been well-documented (Ennew et al., 1994; Devlin and Ennew, 1993). More generic problems facing salesforces in the life assurance industry are discussed by George and Myers (1981) who identified a number of differences between selling goods and selling services. They suggested that consumers were aware of the potential for quality variability, that the purchase of a service was regarded as a potentially risky decision and a not particularly enjoyable process. In the purchase process, consumers tended to undertake fewer price comparisons than they would with physical products and they attached considerable importance to the image of the service provider and the performance of sales staff. The actual sale of a financial service was typically characterized by much greater customer involvement than would be the case for a product and the sales staff were required to spend a significant proportion of their time reducing consumer uncertainty.

Given the significance of contact with individual staff, which George and Myers identify, it is clearly important to ensure that sales staff develop good personal relationships with their customers. To alleviate any doubts or risks which the customer may feel requires a professional orientation by sales staff to illustrate the competency and familiarity with all aspects of the relevant products. This in turn requires the organization to ensure good training and motivation for such staff. Finally, the personal selling approach should ensure that the actual purchase decision is made easy and minimal demands are imposed on the customer.

While personal selling is in many respects central to any service delivery system, it is perhaps equally important as a method of promoting financial services, particularly so in the light of the increasing complexity of the product. When dealing with a complex product, despite the obvious importance of advertising in creating an awareness of the product, effective personal contact becomes of paramount importance in explaining the product to the potential consumer. In addition, personal selling is of central importance in dealing with corporate clients for whom the cost effectiveness of mass advertising is extremely poor.

People are also an important element in the specification of the product component of the marketing mix. The product component of the financial services marketing mix, like that of any service, is affected by the problem of copying (Davison et al., 1989). It is difficult to use specific service attributes as the basis for developing competitive advantage because distinctive attributes are easily duplicated by competitors. By contrast, improvements in the quality of service provision in general, and customer care in particular, are recognized as being important strategies for successful product differentiation as is explained in Chapter 9. In financial services, the quality aspects of a product are inextricably linked with the actual provision of the product which is in turn usually highly dependent on the individual who deals with the consumer. Hence the importance of 'people' in the product component of the marketing mix. However, because individuals will have an important role in creating quality, controlling the process of service provision can be a difficult exercise, requiring investment in staff training and the establishment of a quality oriented corporate culture.

Furthermore, contact with the service provider is often the basis for consumers' reaction to, and acceptance of, the price of that service. Of course, customer service is important to any organization and not the exclusive province of the services sector. Nevertheless, poor customer service with a normal tangible product can be forgotten if the consumer is satisfied with the product. Most services are so closely linked to the service provider that poor customer care can lead to dissatisfaction with the supplying organization. Thus 'people' become an important component of the product, as well as an input to pricing, a method of promotion and a means of distribution.

### 4.3.2 Processes

The process theme focuses on the mechanisms by which the service is delivered, including business policies for service provision, procedures, degree of mechanization etc. The emphasis on process arises from several sources. First, the heterogeneity of services raises the issues of quality management and control. Second, inseparability suggests that the process of providing the service may be highly visible to the consumer and will need to be flexible enough to accommodate potential demand variations. Third, the intangibility of services means that the process by which the service is provided will often be an important influence on the consumer's assessment of service quality. Accordingly, the main concern with process is typically in the context of distribution.

In developing distribution systems for financial services, the boundaries between what constitutes physical distribution and what constitutes channel structure are blurred, as are the distinctions between promotion and distribution. The intangible nature of the product means that there is nothing physical actually to supply to the consumer; the consumer is paying only for a bundle of benefits and the delivery process will need to emphasize this. Furthermore, the variability of service quality leads to pressure for automation in service delivery wherever possible (see for example Howcroft, 1992; 1993). For some services, such as money transmission, this is relatively easy whereas for others, such as financial advice, this is more complex, although recent developments in expert systems are assisting with the automation of some of the more complex services.

Although process is important in relation to distribution, it cannot be ignored as a dimension of the product offering and will also have a bearing on the nature of the price charged through its impact on the monitoring and measurement of production costs. The pricing process is described in more detail in Chapter 7. A key influence on pricing decisions is the pattern of costs associated with supplying a particular service. Although price must be determined in relation to the level of demand and the willingness of consumers to pay, costs cannot be ignored and the price that is set should cover variable costs and make a contribution to fixed costs, although this will depend on the level of sales. Financial service providers encounter a number of problems as far as costs are concerned. First, at a very fundamental level, it is often difficult to distinguish between what constitutes a fixed cost and what constitutes a variable cost. Labour time which is typically thought of as a variable or semi-variable cost in most forms of industrial production could arguably be considered a fixed cost for many financial services organizations. This problem is compounded in those organizations which maintain a large branch network, not just because of staffing but also because of the high fixed costs associated with such a network. Furthermore, the systems for the allocation of these fixed costs are by no means clear, particularly in organizations dealing with a wide range of products. In the case of many insurance products, there is the added complication that pricing decisions may be strongly influenced by actuarial requirements, leaving little scope for a significant input from marketing. Indeed, in some financial services sectors, particularly banking, the combination of a limited knowledge of costs and an oligopolistic marketplace has tended to lead to extensive cross-subsidization (Howcroft and Lavis, 1989). As competition increases, and as price competition becomes important, more detailed information on cost structures and consumer reaction will become crucial to an effective pricing strategy.

### 4.3.3. Physical evidence

The physical evidence component refers to the environment in which the service is delivered and the tangible items which are associated with that service, such as wallets for documents. The need for physical evidence within the marketing mix arises directly from the typically intangible nature of the service. It is generally recognized that physical evidence can be subdivided into two components (Shostack, 1982): peripheral evidence which can be possessed by the consumer but has little independent value (e.g. a cheque book) and essential evidence, which cannot be possessed by the consumer but has independent value (e.g. a bank branch). The provision of physical evidence is likely to be most obvious in the product and place components of the marketing mix, although promotion can play an important role in creating a tangible image for the service and the organization. The campaign used by Access based around the concept of the credit card as a 'flexible friend' is one particularly successful example of this approach.

The process of branding as a tangible cue and the associated forms of peripheral evidence (cheque books, plastic cards, document wallets etc.) is becoming increasingly important in financial services as a mechanism for conveying information to consumers on the quality of a product and as a means of establishing a degree of customer loyalty (Onkvist and Shaw, 1989; Saunders and Watters, 1993). In the financial services sector, it is arguably the customer's image of the organization which is the most important type of branding available (Howcroft and Lavis, 1987). Casual empiricism tends to support this conclusion since most financial products are identified primarily by the supplier's name; the decision of Midland to launch these specifically branded current accounts – Vector, Orchard and Meridian – was a break with this tradition although this move has proved to be less than successful. The combination of organization name and product name – for example, Halifax Maxim or BarclayLoan – has proved rather more effective. Indeed, the importance of the organization's image suggests that the organizational name will continue to be used since it remains perhaps the most obvious source of information and indicator of quality available to customers.

The need for physical evidence is particularly significant in the context of promotion. The particular problem facing suppliers of financial services is that they have no physical product to present to consumers; the task of promotion then focuses on developing a message and a form of presentation which allows the organization to present an essentially intangible product in a tangible form. This outcome can be achieved using some combination of the available promotional tools. The appropriate combination will vary according to the type of market in which the organization operates, with the most marked differences being observed in the promotional mixes for corporate and personal customers. A particular feature of advertising and promotion in the financial services sector has been the use of tangible representations of the product where appropriate or the use of tangible associations. In many cases, the tangible association is with the organization itself, such as the 'Northern Rock' or 'Leeds Permanent', but it could equally well be a 'Flexible Friend' or a 'Black Horse'. It is also interesting that the more successful forms of sales promotion have tended to be those offering tangible items as free gifts (calculators, watches etc.) and competitions rather than simple price promotions. More detail on these activities is provided in Chapter 6.

Physical evidence has an important role to play in creating clear corporate identity. While customer perceptions of the character of an organization are seen to be of increasing importance in the marketing of both products and services, their significance in relation to services is considerable. In the financial services sector it is widely recognized that consumer reactions to the organization are critical in terms of their perceptions of service quality (Howcroft and Lavis, 1987). When faced with a variety of similar products of a highly technical nature from competing suppliers, consumer choice is frequently motivated by the perceived image of that organization. Indeed, Howcroft and Lavis (1987) suggest that image is perhaps the most important form of branding available to the suppliers of personal financial services. An organization's corporate identity can be represented by a variety of visual symbols associated with promotional material, branch layout and design and staff appearance. The branch has long been recognized as an arena through which an organization can project its corporate image to existing and new customers (Greenland,

1994). This process can be reinforced by advertising which can emphasize identity and create images. Indeed, as has been suggested earlier, a large volume of financial services advertising has been concerned with corporate image rather than specific products.

## 4.4 Conclusion

Marketing has been slow to develop in the financial services sector – both as a business function and as an area of study. However, extensive changes in the business environment during the 1970s and particularly during the 1980s have led to marketing playing an increasingly important role in guiding business development. This is reflected at a strategic level in a greater degree of customer orientation and a move towards a greater degree of market segmentation and targeting. The effectiveness of any strategic moves however depends on the development of an effective marketing mix, especially one which recognizes and responds to the distinctive features of service products. In particular, when managing the elements of product, price, promotion and place, marketers in the financial services sector need to pay particular attention to the people delivering the service, the process by which the service is delivered and the physical evidence which represents the service.

# 5 Product strategy

Christine Ennew

## 5.1 Introduction

The product is arguably the central component of any marketing mix; however competitively priced, imaginatively promoted and effectively distributed that product may be, if it does not offer the key features that consumers expect, if it does not satisfy the needs of the target market then the organization lacks an effective basis for long-term success in a competitive market. The product component of the marketing mix deals with a variety of issues relating to the development, presentation and management of the product which is to be offered to the marketplace. As such it covers issues such as developing an appropriate product mix and product line as well as considering decisions relating to the attributes and features of individual products. It also, and perhaps most importantly, deals with aspects of new product development. Extending product ranges, either by new product development or through the modification of existing products is a commonly observed strategy in the rapidly changing and increasingly competitive financial services sector. Furthermore, it is apparent that many aspects of product management, such as branding, which have traditionally been associated with consumer goods markets are becoming increasingly important in the financial services sector.

The concept of a financial service product is a complex one. Financial services are highly intangible and consequently distinguishing the product from its price and the mode of delivery may sometime be difficult. An added complication is that many financial services are long term and consequently the precise benefits that they offer may be uncertain. In order to examine the product component of the marketing mix, it is important to define clearly what is meant by the term 'product'. This chapter begins by examining the concept of the service product and the factors which will influence the development of the product strategy in financial services. Subsequent sections deal specifically with aspects of the product range strategy and the process of new product development in the financial services sector.

## 5.2 The concept of the service product

Like products, any service is purchased by consumers not for itself but for the benefits it offers to the user – that is to say, a service is purchased because it fulfils certain needs. The intangibility of services makes the definition of what constitutes the service product a potentially complex exercise (Cowell, 1984). The marketing literature presents a variety of frameworks for the analysis of the components of a product and these provide a useful framework for examining and defining the service product in general and the financial service product in particular. Kotler (1994), for example, distinguishes between the core benefit supplied, the generic product, the expected (or tangible), the augmented and the potential product, while Levitt (1980) focuses on the generic, expected and augmented components of a product. In each case the analysis is based on the idea that any product can be seen as offering a basic set of features which represent its ability to satisfy certain basic needs. Beyond this products are augmented by a variety of additional features which associate it with a particular supplier, differentiate it from competing products and make it in some sense distinctive. The concept of the potential product includes all future possible additions to the product which could occur in the future and it is at this level, according to Kotler, that organizations are searching for new means to differentiate themselves. A simple outline of the three layers of a product – core, expected and augmented – is presented in Figure 5.1.

In the case of services, we can consider the core or generic element as being composed of those features which provide for certain broad consumer needs. Thus, as in Figure 5.1, the core or generic element of a unit trust is the facility to manage and augment an individual's financial resources which fulfils customer needs for a return on financial resources and the associated ability to defer consumption. The tangible or expected elements give a service a more specific identity by adding shape and

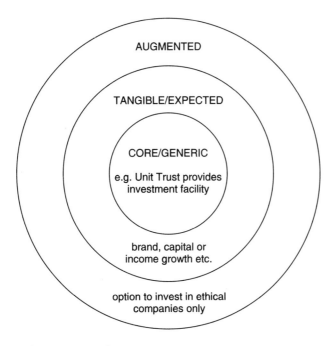

**Figure 5.1** The service product

features to the core or generic product. In the case of a unit trust, this would include an association with a specific supplier (branding), choice of investment realization method (income v. capital growth), projected returns, accessibility etc. The augmented element would then incorporate additional features which go beyond those that would be expected by the consumer. In the case of a unit trust, this might include the option to invest only in 'socially responsible' companies.

Service strategy in the marketing mix concentrates on identifying the core features required in any basic service and on developing the most appropriate peripheral features to augment that service. As Chapter 4 suggests this may require particular emphasis on physical evidence and on people. Indeed, more generally, the development of the product component of this services marketing mix is influenced by certain distinctive features of services:

> *Services are intangible.* A service cannot be seen, touched or displayed. A customer may purchase a particular service but typically has nothing physical to display as a result of the purchase. Money transmission is a service which customers pay for and is performed by banks, but the customer does not obviously have anything to show as a result. The same can be said of many insurance, savings and investment services which may only yield a benefit at some point in the future (ten years, twenty-five years or longer).

> *Services are inseparable.* In general, it is impossible to separate the production and consumption of a service. Most goods are produced and subsequently sold to consumers; by contrast, the service product is typically sold and then produced. As a result, services are perishable – they cannot be stored, they must be produced on demand and often can only be produced in the presence of the customer.

> *Services are heterogeneous.* The quality of the service product is typically highly dependent on the quality of the personnel conducting the transaction. As a result of this, the potential for variability is high. The quality of service a customer receives from a bank when making a loan application will be dependent on the performance of the loan assessor; the bank will be judged on that rather than the quality of the resulting loan. The reduction of quality variability requires standardization in service delivery such as the use of ATMs.

These features are present to varying degrees in financial services products. A key aspect of product strategy for any financial services organization is to confront these issues and attempt to resolve them. A common strategy is to develop a tangible representation of a product in the form of either peripheral evidence (that which can be possessed by the consumer but has little intrinsic value) or essential evidence (that which cannot be possessed by the consumer but which has value) or both. Examples of the latter include the branch environment in which the service is delivered (Greenland, 1994). Credit cards and cheque cards are examples of peripheral evidence which provide tangible representations of money transmission and credit facilities. Indeed, the credit card goes one stage further and provides a facility which effectively enables the consumer to store credit. When the process of direct association is not feasible, an alternative is to rely on developing associations between the service and other tangible items which represent stability. The concept of Access as a 'flexible friend' is one particularly successful example of this approach. Another variant of this approach is to focus on the organization and the nature of the relationship between buyer and seller (hence the attempt by Midland to portray itself as the 'listening bank'). The advantage of such a tangible representation is additionally that it can assist in the process of differentiation and encourage brand loyalty. Furthermore, as is explained in Chapter 6, the notion of developing a tangible representation of the service is crucial in the development of an effective promotional strategy.

## 5.3   Influences on product strategy

Products, particularly service products, are not immutable. The successful organization will undertake a process of monitoring product performance and the requirements of the marketplace to give managers the information necessary to modify existing products, develop new products and withdraw old products. The discussion of the BCG matrix and the product life cycle in Chapter 3 highlighted the importance to organizations of careful and strategic management of a product portfolio. Regular market research is crucial in this respect to provide the organization with the necessary information regarding market developments and market reactions to the organization and its products. Monitoring the environment is necessarily an ongoing process and should be part of any planned approach to marketing. Several aspects of the environment can be identified as having a particular influence on product strategy:

*Consumers.* In the context of product strategy, clearly it is of particular importance to monitor customer needs. In personal markets, customers' tastes and preferences, lifestyles, or patterns of demographic change may be a particular focus of attention. In corporate markets, the focus must be on the objectives and strategies of customers and on understanding the environment in which customers' businesses operate in order to identify likely financial needs. However, in addition to identifying existing needs it is important to be able to anticipate future needs. This process has been described by Hamel and Prahalad (1992) as 'leading consumers where they wish to go'. The launch of First Direct in 1989 provides an example of the successful anticipation of changing customer needs. Having recognized a declining interest in the use of the branch network and a demand for greater convenience and flexibility in accessing banking and financial services, Midland launched a telephone banking service. Despite some initial doubts, First Direct proved to be a highly successful new development and most other major banks have followed suit with their own variants of telephone banking including National Westminster (Prime Line) and Barclays (Barclay Call). The process of identifying and satisfying consumer needs in financial services has also been subject to criticism and some question the extent to which needs are identified or created (Knights, Sturdy and Morgan, 1994). The concept of need satisfaction is certainly problematic for many financial services because many customers may not identify a need for the product in an active sense and this problem has certainly been highlighted by recent scandals concerning the mis-selling of pensions. Nevertheless, problems of this nature should not detract from the importance of trying to identify and understand customer needs as a key component in the development of an effective product strategy.

*Competitors.* The regular monitoring of competitors is an important source of information for guiding the product strategy. Information on changes to a competitor's marketing mix or to their product range may provide guidance on perceived trends in the marketplace. Indeed, given the ease of copying financial products, the monitoring of competitors' products can be an important input to the new product development process. Obviously this provides benefits in terms of savings on development costs and tends to mean the new product will be less likely to fail. However, copying also has its negative aspects in that a simple reliance on copying competitors may lead to a compounding of mistakes, or draw an organization away from its main marketing strategy as a result of purely tactical considerations.

*Government and legislation.* Government policy, legislative and political developments create a range of new opportunities to develop the product range as well as presenting threats to established products. The legislative aspects of the environment have been of particular importance in relation to the financial services sector and their impact on product ranges is discussed in some detail in Chapter 1. Legislative changes can make established products less effective or can create opportunities for the development of new products. The withdrawal of tax relief on mortgage endowments has meant that these policies have become increasingly unattractive as a means of repaying mortgages; by contrast, budgetary changes which provided tax relief on Personal Equity Plans (PEPs) have created an opportunity for organizations to develop (among other things), PEP mortgages.

Throughout the analysis of influences on product strategy, an organization must give careful consideration to how to respond to changes in customer needs, competitor activity and other environmental developments. It is not operationally or financially feasible for an organization to react to every change in the marketing environment; at the same time, no organization can afford to miss key opportunities which may be presented by legislative, social or economic change. Indeed it has been argued that many of the forms of new product development and diversification observed in the late 1980s were a response to the identification of significant windows of opportunity which organizations saw as being too important to miss.

Subsequently as market conditions changed many of these new developments were withdrawn or divested (Ennew et al., 1992).

## 5.4 Product range strategy

The majority of organizations offer a range of products to a variety of customer groups in order to meet a variety of customer needs. In financial services, the prime customer groups are personal customers and corporate customers. In personal markets, it is not uncommon to distinguish high net worth consumers from other groups and in the corporate market, the usual distinction is between large and small businesses. These customer groups have a wide variety of needs. Stevenson (1989) identifies six broad generic needs:

- The need for money (loans)
- The need to earn a return on money (savings and investment)
- The need to move money (money transmission)
- The need to manage risk (insurance)
- The need for information
- The need for advice or expertise

Financial services organizations will look to develop services which meet some or all of these needs, for some or all of the existing customer groups. Most organizations will concentrate on either a subset of customer or a subset of needs or both; only a small number of organizations can aim to cover the entire market. To meet selected needs of select customers requires a range of differing products. A simple example of the product range which might be offered to personal customers is presented in Figure 5.2. The width of the range refers to the number of different broad product types or lines (savings, investment, insurance). Each type or line will consist of a number of related products and the number of such products determines the length of the line. For each product category in the line there may then be a range of different variants; for example, with fixed rate mortgages, a bank or building society may offer two-year, five-year

| | | | Product ranges | | | |
|---|---|---|---|---|---|---|
| | *Money transmission* | *Mortgages* | *Personal lending* | *Savings* | *Investment* | *Insurance* |
| Product line Length | Standard current account | Fixed rate | Overdrafts | Basic deposit account | Unit trusts | House insurance |
| | | Flexible | Car loans | High interest accounts | PEPS | Life insurance |
| | Interest bearing account | Low start | Home improvement loans | | Unit-linked life policies | Car insurance |
| | | | | TESSAs | | |
| | | | | | Share dealing | Health insurance |

**Figure 5.2** Sample product range

and ten-year fixed rates while for home insurance there may be different policies providing different levels of cover and imposing different restrictions on the purchaser.

The product strategy concerns itself with the management and development of this range to ensure that the organization maintains and improves its competitive position in the various markets in which it operates. The first key issue in relation to product strategy is the determination of the range of products to be offered. Decision making in this area is frequently a component of the overall strategic plan because of its implications for diversification and patterns of growth. Traditionally in the financial services sector, organizations have been characterized by a limited product range – banks concentrating on money transmission, building societies on savings and housing finance, and insurance companies on insurance products. In part, the narrow range was determined by legal restrictions on the products that could be supplied by particular types of organization but it was reinforced by the traditionally conservative nature of financial institutions. The combination of deregulation, developments in information technology and the resultant increase in competition have led many organizations to expand considerably their product range, with banks moving into a wide range of insurance activities, building societies expanding into retail banking and housing services, insurance companies expanding into estate agencies and so on.

In the context of the marketing mix, the components of product strategy range from decisions on the attributes and presentation of individual products, through to decisions regarding the most appropriate range of products to offer and on to decisions relating to the development of new products and the withdrawal of existing products. While each of these aspects of product strategy will be considered separately, it should be recognized that they are necessarily interdependent; product attribute decisions have implications for the product range and decisions relating to the product range will also have implications for aspects of the new product development process and for product elimination. (Some of the more important issues relating to product elimination are discussed in Chapter 3, while Harness and McKay (1994) discuss the topic in greater detail.)

### 5.4.1 Product attributes

In developing from the core product to the tangible and augmented stages, a variety of attributes are attached to the generic product in order to differentiate it from the competition and tailor it more specifically to the needs of customers. These attributes normally include quality, style, features, brand name, packaging, labelling and after-sales service. In the financial services sector, marketing managers face similar decisions. The generic service product (money transmission, for example) has to be developed into some tangible or augmented form (the Midland Orchard account or the Halifax Maxim) through the addition of various features such as cheque and debit cards, overdraft facilities, monthly statements

**Table 5.1**  *A sample of current accounts*

| Bank | Delivery | No penalty overdraft | Interest on credit balance | Overdraft arrangement fee | Overdraft charge per month | Rate of interest on overdraft | Interest on unauthorized overdraft | Debit card | Cheque card |
|---|---|---|---|---|---|---|---|---|---|
| Barclays Flexible | Branch | No | – | – | £5 | 19.2 | 29.8 | Delta | £100 |
| Barclays Interest | Branch | No | 0.38 | – | £10 | 19.2 | 29.8 | Delta | £100 |
| First Direct | Phone | No | 0.56 | 15 | – | 16.0 | 31.8 | Switch | £100 |
| Lloyds Classic | Branch | Yes | 0.20 | – | £8 | 19.5 | 26.8 | Delta | £100 |
| Lloyds Current | Branch | Yes | – | – | – | 19.5 | 26.8 | Delta | £100 |
| Midland Orchard | Branch | No | 0.38 | 1.25% | £7 | 17.4 | 31.8 | Switch | £100 |
| NatWest Current | Branch | No | – | – | £9 | 18.1 | 33.8 | Switch | |
| NatWest Current Plus | Branch | No | 0.38 | – | £9 | 18.9 | 33.8 | Switch | £100 |

and so on. An example of the different product features associated with a range of current accounts is presented in Table 5.1.

One of the key issues in developing the service product is to attempt to overcome the problem of intangibility. When purchasing a financial service, the customer cannot see or examine the product and can only accurately judge its performance once the purchase has been made. An important aspect of the organization's attribute decisions is to overcome this problem of intangibility by developing some physical representation of the service product. The most obvious tangible representations of service products are the cheque books, cheque cards and debit cards which accompany all the current accounts illustrated in Table 5.1; building society pass books and well-presented insurance certificates may also be regarded as tangible representations of intangible products.

The range of features offered as part of a particular service product is potentially a mechanism for differentiation to appeal to specific groups of consumers. Thus for example, the main distinction between NatWest Current and NatWest Current Plus is that the former pays no interest on cash balances but has a slightly cheaper overdraft rate and therefore is suited to consumers who hold small amounts of surplus cash and overdraw regularly. By contrast, the Current Plus account pays interest but charges a higher overdraft rate and therefore is more suited to those customers who have larger cash balances and do not overdraw. However, the range of actual distinct features which can be attached to a particular financial service is limited and may not provide a long-term basis for differentiation since such features are easily copied. Offering interest payments on cheque accounts might constitute an extra product feature which can be attached to a money transmission product; if successful, it is easily copied and may not generate much increased business for the innovator.

It is apparent from examining the basic characteristics of these accounts that it is difficult to differentiate in terms of product attributes; with the exception of a some variation in pricing structures, each account offers essentially the same set of features. Only First Direct differs significantly because of its delivery mechanism, although this is increasingly being imitated by other banks (Devlin, 1995). Thus, any attempt to differentiate a product at the expected or augmented level must look beyond simple product features and consider instead issues such as quality, branding and organizational image.

Quality is regarded as an increasingly important product feature and refers to the ability of a product to perform its intended task. As is explained in Chapter 9, quality in the service sector in general and financial services in particular can be a rather more complex concept. Customers' assessment of service quality may be based on both functional (process) and technical (outcome) aspects (Lehtinen and Lehtinen, 1991). The technical or outcome aspect relates to the extent to which a product conforms to specifications and might indicate questions such as: does a capital growth investment trust provide an acceptable rate of capital growth; does a mortgage endowment pay off the mortgage or does the bank pay a standing order on time? The functional or process component by contrast is concerned with the way in which the service is delivered and might include factors such as the way staff behave towards customers, the quality of information provided, speed of response to questions and the extent to which the institution engenders trust. Frequently, these process factors may be as important as outcome factors in the consumer's assessment of quality.

In addition to the commonly made distinction between technical and functional quality, other research in this area has stressed the importance of considering service quality and performance in relation to customer expectations (Parasuraman, Zeithaml and Berry 1985; 1988) across a range of quality dimensions such as tangibles, reliability, assurance, responsiveness and empathy. This perspective focuses primarily on the process by which service is provided rather than dealing explicitly with the technical quality of what is provided. Concepts of service quality and customer care are discussed in much greater detail in Chapter 9. However, it is important to note that process quality in particular may be an important and effective means in differentiating financial services, simply because quality is more difficult to copy than product features.

What is evident from even this brief discussion of quality in financial services is that the management of quality is likely to be a complex exercise. Certainly, the effective management of technical systems and technical skills will be an important component in developing and maintaining outcome quality. Process quality however may be far more dependent on the individuals involved in service delivery – both customer and provider. The importance of staff attitudes and behaviour is widely acknowledged (Bowen and Scheider, 1988) and evidence from the small business sector would tend to suggest that customers who are more involved in the service delivery process tend to perceive a higher level of service quality (Ennew and Binks, 1995b). This tends to suggest that managing process quality becomes rather more difficult and must focus on issues such as staff training and motivation and internal marketing to develop a quality, customer-oriented culture. As a consequence, quality control can be a difficult exercise, requiring investment in staff training and the establishment of a quality-orientated corporate culture. The growing interest in 'relationship banking', particularly in the corporate market, can be regarded as an attempt to improve the quality aspects of banking services (Watson, 1986; Turnbull and Gibbs, 1987; Binks and Ennew, 1991).

Branding is an attribute which is often regarded as being central to the marketing of products but less common in the service sector (Cowell, 1984). Branding is of growing significance in financial services because it provides a means of maintaining a clear identity in a marketplace in which organizational boundaries are becoming increasingly blurred. The process of branding extends beyond simply giving a product a memorable name. Rather, branding is concerned with building a link or a relationship between product and consumer such that the product is identified as having the ability to meet both functional and psychosocial needs. Using the brand to build a relationship between the customer and the product provides a means of conveying information regarding quality, differentiating the product from the competition and encouraging customer loyalty. In the financial services sector, it is arguably the customer's image of the organization which is the most important type of branding available (Howcroft and Lavis, 1987). Casual empiricism tends to support this conclusion since most financial products are identified primarily by the supplier's name; there is some evidence to suggest a move away from the company trade name brand to individual product brands – thus Midland's decision to brand the Vector account and Nationwide Anglia's decision to brand their FlexAccount. Even with these developments, it seems unlikely that the use of the organizational name will disappear since it remains perhaps the most important source of information and indicator of quality available to customers.

A systematic framework for the analysis of branding in financial services has been developed by Saunders and Watters (1993). They suggest that a brand hierarchy can be identified as follows:

*Corporate dominant.* The main element in the brand is the name of the organization itself (Halifax Maxim, Lloyds Classic) or a division of the organization (First Direct as a division of Midland). This approach is generally very effective when the organization's products are closely related and the generic image of the organization is then seen to be applicable to all its products.

*Dual branding.* Dual branding involves combined brand names (Lloyds Abbey Life) or combinations of product brand and corporate brand with the product brand rather more dominant (NatWest Visa Card). Approaches such as this are typically used when an organization wishes to use aspects of its own established brand or image without losing the benefits of being associated with another established brand. Thus for example, when Halifax moved into estate agency, it wished to make full use of its own brand image but did not want to lose the brand image of the established estate agent. Consequently a dual branding approach was used combining the two names. Interestingly, once established in the market, Halifax gradually returned to corporate branding.

*Brand dominant*. Brand dominant approaches essentially de-emphasize corporate associations and concentrate on products. One approach is the simple product brand such as Vector (Midland) or Liquid Gold (Leeds) which attempts to create a distinct identity for the product independent of the organization which supplies it. This approach has not been entirely successful in financial services, partly because of the difficulty of divorcing the product from the provider and partly perhaps because of limited investment in building the brands. Another variant of this approach is 'furtive branding' in which a separate identify is created for a product or group of products in a way that attempts to disguise corporate relationships. Hong Kong and Shanghai Bank appear to be pursuing this approach with Midland in order to protect the existing Midland brand image.

While assessing the value of a brand may be difficult, some indication of the benefits which may be realized is shown in Table 5.2. The table lists a series of different savings accounts. The lowest return is offered by the Halifax; many of the smaller societies are offering far more attractive rates but attract far less in the way of deposits. In part the observed pattern of returns will be related to the branch coverage of the Halifax and thus to added convenience; but it can also be attributed to the strength of the Halifax brand and the trust and confidence associated with the name.

## 5.4.2 Product modification/product development

Irrespective of the attributes that may be assigned to service product when first developed, it is likely that various changes will be made during the course of the product's life. Some of these changes may occur at an

**Table 5.2** *A sample of savings accounts*

| Name | Minimum investment | Access | Interest paid |
|------|--------------------|--------|---------------|
| Bradford & Bingley | £1,000 | Postal | 5.4 |
| Caledonian | £1 | Instant | 5.25 |
| Caledonian | £1000 | Instant | 5.25 |
| Halifax | £1000 | Instant | 3.75 |
| Exeter | £1000 | 90 days | 6.4 |
| Dryfield Trust | £10 000 | 90 days | 6.92 |
| Income Bond (National Savings) | £2000 | 1 year | 6.5 |

early stage in response to initial feedback from the early adopters, but equally further changes may occur at later stages in order to prolong the product's life. Product modification is often pursued in the maturity stage of the life cycle to attract new customers and differentiate the product from the competition. Product modification does not add to the product line as such but instead involves effectively replacing an existing service with a new and improved version. Related to the process of product modification is the process of product development which constitutes a process of modification resulting in the appearance of new but related products. Essentially this will involve some form of product line stretching or product proliferation.

Product modification in financial services aims to improve the performance of an existing product. This may entail making the service easier to use (fixed annual repayments on existing mortgages, for example), improving the quality of the service (personal account managers for corporate clients), improving the delivery system (the introduction of telephone banking) or adding additional features (the opportunity to use American Express cards as Mercury charge cards). The importance of product modification is considerable in an increasingly competitive marketplace. With financial services suppliers diversifying and the number of products proliferating, significant improvements in existing products can be an important strategy for maintaining and expanding the existing customer base. There are clearly risks associated with devoting additional resources to existing products, particularly at the maturity/decline stage of the life cycle, but these risks may well be small in comparison with those associated with new product development and diversification.

Product line stretching or product proliferation entails adding new services to an existing service line and has traditionally accounted for much of the new product development activity in financial institutions. The Lloyds Classic account, the Barclays Interest account and the NatWest Current Plus account shown in Table 5.1 are simple examples of line stretching. New products are added to the existing line that are slightly different from established products and should appeal to a slightly different group of consumers. The rationale for any line stretching exercise is to further differentiate existing products in order to appeal to more specific segments of the market. Since line stretching entails a form of new product development in a market with which the organization is familiar, the risks tend to be relatively low, although there is the danger of oversegmenting in the line stretching process. The potential exists to identify a large number of segments among the consumers of financial services, but many of those segments may be small or insufficiently distinct to justify the addition of a new service line. Excessive product proliferation can then result in overly long service lines which can cause confusion amongst consumers. Consequently, any line stretching exercise must consider not only the potential to add new lines but also the scope for rationalizing existing lines. With the increased competition between banks and building societies, both in personal savings and money transmission, a large range of different accounts appeared, but consumers experienced considerable difficulty in distinguishing between the products on offer. A number of building societies, recognizing this problem opted to rationalize the relevant service lines in order to present a clearer position to their customers of the range of products on offer (Watkins and Wright, 1986). Similar problems were experienced by Midland and over-segmentation was widely seen as one of the reasons for the bank's lack of success with the Vector, Orchard and Meridian accounts. (For more details on the process of segmentation see Chapter 2.)

## 5.5  New product development

One of the most important aspects of product strategy relates to the issue of the development of new products, a strategy which is becoming increasingly important as the intensity of the competitive environment increases. In many organizations, the resources devoted to new product development (NPD) are substantial, yet it should be remembered that much of the work carried out under this heading is not always the production of brand new products; frequently, it relates to the development and modification of existing products. In this section we will consider two specific types of new product development:

*Major innovations*. These are products which are new to the organization and new to the market. As such, while they offer great potential in terms of returns, they are inherently more risky since they will typically require a much higher level of investment, the use of different and new technologies and may involve the organization moving into areas in which it is comparatively inexperienced. Major innovations in the financial services sector, as in many sectors, are comparatively rare. Both First Direct and Direct Line provide illustrations of major innovations but, in both cases, the innovation was in the delivery system rather than in the basic product itself.

*New service lines*. These refer to products which are new to the organization but not new to the market. Since there are competing products already established in the market, the potential returns may be lower, but at the same time the organization is moving into an area with which it is considerably more familiar, either in terms of the technology or the markets. It is one of the more common forms of NPD in the financial services sector, particularly as deregulation has removed many of the barriers which had in the past restricted certain types of organization from offering certain types of product. Thus for example, the decision by many building societies to move into estate agency services, insurance and pensions can be regarded as the addition of new service lines rather than as major innovations. The process of adding to existing service lines and modifying existing service products can also be regarded as a form of NPD, although for the reasons indicated above these are treated separately.

There are a variety of frameworks proposed to guide new product development. The approach suggested by Booz, Allen and Hamilton (1982) is

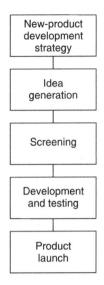

**Figure 5.3** The new product development process

widely accepted as an appropriate framework, although a number of alternatives specific to service industries have been suggested by Donnelly et al. (1985), Cowell (1984), and Scheuing and Johnson (1989). Despite the various formulations suggested the basic components of any new product development process are essentially similar and are outlined in Figure 5.3.

### 5.5.1 New product development strategy

Any exercise in new product development must be systematically organized in order to ensure that effort and resources are devoted to the development of new products in areas which the organization regards as strategically important. The motivations for new product development should be clearly defined in order to provide some guidance in the process of formulating ideas. Thus for example it should be made clear whether the process of NPD is to be orientated towards taking advantage of new market segments; whether it is seen as crucial to the continued competitiveness of the organization; whether it is required to maintain profitability; or whether it is designed to reduce excess capacity or even out fluctuating demands. There are numerous strategic factors which may underlie any process of NPD but it is of considerable importance that these are clearly stated at the commencement of an NPD exercise.

### 5.5.2 Idea generation

The process of generating ideas can take many forms both inside and outside the organization. Inside many organizations there are often distinctive groups or individuals with particular responsibility for NPD; however, Scheuing and Johnson (1989) suggest that this particular management function was relatively under-developed in the financial services sector. Of equal importance in generating ideas may be the feedback that reaches management from the experiences of staff in their dealings with consumers. The results of market research studies and information collected from consumers have traditionally been seen as an important breeding ground for new product ideas, although recent research would tend to suggest that this facility is relatively under-used in the financial services sector (Davison et al., 1989). A significant number of new product ideas are developed from external sources which may include the use of specialist new product development agencies, learning from overseas or simply copying the competitors. Survey work reported by Davison et al. suggested that copying from competitors was a major source of NPD in the financial services sector primarily because of the ease with which products could be copied and the lower risks and costs associated with doing the same as the competition but attempting to do it rather better. More recently, evidence from the building society sector suggested that market and competitive factors were the main drivers of NPD and that societies had started to move away from a technology-driven approach (Edgett, 1993). The dangers associated with a product/technology-driven approach to generating new product ideas is clearly illustrated in the failure of home banking. Home banking was launched as early as 1985 by Nottingham Building Society but the exercise failed dismally because insufficient attention had been paid to the needs and expectations of customers and to the availability of the appropriate technological infrastructure.

### 5.5.3 Screening

The variety of ideas produced at the idea generation stage must be screened to ensure their consistency with the organization's existing strategy, the extent to which they fit the image of the organization and its capabilities, their appeal to particular segments and their cost and profitability implications. In any NPD exercise, the evaluative criteria should be determined in advance of the process of idea generation and should constitute, at least in part, the strategic guidelines to be used in NPD. Screening requires thorough evaluation; the application of weights to the different criteria and the development of rankings for the various ideas in terms of the suitability. Often, the screening process passes through several stages; initially all ideas are screened, using simple criteria to eliminate any obviously unattractive suggestions. As the screening process moves on it becomes rather more complex and typically rather more expensive.

Following on from these preliminary screenings a number of product ideas would be selected and subjected to a more detailed examination of their operational and financial viability, with this process often requiring a degree of product specific market research.

### 5.5.4 Development and testing

Those ideas which have survived the screening process must then be translated into specific service concepts – that is to say the ideas which constitute the new product must be translated into a specific set of features and attributes which the product will display. A particular feature of this process is that of establishing an appropriate position for the product vis-à-vis competing products – that is to say, determining the way the product should be conceived by the customer. The two basic options are whether to position the product in direct competition with existing products, trying to offer something extra, or positioning away from the competition to ensure that the new product is perceived as something quite different although still fulfilling the same basic needs.

At this stage it is common to test this newly defined product and to identify consumer and market reactions in order to make any necessary modifications to the product before it is launched. The problem with test marketing in the financial service sector is that it gives competitors advance warning of an organization's latest ideas and given the ease of copying products it offers competitors the opportunity to imitate. As a consequence, test marketing of financial services is comparatively unusual, being avoided by many organizations because the actual costs of developing a new products are often low but the losses from giving advance warning to competitors may be quite high (Davison et al., 1989). However, Donnelly et al. (1985) argue in favour of more extensive test marketing for financial services despite these perceptions of cost. They argue that there are significant benefits, not only in terms of feedback but also in terms of developing an appropriate marketing campaign to guide the product launch and that it is 'better to be second with a good service – one that is thoroughly tested, and debugged – than it is to be first with a faulty service' (p.153). Recent evidence for Europe (Mohammed-Salleh and Easingwood, 1993) suggests that the extent to which test marketing is used is still limited, partly because testing a service is difficult and partly because testing may give competitor a chance to pre-empt a new development.

### 5.5.5 Product launch

The product launch is the final stage and the true test of any newly developed product; it is the point at which the organization makes a full scale business commitment to the product. At this stage, the major decisions are essentially of an operational nature – decisions regarding the timing of the launch, the geographical location of the launch, and the specific marketing tactics to be used in support of that launch.

There are numerous different ways in which the success of new products can be measured and the evaluation of a new launch can vary according to which measure of success is used. Despite the difficulties associated with the measurement of success there is a growing body of research which attempts to identify key success factors in NPD. In a study of product innovation in commercial banks, Johne and Harborne (1985) identified a number of other general factors which they consider central to the success of NPD programmes. First, they suggest that it is important to maintain regular contacts with the external environment to identify changes in market characteristics and customer requirements. The importance of this factor is reflected in a subsequent study of insurance companies (Johne, 1993). Second, the organization should develop a corporate culture which is receptive to innovative ideas – what Donelly et al. (1985) describe as 'creating a climate of trying'. Third, they stress the importance of flexible management which stimulates and encourages the NPD process. Finally, they mention the benefits of identifying key individuals with specific responsibility for the NPD process. More generally both de Brentani (1993) – corporate financial services – and Johne and Vermaak, (1993) – insurance – stress the importance of both support and environments and support and commitment from head office/senior managers. Finally, Storey and Easingwood (1993), focusing specifically on consumer financial service, identify effective communications, a product which fits well with the company, selling strength, product quality, market knowledge and customer understanding as making significant contributions to the success of new product development programmes.

Clearly, the simple structured framework outlined above will not by itself ensure success. However, research suggests that if this is accompanied by a supportive environment, high market and consumer awareness and the careful selection and design of products to ensure quality and company fit, then the chances of success will be considerably enhanced.

## 5.6  Conclusion

The intangibility, heterogeneity and inseparability of services inevitably create some difficulties in the process of developing an appropriate product strategy. Particular strategies to deal with these problems include the association of tangible items with the intangible service and focusing attention on the relationship between the service provider and the service consumer. In this context, the development of a corporate image is becoming increasingly important and will be discussed in more detail in the following chapter.

The key to a successful product strategy is the development and maintenance of an appropriate product range. This requires that a financial service is developed with a set of features which correspond to consumer requirements and that this range is constantly monitored so that existing services can be modified and new services can be developed. The process of new product development in the financial services sector has tended to concentrate on the redesign of existing products within an organization's portfolio and the development of products which are new to the organization, though not necessarily new to the sector. The perennial problem which faces the provider of financial service products is the ease with which such products may be copied and the consequent importance of ensuring rapid market penetration in the desired segment when new products are launched.

# 6 Advertising and promotion

## Des Thwaites

## 6.1 Introduction

Advertising and promotion are the means by which organizations provide information about themselves, their services, pricing structures and delivery channels to a variety of audiences, including existing and potential customers, intermediaries, employees and the media. The communications process in marketing has traditionally stressed the attributes and benefits of a particular good or service in order to create awareness, stimulate interest and encourage purchase. However, in practice, the role of communications is much broader, encompassing all aspects of the image of an organization and the way that image is presented to a variety of interest groups within society. Generally defined as 'promotion' within the marketing mix, communication provides an opportunity for organizations to differentiate themselves at both corporate and brand levels. Communicating effectively requires a thorough and systematic approach to promotional planning to ensure that the message is correct and consistent with the desired image of the product or organization.

The promotion of financial services has many similarities with the promotion of physical products, although some differences do characterize service promotion, either as a result of the nature of the service industries themselves or as a result of the characteristics of services. In developing a communications strategy, the particular problem facing suppliers of financial services is that they have no physical product to present to consumers and consequently a major requirement of promotion is to develop a message and a form of presentation which allows the organization to present a product which is essentially intangible in a tangible form. This chapter addresses the issues surrounding the development of an effective promotional strategy in financial services. Section 6.2 provides an overview of the communications process in financial services and section 6.3 examines the development of promotion campaigns. The relative merits of different forms of promotion are discussed in section 6.4 and conclusions are presented in the last section.

## 6.2 Communications: An overview

To communicate effectively it is necessary to appreciate the process through which communication works and to develop a systematic framework for promotion activity. The essence of the communications process can be described in terms of who says what to whom, through which channels and with what effects. The elements of a simple model based on this frame-work are presented in Figure 6.1 and described in greater detail in general marketing texts (e.g. Kotler, 1994). There are basically nine components:

- *Source*. The party sending the message, either the organization itself or a quasi-independent body.
- *Encoding*. Finding some verbal or symbolic representation for the concepts used.

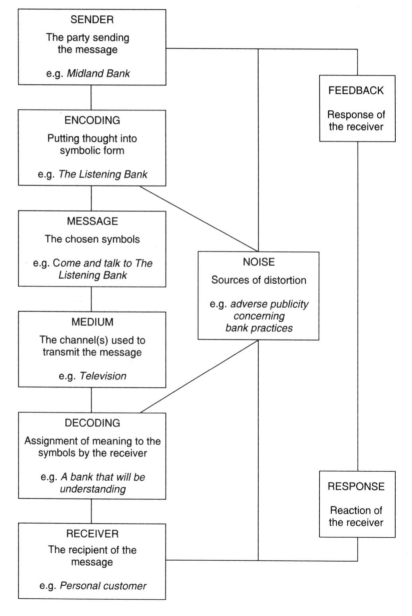

**Figure 6.1**  The communication process

*Source*: Based on Kotler (1994)

- *Message.* The set of words and symbols that the sender transmits.
- *Medium.* The channel through which the message is transmitted, either personal (sales staff) or nonpersonal (advertising, publicity or sales promotion).
- *Decoding.* The process whereby the receiver assigns meanings to the message that has been transmitted.
- *Receiver.* The party receiving the message.
- *Response.* The receiver's reaction to the message.
- *Feedback.* Information on the receiver's response which is transmitted back to the sender.
- *Noise.* Unplanned interference with the communications process which distorts the message.

This basic model highlights many of the important components of effective communication: the need to identify an audience, to develop an appropriate message, present it in a form which will attract the attention of the target audience and minimize the effects of noise. The presence of noise in the marketing environment is unavoidable and there will inevitably be some distortion in the message; the target audience may receive only part of the message being communicated, they may interpret it in accordance with their own preconceptions and they may recall only parts of the message. Effective communications will aim to minimize distortions of this nature by keeping messages brief, distinctive and unambiguous.

Through the communication process, organizations stress the attributes and benefits of a particular service, create awareness, develop interest and encourage purchase. Increasingly within the financial services sector promotion has been used to create and present a positive image of the institution to a broad range of constituencies. Indeed it has been suggested that the development of a positive corporate image is an essential ingredient in the strategic portfolio of players in the personal financial services market (Watkins and Wright, 1986; Howcroft and Lavis, 1987; Stewart, 1991).

The development of an effective communication programme involves, *inter alia*, the integration of several components of the promotion mix. These elements are commonly classified as:

- *Advertising.* Any paid form of non-personal presentation and promotion of ideas, goods or services by an identified sponsor, e.g., television, radio, cinema, newspapers.
- *Personal selling.* A process of encouraging and persuading prospects to purchase a good or service, or to respond to any idea presented orally, e.g., sales presentations, meetings, telemarketing.
- *Sales promotion.* Activities which provide predominantly short-term stimulation to purchase (or sell) through the use of incentives, e.g., contests, coupons, rebates, gifts.
- *Public relations.* Non-paid, non-personal stimulation of demand through the presentation of commercially significant news about the organization or its services in the media, e.g., speeches, reports, media publications.

Whilst there are similarities between the promotion of goods and services there are also differences based on the specific characteristics of services or particular service industries (Cowell, 1984). For example Kirk (1994) suggests that advertising by the financial services sector must not only contend with the dynamic and competitive environment but with other industry specific traits:

- *Consumer apathy.* Products are recognized as important but not interesting.
- *High risk.* May involve substantial commitment without scope for trial. Benefits are intangible.
- *Plethora of information sources.* Consumers can obtain information from a wide variety of sources in addition to advertising (which may support or conflict with the advertising message).
- *Minority of consumers in the market.* Only a small minority of the population will be in the 'decision window' at any one time.
- *Commodity purchase.* Numerous suppliers of similar products.

The particular features of services have been acknowledged in the development of advertising guidelines for service institutions. These are summarized in section 6.4 and discussed more fully by Cowell (1984) and Hill and Gandhi (1992).

The importance which financial services institutions attach to communication is highlighted by the substantial sums devoted to a variety of promotion activities. Advertising remains the most popular amongst financial institutions and now attracts sums in excess of those spent by the traditionally heavy advertisers in the fast-moving consumer goods market. The expenditure is heavily skewed towards the larger institutions (Kirk, 1994). Table 6.1 provides a breakdown of spending on television, radio, press, outdoor and cinema for a selection of financial services for the period 1989 to 1993.

Although promotion has contributed significantly to strategies such as market growth, penetration, product development and the cross-selling of related products (Gavaghan, 1994), public perception of financial services institutions is not particularly encouraging (Mintel, 1993b; Devlin, Ennew and Mirza, 1995). This is attributed to a failure by organizations to live up to the expectations built up through advertising (Nicholas, 1994; Gavaghan, 1994; Joseph, 1994). Promotional activity is merely one source by which institutions communicate with their public. Where these messages are not compatible with information received from other sources the impact will be sub-optimal. Cheese (1994) suggests that the opinions customers have of their bank will be developed more through their experiences of the distribution channels than through advertising. Financial services institutions should therefore seek to present a consistent message through all the sources by which customers acquire information and ensure that the claims made in their advertising can be delivered in practice.

**Table 6.1**  *Advertising expenditure[1]: Selected financial services 1989–93 (£ million)*

| Source | 1989 | 1990 | 1991 | 1992 | 1993 | Total |
|---|---|---|---|---|---|---|
| Building Societies and Mortgage Companies | 98.6 | 112.3 | 106.5 | 112.5 | 101.1 | 531.0 |
| Credit and Charge Cards | 23.8 | 16.3 | 17.1 | 18.3 | 33.2 | 108.7 |
| Financial Services[2] | 34.2 | 39.0 | 24.8 | 21.8 | 30.4 | 150.2 |
| Insurance and Assurance Companies[3] | 35.3 | 40.4 | 31.9 | 27.1 | 28.7 | 163.4 |
| Insurance – Life and Pensions | 25.3 | 25.4 | 23.7 | 14.6 | 33.1 | 122.1 |
| Insurance – Motor | 16.0 | 20.3 | 17.9 | 13.0 | 21.1 | 88.3 |
| Insurance – House and Contents | 7.5 | 7.3 | 6.3 | 5.7 | 7.9 | 34.7 |
| Insurance – Welfare | 5.5 | 10.0 | 5.2 | 9.9 | 12.9 | 43.5 |
| Investment Bonds | 9.5 | 5.4 | 8.7 | 15.6 | 18.1 | 57.3 |
| Investment Trusts | 2.5 | 3.8 | 4.6 | 4.0 | 4.5 | 19.4 |
| Banks – High Street | 112.1 | 108.2 | 74.2 | 55.4 | 74.0 | 423.9 |
| Banks – Foreign | 10.0 | 9.1 | 7.8 | 7.7 | 11.0 | 45.6 |
| Banks – Merchant | 2.7 | 2.4 | 1.1 | 1.1 | 1.3 | 8.6 |
| Credit and Loan Companies | 10.1 | 6.5 | 2.6 | 0.8 | 1.2 | 21.2 |
| Solicitors and Accountants | 3.4 | 2.0 | 1.0 | 1.3 | 2.2 | 9.9 |
| Stockbrokers | 1.4 | 0.7 | 1.0 | 0.6 | 0.4 | 4.1 |
| Unit Trusts | 15.8 | 15.7 | 9.6 | 10.6 | 19.9 | 71.6 |

[1]includes all TV, radio, press, outdoor, cinema
[2]excludes those defined more specifically
[3]excludes life and pensions, motor, house and contents, and welfare
*Source*: MEAL

## 6.3   Developing the promotion mix

Because the promotion mix involves several different components, each exhibiting particular strengths and weaknesses, careful integration will be an essential element in a successful campaign. The process will be made easier by the development of a systematic framework for marketing communication based on the key stages outlined in Figure 6.2. The key stages can be described as follows.

### 6.3.1  Situation analysis

At the outset it is helpful to place the impending promotion in context by assessing features of the customer, the competitive situation and the environment.

*1. Customer*
Identify target audience's:
• demographics and lifestyle
• usage levels
• perceptions of services and organization
• buying process.

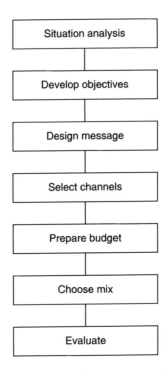

**Figure 6.2**  Decision framework for marketing communications

*2. Competitive situation*
Assess:
- industry structure
- competitive groupings
- threat of substitutes
- strengths of competitors
- perceived differentiation among competitors.

*3. Environment*
Examine the:
- internal environment – company objectives, resources, other components of the mix.
- external environment – political, economic, social, technological.

## 6.3.2 Develop objectives

Once the target audience has been identified and any constraints evaluated, a range of promotional objectives can be considered. While purchase may be the ultimate goal of many communication programmes, the consumer will pass through a number of decision stages before taking the desired action. Communication objectives may differ depending on the relevant stage in the process. For example, using the hierarchy of effects model (Lavidge and Steiner, 1961) the desired response may be to put something in the mind of the prospect (cognitive), to change attitudes (affective) or to generate action (behavioural). At the cognitive stage promotion is aimed at creating awareness and knowledge; subsequently during the affective phase the focus changes to creating liking, preference and conviction. Enticing prospects into the final step which results in a sale is the aim of the behavioural stage.

In most instances, the desired outcome of any promotional strategy is to increase sales of a product; however, as mentioned earlier, an increasing number of promotional campaigns are targeted at creating, reinforcing or changing an organization's image in relation to specific groups. Increasing sales and developing corporate image can perhaps be considered the two key objectives of any promotions campaign.

The objectives for each element of the promotion mix should be carefully integrated and co-ordinated with the other components of the marketing mix. Specifying the target audience, degree and nature of change and a time scale for each objective will provide a basis for subsequent evaluation of the effectiveness of the promotion campaign.

### 6.3.3 Design message

The nature of the message will be influenced by the specific objective of the promotion and by the type of appeal which is most likely to encourage the audience to respond positively. Several options are available:

- rational – stresses product benefits
- emotional – stresses good feelings associated with the use of the product or the negative side of not using the product
- moral – appeals to audiences' sense of right and wrong.

Financial services are often products which consumers do not actively seek to purchase; consequently advertising messages frequently concentrate on emotional and moral appeals rather than rational appeals. When rational appeals are used, they appear most commonly at the point of sale either through detailed product information or through sales presentations.

Fear is an emotional appeal which is often used in the promotion of insurance services. Examples include the problems experienced by a family in the event of the death or injury to the breadwinner, the difficulties encountered through the loss of travellers cheques (American Express) or damage to recent purchases (Barclaycard).

Humour has also been a feature of advertising by financial services institutions and can be used positively. Scottish Amicable received several awards for its advertisements featuring funny home video clips, although its move to 'Captain Chaos and the Amicable people' was less widely appreciated and some of the target audience failed to see the joke (Richards, 1994). Humour can also trivialize important issues, for example Joseph (1994) criticizes the Lloyds Bank campaign featuring knights and mythical trolls for being inconsistent with the more serious aspects of the products being advertised. There is an additional risk that the humour is so strong that the audience is distracted and fails to appreciate the message. For example, the popular Prudential campaign which revolved around the theme – 'I want to be . . .' – was subsequently replaced with a campaign drawing on the theme and character of 'Prudence', because the original campaign apparently failed to generate a strong association with the company.

Once the appeal has been determined, consideration must then be given to the structure, format and source of the message to secure acceptance and credibility amongst the target audience. This process is typically the responsibility of an external agency in conjunction with the organization's marketing staff.

### 6.3.4 Select channels

The message can be communicated to the audience through personal or non-personal channels. Within personal channels Kotler (1994) draws a distinction between advocate channels which comprise company sales staff focusing on the target audience and expert channels consisting of independent authority figures. Friends, neighbours, family and other reference groups may constitute social channels involving word of mouth transmission. This route is invariably the cheapest and often the most credible approach to promotion and word of mouth has been identified as being of particular significance in the small business sector (File and Prince, 1992). Indeed, one of the most commonly cited benefits of retaining satisfied customers is the increased likelihood of such customers engaging in positive word of mouth communication (Reichheld and Sasser, 1990). Word of mouth communication is particularly appropriate where the product is expensive, risky, purchased infrequently or has social status. Several financial services could be described in this manner.

Non-personal communication channels include print, broadcast, electronic and display media. Each has its strengths and weaknesses and must be evaluated accordingly. In addition the organization can develop an atmosphere (packaged environment) which creates or reinforces a particular image of the organization or encourages purchase. Events can also be organized with the intention of conveying particular messages, for example seminars and conferences.

### 6.3.5 Prepare budget

The methods used to determine the budget vary considerably between industries and even between companies within the same industry. While it can be argued that spending on promotion should continue provided the marginal revenues exceed the marginal promotion costs, this is not easy to implement in practice. Difficulties arise in estimating the marginal revenue where sales are a function of many variables, of which promotion is but one (Boyd and Walker, 1990).

Of the methods in common use, most are described as 'top down' in that the total promotion budget is established and then broken down

| Method | Claimed strengths | Claimed weaknesses |
|---|---|---|
| Affordable/residual | • Simple | • Makes long-range planning difficult<br>• Treats promotion as a luxury |
| Percentage of sales (actual or anticipated) | • Linked to what the company can afford<br>• Encourages managers to think of the relationship between promotion cost, price and profit<br>• Encourages competitive stability | • Assumes sales cause promotion<br>• Restricts long-range planning<br>• Ignores product opportunities in favour of availability of funds |
| Competitive parity | • Based on collective wisdom of the industry<br>• Limits promotion wars | • Assumes competition is right<br>• No empirical evidence that it prevents promotion wars |
| Objective and task | • Rational<br>• Requires clear identification of objectives and the strategies necessary to achieve them. | • May not be affordable<br>• Can prove complex and difficult to implement |

**Figure 6.3** Methods of establishing the promotional budget

*Source*: Based on Kotler (1994)

between the various elements of the mix. However, the approach most frequently advocated, 'objective and task', assesses the activities necessary to achieve the organization's communication objectives, estimates the cost, and allocates the appropriate budget. Figure 6.3 highlights the strengths and weaknesses attributed to some of the more popular methods of determining the promotion budget.

### 6.3.6 Choose mix

The choice of the various elements of the promotion mix will be influenced by the objectives and resources of the institution and the nature of the product. For example, Boyd and Walker (1990) stress the importance of advertising where the benefits to be communicated are relatively simple, there is a need to develop awareness in a mass market, brand names are available and products are purchased frequently. Personal selling is more appropriate where the product is complex and requires explanation or demonstration. Other influences on the form of promotion include the life cycle stages, characteristics of the market and product, price and distribution decisions. The characteristics of the different promotional tools are discussed in greater detail in section 6.4. Particular emphasis is given to the increasingly popular areas of direct marketing and sponsorship.

### 6.3.7 Evaluate

Given the large sums spent on promotion by the financial services sector it is essential to assess the effectiveness of the various components of the mix. This may involve both pre-testing and post-evaluation. However, the

process is not always as easy as it appears and several factors may con-
spire against the achievement of meaningful results, for example:

- the carry-over effect of earlier activities
- synergy derived from marketing communication variables
- exogenous environmental factors
- pursuit of multiple objectives
- discretionary nature of media coverage
- the competitive context.

Despite these difficulties a range of evaluative techniques are suggested in
the literature broadly consisting of measures of, for example, exposure,
awareness, image, sales effectiveness and guest feedback. Information
can also be secured through continuous tracking or ad hoc dipstick
approaches, such as before, during and after a specific event or promotion. Each of the different techniques for evaluating promotional effectiveness has advantages and disadvantages. Pre-testing attempts to predict
the likely effectiveness of a campaign and eliminate weak spots, but does
not guarantee effectiveness and many successful advertisements have
failed pre-tests. Commercial market research is widely used to determine
levels of recall and comprehension, but recall and comprehension surveys
can often only indicate whether a communications link has been established and may be less suitable for assessing how effective a campaign has
been in terms of encouraging purchase. Statistical and econometric analysis is often used to assess the impact of promotion by comparing sales
on a 'before and after' basis; such approaches can identify correlations
between promotions and sales but their ability to identify whether promotion has actually 'caused' an increase in sales is more limited.

Ideally, evaluation of promotion should be organization/product specific, with clearly defined objectives and statements of what is to be measured and how; in practice, the costs of this approach often lead to a
reliance on general, commercial studies and an acceptance of some loss
of detail and relevance in the evaluation. Figure 6.4 illustrates part of the
evaluation of Lloyds Bank's sponsorship of Clothes Show Live.

## 6.4  Forms of promotion

As the previous section has indicated, there are a range of different promotional tools available to suppliers of financial services. This section
discusses some of the more important methods of promotion in greater
detail and highlights their strengths and weaknesses.

### 6.4.1 Advertising

The distinctive characteristics of services; intangibility, perishability,
inseparability and heterogeneity are well-documented in the literature
(see, for example, Chapter 4 of Edgett and Parkinson, 1993 for a review)
and pose specific problems for marketing communications. Services are

**1991 CLOTHES SHOW LIVE**

**Sponsorship evaluation**

**Awareness**

|  | All attendees | LB customers |
|---|---|---|
| Spontaneous | 74% | 92% |
| Total (spontaneous and prompted) | 88% | 98% |

**Suitability**

How suitable is LB as sponsor of Clothes Show Live?

|  | All attendees | 15–24s | LB customers |
|---|---|---|---|
| Very suitable | 31% | 28% | 30% |
| Fairly suitable | 46% | 58% | 46% |
|  | 77% | 86% | 76% |

**Image**

|  | All attendees | General population* |
|---|---|---|
| Understands the needs of young people | 58% | 18% |
| LB is a bank I would consider joining | 46% | 18% |
| LB is a bit different to other banks | 26% | 4% |

*Source*: Millward Brown Tracking Study 26/8/91–20/10/91

**Effect**

Effect of sponsorship on likelihood of banking with LB in future

| More likely | 21.0% |
|---|---|
| Less likely | 0.5% |
| No difference | 78.5% |

Note: A random sample of 250 spectators were recruited and profiled by RSL and interviewed within seven days from time of recruitment.

**Figure 6.4** Lloyds Bank evaluation of Clothes Show Live
*Source*: Lloyds Bank PLC

also characterized as an act performed for a specific person. Based on these distinctions a number of advertising guidelines have been developed and are summarized by Hill and Gandhi (1992).

1. *Intangibility and concreteness*
- Present services more tangibly through the inclusion of physical evidence and artifacts showing service delivery points. Houses are often used to highlight mortgage facilities and branch offices to illustrate the delivery point. Norwich Union use the Great Wall of China to overcome the intangible elements of security and protection.
- Use concrete, specific language and symbols and establish creditability through word of mouth endorsement.

2. *Inseparability/perishability and reputation*
- Include the service deliverer and the customer in the advertisement.

3. *Heterogeneity and documentation*
- Document the scope, characteristics, performance record or effects of the service with concrete information thereby gaining credibility and confirming consistency of performance.

4. *Characterization as sequence of events*
- Highlight the sequence of events which comprise the service experience. Insurance companies may show damage to a car, the claim, subsequent repair and ultimately a satisfied customer. Advertisements documenting the loss and replacement of travellers cheques are another such example.

Hill and Gandhi (1992) then extend the guidelines and suggest that:

- The more intangible the service the greater the need for concrete cues in the advertisement.
- The greater the inseparability the greater the need to show participation of customers in service production and delivery.
- The greater the heterogeneity the greater the need to stress quality.
- The greater the specificity of context, customers and service settings, the greater the need to characterize the service through illustrating a sequence of events.

Further refinements can be achieved by considering these guidelines in relation to the nature of the service, the organization's relationship with customers, service delivery and demand and supply relationships. For example, where the nature of the service delivery is continuous and there is a formal relationship with customers, such as insurance, Hill and Gandhi (1992) recommend that advertising emphasizes concreteness, representation and sequence of events and, to a lesser degree, documentation. Where the nature of the interaction between the customer and the provider is at arm's length, such as mail or electronic communication and the service delivery is focused on a single location (e.g. credit card companies), high levels of concreteness and documentation are suggested and moderate emphasis is given to representation. For such products, the emphasis on sequence of events is generally inappropriate.

Cowell (1984) stresses the importance of clear unambiguous messages and the avoidance of unnecessary technical detail for press and television advertising. However, the provisions of the Financial Services Act 1986 (discussed in Chapter 1) do impose restrictions on the content of financial services advertising. Television advertisements generally fall into category A and must concern themselves with simply announcing and drawing attention to the product or the company. Advertisements which actually attempt to sell a product are required to give full details of the small print surrounding an investment product. These compliance requirements create substantial problems for the preparation of copy, particularly for press advertisements. As a consequence, many such advertisements are moving towards category B – namely adverts which invite consumers to respond for further information, thus reducing the compliance costs for the sponsors.

Advertising to employees is also advocated as part of the process of internal marketing; this reflects the key role played by customer contact staff and the need to ensure that they are fully convinced of the benefits of the service before they attempt to sell to potential customers. If staff are not fully aware of product specifications or target audience or, are not fully convinced of the product benefits, they may miss potential sales or may fail to perform effectively in the sales process.

People

The fact that customers are not continually in the market for financial services leads Cowell (1984) to suggest that the use of a common theme in advertising helps to maintain the image of the institution in the mind of infrequent purchasers. Examples include the 'black widow' in Scottish Widows' advertising and the 'black horse' used by Lloyds Bank. The use of advertising to reduce post-purchase anxiety is also recommended, particularly for financial services where there is no tangible object for consumers to evaluate after purchase and where the benefits from purchase may not be realized for many years (e.g. ten or twenty-five-year savings policies). An increasing number of financial institutions use advertisements in their own customer magazines as a means of reducing post-purchase anxiety.

Kirk (1994) suggests that the role of advertising in the financial services market is often to offer new services or provide specific new information. In this respect advertising is seen to work in the traditional manner whereby new, relevant and interesting information sets a process in motion which leads to an increase in sales in the short term. However, advertising can also generate sales in the longer term by building an association between the institution and the service. Where the same advertisement is repeated the institution may immediately spring to mind when the customer enters a 'decision window' for a particular service. Furthermore, Kirk suggests that advertising images may enhance the perception of the institution and its brands through increasing awareness of strengths, providing simplification, generating positive social feedback and transforming claims into beliefs.

### 6.4.2 Personal selling

Personal selling offers benefits in both the corporate and personal sectors of the financial services market and can contribute to a range of objectives, for example:

- gaining acceptance of new products by existing customers
- attracting new customers for existing products
- maintaining customer loyalty
- facilitating future sales by the provision of advice to prospects or influencers
- gathering market information.

Unlike many other components of the promotion mix, personal selling provides the basis for dialogue and offers a focused approach with immediate feedback. Nevertheless these benefits are not without cost as personal selling is generally more expensive than other elements of the mix and is more difficult to turn on and off. Attention must also be focused on important issues such as the organization, training and motivation of the salesforce. Morgan (1994) provides three case studies which highlight different approaches to the operationalization of bancassurance and in particular the personal selling role. Key distinctions revolve around the control, location and remuneration of the salesforce. In each case the financial institution has its own branch network, and owns an insurance company. Insurance products are sold almost exclusively to the institution's customer base. In the first scenario enquiries are screened and passed to the appropriate sales channel. General insurance and mortgage products go to the institution's customer service representatives located within the branch network, whereas investments regulated under the Financial Services Act 1986 are referred to representatives of the insurance company. Interviews are sometimes arranged at the branch but are more likely to involve a home visit. Customer service representatives are remunerated according to the institution's normal salary scale with small amounts of commission; the insurance company representatives operate on commission only.

The second example is similar except that enquiries are screened by branch cashiers who refer prospects to either the institution's in-branch salesforce or the insurance company representatives. While both groups are qualified to deal with a full range of insurance and investment issues, the more complex products usually go to the insurance company representatives who operate solely through home visits. They receive a small salary with a high commission element, unlike the in-branch sales team who are paid in accordance with the institution's salary scales plus marginal commission.

The final example is quite different in that specially trained branch staff traditionally dealt with enquiries, predominantly from the branch location and on a no-commission basis. This approach did not prove successful and a revised format is to be introduced involving a specialist salesforce carrying out home visits. Payment will involve a basic salary and commission. Control of the salesforce will remain with the institution rather than the insurance company.

These examples highlight many of the problems associated with the development of personal selling among bancassurers. Attempting to develop selling skills among established branch staff may in many instances prove problematic because the traditional banking culture may be not be conducive to the development of a sales culture. At the same time, attempting to integrate sales staff (primarily remunerated by commission) and branch staff (remunerated by salary) may introduce significant tensions. The institutions described above each adopted different approaches to dealing with these dilemmas although, as yet, there is little evidence to suggest that one is any more appropriate than any other.

### 6.4.3 Public relations

Public relations (PR) was traditionally viewed as sending out press releases and seeking good publicity. This notion is no longer appropriate. PR has become more sophisticated and uses a variety of tools to create and enhance a positive image of the institution and its services, for instance:

- annual reports/surveys
- speeches
- seminars
- charitable donations
- in-house magazines
- press releases.

Specific examples include Halifax Building Society's surveys on house prices and childrens' pocket money and the Leeds Permanent magazine *The Leeder*. PR seeks to establish and maintain mutual understanding between the organization and those with whom it comes into contact. In addition to customers this may include other interested parties such as employees, intermediaries, the financial community and government. To maximize its effectiveness PR should be deliberate, planned and continuous rather than an ad hoc, damage limitation exercise, aimed only at minimizing the negative impact of a particular situation.

Palmer (1994) suggests that because PR is involved with more than just customer relationships it is often handled at a corporate rather than a functional level thereby ensuring a consistent image. Corporate image is of particular importance to financial services institutions not least because of the tendency of customers to evaluate the quality of an intangible service through an assessment of the corporate image of the organization. Additionally, where customers are faced with a plethora of similar, complex offers, they may revert to their perception of the institution as a basis for differentiation. The development of a clear corporate image is increasingly viewed as an important element of competitive strategy and represents a valuable marketing asset, particularly for service institutions (Leonard and Spencer, 1991; Stewart, 1991; Dowling, 1993). Unfortunately the failure to develop a clear terminology has hindered progress. Mintel (1993a) provide the following descriptions.

- Corporate identity is not merely a company logo. It is about what the organization is, its personality; the sum total of its expertise, history, philosophy, culture, strategy and structure.
- Corporate image is how an organization's audiences (the public, staff, city financiers, customers) perceive its corporate identity.
- Corporate communications is the way in which an organization projects its identity (or what it would like its identity to be) to the outside world via the media.
- Corporate manifestation is the way an organization presents itself through its visual identity, staff, buildings, sponsorship etc.

Balmer and Wilkinson (1991) suggest that building societies have spent considerable sums on achieving visual identities but have failed to establish corporate identities based on factors such as philosophy and culture. It is argued that these elements form the foundations of corporate identity and provide the key to differentiation. Whilst many building societies have introduced symbolic representations (logos, letterheads etc.) of how they wish to be seen, for example, easy to deal with and friendly, there are often differences between perception and reality.

Another important consideration in the development of a corporate image is the existing image of the whole industry. Difficulties can be experienced when institutions seek to promote an image which is at odds with the prevailing image of the industry (Balmer and Wilkinson, 1991). The traditional values associated with financial services institutions are changing and accordingly new identities are required to reflect these. Stewart (1991) provides a case study of Allied Irish Banks PLC which illustrates the attempt of one institution to develop a new identity which more accurately reflects corporate reality and facilitates repositioning from an Irish bank to an international financial services provider.

Although financial services institutions have similar PR requirements there are also differences brought about by the nature of their core business (Wragg, 1992). While both building societies and banks are concerned about raids on their branches, the PR problems created by foreclosing loans and forcing businesses into receivership are of sole concern to the banks. Building societies must overcome the negative impact of mortgage repossessions whereas insurance companies contend with the bad publicity generated by the sale of personal pension plans to clients who would have been better to remain within their occupational schemes.

### 6.4.4 Sales promotion

Sales promotion is used predominantly to encourage trial and generate brand switching, although without support from other media it is unlikely to develop brand loyalty. Palmer (1994) suggests that sales promotion is used to break down brand loyalty whereas advertising is used to build it up. The range of sales promotion tools continues to increase and several have proved popular with financial services institutions. The banks have used a variety of approaches within the student market including cash incentives and the provision of rail cards, book tokens etc. Gifts are now commonly available to those who respond positively to a particular promotion. For example, Commercial Union provided a torch for anyone applying for a home contents quotation, Northern Rock offered a calculator or radio alarm for anyone taking out a particular type of insurance policy. Cashback offers are increasing in popularity and a number of building societies have adopted this approach. The Alliance and Leicester currently offers £400 cashback and a free valuation for customers accepting a specific mortgage contract. Special concessions for first time buyers are also in evidence as are coupons offering price discounts on mortgage and insurance products.

Barclays' offer of gifts from a catalogue (*Profiles*) based on points generated through spending on Barclaycard is another illustration of sales promotion. This approach may also create an element of loyalty if customers are tied into saving for goods which will require high points scores. Recent growth of activity in the market for credit cards has led to a variety of schemes aimed at encouraging brand switching. For example the Bank of Scotland, in connection with the launch of the University of Leeds affinity card offered:

- no fee in first year
- no fee, or low fee in subsequent years subject to spending patterns
- a credit of up to £60 for transferring balances from other card issuers
- up to fifty days' interest free credit,
- free purchase cover up to £2500 for 100 days.

Peattie and Peattie (1994) note that the use of competitions is evolving gradually within the sector, with the banks leading the way. Prizes vary considerably from an E-type Jaguar and four MG Midgets (Lloyds Bank), to a trip on the Orient Express (Staffordshire Building Society) and a weekend for two in Madrid (Birmingham Midshires Building Society). The authors conclude that there is room for improvement in the use of competitions by financial service institutions and scope for joint promotions such as the one between Kelloggs and Barclays Bank aimed at attracting young savers.

It should also be recognized that sales promotion activity to expand sales of particular products can be focused on staff and intermediaries as well as potential customers. The use of competitions to encourage the salesforce to increase their level of activity is one widely used example of this type of sales promotion.

## 6.4.5 Direct marketing

Direct marketing is described by the US Direct Marketing Association as an interactive system of marketing which uses one or more advertising media to effect a measurable response and/or transaction at any location.

It aims to create and exploit a dialogue between the service provider and the customer and offers several potential benefits (Betts and Yorke, 1994):

- targeting precision
- testing (markets, offer, services, timing, creative, format)
- is measurable and accountable
- provision of new distribution channels and support for existing channels
- control of timing
- advertising cost effectiveness
- more effective segmentation
- invisible to competitors.

Unfortunately the potential benefits are not always realized and the image of direct marketing has suffered accordingly. Betts and Yorke (1994) suggest several reasons for this negative image:

- poor targeting
- unscrupulous operators
- incorrect personalization
- misuse of sensitive information
- association with down-market mail order
- self-regulation historically poor
- journalistic sensationalism
- inadequate training and education.

Direct marketing activity has grown considerably during the last decade, particularly by financial services institutions. A 1992 study of 105 banks, building societies and insurance companies revealed that 75 per cent of respondents used direct marketing although 65 per cent of these had only adopted this approach post-1986 (Thwaites and Lee, 1994). While budgets were related to organization size it was noted that seventeen institutions spent in excess of £2 million in 1991. Direct mail proved the most popular media although a number of alternative approaches were commonly used, as shown in Table 6.2.

The growing use of leaflet inserts, highlighted by Firth and Lindsay (1989), had continued probably due to the tighter advertising restrictions brought about by the Financial Services Act 1986 which required the provision of more detailed information to prospective customers. The most significant growth was in relation to telemarketing which offers a variety of benefits in relation to building and maintaining databases, developing and cleaning lists, market measurement and testing, generating retail traffic, direct selling and customer care programmes. Telemarketing was seen as an important facility through which various elements of the direct marketing campaign could be integrated.

No differences were apparent between the three institutional groups in relation to their use of different media other than in the area of off-the-page advertising. The complexity of many insurance and pension products and the need for wider disclosure under the Financial Services Act 1986 may have encouraged insurance companies to move towards

**Table 6.2**  *Use of direct marketing media*

| Media | Institutions using the media (%) | | |
| --- | --- | --- | --- |
| | *1989*<br>*Firth and Lindsay*<br>*(n = 70)* | *1992*<br>*Thwaites and Lee*<br>*(n = 77)* | Percentage<br>increase |
| Direct mail | 97 | 97 | 0 |
| Leaflet inserts | 67 | 85 | 27 |
| In-house piggybacks | 60 | 78 | 30 |
| Off-the-page press advertising | 63 | 76 | 21 |
| Two-stage press advertising | 59 | 73 | 24 |
| Door-to-door leaflets | 41 | 52 | 27 |
| Third-party piggybacks | 33 | 47 | 42 |
| TV direct response | 23 | 35 | 52 |
| Telephone marketings | 21 | 57 | 171 |
| Radio direct response | 20 | 26 | 30 |

*Source*: Thwaites and Lee (1994)

leaflet inserts. Off-the-page advertising  is now used largely to generate leads, qualify prospects, encourage requests for additional information and to sell products which do not require complex and lengthy explanations.

Thwaites and Lee (1994) also identified several roles for direct marketing. Financial services institutions found opportunities for cross-selling the most valuable although trading-up and lead generation were also important. There were, however, differences of emphasis between institutions. Banks placed greater value on direct marketing for cross-selling and encouraging existing customers to trade up. Building societies also stressed cross-selling and trading-up but less strongly than banks. They found direct marketing particularly useful for retaining existing customers. Insurance companies were broadly similar to building societies except that they used direct marketing more extensively for lead generation and selling to new prospects.

Specific advantages of direct marketing compared to other communication methods were accountability and measurability, and precise targeting. Some support was also found for control and flexibility and one-to-one communication. Nevertheless, some problem areas were identified. Cost was cited by 69 per cent of institutions and was of particular concern to insurance companies. Accurate and up-to-date lists were mentioned by 46 per cent of institutions, particularly banks. Both building societies and banks experienced problems with analysis although this seemed of little concern to insurance companies. Creative problems, cited as a major worry in 1989 (Firth and Lindsay) were less apparent in 1992, perhaps suggesting that financial services institutions have come to terms with the creative constraints and implications of the Financial Services Act 1986.

In conclusion Thwaites and Lee (1994) suggest there is scope for a greater appreciation by some institutions of the strategic value and workings of direct marketing. Attention could usefully focus on a fuller integration of direct marketing with other communication and marketing activities, and improving database quality and sophistication (Fletcher and Wright, 1994).

### 6.4.6 Sponsorship

The highly versatile and adaptable nature of sponsorship has created difficulties in the development of an enduring definition. Head (1981) likens the exercise to 'trying to harpoon a butterfly in a gale'. There is, however, general agreement that sponsorship has a commercial dimension and is not patronage. An organization seeks to exploit the commercial potential associated with an event or activity in return for an investment of cash or kind. Nevertheless the increase in, for example, environmental and community sponsorship may have limited the degree of material benefit required by the sponsor.

The complex nature of sponsorship has also presented difficulties in relation to functional control. Shanklin and Kuzma (1992) note that initially organizations tend to locate sponsorship within their advertising and sales promotion functions, but with greater experience they treat sponsorship as an extension to traditional marketing functions rather than a component of them. Witcher, Craigen, Culligan and Harvey (1991) found that where organizations had both a marketing and public relations (PR) department, sponsorship was more likely to fall within PR. In the cases where marketing took control, the sponsorship was invariably of a sporting nature.

While it is sometimes suggested that sponsorship is merely another form of advertising this is strongly refuted in the literature (Hastings, 1984; Jones and Dearsley, 1989; Meenaghan, 1991). Sponsorship works differently from advertising in that the sponsorship fee generally represents the cost of buying an association. This investment must then be leveraged through the use of additional advertising and promotional material. The form and extent of the leverage will depend on the specific objectives of the programme but additional investments at least equivalent to the original fee are often cited. While sponsorship can be used independently it is more effective when integrated with other advertising and promotion media thereby generating communication synergy (Witcher et al., 1991). Meenaghan (1991) uses the analogy of an orchestra with each section contributing to the performance.

Marshall (1993) suggests that sponsorship can endow the sponsor's communication with elements of value which are unlikely to be available through mainstream advertising. Added value is based on credibility, imitation, image transference, bonding and retention as shown in Figure 6.5.

Sponsorship can also contribute to a wide range of objectives at both corporate and brand level. The following list is indicative although not exhaustive:
- increased corporate or brand awareness
- increased media attention

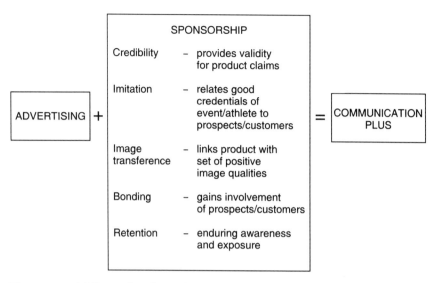

**Figure 6.5** Adding value through sponsorship
*Source*: Marshall (1993)

- community involvement
- corporate hospitality and goodwill
- increased new product awareness
- counter adverse publicity
- aid staff recruitment or relations
- lead generation of sales.

Furthermore a wide range of constituencies can be targeted through sponsorship, for example:

- shareholders
- suppliers
- workforce
- media
- customers/potential customers
- general public
- politicians.

While various activities form the basis for sponsorship programmes sport has proved the most popular among financial services institutions, for example,

- Snooker   Pearl British Open
- Athletics   GRE Clubs Cup Final
- Soccer   Endsleigh League
- Motor racing   Norwich Union Classic
- Cricket   NatWest Trophy
- Horse Racing   General Accident – 1000 and 2000 Guineas
- Tennis   Midland Bank Championships

- Rugby Union   Save and Prosper Internationals
- Rugby League   Co-operative Insurance – The Charity Shield.

Sleight (1989) suggests sport offers a number of advantages such as high levels of visibility and the ability to capture a full range of demographic segments. It can be used to target mass markets or specific niches and is capable of transcending national boundaries and breaking down cultural barriers. Television coverage is also encouraged through the provision of all-round entertainment and low production costs. Many of these features were instrumental in Barclays' decision to sponsor the Football League:

- appeal to youth – a key recruitment area
- national coverage – the home ground of every league club has at least one Barclays' branch nearby
- interests all ages and sociological groups – specific target groups can be isolated
- television coverage
- scope for corporate entertainment – complementary tickets to all home league games
- availability of other communication media – programme advertising, perimeter boards, logos on Football League material etc.
- links with community – competitions for National Association of Boys' Clubs.

While sport remains a popular focus for sponsorship activity it does not fulfil the needs of all institutions. For example General Accident took a decision to move away from sports sponsorship in 1992 based on their experience of the Guineas Horse Racing and the European Open Golf Championship. A key concern was to ensure that future sponsored activities had relevance to the business. This can be achieved at various levels, for example:

- product linkage – the product is related to the sponsored activity
- product image linkage – the image created by the product relates to the sponsored activity
- corporate image linkage – the image created by the organization is related to the sponsored activity.

Part of the solution for General Accident was to enter community sponsorship through the Neighbourhood Watch Scheme. The question of relevance and the fit between the sponsor and the activity is often cited as a feature of many successful sponsorship programmes.

A study of sponsorship activity by banks, building societies and insurance companies during 1992 (Thwaites, 1994) highlighted the growing popularity of this form of communication. Of the eighty-seven respondents to the survey sixty-three (72.4 per cent) were involved in some form of sponsorship. Sporting activities were sponsored by fifty institutions and proved the most popular form of sponsorship. The main purposes of sports sponsorship were to generate awareness of the institution, increase media attention, provide a mechanism for community involvement and a forum for corporate hospitality. Key influences on the choice of activity were the ability to link the sponsor's name to the event, a clean image, availability of a sole sponsorship and the provision of a good fit with brand or corporate positioning.

While the study revealed evidence of a professional approach to the management of sports sponsorship programmes by some institutions, particularly banks, this pattern was by no means universal. The general picture suggested that sports sponsorship was used on an ad hoc basis and appeared unhinged from broader strategic considerations. In particular there was often no clear rationale for sponsorship involvement and a failure to integrate sport with other sponsorship initiatives or indeed with elements of the wider communication mix. A lack of appreciation of the workings of sponsorship was highlighted in a failure to leverage the sponsorship through additional expenditure. The selection of sponsorship projects was often reactive and there was evidence of a lack of clarity in the development of focused objectives capable of subsequent measurement, particularly by building societies.

The budget allocation for sports sponsorship among financial institutions averaged 5 per cent whereas advertising, for example, reached 55 per cent. It may therefore be argued that the development of a systematic framework for sponsorship management is unjustified given the limited expenditure. Furthermore it is suggested social, environmental and community sponsorships are not overtly commercial. Notwithstanding these arguments, at a time of increasing competition and a desire to control costs and ensure business activities deliver measurable benefits such cavalier attitudes to sponsorship are unrealistic. Although Thwaites (1994) reports predominantly on sports sponsorship there is no reason to suggest that attitudes differ in relation to other forms of sponsorship.

The arts have proved a focus for many financial service sponsorships, for example Royal Insurance Company's support of the Royal Shakespeare Company, the Royal Bank of Scotland's Mozart Gala Concert with the BBC Philharmonic Orchestra and Lloyds Bank's sponsorship of the Young Musician of the Year competition. Lloyds has also focused attention on fashion through an integrated package of measures as outlined in Figure 6.6. Fashion offers the bank an opportunity to target three distinct markets: the general public, the youth sector and affluent adults. Prime objectives of the sponsorship package were to 'reposition the bank towards a modern approachable image' without prejudicing the existing quality image and to differentiate the bank from other financial services institutions. Figure 6.4 above provides an evaluation of one of the initiatives, Clothes Show Live.

Although two-thirds of sponsorship budgets are applied to sport (44 per cent) and the arts (22 per cent), social and environmental activities have also attracted attention. Barclays, for example, became involved in sponsoring the Woodland Trust in 1990. The promotion was linked to the Barclayloan and offered respondents the opportunity of winning several prizes including a Land-Rover Discovery. Barclays donated £1 to the Trust for each of the first 100,000 entries, which facilitated the planting of 12 500 trees throughout Britain (Mintel, 1991). The Royal Bank of

---

### LLOYDS BANK FASHION SPONSORSHIP

Lloyds Bank has embarked on a pioneering programme of fashion sponsorship, spanning three of the UK's premier fashion events. The threefold package encompasses all levels of Britain's fifth largest business sector – from youth fashion to high street fashion to designer fashion:

- LLOYDS BANK FASHION CHALLENGE – Britain's largest youth fashion competition encouraging 11 to 18-year-olds to design an outfit for a favourite celebrity. The best designs are made into garments and modelled professionally in a televised catwalk show. Over 90 000 entries have been received in its first four years and media exposure has included extensive coverage by BBC TV's 'Clothes Show' and ITV's 'Motormouth'.

- CLOTHES SHOW LIVE – the sole major sponsor of this six-day event, the largest public fashion exhibition in the UK. It features the 6500 seat Lloyds Bank Fashion Theatre and is run in association with the highly successful Clothes Show television programme. Over 200 000 visitors attended the 1992 event.

- BRITISH FASHION AWARDS – the Oscars of the fashion industry and one of the most prestigious events in the British fashion calendar. Now retitled the Lloyds Bank British Fashion Awards, the awards acknowledge design excellence from the country's top designers and attract network television coverage.

*Benefits*

- Image – associates the Bank with modern, quality image.

- Media – all three events attract substantial mass media promotion with primetime television coverage.

- Dominance – fashion is new territory for sponsors, providing substantial rewards for those first in to secure the key events.

As a major provider of financial services to the fashion world, Lloyds Bank is committed to the success of the British fashion industry. The Bank's position as the UK's premier fashion sponsor endorses that commitment.

**Figure 6.6**   Lloyds Bank fashion sponsorship
*Source*: Lloyds Bank PLC

Scotland also supported the Woodland Trust through an affinity card scheme.

Broadcast sponsorship has also attracted several financial services institutions such as Legal and General (regional weather forecasts) and Barclaycard (*Wish You Were Here*). The ability to target on a regional basis has proved particularly useful and has encouraged smaller organizations to become involved. For example the Heart of England Building Society supported community service announcements on Central Television (Mintel, 1991). Education is another area which has attracted financial services institutions and appears likely to grow at primary, secondary and college or university levels. Several institutions have already funded Research Fellowships or Chairs in universities, including Halifax Building Society (Loughborough), Britannia Building Society (Stafford), Yorkshire Bank (Leeds), Norwich Union (Nottingham) and Midland Bank (Nottingham and Loughborough).

## 6.5 Conclusion

The market for financial services has undergone a period of rapid change during the last decade. Traditional lines of demarcation between institutions have been eroded and greater competition now takes place over a wider product range. Forces such as deregulation, increased consumer sophistication and technological developments have contributed to the more turbulent environment which has been accompanied by a rapid growth in marketing activity. Financial services institutions now spend significant amounts on communicating a variety of brand and corporate messages to a range of interest groups. To be effective the different forms of promotion used in this task should be complementary and integrated with other components of the marketing mix. Attention must also be given to the specific characteristics of services and the traits of the financial services market which will condition the form and nature of the messages used and the medium through which they are transmitted. Furthermore, corporate communication is not the only channel through which an institution's audiences receive information about its performance and accordingly promises made in promotion campaigns should be realistic, deliverable and compatible with information derived from other sources. Through an appreciation of how the communication process works and the development of a systematic framework for promotion planning financial institutions should be better placed to capitalize on their substantial investments in communication activities.

# 7 Pricing

### David Llewellyn and Leigh Drake

## 7.1 Introduction

In all industries, pricing strategies are determined largely by the prevailing competitive environment. The pricing of retail financial services has become a major strategic issue and of increasing significance in marketing strategies. However, under pressure from regulatory authorities, it was only in January 1995 that life assurance companies, for instance, were required to make their pricing transparent. Clear statements about the charges levied by banks are also only a recent phenomenon.

Traditionally, pricing has not been the key issue in marketing strategies for financial services that it has been in other industries. There are several reasons for this. Firstly, competition has not been as intense in retail finanical services as in most other industries. As noted by Howcroft and Lavis (1987), banking has operated in a 'cartelised-oligopoly' and price competition has been weak. Similarly, building societies operated an interest rate cartel until 1983. The cartel not only limited price competition, but operated in a way that enabled less efficient societies to survive (Drake, 1989). Secondly, regulation had the effect of limiting competitive pressures and created what amounted to economic rents in many sectors of finance (Benink and Llewellyn, 1995; Bank for International Settlements, 1992). Profits were reasonably stable and secure which reduced the pressure to compete through pricing. In this conducive and largely protective environment, competitive strategies took the form of non-price competition which had the effect of raising costs. In effect, the economic rents created by regulation were appropriated by higher costs rather than profits. Thirdly, and partly because there was no necessity, banks in particular had only limited information about the costs of their services.

Since the early 1980s competitive pressures have intensified in retail financial services for two main reasons: public policy priorities have shifted towards emphasizing the benefits of competition in financial services (Organisation for Economic Co-operation and Development, 1989; Llewellyn, 1991; 1992), and entry barriers have been eroded which means that the range of competitors in each sub-sector of the retail financial services industry has widened. For instance, Marks & Spencer now offers a range of financial services (including consumer credit and unit trusts, and plans also to offer life assurance contracts). In January 1995, Virgin (the airline and music retailer) announced that it plans to offer retail financial services (pensions, life assurance and personal equity plans) and has applied for membership of the relevant regulatory body – the Personal

Investment Authority. It claims to be able to undercut the prices of existing financial institutions by up to 40 per cent. In addition, consumers have become more sophisticated and demanding, and the financial press has given increasing emphasis to the price and quality of financial services.

At the same time there has been a growing demand for more transparency in the pricing of financial services. Because of the wide range of pricing modes in financial services (discussed in Section 7.2.2) consumers often cannot readily determine how much they pay for their banking services, life assurance contracts, personal pension plans and personal equity plans. This is not a feature of services in general as consumers know the price of dry-cleaning, car servicing, window cleaning, etc. Finance seems to be peculiar in that pricing often lacks transparency. Readers could be challenged to identify what they pay for their life assurance, endowment mortgages, personal pensions, etc. They will know what they pay for their car insurance but probably not their life assurance policy.

As competition has intensified, price competition in retail financial services has become a more important and visible aspect of marketing strategies. This has been reinforced by regulators' demands for more transparency in pricing and costs. It is also evident that price competition will increase most notably in the insurance sector. This sets the scene for the analysis to follow.

The focus of this chapter is on the pricing of retail financial services, i.e. those of relevance to personal as opposed to corporate customers. Even this restricted range is far from a homogeneous set of services and contracts as the different services within it (see Tables 7.1 and 7.2 for a summary) embody different combinations of characteristics. As the focus is upon a heterogeneous set of financial contracts and services, generalizations about pricing can be made only with extreme caution.

This chapter comprises two main sections. Section 7.2 reviews the special characteristics of retail financial services that have a bearing on pricing and consumers' responses. Ten financial services, products and contracts are identified and the relevant characteristics defined. Space precludes an analysis of the pricing characteristics of all of these services. Section 7.3 therefore, focuses upon banking services in particular as a case study. An analytical framework for the banking firm is established in which to discuss the pricing of two aspects of the business of banking: financial intermediation (the setting of lending and deposit interest rates), and the pricing of bank payment services such as ATM transactions, cheque processing etc.

## 7.2  Special characteristics of retail financial services

While there are common issues of relevance to pricing in all products and services, several special characteristics of retail financial services add unique complexities.

The nature of the service being demanded or supplied is not always clearly defined partly because it is multidimensional and involves a bundling of different implicit services. Thus, a life assurance contract is both a means of saving (with a sum repaid if the consumer survives the maturity of the contract) and a form of insurance (the spouse, for instance, receives a sum from the insurance company if the life assured does not survive the maturity of the contract). There are, in effect, two services within a single contract and they raise different pricing considerations. Similarly, a bank deposit may embody a savings product, a payments service, and access to several ancillary services. Also, use of a credit card is a means of either making transactions and securing credit or both. Although, in principle, different embodied services can be unbundled and supplied and priced separately, this is infrequent in practice. Thus, it is not always clear what precise service is being demanded and priced when financial services and contracts are purchased. Financial services and contracts are frequently analogous to joint products. Indeed, 'packaging' of a collection of services may be part of a marketing strategy.

Some services (e.g. those associated with bank accounts) involve a complex and continuing relationship between the supplier and consumer. Several services are implicit in the arrangement, not all of which are continuously demanded. Thus, many of the services consumers demand (and have access to) through a bank account are only intermittently demanded.

This continuing relationship involving several services in turn gives rise to the potential for suppliers of financial services to price on the basis of cross-subsidies. Thus, depending on the elasticity of demand and competitive conditions in different markets, one service or contract may be priced low relative to cost and risk and subsidized by other services (or different customers) which are priced high relative to cost and risk. Bank pricing frequently involves a network of complex cross-subsidies between sectors, customers and products (Howcroft and Lavis, 1989).

Because of the complex nature of the relationship in some financial services, and the multidimensional nature of the relationship, the transactions costs of switching suppliers may be substantial. There is, for instance, substantial inconvenience in switching bank accounts as the whole relationship is switched and some of the information advantages derived through the ongoing relationship may be lost. Similarly, substantial penalties may be incurred if long-term life assurance contracts are cancelled ahead of maturity perhaps because the consumer wishes to switch funds to another company.

Some services or contracts give rise to special kinds of risk to the supplier, and risk-averse suppliers will need to price for the risks involved. Thus, the making of a loan necessarily involves a bank in the risk that the borrower may default. Similarly, some services (e.g. insurance) are demanded because the consumer wishes to shift risk on to the supplier of the contract.

Many financial contracts involve a future consumption in that the benefit of the contract is not made available at the point of purchase. Savings or pensions products fall within this category. These may also give rise to complex principal agent issues, and hence to the necessity of trust and monitoring of the supplier of the service or contract. The economies of scale in monitoring by regulatory agencies are discussed in Llewellyn (1995).

Similarly, there is often a fiduciary relationship between the consumer and supplier as a financial institution may be acting on behalf of the consumer on a continuing basis. Thus, a unit trust fund manager or supplier of a personal pension contract is in effect managing assets on behalf of the consumer. This also gives rise to the necessity of monitoring the behaviour and performance of the institution on a continuing basis after the point of purchase.

It follows from this that, unlike with most purchases, the consumer has a continuing interest in the standing, behaviour and solvency of the firm supplying financial services and contracts. It is of no concern to a consumer if a restaurant goes out of business the day after he or she has bought a meal, whereas, because of the long-term nature of a contract or service and the fiduciary role that exists, it matters a great deal if a bank or insurance company collapses. These factors necessarily have some bearing on pricing, and considerations other than price clearly influence consumer demand.

It is also for these reasons that regulatory authorities monitor and set standards for certain types of financial services and contract (see Llewellyn, 1995 for a discussion of this dimension).

As already noted, there is often a lack of transparency in the pricing of financial services. The consumer is frequently unaware of the price being paid at the point of purchase. This is partly because unlike other services and purchases of goods, the supplier effectively has access to the customer's funds which have been handed to the institution. For instance, with life assurance and private pensions contracts, the consumer contracts to pay a single or regular premium. The costs of the service are deducted from these premium payments before the consumer's funds are invested. The consumer is often unaware of this fact or of the amount deducted. Similarly, with the purchase of a unit trust personal equity plan, typically 3 per cent is deducted from the initial payment together with a 1.5 per cent annual charge. This lack of transparency, and evidence that consumers are frequently unaware of the charges being made, has been a concern to the regulatory authorities. From January 1995, sellers of life assurance contracts are required to state clearly at the point of purchase how much is being deducted from premium payments in charges, what a salesperson's commission is, any incidental charges, and how much the consumer will receive if a contract is surrendered ahead of maturity. Some life assurance companies have made public statements that this disclosure is likely to reduce the demand for such products.

Because of the long-term nature of some financial services and contracts, in many cases it is difficult for the consumer to ascertain the value of a service or contract at the point of purchase. This suggests that reputation as well as price is likely to have a powerful influence on consumers' decisions. Indeed, in many cases the quality of a contract or service is revealed only after several years. Thus, the return on a life assurance contract is determined by the quality of the investment management of the insurance company, and this is revealed only after a period of time. When the contract has a long maturity (e.g. twenty years) past investment performance may be a poor guide to future performance. Evidence indicates that the relative investment performance of different companies varies considerably from one year to another. It is therefore difficult for the consumer to judge whether a high price reflects superior quality and performance. This means that price may be only a small consideration in the decision to choose a particular company. A 10 per cent difference in the price of a life assurance contract may be trivial even if there is only a small difference in the investment performance of the insurance company. And yet the performance is not known *ex ante* when the decision to purchase is made. This means that an insurance company has a strong interest in attempting to signal quality and, if it is successful in this, price may be a minor consideration in the marketing mix. Thus, compared with many goods and services, the price of financial services and contracts might be only a minor consideration to the consumer.

In addition, the value of a service or contract is often contingent. It frequently, for instance, depends upon the performance of the firm after the point of purchase. Thus, the value of a pensions contract is determined by the fund-management and investment performance of the insurance company. In other words, again the value of the service is unknown at the point of purchase. The value of a contract may also be unknown because it depends on outcomes rather than the firm's performance. In the case of insurance, for example, the ultimate outcome depends upon whether the insured event occurs though such contracts should be viewed as payments being made for peace of mind lest the event does occur.

Many of the special characteristics of financial services and contracts derive ultimately from information problems; in particular, the problem of identifying quality (and hence value for money) at the point of purchase. This is a major issue for the consumer. It is axiomatic that, as in all areas, consumers of financial services relate price and quality and are prepared to pay prices which reflect quality. The fundamental problem with many financial services is that quality cannot be determined at the point of purchase, whether it relates to the quality of advice or of investment performance which determines the ultimate value of life assurance or personal pension contracts. An additional dimension to this general problem is that many financial services and contracts are purchased only infrequently. It is not many times in a lifetime that a consumer purchases, for instance, life assurance or a personal pension plan. There is therefore only limited opportunity to test the market, compare services and contracts offered by alternative suppliers, or to learn from experience.

In conclusion these considerations indicate that financial services and contracts involve issues that do not arise in most other goods and services. Some of these have a bearing on pricing strategies and influence consumers' decisions.

## 7.2.1 Retail financial services

The main retail financial services are listed in Table 7.1 with an indication of which of the above characteristics are relevant for each. In the table, 'financial intermediation' services relate to institutions which accept deposits and acquire assets such as loans. Two securities services are indicated: market making (where an institution stands ready at all times to sell securities to, or buy them from, investors) and, more relevant for retail transactions, broking (where a firm arranges for such sales or purchases). A group of financial advisory firms give advice on a wide range of financial services and contracts to consumers. Payment for such advice is either explicit (where fees are charged directly to consumers) or through the supplier of a contract (e.g. an insurance company) paying commission to an agent. Private pensions are essentially savings arrangements whereby a consumer pays either a single lump sum or a series of monthly or annual payments to an insurance company in return for an annuity or cash payment on the maturity of the contract.

At the risk of over-simplifying what, in practice, is a complex matrix, Table 7.1 identifies the characteristics which are relevant to each product class. A distinction not so far made explicit is whether the service involves business taken on the balance sheet of the institution supplying the service through the acquisition of assets and liabilities. The two that do not are securities broking (where the institution does not itself buy or sell securities on its own account but acts solely as an agent) and financial advisers.

This is also related to the question of risk for the supplier of the service. Risk is created for a firm if the value of the liability is set independently of the performance of the firm itself or the value of its assets. Thus, a bank is contracted to repay deposits in full irrespective of whether borrowers repay loans. It is ultimately for this reason that banks have equity capital which acts as an internal insurance fund. The suppliers of equity capital are providing risk capital to enable the bank to honour the commitment to depositors in the face of an uncertain value of assets. But equity holders need to be compensated and this consideration must be incorporated into the bank's pricing decisions. Similarly, an insurance company must pay in the event that insured risks materialize and this requirement is independent of its own performance. As shown by the experience of Lloyds of London, this can prove to be hazardous. A market maker takes risks – when it buys securities from a seller at a stated price it does not know for certain at what price, if at all, it can subsequently sell the securities to a purchaser. A firm's bid-ask spread (the difference between its posted buying and selling prices) partly reflects this risk. With respect to payments services, a bank is at some risk against other banks which are the counterparty, and credit-card companies face the risk that those who take credit do not repay.

On the other hand, while unit trusts and suppliers of private pension plans conduct business through their balance sheets, the risks noted above do not apply because the value of liabilities is, in general, not set

**Table 7.1** Characteristics of selected retail financial services

| | Risk to supplier | Service involves balance sheet position | Fiduciary role | Future consumption | Multi-relationship | Contingent value | Uncertainty over consumption |
|---|---|---|---|---|---|---|---|
| Banking: Financial Intermediation | ✓ | ✓ | ✓ | | ✓ | | |
| Securities Trading: Market Making | ✓ | ✓ | | | | | |
| Securities Trading: Broking | | | | | | | |
| Life Assurance | (✓) | ✓ | ✓ | ✓ | | ✓ | ✓ |
| Insurance | ✓ | ✓ | ✓ | ✓ | | | ✓ |
| Fund Management: Unit Trust | | ✓ | ✓ | | | ✓ | |
| Financial Advice | | | | | ✓ | | |
| Private Pensions | | ✓ | ✓ | ✓ | | ✓ | |
| Payments Services: Bank | (✓)* | ✓ | ✓ | | ✓ | | |
| Payments Services: Cards | ✓ | ✓ | | | | | |

*Inter-bank

independently of the performance of the firm itself. In the case of unit trusts, the payments made to sellers of units are determined precisely and automatically by the value on the underlying assets in the portfolio. Similarly, the value of pay-outs on pensions (and on 'with-profits' life assurance contracts) are determined by the underlying performance of the insurance company, though the calculation is complex as companies tend to smooth volatile profits when making their calculations.

## 7.2.2 Pricing issues

Abstracting from these special considerations, pricing is often also more complex with financial services than with goods and other services because a variety of pricing modes are adopted. Three in particular will be considered: *explicit pricing*, *implicit pricing*, and *spread pricing*. With explicit pricing, specific and identified charges are made on the purchaser of a service. Thus a bank may make charges for some payments transactions and a broker levies fees for its services. Frequently, however, charges are implicit, such as when a bank offers allegedly 'free' payments services (no charges are made for clearing cheques etc.), but the consumer effectively pays by receiving no interest on credit balances. This is considered in detail as one of the examples provided later in the chapter.

Similarly, an insurance company does not make explicit charges for its services but absorbs, for instance, a large proportion of the first year's premiums to cover costs. The consumer who contracts to pay, for example, £1000 per annum for fifteen years towards a life contract or pension may be unaware that virtually none of the first £1000 payment contributes to his or her fund or investment.

In the third pricing mode – spread pricing – the price of the service is reflected in the bid-ask spread. As an example, on 28 December 1994 two prices were quoted for the Global Managed Fund of Henderson Administration: 461.5p and 491.0p. This means that if an investor bought £5000 worth of such units but immediately sold them back (an admittedly absurd outcome), he/she would receive only £4700. This 6 per cent difference between the buying and selling prices is the effective price of the unit trust service.

This means that the price of many financial services and contracts is not readily transparent to the consumer at the point of purchase. It is for this reason that the Personal Investment Authority is requiring the sellers of such products to give more prominence to the form and extent of their charges. The consumer may not be aware of the commissions paid by insurance companies to selling agents which are taken from premiums paid by the consumer. In order to increase transparency of charges, insurance companies are required to state these charges as from 1 January 1995.

## 7.2.3 Pricing considerations

In a marketing framework, pricing strategies in financial institutions may be governed by a range of alternative business objectives: market share, balance sheet size, enhanced customer loyalty, profit maximization, max-imizing profits from individual customers or customer groups rather than particular products and services (relationship banking) etc. We do not consider these alternative strategies in any detail. The focus in this section is upon the institution as an entity whose ultimate objective in a compe-titive market environment is to maximize shareholder value by maximiz-ing the risk-adjusted rate of return on equity capital. We abstract from the complication that this might be viewed as a misleading definition of business objectives for mutual financial institutions (building societies and some life assurance companies) though elsewhere the authors have questioned the behavioural distinctions between mutual and PLC finan-cial institutions (Llewellyn and Drake, 1988). Within this broad frame-work, pricing must ultimately reflect four inter-related considerations:

- the fixed and variable costs of the services provided
- risk needs to be priced
- equity capital must be remunerated
- there needs to be an internal generation of capital through retained profits.

The relevance of these is given in Table 7.2 for each of the services con-sidered in Table 7.1.

A major problem with all multi-product firms is to identify the precise costs of individual products and services and what proportion of the firm's fixed costs (e.g. the cost of a branch network) are to be allocated to particular products and services. The allocation of fixed costs is more of an art than a science (Ward, 1989). Nevertheless, for the institution overall, costs must be covered even if, through cross-subsidies, individual pro-ducts and services may be priced in a way that means costs are not fully recovered.

Risk is a cost to an institution although, as noted in Tables 7.1 and 7.2, not all financial services and products give rise to risk to the supplying institution even when the service involves a balance sheet position. In the

**Table 7.2** *Revenue requirement*

|  | Risk | Cost of specific service | Remuneration of capital | Internal generation of capital |
|---|---|---|---|---|
| Banking: Financial Intermediation | ✓ | ✓ | ✓ | ✓ |
| Securities Trading: Market Making | ✓ | ✓ | ✓ | |
| Securities Trading: Broking | | ✓ | | |
| Life Assurance | ✓ | ✓ | ✓ | ✓ |
| Insurance | ✓ | ✓ | ✓ | ✓ |
| Fund Management: Unit Trust | | ✓ | | |
| Financial Advice | | ✓ | | |
| Private Pensions | | ✓ | | |
| Payment Services: Bank | ✓ | ✓ | ✓ | |
| Payment Services: Cards | ✓ | ✓ | ✓ | |

absence of cross-subsidies, if a bank consistently does not incorporate risk premiums in its interest rates on loans, its equity capital will eventually be depleted and it will become insolvent. In effect, borrowers who repay and service their loans pay for those who do not. If a bank knows from experience that $x$ per cent of borrowers default, though does not know *ex ante* which $x$ per cent, all borrowers pay the relevant risk premium to cover the risk to the bank associated with the $x$ per cent who default. Obviously, an insurance company must price its contracts on the basis of an actuarial judgement about the nature and probability of the risks being incurred. As with banks, contracts which do not subsequently involve claims pay for those which do. Similarly, a market maker in securities needs to reflect its risks in the bid-ask spread.

The suppliers of risk-capital (equity holders) need to be remunerated so as to compensate them for taking risks. Equity holders are remunerated in three ways: through dividends, through capital appreciation and through undistributed profits which increase the equity holders' claim on the company. The case of banks is instructive. A wealth-holder has two options when allocating funds to a bank: either through a riskless deposit or through equity holding. If a wealth-holder has the option of investing in a bank through a riskless deposit, the expected rate of return on equity must be greater than that on deposits as there needs to be compensation for absorbing risk. The cost of capital to a bank will be determined by the riskless rate of return available to investors, perceptions about the risk characteristics of the bank, and the degree of risk aversion by potential equity holders. If equity is not adequately remunerated, there will be no further external supplies of risk capital though in itself this may not be important if the bank plans no further balance sheet growth. However, even in this case the bank's share price will fall and the institution will become vulnerable to a take-over.

Table 7.2 also indicates that, if an institution is expanding, it needs to generate internal capital through retained profits so as to maintain its capital–assets ratio set either by regulators or voluntarily on the basis of its own judgement about capital adequacy. While capital can be injected from the capital market (rights issues etc.) it is unlikely that this would ever be a sustainable source for institutions which were unable to generate their own capital. Leaving aside the risks to shareholders of such a strategy, the dilution of earnings per share sets a practical limit on any company issuing new capital unless, as a result, the institution can convince actual or potential shareholders that the profits stream will be significantly enhanced.

Overall, therefore, institutions that absorb risk need to set the prices of their products, services and contracts not only to cover operating costs but also to reflect risk, remunerate the suppliers of risk capital, and to generate internal capital. While other marketing considerations might and do apply in the case of individual products and services and between different customer groups, in the final analysis these four imperatives must ultimately dominate pricing strategy.

Having considered some general issues which have a particular relevance to the pricing of financial services, two case studies are reviewed to illustrate some of the issues involved: the financial intermediation role of banks; and the pricing of payments services.

## 7.3 The pricing of bank services

Banks are firms and use economic resources to provide a wide range of services. In one way or another, their costs need to be covered and an appropriate risk-adjusted profit earned. In several ways the banking firm is a complex institution with respect to pricing and charges because of the nature of its diversified business. A wide range of pricing and charging strategies are levied by banks including the non-charging for some services, a range of *explicit* charges, and a structure of *implicit* charging. Furthermore, some charges are designed specifically to cover the costs of providing services while others are designed as a penalty.

Over the years, there has been a trend towards making more explicit charges and this partly reflects changes in the nature of the business of banks. This can be seen in Table 7.3 which shows the increasing proportion of banks' income earned from fees and commissions etc. and the declining proportion of income earned through the interest margin.

At the outset, a distinction needs to be made between explicit and implicit pricing and charging of bank services. Implicit pricing includes requirements on customers to maintain a minimum balance, and the non-payment or low-payment of interest on some credit balances. Banks earn interest on using these interest-free deposits to acquire interest-earning assets and this contributes to the costs of running current account services. When interest rates are high they also generate 'endowment profits'. Such interest-free accounts represent a cost to the consumer and contribute to covering the costs of the bank; they represent implicit payment to the bank for services. A major issue in bank pricing, therefore, is whether services are priced explicitly or implicitly. It follows that the pricing and charging of individual services cannot be viewed in isolation; the whole vector of a bank's pricing and charges needs to be considered.

### 7.3.1 Analytical framework

*The banking firm*

The starting perspective is that banks are firms in the traditional economic sense of the term and operate in a wide range of competitive markets. They are multi-product firms in that they supply a wide range of on- and off-balance-sheet services and products. In many senses a bank is a conglomerate market for a wide range of services with sometimes substantial degrees of bundling between them. Some of the services of banks are produced on a joint basis and share substantial resources (most especially overheads) on a common basis. Not only is the supply of services frequently undertaken on a joint basis, customer demand for services is often interrelated.

**Table 7.3** *Structure of UK banks income and expenses**

| | Year end December (£) | | | | | | | | | | | |
|---|---|---|---|---|---|---|---|---|---|---|---|---|
| | 1980 | 1981 | 1982 | 1983 | 1984 | 1985 | 1986 | 1987 | 1988 | 1989 | 1990 | 1991 |
| Interest Income | 14 245 | 19 103 | 23 108 | 22 040 | 27 008 | 26 399 | 25 711 | 25 555 | 29 292 | 42 047 | 45 451 | 40 339 |
| Interest Expenditure | (10 021) | (14 144) | (17 315) | (15 517) | (19 634) | (18 563) | (17 372) | (16 778) | (19 450) | (31 071) | (34 438) | (28 921) |
| Net Interest Income | 4224 | 4959 | 5793 | 6523 | 7374 | 7836 | 8339 | 8777 | 9843 | 10 976 | 11 014 | 11 418 |
| Non-Interest Income | 1469 | 1843 | 2476 | 3068 | 3894 | 3735 | 4272 | 4877 | 5562 | 6730 | 7300 | 8450 |
| Total Operating Income | 5693 | 6802 | 8269 | 9591 | 11 268 | 11 571 | 12 611 | 13 654 | 15 405 | 17 706 | 18 314 | 19 868 |
| Personnel Expenses | (2648) | (3190) | (3793) | (4220) | (4688) | (4675) | (5103) | (5490) | (6165) | (6893) | (7249) | (7491) |
| Premises and Equipment Expenses | (600) | (758) | (1016) | (1209) | (1429) | (1435) | (1502) | (1637) | (1900) | (2095) | (2396) | (2752) |
| Other Expenses | (739) | (946) | (1256) | (1345) | (1638) | (1616) | (1791) | (2088) | (2295) | (2733) | (2911) | (3094) |
| Total Operating Expenses | (3987) | (4894) | (6065) | (6774) | (7755) | (7723) | (8396) | (9215) | (10 360) | (11 721) | (12 556) | (13 338) |
| Net Operating Income | 1706 | 1908 | 2204 | 2817 | 3513 | 3848 | 4215 | 4439 | 5045 | 5985 | 5758 | 6530 |

*Barclays Bank, Lloyds Bank, Midland Bank and National Westminster Bank

As a multi-product firm, a bank offers three major services:

- Financial intermediation services (the offer of deposit and loan facilities)
- A range of payments services
- A wide range of other specific services.

A bank is both a financial intermediary (in that it accepts deposits with one set of characteristics and acquires loans and assets with a different set), and also a supplier of on- and off-balance-sheet services. This diverse range of services complicates the allocation of costs and pricing within the banking firm. The major area where British banks do not make explicit charges for services is in the payments system for personal customers providing the account is maintained in credit. In effect, the cost of providing payment services is borne largely by the way prices are set in the provision of financial intermediation services. However, these are separate activities and can be priced separately. In the main, the costs of the payments system are borne through the implicit charging for financial intermediation services and most especially by either requiring minimum balances before interest is paid on deposits, or by setting deposit interest rates at comparatively low levels.

## Costs and revenue

The multi-product nature of the banking firm influences the structure of costs. As the banking firm provides both financial intermediation and other services, the costs can equally be divided between the costs of providing financial intermediation services and the costs of providing other services. These raise different issues with respect to pricing. On the basis of these distinctions, the costs of a bank can be divided as follows:

1. Financial intermediation costs
   - The cost of deposits (in the form of the rate of interest paid).
   - The cost of risk capital supplied by shareholders.

2. Business costs
   - Staff and management costs (some of which are fixed and some variable).
   - The overhead and infrastructure costs in managing the branch network.
   - The infrastructure costs of supplying money transmission services (e.g. the substantial capital costs involved in developing adequate capacity for administering the payments system).
   - Variable costs in the provision of services (e.g. the costs associated with the volume of money payments transactions).

In terms of pricing, the key distinction is between *financial intermediation costs* and *business costs*. With respect to business costs, these can also be sub-divided into the fixed costs of the bank (e.g. in the development of the infrastructure of the branch network), certain fixed costs associated with each customer (e.g. the costs of opening and managing an account on an ongoing basis irrespective of the use made of that account), and variable costs which are dependent on the use that consumers make of the services provided. An overview of the broad structure of a bank's costs is given in Table 7.3. It is evident that banks have in recent years been under considerable pressure to reduce the level of business costs.

Having outlined the general nature of the costs of a bank, attention needs to be given to the sources of revenue and how costs are covered. In general, five broad sources of revenue can be identified and again this reflects the nature of the banking firm as both a financial intermediary and a supplier of services:

1. The interest earned on assets including loans.
2. Fees charged for on-balance-sheet business.
   - Some penalty charges (e.g. penalty charges levied on customers making unauthorized overdrafts).
   - Arrangmement fees for loans.
3. Commission charges.
4. Explicit charges for off-balance-sheet services.
5. Explicit charges made for payment services.

The key issues are centred on how costs are allocated to individual services within the banking firm, and the extent to which pricing is based explicitly on the costs of individual services. This in turn raises issues with respect to who pays for which services and how payment is made, and most especially the balance between implicit and explicit pricing. Overall, a major issue is the balance to be struck in how total cost are to be covered within the intermediation business of banks (the difference between the interest payments on deposits and interest receipts on assets) through the interest margin, and the explicit charging and pricing of specific services. In the following analysis we deal with these two key areas of banks' pricing decisions in turn.

## 7.3.2 The pricing of financial intermediation

The overall interest margin for banks is determined by: the difference between deposit and loan interest rates, and the extent of interest-free deposits.

*The difference between deposit and loan interest rates*

This first influence on the interest margin can be illustrated using a simple model of the competitive credit market comprising fairly homogeneous institutions illustrated in Figure 7.1.

Assets are funded by deposits and capital. Holding all other interest rates constant, deposit-taking intermediaries face an exogenous upward-sloping supply curve of deposits ($S_D$). For a given supply curve of deposits, the institution's endogenous supply of loans ($S_L$) is also a rising function of the loan rate. The interest margin (AB – the supply price of

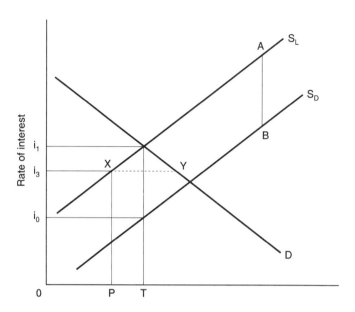

**Figure 7.1**   Interest margins in a competitive credit market

financial intermediation) is effectively the price paid by consumers for the financial intermediation service of banks. It is determined by non-deposit costs (management and technology costs etc.), the cost of capital (which increases as either the required capital/assets ratio or the price of capital rises), risk premiums charged on loans, tax payments, and the institution's internal generation of capital. The margin will also be influenced by competitive pressures within the banking sector and from actual or potential external competitors: non-bank financial institutions, non-financial banking institutions and the capital market. Competitive pressures impact on costs and profits but may also induce banks not to fully reflect risk premiums in loan rates in the short run and in order to maintain market share.

The demand curve for loans is given by $D_0$. In equilibrium the volume of deposits and loans is OT with a deposit rate of $i_0$ and a loan rate of $i_1$. The model is useful in stressing that the price of loans has to incorporate the necessary risk premiums in addition to other non-interest costs and contributions to profits etc. While this has always been an important issue for financial institutions, it has become increasingly important in recent years as increasing competition combined with more stringent capital adequacy requirements have forced banks to quantify more formally the returns associated with their various activities and the risks associated with these returns. In turn, this has led to the widespread adoption in banking of Risk Adjusted Profitability Measures (RAPMs) such as the Risk Adjusted Return on Capital (RAROC), and the Return on Risk Adjusted Capital (RORAC). The recent problems experienced in the Scandinavian banking markets bear testament to the problems which can occur if banks persistently fail to incorporate the risk premiums into their pricing of loans (Benink and Llewellyn, 1995).

Different types of loans carry different degrees of risk and this has implications for the differential pricing of loans. A good example is the contrast between mortgage lending, which is secured lending and has traditionally represented low risks to lenders, and unsecured lending such as overdrafts and credit card lending which represents much higher risk lending. As a consequence of these differential risks, it has been common in the past to see mortgage rates priced at a margin of around 2 per cent over base rates (or three-month money market rates) while credit card and other unsecured lending was priced at over twice the base lending rate.

This particular case also provides an example of the various factors which can impinge upon the pricing decision in financial products/ services. It is common in discussions of pricing, for example, to see reference made to the influence of 'what the market will bear'. This really combines two separate but related influences: the demand characteristics of the borrowers, and the extent of competition in the marketplace (both internal competition within the sector and external competition). With respect to the former, this issue centres around the elasticity of demand of the particular borrowers: how sensitive is the demand for a particular category of lending to the interest rate charged? While a large part of the historical differential between the margins charged on mortgage lending and unsecured lending has undoubtedly been attributable to the differential risk premiums; a further important factor was probably that unsecured borrowers (particularly personal sector credit card borrowers) were relatively less sensitive to the margins charged. Anecdotal evidence for this can be found in the massive increase in credit card and store card borrowings following the de-regulation of the credit market in the 1980s.

The impact of the extent of competition can be seen in this example in the sense that the differential between the lending margins on credit cards and mortgages was at its highest in the UK in the early and mid-1980s when the market was dominated by the major banks via Barclaycard and Access (subsequently Visa and Mastercard). In the mid- to late 1980s, however, the margins on credit card lending were reduced in response to external competition. The 1986 Building Societies Act gave building societies the power (from January 1987) to enter the credit card market and in order to gain a foothold in the market they began significantly to undercut the margins being charged by the incumbents. The banks also faced stiff competition in this market from other non-bank institutions such as Save and Prosper which also launched highly competitive credit cards.

The mortgage market also provides an interesting example of the complex interactions between the various factors which influence pricing decision. If we take the specific example of first-time buyers in the mortgage market, it is generally accepted that they represent a higher risk to lenders than do 'seasoned' borrowers. They have, for example, no track record in terms of making repayments and they also typically have less equity to put into the property. If we look at the terms offered to first-time buyers, however, we find that they are invariably favourable compared to those offered to existing owner occupiers and take the form of discounted mortgage rates, cash-back schemes, assistance with legal fees etc. There are three main reasons for the preferential rates offered to first-time buyers in spite of their intrinsically higher risk: (a) they typically have much higher elasticities of demand (i.e. they are much more sensitive to interest rates than are more established borrowers); (b) it is also the beginning of a long-term relationship with the lender and hence the lender has an incentive to tempt the customer by a low interest rate; and (c) first-time borrowers do not incur the transaction costs of switching between lending institutions and hence are not 'locked-in'. In this type of situation where distinct sets of customers have different degrees of 'price' sensitivity, it is common for suppliers to maximize profits by charging differential prices for essentially the same product, with the least price sensitive customers being charged higher prices. Similar examples include the use of student and senior citizen railcards, differential electricity prices for businesses and households, and (in the past) higher telephone charges during 'business' hours.

A further important reason for the favourable terms offered to first-time buyers, however, is the increasingly important concept of relationship pricing which is tied in with the concept of relationship banking. It is well known that most customers make use of several different banking services and the importance of paying attention to the whole customer relationship is now increasingly recognized in retail banking. Hence, relationship banking places particular emphasis on cross-selling, i.e. inducing the customer to purchase a wide range of services from one bank. This is achieved via the use of relationship pricing whereby more advantageous prices are charged for users of combined services. Clearly, first-time buyers in the mortgage market represent a prime target in terms of cross-selling opportunities. They will have no existing contents or buildings insurance and possibly no existing life assurance cover. They also present valuable cross-selling opportunities with respect to endowment policies etc. Further down the line these first-time buyers offer the prospect of a long-term, profitable banking relationship as they come to require products such as unit trusts, personal pensions, savings accounts etc. This idea of relationship pricing should not be confused with the concept of loss-leaders, however. Relationship pricing should be implemented on the basis of rational full cost recovery pricing, but with the overall pricing structure geared towards the particular needs of individual segments of the market. In the case of first-time buyers in the mortgage market, therefore, their particular demand characteristics, combined with the potential for cross-selling and long-term profitable banking relationships, dictates that they be offered favourable pricing on mortgages.

A further element which is typically incorporated into the interest margin, or price for financial intermediation, but which has not yet been mentioned is what might be termed an 'implicit interest charge'. This charge is imposed via the lending rate being higher and the deposit rate lower (or some combination of the two) than is necessary to cover all the costs and the contribution to profits outlined previously. The need for this type of implicit interest charge has been evident in the tendency for UK banks not to charge (or not to charge fully) for the costs of payments services such as cheque processing, ATM transactions etc. The fact that these types of financial services have traditionally not been explicitly charged for has resulted in a system of implicit pricing and cross-subsidization which is discussed in more detail in the next section.

### The extent of interest-free deposits

The second influence on the overall interest margin of banks is the extent of interest-free deposits. The greater is the volume of interest-free deposits (such as zero-interest current accounts), the more net interest income rises as the general level of interest rates rise. This is illustrated in Figure 7.2 below.

The diagram shows a series of deposit (D) and loan (L) curves with an interest margin equal to CD (= EF). With $D_1$ and $L_1$ if OA is the volume of interest-fee deposits, the bank's net interest income with a volume of business of OB equals $(AB \times CD) + (OA \times BC)$. If the level of interest rates rises (with the differential unchanged, i.e. D2, L2) net income rises to $(AB \times EF) + (OA \times BE)$. This implies a higher net interest income as while $(AB \times CD) = (AB \times EF)$, $(OA \times BE) > (OA \times BC)$.

The benefit to profits which banks gain from the presence of these interest-free deposits at high levels of market interest rates is often referred to as the endowment effect. The benefit of this endowment effect has been eroded in recent years, however, as competition (from building societies, for example) has forced banks to pay interest on a higher proportion of their deposits, and as the relatively low level of market rates has reduced the benefit available from that proportion of interest free accounts which remain. It is these pressures, amongst others, which

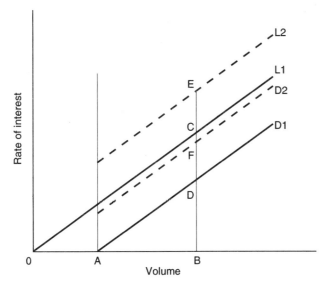

**Figure 7.2** Interest margins and interest-free deposits

have led banks to re-appraise their traditional practice of implicit rather than explicit charging for payments services. This is discussed in more detail in the next section.


### 7.3.3 The pricing of bank payment services

The previous section established a simple analytical framework for banking firms which was used to examine some of the key issues relevant to the pricing of deposits and loans. One of these issues was the requirement to recover some of the costs of providing payments services via the levying of implicit interest charges. It was stressed that this requirement was driven by the traditional practice of implicit pricing and cross-subsidization in respect of the payments system. In this section, therefore, we examine the pricing of bank payment services in greater detail, paying particular attention to the choice between explicit versus implicit pricing.

The analysis of the pricing of bank payment services is highly topical as a number of banks have intimated that they would like to move away from the practice of Free if in Credit (FIIC) banking which was introduced in the mid-1980s. Indeed, although FIIC banking still remains, we have seen a general shift towards greater explicit pricing for bank services in recent years.

The analysis of the pricing of bank payment services allows us to illustrate some of the pricing issues which are peculiar to banking, and also to illustrate how elements of basic economic pricing theory can be applied to the pricing of bank payment services.

*Alternative pricing mechanisms*

Banks have a wide range of pricing and charging options with respect to:

1. The **form** of pricing (between *implicit* and *explicit* mechanisms).
2. The **strategy** of pricing (between 'Disneyworld' (i.e. fixed annual free), transactions charges and a two-part tariff).
3. With respect to **tariff** levels.

With respect to the pricing of current account and payments services, the major variables at the disposal of a bank are:

(a)  explicit transactions charges
(b)  quarterly or annual fees
(c)  zero interest on current account deposits
(d)  payment of interest at below the market level on current account deposits
(e)  the requirement to maintain minimum or average balances in the account in order to qualify for non-explicit charging
(f)  a fixed quarterly fee which includes a specified number of transactions that can be made free of charge
(g)  differential prices attached to different payment media

**Table 7.4** *Pricing matrix*

|  | *Explicit* | *Implicit* |
|---|---|---|
| Disneyworld | ii and vi | iii, iv and v |
| Transactions Charge | i, vii and viii | – |
| Two-Part Tariff | i, ii, vi, vii and viii | iii, iv and v |

(h)    notional calculated charges which are reduced on the basis of the size of the average balance maintained in the transaction period.

These implicit and explicit charges can be combined in various ways. Table 7.4 shows a matrix of the form of pricing together with the strategy of pricing. In general, each strategy can be operated either through implicit or explicit charges. However, a notable feature of the matrix is that there is no implicit form of charging which can be related to the use made of services, i.e. related to the consumers' volume of transactions.

A major weakness, therefore, of implicit charging is that it offers no incentive to the consumer either to economize on the number of transactions, or to choose transactions with low costs.

Apart from transactions charges, any explicit charge has an implicit equivalent. It follows that the combination of implicit and explicit charges can be rearranged to produce a trade-off that gives the same revenue to the bank. Using the Federal Reserve's Functional Cost Analysis for US banks, Whittle and Handel (1987) show how the trade-off between fees, interest payments and average balances works to yield the same revenue for banks. However, some methods of pricing also have the effect of influencing consumer behaviour and of reducing the costs of providing payments services. In this sense, a bank would not necessarily be indifferent between alternative pricing mechanisms which yield the same revenue. Alternatively, implicit or explicit charges can be set at levels which either yield the bank the same revenue, or produce a lower revenue but also lower costs. In terms of the allocation of resources within the payments mechanisms, the preference should be in favour of mechanisms which have the effect of reducing costs.

Table 7.5 compares some of the properties of alternative pricing mechanisms.

## 7.4    Implicit versus explicit pricing

The essence of implicit charges for current accounts is that banks receive interest on assets acquired through zero or low-interest deposits. This (endowment) revenue is compensation for the provision of free current account services. In effect, the consumer pays through an interest-free loan (or low-interest loan) made to the bank. It follows, therefore, that the cost of the current account to the consumer and the implicit revenue to the bank is determined by the level of interest rates: both fall with a fall in the level of interest rates. When interest rates are high, the absence of

**Table 7.5** Properties of pricing modes

| | Induces cost reducing behaviour | Implicit cross subsidies | Cost/revenue interest rate sensitive | Benefit to low volume transactions | Certainty of costs | Subsidy to large volume transactors | Transparency |
|---|---|---|---|---|---|---|---|
| (a) Explicit transactions charges | ✓ | x | x | ✓ | x | x | ✓ |
| (b) Fixed quarterly fee* | x | ✓ | x | x | ✓ | ✓ | ✓ |
| (c) Zero interest on balances | x | ✓ | ✓ | – | ✓ | – | x |
| (d) Minimum balance requirements | x | ✓ | ✓ | – | ✓ | – | x |
| (e) Fixed quarterly fee incl. X transactions* | (✓) | ✓ | ✓ | ✓ | (✓) | x | ✓ |
| (f) Differential transactions charges | ✓ | x | x | x | x | x | ✓ |
| (g) Rebates on basis of balances | x | ✓ | ✓ | x | x | x | x |

*Explicit charges

explicit transactions charges is of little concern to banks if they are receiving deposits upon which they do not pay a rate of interest or deposits upon which the rate of interest is held below market levels. In this case, at high interest rates a high proportion of the costs of running the payments system is covered by the interest receipts on the assets financed by the given level of average balances. In general, the higher the levels of minimum balances and the wider the differential between deposit interest rates and the level of market rates, the greater benefit the bank receives in a period of high interest rates. Similarly, the effective cost to the consumer also rises with the level of interest rates in such cases. This represents one of the major problems associated with implicit charging: effective costs and revenue vary with the level of interest rates whereas the costs of supplying current account services are independent of the level of interest rates.

## 7.4.1 Case for implicit pricing

Providing implicit and explicit pricing variables can be infinitely varied, they can be made equivalent in terms of revenue and cost implications. Put another way, implicit charges represent the equivalent interest rate cost (in the sense of interest on deposits foregone) of the provision of a range of current account services. In the complete absence of cross-subsidies, depositors would receive the market rate of interest on all credit balances but pay the economic cost of all services consumed.

The alternative is not to make explicit payments for services consumed but instead to receive a lower rate of interest on deposits held at the bank. There are four main arguments in favour of implicit charging of current account services (i.e. paying for services in terms of minimum credit balances and/or low rates of interest on credit balances):

1. The overwhelming advantage is its potential tax efficiency. Tax is levied on interest received on deposits but is not levied on the implicit interest received through the provision of free banking services. This implies that, compared with the zero cross-subsidy outcome, implicit charges have the effect of reducing the overall tax liability of bank customers.
2. A major advantage of implicit charging is its simplicity both for the bank and the consumer.
3. The consumer has a high degree of certainty about the level of charges. A problem with explicit charges for transactions is the uncertainty for the consumer about the future cost of the account. This uncertainty is removed through implicit charging although, in truth, the effective cost of 'free banking' is not known in advance because it is determined by the level of interest rates.
4. Implicit charging is also a low-cost form of charging for the bank; administration costs are low compared with explicit charging where charges are levied for each transaction and hence there needs to be a regular monitoring procedure for calculating the transactions costs for each consumer.

There is a trade-off to consider between welfare and tax efficiency. In principle, the norm is that consumers value income more highly than the provision of free services. This is because, with income, consumers are free to choose the preferred combination of services. However, if consumers receive no intrinsic benefit from transactions *per se* then the use of such services may not be greatly affected because they are not charged. In this case, the consumer consumes a volume of banking services which is not substantially greater compared with a situation where interest is received on credit balances and the economic cost paid for the services utilized. In this case, the tax efficiency gain is likely to outweigh the potential welfare loss through the provision of free services rather than income.

### 7.4.2 Disadvantages of implicit pricing

On the other hand, there are clear disadvantages and hazards to pricing mechanisms based exclusively on implicit charges:

1. A major problem is that both the cost to the consumer and the revenue to the bank are interest-rate sensitive. As interest rates fall, the implicit cost of services to the consumer goes down with a corresponding decline in net revenue to the bank, though the cost of providing services does not fall.
2. There is a particular problem at low levels of market interest rates. It is possible that at some low levels of interest rates, the break-even implicit charge would imply a negative deposit rate of interest. At some low level of interest rates, the overall cost of supplying current account services cannot be met from the interest received on the basis of balances upon which the bank does not pay a rate of interest. In this case, the implicit charge does not cover the full costs of the service.
3. Implicit pricing has the general effect of leading to an over-supply of services and for the consumer to over-use some bank services such as transactions facilities (Higgins, 1977). This in turn has the effect of raising the overall costs of banks. The failure to charge for transactions is allocatively inefficient in the sense that consumers are provided with costly services which are valued very little at the margin. This in turn implies little incentive for the consumer to economize on the use of bank services as there is no price signal in operation. To the extent that this raises the costs of the bank, the level of implicit charges must be higher than the level of explicit charges.
4. In general implicit pricing is sub-optimum for the consumer. Leaving aside the question of tax, free goods are valued less than the equivalent taken in income (such as through the payment of interest on credit balances). The consumer is indifferent between implicit and explicit pricing only in the case where precisely the same quantity of services as are being offered free with implicit pricing are chosen when they are charged for explicitly. This is unlikely and hence there is a net welfare loss to the consumer through implicit pricing. This implies that the consumer could be

compensated by a smaller rise in interest on credit balances than the equivalent benefit given in the form of free services. Overall, this would leave the consumer in the same position but the bank with lower costs. In this case, although in general the consumer prefers income to the provision of free services, if that excess welfare is less than the taxation liability that derives from receiving income, the consumer would prefer implicit rather than explicit charges combined with interest on credit balances. The taxation system has the effect of distorting the way bank services are priced.

5. A major hazard of implicit pricing (as noted in Table 7.5) is that there is no system that can be related to the extent to which the consumer uses the account. This means, therefore, that implicit pricing has the disadvantage of offering encouragement to consumers to over-use their accounts and thereby raise the costs of the bank.

6. Implicit pricing has a general disadvantage of a lack of transparency. The consumer is unaware of the benefit received (and its interest rate sensitivity) and is unaware of the costs that different behaviour patterns impose upon banks.

7. A product of implicit charging is that it creates a series of potential cross-subsidies between products and consumers. This raises the question of the sustainability of cross-subsidies in two respects: (a) competition may cause the banks to lose the subsidizing part of the business because this is priced too high, and (b) to the extent that some of the over-priced products lead to a reduction in their use this too reduces the cross-subsidy potential.

8. The absence of explicit pricing means that, unless the bank places a limit on the number of free transactions, there is no incentive for the consumer to use cheaper forms of payment. Again this has the effect of raising the overall costs of the bank. This issue arises because different payments media have different costs. In principle, if a consumer is indifferent between using two alternative payment mechanisms, a rational pricing structure would induce increased use of the least costly forms. In the absence of any explicit pricing of transactions there is no incentive to induce consumers to choose cheaper forms of payment.

Overall, therefore, there is a presumption in favour of explicit rather than implicit pricing. However, as frequently noted, the comparison is greatly complicated by the taxation effect. While it is certainly true that in the presence of income tax on interest income, the rational consumer will generally prefer at least some portion of return to be in the form of implicit interest, there will be a whole spectrum of pricing structures involving a mixture of implicit and explicit pricing, and it cannot be presumed that a structure involving zero service charges is in any way optimal.

## 7.4.3 Implications of implicit pricing: Cross-subsidies

Within a regime of implicit pricing, some services are not priced at all according to the level of use, while a non-directed implicit payment is made for a collection of services independent of use. Thus the implicit cost charged through the requirements to hold a minimum balance is a cost to the consumer which is fixed and independent of the volume of transactions made and the use of current account services.

'Free banking' is a total misnomer. If a particular service is not charged then payment is made elsewhere within the banking firm. This may take one of four forms: (a) the shareholder implicitly pays to the extent that profits are lower by virtue of non-pricing, (b) another customer pays through higher charges, (c) a different product effectively pays for the free good to the extent that it is priced higher than would otherwise be the case, or (d) the lending margin on intermediation business is wider (which implies either that the deposit interest rate is lower or the loan rate is higher than would be the case were charges made for all services). Therefore, if a particular service is not charged for, then it is a question of who pays and how payment is made. This in turn again raises the issue of cross-subsidies between different products and/or different customers.

Cross-subsidies are at the centre of issues regarding implicit or explicit charging for services. One of the implications of non-charging for some services is the existence of cross-subsidy which in turn requires there to be subsidizing and subsidized parts of the business. In the former, prices are set above, while in the latter they are set below, costs. The absence of pricing for some services means that some users of banking services effectively impose costs on others. There is no obvious rationale for this. If pricing policy is changed in the direction of making explicit charges for all services, subsidizing customers would gain while subsidized customers would lose. This is a question of redistribution between customers rather than from the customer base to the bank.

There are substantial problems associated with cross-subsidies between products and customers:

1. Because they imply subsidizing and subsidized parts of the business, there is always the potential that competition erodes the capability of banks subsidizing parts of the business as competition is likely to develop in the subsidizing part of the business which then makes the under-pricing of subsidized parts untenable. Cross-subsidies imply that the supplier of services is able to maintain all parts of the business. An example of how cross-subsidies can be competed away is given by the experience in the mortgage market in the early 1980s when the entry of banks forced building societies to lower the price of large mortgages and raise the price of small mortgages. Building societies' previous strategy implied a cross-subsidy from borrowers of large mortgages to borrowers of small mortgages. A similar example is the pressure on banks to pay interest on current accounts which erodes endowment profits and the ability of 'free' deposits to generate net income to subsidize other parts of the business.

2. Cross-subsidies are clearly unfair to some consumers. The question arises as to why some consumers should pay more for services or products while others pay less than costs.

3. Cross-subsidies imply a misallocation of resources because they tend to encourage over-use of under-priced services and under-use of over-priced services. The clear presumption is that consumers should choose optimum scales of services as determined by demand and costs.
4. There is no rationale for a consumer not paying at least the marginal cost of the services consumed.
5. They frequently imply a lack of transparency and information for consumers with respect to the effective cost of services.

Again the point is emphasized that a change in the structure of prices causes a redistribution of costs and benefits within the customer base. Some consumers gain while others lose. However, those that lose may also be in a position to reduce their costs through changes in the way they use the account.

The focus on cross-subsidies highlights the distinction between whether, if explicit charges were introduced, the motive would be to raise the net revenue of the bank, or designed to change the structure of pricing and thereby remove some of the cross-subsidies (leaving the bank with the same net revenue as before). In the latter case, the introduction of explicit charges for current account services would be accompanied by the payment of more interest on credit balances, lower prices for some other services, lower levels of penalty charges etc. Thus the previously subsidizing customers would gain relative to those who were previously subsidized. As already noted, in the absence of the tax effect, the complete elimination of cross-subsidies would involve banks paying the market rate of interest on all credit balances while at the same time charging the economic cost of all services provided and consumed.

However, the additional dimension is that the imposition of transactions charges could also have the effect of lowering the overall costs of banks which would ultimately be to the benefit of consumers and would reduce the resources involved in the payments system. If explicit transactions charges were differentiated to reflect the marginal costs of different transactions media, explicit charging would create an environment conducive to the development of the most efficient payment system in the long run.

## 7.4.4 Alternative pricing strategies

As noted in an earlier section, banks have a wide range of instruments to implicitly or explicitly price their services: explicit charges, the interest margin, the size of free balances, the number of transactions allowable free of charge etc. There is a trade-off between them and they can be set in various combinations in order to yield the same revenue to the bank. On the other hand, some are more beneficial to some customers than others.

We now consider the analysis of explicit prices for current account transactions and services. Three generic alternative pricing strategies are considered:

1. Disneyworld pricing: the imposition of a flat (e.g. quarterly) charge irrespective of the use of the account with no additional transactions charges.
2. Transactions-charges only which cover fixed and variable costs.
3. A two-part tariff which incorporates a fixed quarterly charge (irrespective of use of the account) plus transaction charges related to the cost of each transaction.

As will be shown, each have different implications for different customers, different tax implications, and imply different incentives for the consumer with respect to the use of the account and alternative transactions mechanisms. Indeed, by changing behaviour and switching between alternative payment mechanisms, the consumer is able both to reduce his or her own charges and the costs of the bank. For instance, if transactions charges are related to the type of transaction (e.g. cheques, credit cards, debit items etc.) the consumer is able both to minimize the cost of the acccount and also the overall costs of the bank to the extent that the bank sets charges in a way that creates incentives for consumers to choose less costly payments media. For a more formal analysis of the market for different payment media, see Whitesell (1992).

One of the major issues in pricing is how to recover fixed costs. In banking these may be of two kinds: *customer costs* (i.e. those costs incurred by the bank when an account is opened and maintained irrespective of the use made of that account by the consumer), and *bank costs* (i.e. those costs of the bank which are not related to specific accounts, e.g. the cost of technology in setting up a payments system). If marginal costs are lower than average costs, and only marginal costs are charged, then fixed costs are not covered and the industry becomes potentially unstable. However, the way that fixed costs are incorporated in pricing policy also has implications for different consumers. For instance, single fixed charges with no transaction charges benefit high users of current accounts. On the other hand, when fixed and variable costs are incorporated in transaction charges, low users of current accounts benefit as high users carry a large share of fixed costs. In other words, whatever pricing policy is adopted has distributional implications between different categories of customer.

We now turn to a consideration of each of the three alternative pricing strategies outlined above.

*Disneyworld pricing*

The norm in pricing is for the consumer to pay for what is purchased and pay according to the quantity purchased, as pricing is designed to reflect the use of resources and the costs imposed on the supplier. However, this is not always the case as there are examples where charges are set irrespective of the volume of purchases by consumers. A good example is in the case of Disneyworld, theme parks, and ski-lifts in holiday resorts, where consumers pay a single price which grants access to services, but thereafter no prices are charged according to the use made of the facilities.

The parallel with banks is where a fixed quarterly charge is levied on current account holders with no additional transactions charges.

In the case of theme parks the consumer pays an entry fee but thereafter all rides are free. The fixed charge can be calculated to cover fixed and variable costs based on assumptions about average use of facilities (in which case those consumers who use more than the average gain). Thus, the theme park may estimate how many rides will need to be supplied during the time it is open, or alternatively it may run the rides continuously in which case it is able to calculate the overall running costs. Either way, fixed and variable costs can be covered through the single entrance fee without charges being levied on consumers as they use each ride. In effect, a single charge is an entrance fee which gives access to facilities even though the consumer may not make full use of them. On the face of it, this seems an irrational system of pricing as it contains no incentive for consumers to economize on use. It would appear that there is an incentive to over-consume the service for which no usage charge is made. However, this has been analysed in some detail by several authors (e.g. Cowen and Glaiser, 1991; Barro and Romer, 1987) and it can be shown that, under some circumstances, it is an efficient form of pricing.

The obvious problem is that, as no charge is made for use, there is an incentive for consumers to make substantial demands on the supplier. This could have the effect of raising the supplier's costs which are then not compensated by usage charges. In this case, there needs to be an alternative equilibrating mechanism other than price. In the case of ski-lifts and theme parks the equilibrating mechanism is in the form of queues. Also, the consumer is not able to overload costs onto the supplier because the supply is effectively limited by the number of rides that can be supplied within the opening hours of the park. In effect, therefore, the effective price does rise with substantial consumer use if a measure of the consumer's time in queuing is incorporated into the calculation of the effective price. The important aspect of ski-lift and theme park pricing, however, is that the consumer does not increase the costs of the supplier. This is likely to be different from the case of a single charge levied by banks because consumers are able to increase the costs of banks by 'excessive' use of current account services. To reinforce the point, it is also noted that theme parks do charge for purchases of food which are not included in the entrance price. It would seem, therefore, that a single charge without transactions charges is viable only in situations where it does not lead to behaviour by consumers that adds to the costs of the supplier.

The conditions under which 'Disneyworld pricing' are viable may be summarized as follows:

- Where the marginal costs are low most especially relative to fixed costs.
- Where the enforcement costs of transaction prices are high (perhaps because a system of collecting charges has to be established which may be expensive, and where the behaviour of the consumer needs to be monitored)

- Where the supply of the service or commodity is fixed, i.e. the consumer by his or her behaviour does not increase the costs of the supplier.
- Where it is particularly inconvenient for the consumer to pay on each occasion.
- Where the customer places a high value on knowing precisely what the level of expenditure is likely to be in advance.
- Where there are alternative equilibrating mechanisms which induce appropriate responses from consumers.

Such a pricing policy has several advantages: it is comparatively cheap to administer, it creates certainty for consumers as to total expenditure, and it is simple for consumers to understand. In particular, if the marginal cost of each use of the service is particularly low there is a high probability that the administration costs of charging for usage could be disproportionate to the marginal cost of the service itself.

A single charge without any transaction charges is one of the options available to banks in the pricing of personal current accounts. The charge can be either implicit or explicit: it can take the form of a required minimum balance without interest being received by the depositor, or alternatively an explicit quarterly charge can be levied.

Overall, a single fixed charge is unlikely to be optimum as a means of pricing current account services. Firstly, the supply of the service is not fixed and consumers are likely to over-use the service if there is no charge levied on each transaction. Secondly, it follows that in this case the behaviour of the customer influences the costs of the supplier of banking services. Thirdly, there is no incentive for the consumer to economize on the use of the current account or to arrange transactions to give priority to low-cost media. In practice, this last problem is likely to be significant because different payment media have different cost structures. In many cases the consumer is faced with a range of alternative means of payment and in many instances is likely to be indifferent between them. In such a case, the costs of the bank are likely to be reduced if there are differential prices which create an incentive in such a situation for the consumer to choose a lower cost medium. If the consumer is indifferent between different payment media, and yet the costs to the bank can be reduced by particular methods, a rational pricing system would encourage behaviour to minimize the costs of the bank. This would be of benefit either to the bank and/or to the consumer dependent upon how the bank distributed the net benefit so generated. Once a fixed charge has been paid, there is no incentive for the consumer either to economize on total transactions or to direct transactions to low cost media.

A slight modification to the fixed charge system is for the charge to include a limited number of free transactions with prices charged on transactions which exceeded this amount. This would be one way of guarding against the hazard of a fixed charge inducing consumers to over-use the facility. This is a fairly common practice in many Continental countries and in the US where banks impose a fixed quarterly or monthly charge.

Overall, therefore, a single fixed charge (Disneyworld pricing) is unlikely to be optimal for bank pricing of current accounts. However, it has the substantial potential marketing advantage of ensuring that consumers know in advance what the current account will cost. Although there are ways of reducing costs with explicit transactions charges (e.g. by rearranging monthly transactions and selecting media which have a lower cost), the consumer may nevertheless put a high value on the reduction in uncertainty implicit in a fixed charge.

## Single transactions charge

An alternative strategy is to levy charges on each transaction. This has the general advantage of at least creating some form of rationing mechanism within the payments system and is, after all, the norm for most consumer expenditure. There are two alternatives: for the price to reflect only the marginal cost of production, or the single transaction charge can be an inclusive charge to cover fixed and variable costs. The obvious problem with the former is that fixed costs are not recovered within the price and creates an obvious difficulty if fixed costs are a substantial proportion of the total. On the other hand, the second alternative disadvantages below-average users of current account services, as they pay a disproportionate share of fixed cost. Also, if the price is set above marginal cost, then this will have the effect of reducing demand. As with all pricing formulae, different consumers will be affected differentially by either of the two single prices on transactions. Compared with the cross-subsidies implicit in either not making explicit charges or with implicit charges which do not cover full costs, there is no system of pricing that can benefit all consumers. Some gain and some lose: a cross-subsidy implies a subsidizing and a subsidized part of the business and if prices are set to eliminate cross-subsidies the consumer of subsidized products and services loses relative to the consumer of subsidizing goods and services. It follows, therefore, that the costs and benefits depend on the type of consumer involved although behaviour can change in response to any particular pricing method.

## The two-part tariff

The third general method of pricing is to combine elements of the first two into a two-part tariff structure. This is a common feature of pricing structures with utilities such as gas, electricity, and telephones. A two-part tariff involves a fixed charge (the level of which is not determined by the consumer's consumption of the product or service), together with a charge which is paid on the level of service consumed. The nature and rationale of a two-part tariff is described well in the quarterly statements issued by utility companies. For instance, the East Midlands Electricity Board states:

The standing charge covers the rental and maintenance of the local mains and cables to individual premises together with the provision of the meter and other equipment on the premises, and meter reading and billing. These costs have to be met on a continuing basis and are not affected by the level of consumption of electricity in the premises.

As is implied in the above statement, a two-part tariff is a method of specifically covering fixed costs while at the same time charging the consumer the marginal cost of producing the good or service. It avoids some of the distributional problems in either of the two single charges discussed above, and also addresses the problem of single charges which do not create incentives for consumers to minimize the costs of the supplier. It is based on the general principle that fixed costs should be recovered somewhere within the pricing structure, and that all of the costs created by consumers' behaviour should be reflected in prices. It can be shown that, when marginal costs are below average costs, it is superior to recoup fixed costs via a single charge, and to charge usage at marginal cost, rather than to recover fixed costs through usage pricing.

Fixed costs need to be recovered irrespective of how the consumer behaves. Fixed resources give the consumer access to facilities and if these costs are not covered the consumer will be unable to secure access. In effect, the fixed charge is in the nature of an entrance fee into the service being provided by the supplier. They give access to services while the transaction charge reflects the actual costs involved in producing additional items. The standard analysis of two-part tariffs is provided by Lewis (1949). It is a pricing system which is often used when fixed costs represent a high proportion of total costs and when marginal costs are relatively low. In such a case marginal cost pricing has problems because it implies that fixed costs are not recovered. Overall, the objective of the two-part tariff from the supplier's point of view is to extract the consumer surplus that is implicit in single charges. The fixed charge is in the nature of an entry charge and to that extent is analogous to Disneyworld pricing. However, the major difference between this and Disneyworld pricing is that the consumer is also charged according to the use of the service.

A two-part tariff is designed in part to circumvent some of the problems implicit in marginal cost pricing. If prices are based on marginal cost, and marginal cost is equal to or greater than average cost, then a two-part tariff is unnecessary as the marginal cost price would cover all costs. However, if marginal costs are less than average costs (i.e. average costs are falling with rising output) marginal cost pricing would not cover the supplier's total costs. It follows, therefore, that marginal cost pricing is inappropriate in a situation where marginal costs are below average costs and where fixed costs are a large proportion of the total. This represents the position of banks supplying payment services. Therefore, if all costs in such an industry are to be covered then the pricing policy must involve either a single price which is set above marginal cost, or the adoption of a two-part tariff.

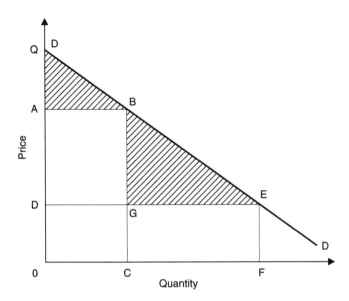

**Figure 7.3**  Two part tariffs and consumer surplus

It can be shown that a two-part tariff can be beneficial to both the supplier and consumer. In Figure 7.3, the demand for the product is given by DD. If price is set at the level of average costs (OA) the quantity demanded is OC. In this case the total revenue of the firm is given as OABC and consumer surplus is measured as AQB. If, alternatively, the supplier adopts a two-part tariff and levies a fixed charge of DABG and prices the product at the marginal cost (OD), the quantity demanded rises from OC to OF. In this case the firm's total revenue is equal to DABG plus ODEF which must necessarily be greater than the original revenue of OABC as ODGC is common to both and GECF is added. It follows, therefore, that the supplier receives a larger revenue and increased profit. However, it also follows that the consumer gains because consumer surplus is now equal to AQB (as before) plus BGE. The effect of the two-part tariff compared with charging a single price equal to average cost is that the quantity demanded rises and the total revenue and profits of the supplier are increased. Consumer surplus is also greater in this case.

When applying a two-part tariff two elasticities of demand need to be considered: the income-effect of the fixed charge, and the responsiveness of transactions to the transaction charge. The first tariff (i.e. the entry charge) may have an income-effect which reduces the consumer's income and hence either consumption or whether or not the firm is entered at all. The analysis above implicitly assumes that the income-effect is zero and that the imposition of the flat tariff does not influence either the consumer's ability to buy the product or the willingness to do so. The danger is that the first tariff will deter consumers from buying the service at all; the consumer has an incentive to seek an alternative supplier which is not charging an entrance fee. Two-part tariffs are frequently applied in industries where the consumer does not have such a choice.

As already noted, the fixed costs of a bank in supplying current accounts have two components: those related to individual customers (customer costs), and those which relate to the bank (bank costs). If these fixed costs are a high proportion of total costs, a two-part tariff is likely to be a viable pricing strategy for banks to apply to current accounts. Indeed, in many countries a two-part tariff is the norm with a fixed quarterly or monthly charge (which may also include a limited number of transactions free of charge) plus charges related specifically to each transaction. The first part of the two-part tariff can be either implicit or explicit. The two-part tariff can, therefore, be applied in various ways within the banking firm. It may take the form of explicit charges for both tariff one and tariff two as is the case in many European countries. Alternatively, the fixed charge element of a two-part tariff might be imposed through the establishment of a minimum balance before any interest is received by the depositor. This is equivalent to a flat charge although, as already noted, the effect of this charge and the implicit revenue received by the bank varies with the level of interest rates. It is also interesting that prior to the establishment of 'free if in credit banking' in the middle 1980s, the norm for British banks was for a two-part tariff. A proxy for a two-part tariff can also be found in the non-payment of interest on all current accounts except where balances exceed a high figure. One rationale of this strategy is that the volume of services consumed is often proportionate to the balance the customer maintains at the bank. In this case, the consumer is effectively paying both a fixed charge and one related to the volume of transactions. However, it is an imperfect representation of the two-part tariff and can lead to implicit cross-subsidies and distortions.

The rationale and superiority of a two-part tariff for explicit charging of current account services may be summarized as follows:

1. There is no obvious rationale for consumers not paying for services actually used, and therefore at least the marginal cost of services should be charged. However, because of the nature of the cost structure of a bank, pure marginal cost pricing is unlikely to recover full costs.
2. Marginal costs are likely to be low relative to fixed costs and this is one of the instances where a two-part tariff is a viable pricing strategy.
3. Because transactions are explicitly charged (and charges levied can be related to the particular payments medium and service used) a two-part tariff creates incentives for the consumer to minimize the costs of the bank. This is particularly relevant when the consumer faces a choice of payment media (but is indifferent between them) but where the bank has a clear advantage in inducing use of one particular method.
4. The nature of fixed costs are such that customer costs exist in banking in that there are costs of servicing accounts irrespective of the use made of them. For instance, cheque books have to be issued (because the consumer wants access to the payments system), the

account needs to be managed and monitored, and there are set-up costs involved with opening accounts. None of these costs are dependent upon the use of the account once opened. There is also a very substantial amount of capital equipment involved in the payments mechanism which is needed in order to cope with potential demand. The volume of capacity also needs to be related to the peak of potential demand and in this respect it is parallel to the peak-load problem found in some utilities.

5. One aspect of the service of the bank is to offer customers access to facilities and this is inappropriately charged for on a single-price basis.

Overall, therefore, given the nature of the cost structure of the banking firm and the nature of the services offered, a two-part tariff seems an appropriate pricing strategy for current accounts of the personal sector. A two-part tariff also avoids some of the problems implicit in the single price tariff outlined earlier.

## 7.4.5 Choices to consumers

The two-part tariff structure suffers the disadvantage that consumers do not know in advance the cost of banking services because of an inability to accurately predict the use of the account over a month. However, all transactions charges have this problem and at least the two-part tariff (to the extent that the transactions charge is lower than would be the case if all costs were put into transaction charges) reduces the degree of uncertainty faced by the consumer. It is also the case that consumers are able to respond to differential prices for different payment services. Overall, because consumers differ in their pattern of usage (e.g. with respect to average balances, number and type of transactions etc.) any pricing structure affects different consumers differentially.

It is for this reason that it is preferable to offer consumers a choice of pricing strategies. In effect the bank can offer a limited range of self-selecting contracts. A choice could be offered in advance where the consumer could choose either a single pricing tariff (either of a fixed kind or related to transactions), or a two-part tariff as described above. The consumer, to the extent that future payments behaviour (including responses to different prices) can be predicted, is then in a position to minimize costs by an appropriate choice of tariff system. Although this makes for a more complex pricing system which may create some confusion (and may be more expensive for the banks to operate) an element of choice is likely to be beneficial to consumers. Those consumers who place a high value on the certainty of costs, and which tend to use their accounts at a rate above the average, might tend to opt for a single fixed charge. On the other hand, those consumers who do not use their account substantially would tend to favour transactions charges. The offer of a choice is not likely in practice to make it more difficult for the bank to forecast the revenue received from charges. This is because, if any new system of charges is imposed, the bank would need to forecast the behavioural responses of customers and this in practice is likely to be very difficult. The additional uncertainty implicit in offering a choice is unlikely to be very substantial. The analysis of choice is considered more formally in Llewellyn and Drake (1993).

The spectrum of charge systems ranges from a uniform price (set at a level equal to average cost) to a two-part tariff where the transactions charge is set equal to marginal cost. These can be constructed in a way that yields the bank the same revenue. A more detailed analysis of two-part tariffs and their applications can be found in Brown and Sibley (1986) and Faulhaber and Panzar (1987).

### 7.4.6 International experience

The authors conducted a questionnaire survey of banks in eleven countries with respect to the pricing of personal bank account services. There has been a widespread trend towards the explicit charging of personal current account services. Of the countries surveyed, the UK is alone in both paying interest on credit balances and not making explicit charges for transactions. Increasing emphasis has been given in recent years towards more explicit and directed charges for money transmission services. Common pressures have been: increasing cost pressures faced by banks, the competitive and deregulation pressures inducing the payment of interest on a wider range of accounts, the widening cost differential between different payment media, and the strategic objective of inducing consumers to switch towards electronic media. In addition, deregulation has removed economic rents from many national banking systems and competition has intensified in all banking markets, products and services. Both have had the effect of eroding banks' capacity to sustain a network of cross-subsidies. The common pattern that emerged from the international survey may be summarized as follows:

- Explicit charges are the norm.
- The norm is for a two-part tariff (a monthly or quarterly fixed fee plus transactions charges) with the fixed charge frequently including a specified number of transactions free of charge.
- Consumers are often offered a choice of charging structures.
- Charges are almost invariably waived if the account is maintained in credit at or above a specified minimum level in the accounting period.
- Transactions charges are usually differentiated between different payments media.
- The charging for automatic teller machine transactions, while not universal, is not uncommon.

Thus, international experience seems to confirm the conclusions derived from the formal analysis outlined in earlier sections of this chapter.

## 7.5  Conclusion

In this chapter we have analysed the pricing of retail finance services. While it will be apparent that some of the features of the pricing of financial services are common to those of other products, we have stressed throughout this chapter that retail financial services do have some special characteristics which necessarily have implications for pricing. One feature which was stressed is that some financial services, such as loans, carry risks for the supplier. In turn, these risks must be adequately priced in order to remunerate the supplier of risk capital and generate internal capital.

We have also stressed in this chapter that the term 'retail finance services' actually covers a highly heterogeneous set of products displaying different combinations of these special characteristics. Consequently, it is difficult to make generalizations about the pricing of retail financial services. For this reason, we chose to illustrate some of the detailed issues involved in the pricing of retail financial services in the context of two particular cases: the pricing of financial intermediation and the pricing of bank payments services. The former illustrates the many factors which impinge upon the pricing of financial intermediation and the inter-relationships and trade-offs between them. The latter demonstrates the application of basic pricing theory to a particular financial service. The analysis suggests that the current UK system of implicit pricing and cross-subsidies will gradually be eliminated due to the twin pressures of competition and costs. It is likely to be replaced by a system of explicit pricing for bank payment services.

Although there are a wide range of explicit pricing options available to banks, the chosen systems are likely to offer consumers a choice of tariffs based around a two-part tariff structure. It is also likely that differential pricing will be applied to different payment media in order to facilitate an efficient use of resources. A survey of international experience seems to confirm these conclusions and highlights that the current UK system is unique in respect of the pricing of bank payment services.

# 8 Distribution channels

Barry Howcroft and Julia Kiely

## 8.1 Introduction

Distribution channels are an important means of delivering products and communicating effectively with the marketplace. In the basic banking market, branch networks have fulfilled both these functions with considerable success. As distribution channels, however, branch networks have certain inherent disadvantages which have become only too apparent with the progressive deregulation of the financial services markets. Alternative distribution channels, particularly those which utilize advanced technology, have partially remedied some of these weaknesses by complementing and supplementing the branch networks. The emergence and very existence of these alternative distribution channels, however, has also introduced some far reaching and potentially challenging strategic implications for financial institutions (Friars et al., 1985).

In banking, the pre-eminence of the branch was largely due to the difficulties associated with marketing financial services. Branch networks evolved to attract relatively cheap retail deposits through the convenience of branch locations and branch-based payment systems. Traditionally, they have provided a highly effective, though increasingly costly, mechanism for administering, collecting and delivering cash. They have also, simultaneously, facilitated the provision of an extensive range of associated lending and ancillary services.

The cartelized oligopoly operated by the London Clearing Banks (LCBs) until 1971 precluded price competition but other forms of competition, particularly, 'functional' competition aimed primarily at increasing (maintaining) market share by increasing customer satisfaction was prolific. The most obvious example of this competition was the growth in the number of bank branch networks in the 1960s.

After 1971, various changes in the financial services markets, collectively referred to as 'deregulation', have systematically changed the nature of competition in the markets. Not only have the traditional constraints on price competition been removed but the demarcation lines between the various financial institutions and their respective markets has been considerably eroded. As a consequence, different types of financial and non-financial institutions which traditionally never competed are now actively competing against each other in an increasingly universal financial market. The net effect has been to introduce a range of new competitors who do not have branch networks.

These non-branch competitors and the increased cost constraints now experienced by branch orientated institutions are primarily responsible for the increased emergence of 'product' rather than 'relationship' strategies. This change in marketing philosophy poses a potential threat to the branch infrastructure because at the extreme a product strategy emphasizes the sale of financial products through non-branch distribution channels. This is in stark contrast to the relationship strategy, traditionally associated with the LCBs and building societies, which typically utilizes the branch network to attract customers and develop personal relationships as a basis for selling financial services (Kimball, 1990).

Against this background this chapter discusses the main forces which are changing the patterns of competitive behaviour in the financial services markets and examines the important strategic challenges which currently confront financial institutions as they attempt to provide products and services utilizing the most appropriate delivery channel. The chapter examines both indirect distribution channels, such as branch networks, ATMs, EFTPOS and home banking; and, direct distribution channels including direct mail, direct response advertising and direct salesforces.

## 8.2 The strategic issues

The emergence of new delivery channels has meant that financial institutions now think in terms of a delivery mix rather than exclusively relying upon one dominant channel. The key to successful management of this delivery mix is to balance product delivery costs with potential revenue in an endeavour to maximize profitability. Costs will include product and systems development, advertising, support activities, overheads and a gross margin. As a substantial proportion of the costs will be fixed they will not be significantly affected by the volume of business processed, thereby introducing opportunities to increase profitability from economies of scale. Revenue, on the other hand, will be determined by the numbers of potential customers, market share, products purchased per customer and the gross margin per product. This suggests that successful management of the delivery mix will necessitate an increase in both the number and variety of distribution channels in order to maintain and increase sales volumes (Kimball and Gregor, 1989).

The optimum mix of distribution channels is another important strategic issue confronting management in financial institutions. The eventual choice will influence both the product range and its impact within the marketplace. Both these considerations are important determinants of ultimate market share but an even more important consideration is how the mix of distribution channels affects the basic cost structures of financial institutions and, therefore, their price competitiveness and overall profitability (Chandler et al., 1984).

In deciding upon the mix of distribution channels, financial institutions are effectively determining their overall ability to operate successfully in the financial markets. The choice is based upon the following considerations:

- Maintaining a strong market position through attracting and retaining a large, profitable customer base.
- Introducing new distribution channels to counteract the cost-benefit characteristics of the branch network.
- Building a distribution channel mix that can respond flexibly to changes in competition and the marketplace.

In deciding upon the mix of distribution channels, the clearing banks probably face the most difficult problem because their dominant position in the marketplace is still based primarily upon the branch network. Any change in their strategic distribution system would, therefore, appear to necessitate either a radical reduction in the size of branch networks and/ or a change in the primary functions (Howcroft and Lavis, 1986).

Technology has also become an important determinant of strategic direction. Not only is it changing the economics of the marketplace but it is also providing both an opportunity and a challenge to incorporate technology characteristics into product designs. Corporate cash management terminals, electronic cash dispensers and company cash management services already utilize technology to this effect. Technology-driven distribution channels can be utilized to focus products and target customers by ensuring that products are sufficiently differentiated from competitors.

Strategies are, therefore, increasingly determined by considerations and options provided by technology, or solely in response to competitive and external market forces. Financial institutions are consequently becoming less capable of determining their future policies solely by reference to predominantly internal considerations and are becoming more responsive to the market.

## 8.3 Arbiters of change

There are two basic factors which underlie changes in the nature and structure of distribution systems in financial services, competition and technology.

*Changing patterns of competition.* The basic problem facing the branch networks of banks, building societies and estate agents etc. is that they are essentially 'passive', i.e., the emphasis is on the customer to make the effort and visit the office. By contrast the 'active' sales medium is the tied salesforce typical of industrial life offices, unit linked offices and major retail brokers, which involves company representatives visiting customers at their convenience, i.e. usually at home and typically outside normal banking hours. Moreover, branch networks may be eminently suitable for relatively simple packaged insurance products, e.g. endowment mortgages or house content policies, but they are certainly less suitable for the more complex life or pension products which require more detailed information and individual tailoring (Belton, 1989).

**Table 8.1** *Polarization: Designation of branches*

| Bank/Building Society | Status | Company represented |
|---|---|---|
| *Bank* | | |
| Barclays | CR | Barclays Life |
| Lloyds | CR | Black Horse Life |
| Midland | CR | Midland Life |
| National Westminster | CR | National Westminster Life |
| Bank of Scotland | CR | Standard Life |
| Royal Bank of Scotland | CR | Royal Scottish Assurance |
| TSB | CR | TSB Life |
| Yorkshire | II | – |
| Abbey National | CR | Abbey National Life |
| | | |
| *Building Society* | | |
| Halifax | CR | Standard Life |
| Nationwide | CR | Guardian Financial Services |
| Alliance and Leicester | CR | Scottish Amicable |
| Woolwich | CR | Sun Alliance |
| National and Provincial | CR | National and Provincial Life |
| Britannia | CR | Britannia Life |
| Bradford and Bingley | II | – |
| Cheltenham and Gloucester | II | – |

The Securities Investment Board's (SIB) polarization regulations have further complicated the situation by insisting upon the designation of retail salespeople as either company representatives (agents) or independent intermediaries (principals) but as Table 8.1 indicates the response over time has been fairly uniform. A minority of institutions have independent intermediary status and, therefore, offer a full brokerage service. The majority of clearing banks and building societies, however, have become company representatives and, therefore, will in the first instance endeavour to sell the insurance products of the companies they represent. In the case of Barclays, Lloyds, Midland, NatWest and TSB, these are associated companies or subsidiaries of the banks in question. This dichotomy in the market is potentially confusing to the average customer and the bias towards company representatives effectively reduces the outlets for independent insurance companies which desire to remain independent but which do not have their own salesforce. This places a serious question mark against whether the best interests of the customer are being met under these circumstances.

*Electronic technology.* In distribution terms there are essentially two types of technology – that which complements a branch's function, e.g. front office terminals, cheque truncation etc., and that which provides an alternative means of distribution, e.g. ATMs, EFTPOS, plastic cards, direct banking etc. New technology initially supported branch networks and thereby facilitated greater volumes of transaction business. The general availability of this technology, however, has meant that no significant competitive advantage has emerged.

As an alternative distribution channel, new and emerging technology is changing the pattern of competitive behaviour. By reducing reliance upon the branch network, the single most important barrier to entry into the basic bank markets has been significantly reduced. This has enabled credit card organizations, particularly the non-bank American Express and highly centralized financial service groups to access the market. Insurance groups, data processing companies and retailers, similarly, now have the potential to offer a comprehensive range of financial products throughout the UK. Moreover, substantial capitalization combined with technology has introduced another competitive threat in the form of large Japanese and American banks with the potential to provide personal and corporate financial services throughout Europe.

The combined net effect of new technology and increased competition has fragmented the marketplace and eroded the traditional homogeneity of the various financial institutions. As distribution channels based upon technology have the capability to offer specific bundles of services, the traditional interdependence between savings, payment systems and lending products has also started to break down. This has facilitated the emphasis upon market segmentation and introduced the potential and opportunity to design products which increasingly incorporate reliance upon specific technological distribution channels (Nicholas, 1985).

## 8.4  The development of delivery systems in the UK

There is an increasing diversity of distribution systems in evidence in the UK financial services sector and an increasing reliance by suppliers on the simultaneous use of more than one channel (multi-channelling). This section outlines a number of the most important distribution systems.

### 8.4.1  Branch networks

The development of large branch networks in the UK, as shown in Table 8.2 is largely a consequence of evolutionary and unplanned growth. As a result the past two decades witnessed a gradual reduction in the size of branch networks. The early 1990s have, however, seen a more radical reduction in the size of branch networks.

The factors responsible for this reduction derive basically from two sources: the first is that customers are increasingly seeking both greater control and greater convenience in the conduct of their financial affairs. The second factor relates to the vulnerability of branches to excessive costs. The situation has been exacerbated by the traditionally low levels of cost recovery on payment systems and by the emergence of alternative cost-effective technology-driven distribution systems (Hammond, 1981).

Building society branch networks have in the past been cited as examples to illustrate the deficiencies of clearing bank branches, particularly in terms of style and operating efficiency. The expansion of the societies'

**Table 8.2** *Branch networks in the UK*

|  | *1983* | *1993* |
|---|---|---|
| Girobank | 22 301 | 19 958 |
| National Westminster | 3226 | 2545 |
| Barclays | 2912 | 2119 |
| Lloyds | 2276 | 1860 |
| Midland | 2345 | 1713 |
| TSB | 1604 | 1321 |
| Royal Bank of Scotland | 894 | 752 |
| Bank of Scotland | 559 | 455 |
| Clydesdale | 381 | 314 |
| Yorkshire | 215 | 270 |
| Co-operative | 75 | 109 |
| Standard Chartered | – | 4 |
| Total Banks | 36 788 | 31 420 |
| Total Building Societies* | 6643 | 5765 |

\* The number of building societies had declined from 206 in 1983 to 87 by 1993
*Source: Annual Abstract of Banking Statistics* (various)

networks, shown in Table 8.2 has, undoubtedly, undermined the clearing bank's competitive advantage of convenience and has had the almost incidental effect of providing direct price competition. Nevertheless, despite the similarities, not least those afforded by the building societies' pre-1983 cartel, there are fundamental differences in the traditional business conducted by building societies and clearing banks. In essence the traditional building society function has been more simple and limited in range, compared to the traditional business of the clearing banks. These differences reduce to some extent, the validity of a direct comparison between bank and building society branches. However, in the aftermath of the Building Society Act (1986) and the Financial Services Act (1986) building societies are beginning to incur problems not entirely dissimilar to those experienced by the clearing banks, particularly those relating to the functional and cost efficiency of branches, compared to new and emerging distribution channels (Barnes, 1985).

Estate agency business exhibited massive increases in the number of outlets operating in the market between 1986 and 1989. This increase was paralleled by an equally impressive change in the diversity of ownership of these outlets, away from the specialist estate agency towards banks, building societies and insurance companies. With approximately 80 per cent of new mortgage business being conducted on an endowment, rather than a traditional capital repayment basis, these structural changes were to a large extent attributable to the critical link between housing transaction and brokerage income. The collapse of the housing market in the 1990s has, however, seen a reduction in the number of estate agent outlets and a certain degree of retrenchment has taken place as agency chains purchased in the boom years of the 1980s have been sold at substantial loss during the recessionary period of the early 1990s. A good example of this retrenchment was the sale of NEA, the estate agency business of Nationwide Building Society, to Hambro Countrywide in 1994. Countrywide paid £1 for NEA which had assets totalling £5.2m and included 300 branches. Similar deals at nominal prices have taken place but in this particular instance the price reflects that Hambro was taking on a business which had originally cost Nationwide more than £200m but made a loss of almost £14m in 1993.

The advantages associated with a comprehensive branch network, however, must not be underestimated. Branches still constitute a substantial barrier to competitive entry and remain a most effective distribution channel in the basic bank markets. Information technology has facilitated their importance by making them more cost effective. Automation of a significant amount of processing, administration and routine customer service has reduced the branches' overall requirement for traditional bank clerk staffing whilst simultaneously increasing their output capacity. Technology has also reduced the administrative pressures on branches and provided the opportunity to increasingly regard them as marketing or retailing centres, with the potential to project corporate image (Faust, 1990).

A significant amount of investment has already taken place at certain preselected branches in an endeavour to reflect this change in image. Branches have been selected using social and demographic information both to justify the cash investment and to match it more accurately with the potential of the branch. The criteria for selection typically includes detailed analysis of the population and workforce around the branch and the specific appeal of any branch, including the amount of floor space and shopping trends in the surrounding area.

The general atmosphere within these branches has been substantially changed by simply facilitating closer physical contact between staff and customers. (The design and layout of branches is discussed in much greater detail in Greenland, 1994.) Bandit screens are less in evidence and a more welcoming image is projected through open planning, branch decor and the general attitude of staff. Improvements in customer service too, have been attempted by the adoption of a 'zoning' policy by some clearing banks. This strategy involves designating the floorspace of certain key branches for specific banking transactions. For example, customers requiring a quick service, typically associated with money transmission, balance enquiries, statements, etc. are allocated a high-tech, self-service area, typically near to the entrance of the branch. 'Off the shelf' products, such as account openings, simple loans, credit card applications etc. are provided in a completely separate area of the branch, incorporating an essentially open plan, face-to-face environment. Finally, for more complex products, such as personal financial services and mortgages, a slower, more personal approach is used, using a private part of the branch set well back from the entrance.

This policy of zoning is also conducive to 'hub and spoke' branching whereby a core branch offers a full service (possibly zoned) with satellite branches offering a more limited, sometimes highly automated service. The logistics of the system vary between different banks but it is typically structured around an area office which has responsibility for between four and fifteen satellite branches. The area office is referred to as a 'key branch' or 'corporate banking centre' and in addition to controlling the satellite branches has direct responsibility for generating corporate business and other pre-designated key accounts. The satellite branches, themselves, concentrate upon personal banking services or banking for small businesses and are usually designated general, support, counter or agency branch status depending upon their primary function (Caron, 1987). Implicit in this system is the removal of the processing function to a centralized department.

Apart from centralization of the processing function, hub and spoke branching also has the propensity to reduce costs by focusing specialized management in key branches, thereby avoiding the duplication of expensive management skills so abundantly obvious in the traditional branch network system. Satellite branches operated by staff at a lower premium can then be utilized to provide basic banking services and to sell financial products. Hub and spoke branching is also highly conducive to niche market strategies and is easily reconciled with the desire to maintain some form of physical high street presence in an endeavour to sell financial products and project corporate image. Indeed, the combination of such considerations may well lead to an eventual increase in the number of branches operated by the clearing banks. However, satellite branches with their limited and specialized services need to be located with particular care to maximize both revenue and customer satisfaction (Meidan, 1983). Branches specializing in the needs of small business customers have already emerged on the peripheries of towns and cities. Cash shops, offering essentially encashment facilities, have similarly been opened within supermarkets and shopping precincts (Brantley, 1989).

Zoning and hub and spoke branching have also introduced the opportunity for banks simultaneously to pursue both product and relationship strategies through their branch networks, thereby dispelling the view that the two strategies are either mutually exclusive or that product strategies cannot be effected through branches. For instance, in hub and spoke branching, relationships are of paramount importance in many satellite branches which are typically used to attract new customers and provide basic bank services. Opportunities which are identified or present themselves for selling financial products can then be referred to the product managers located in key branches.

The zoning of key branches themselves is similarly a recognition of the advantages of both relationship and product strategies depending upon the type of product being sold. Apart from the day-to-day account transactions which can be automated to some extent, other basic transactions such as account opening, general enquiries etc. need a personal approach which necessitates creating a relationship between banker and customer. Favourable corporate image and culture can then be projected to attract both new customers and strengthen relationships with existing customers. Ideally, successful relationship banking will result in customers being more inclined to purchase more sophisticated products from their primary bank then elsewhere. Opportunities to sell sophisticated financial products can also be more readily identified from the relationships, at which point customers can be referred to the specialist or product manager located in a separate zone but within the same branch.

In essence banks and building societies are currently endeavouring to improve their overall branch delivery system by adopting the following strategies:

- Attempting to provide a service when the customer requires it, by extending branch opening times to incorporate evenings and Saturdays.
- Reducing the amount of processing done at the branches by centralizing back-office work at more cost effective locations.
- Changing training priorities for staff, with a greater emphasis being placed upon selling.
- Investing in certain key branch locations to upgrade the premises and project a corporate identity compatible with retailing financial services in the 1990s.
- Researching products more vigorously and targeting them towards specific customer segments.
- Increasing investment in self-service equipment, particularly ATMs, for money transmission and enquiry services.
- Adopting a more segmented approach towards the personal and business markets in an attempt to enhance the quality of service to both.

### 8.4.2 Technology

The need to make branches more cost and functionally efficient has resulted in the wide-scale introduction of Automatic Teller Machines (see Table 8.3). This development has helped to make twenty-four-hour branch banking a reality. In addition to cash dispensing services, ATMs provide balance enquiries, statements, cheque book request services and in some instances, deposit collection facilities. Marketing messages can also be transmitted onto the ATM screens (Choraphas, 1988).

Multifunctional ATMs, however, are not necessarily conducive to providing the most cost-effective and efficient service. Not only are they more likely to malfunction, compared to more basic machines, but their ability to deliver combinations of banking transactions can lead to lengthy queues and consequently to customer delays. Significantly, the market has witnessed an emphasis by some banks (notably Midland Bank) towards single transaction machines in an attempt to service customer needs quickly and efficiently.

Although the traditional rationale behind the introduction of ATMs was essentially concerned with alternative cost displacement, particularly in terms of the branch infrastructure, another subsequent consideration has emerged which is concerned with the revenue generating capabilities of ATMs. Fundamental to this development is the question: are ATMs distribution systems or financial products? In reality they have qualities and attributes which are indicative of both but this mutuality has impor-

**Table 8.3** *Installed cash dispensers and ATMs*

|  | 1983 | 1993 |
| --- | --- | --- |
|  | **No** | **No** |
| National Westminster | 1304 | 2815 |
| Lloyds | 1535 | 2463 |
| TSB | 445 | 1916 |
| Barclays | 683 | 2805 |
| Midland | 703 | 1938 |
| Royal Bank of Scotland | 469 | 787 |
| Bank of Scotland | 203 | 406 |
| Clydesdale | 194 | 303 |
| Yorkshire | 92 | 321 |
| Girobank | – | 189 |
| Co-operative | – | 119 |
| Total Banks | 5628 | 14 062 |
| Abbey National* | – | 940 |
| Halifax Building Society | – | 1600 |

\* Classified as a bank in 1989
*Source: Banking World* (various)

tant implications for pricing strategy. Currently ATM pricing strategy reflects both these considerations. Access to account information, for instance, is not charged, reflecting the delivery function of ATMs, but account transactions etc. are typically charged in accordance with the bank's pricing tariff, reflecting the product function of ATMs. The future resolution of this question or indeed any changes in the bank's own views on the primary function of ATMs will, therefore, have a marked effect upon pricing strategy.

The move towards ATM-sharing agreements has largely been caused by the desire to reduce both variable and fixed costs, and to spread the risks associated with the new technology. The actual company groupings typical of Matrix and Link, for example, have largely been based upon technological compatibility rather than any other consideration but it does, nevertheless, raise the possibility of future power groupings. This possibility constitutes another reason why financial institutions should attempt to establish distinctive market positions and so endeavour to safeguard corporate identity and market share.

EFTPOS (Electronic Funds Transfer at Point of Sale) is essentially a payment system which may also be described as a distribution channel. The joint development of an EFTPOS network, however, has the potential to create a barrier to the entry of other groups and thereby maintain the market position of individual institutions in the same way that the payment systems oligopoly did. As a consequence attempts were made to establish a national EFTPOS system involving the LCBs and some of the larger building societies. This attempt failed due largely to delays caused by attempting to incorporate central clearing into the system and by adopting the principle of open membership to any 'qualified' financial institution. These delays effectively encouraged and gave ample opportunity for the banks to develop and install their own less ambitious but, nevertheless, successful EFTPOS systems independently of the national system.

The introduction of EFTPOS and the growth in debit cards is a major initiative in using technology to reduce the amount of cash in circulation and control the growth in overheads, but it potentially weakens the traditional role of the branch network. Nevertheless, this trend towards a cashless society will continue with the eventual introduction of smart cards or 'electronic purses' which store electronic money usually drawn from the user's bank account. Although reducing the need for traditional branch networks debit and smart cards might actually strengthen the need to have highly visible 'retail' outlets whose primary function is to project images and sell financial services rather than provide traditional payment services. Such an approach, however, raises the most difficult problem of how to attract customers into branches which do not have money transmission facilities.

Home and direct banking have even more far reaching implications because they rely even less than ATMs and EFTPOS upon an established customer franchise and marketing base. They are also not dependent upon co-operative schemes with other financial institutions, although direct banking does require the intermediation of a communications company to provide the interactive communication networks. This distribution channel uses technology in the form of videotext systems based upon either telephone lines using packet switching techniques or cable television systems utilizing their ability to carry several hundred channels simultaneously. Much will depend upon the demand for these technologies by the general public in determining the future success of home banking. The success of financial institutions in developing software packages capable of delivering an appropriate product mix, with a high degree of interactivity between customer and institution, will also be critical in determining future long-term success.

### 8.4.3 Direct mail

Of the media-based methods of direct distribution, direct mail is perhaps one of the best known and most widely used. The objectives of direct mail may be confined simply to informing the consumer and stimulating interest in a product or it may be concerned with more directly soliciting a purchase – via direct response advertising.

There has been a noticeable increase in the use of direct mail in the financial services sector (Thwaites and Lee, 1994). This is in part attributable to the various restrictions which operate with respect to the advertising of financial services, but it also reflects the fact that direct mail possesses a number of characteristics which make it particularly suitable for the communication and distribution of financial products.

Firstly, when dealing with products which are relatively complex and often difficult to understand, an initial mail communication will give the consumer time to consider the product and his or her reaction to it prior to moving into a buying situation. As such, it is thought to increase consumer confidence in the organization. Furthermore with the opportunities to personalize and tailor the message to specific individuals and groups, the image of direct mail as 'junk mail' is reduced and the power of the message increased. Secondly, direct mail allows an organization to be highly selective in terms of which consumers it approaches. Despite the higher costs associated with mailshots, the ability to target directly reduces the level of wastage in the communications process, making it potentially highly cost effective.

A third characteristic of direct mail is that it is a more versatile and controllable medium for communication and distribution. The organization has a high degree of discretion regarding the quantity and layout of information available to the consumer. Furthermore by allowing the organization to control which consumers receive which types of information and when they receive it, direct mail presents an organization with the opportunity to monitor with a high degree of accuracy the effectiveness of communication and distribution campaigns. At the same time, one important implication of this degree of control is that the message reaches the consumer at a time chosen by the organization rather than at a time chosen by the consumer. This would tend to suggest that a proportion of direct mail may be 'lost' because it does not coincide with a period of information search instigated by the consumer. However, it can be argued that direct mail will have the potential to generate responses until it is physically disposed of by the consumer.

The organization of an effective direct mail campaign requires that considerable care is taken in selecting the target group of consumers, identifying the product to be promoted and formulating the offer. Although a direct mail campaign may be undertaken in-house, it is common for organizations to employ specialist agencies (see, for example, Simmonds, 1988).

In terms of choice of mailing lists and customer targeting, there are obvious advantages in using 'in-house' lists. For long-term success in direct mailing it is preferable to build up specific lists which are customer based; the disadvantage of account-based lists arises from the fact that multiple account/product customers will receive multiple mailings and this will tend to damage the quality of the message. The benefits of combining customer-based lists with specific information on purchase patterns is discussed in some detail by Worthington (1986) and this study illustrates some of the particular gains which can be made from the precise targeting of direct mail.

### 8.4.4 Direct response advertising

Direct response advertising covers both direct mail and press/leaflet advertising. In its direct mail form it essentially involves providing the consumer with all the information required to make a purchase with minimal further assistance from sales staff. In the press/leaflet format, the product is distributed by a two-stage process which requires the consumer to respond to an initial offer and collect further details prior to the actual purchase. The essence of direct response in each case is that the distribution of the product occurs largely without the involvement of an agent – either in the form of an intermediary or a salesperson.

Through press and leaflet advertising, direct response presentations can target specific groups of customers, although typically with a lower degree of accuracy than that achieved by direct mail. Although there is a loss of accuracy through the use of these media there is, nevertheless, a cost saving and it has been suggested that the increased use of direct response advertising for financial services products is as much cost driven as market driven (Watkins and Wright, 1986). At present, the financial services sector is probably the largest single use of press-based direct response advertising and in the context of press advertising by financial services organizations, direct response is the most common format used (*Marketing*, 1989).

Although a tremendous variety of products are presented to the customer via direct response advertising, this method of distribution has tended to be most successful for 'low advice' or standardized offerings. However, with the recent developments in information technology and the growing flexibility of information systems, direct response advertising is increasingly being used in a two-stage format to provide personalized quotes for products such as non-life insurance.

### 8.4.5 Telemarketing

The growth of the telephone as a channel for distributing financial services has already been mentioned. For the purposes of direct marketing the telephone may be considered as an attractive alternative to mail because of the opportunities for interaction with the customer. First Direct and Direct Line are perhaps the best known examples of telephone distribution systems and both have successfully expanded the range of services offered by phone. More recently, many of the leading banks have launched their own telephone banking systems and a number of banks and building societies including the Woolwich, TSB and Cheltenham and Gloucester now offer mortgages by phone to low risk customers.

### 8.4.6 Direct salesforces

The importance of personal selling is likely to increase as competition within the financial services sector intensifies and product ranges both expand and become more complex. Direct mail and direct response are more appropriate for conveying a standard message targeted at the typical customer in a particular market segment. The opportunity to modify sales strategies and approaches according to the needs and nature of the customer suggests that the part played by the direct salesforce will remain crucial.

There has recently been a considerable increase in the numbers of salespeople employed in financial services. This is partly because of the growth of owner-occupation in the 1980s and, accompanying this, a rapid growth in endowment mortgages. The increase is also related to the falling number of independent intermediaries, as the cost of compliance with the Financial Services Act impacts severely on the small independent broker. Many of the major salesforce groups wishing to develop their salesforces have been approached by, or have themselves approached, small independents who are at least partly trained in the sale of life products. Of even greater impact is the decision by many banks and building societies to employ a salesforce that can work closely in co-operation with their branches.

The development and management of an effective salesforce, however, requires that considerable attention is paid to the attraction, retention and motivation of salespeople. Implicit in such issues are matters of ensuring continuity of high performance by adopting appropriate financial and non-financial remuneration packages alongside performance monitoring and career development considerations.

## Recruiting and selecting the salesforce

As with all jobs there is a requirement to match the individual to the job specification. With regard to the selling function, successful recruitment and retention requires that full consideration is given to the following factors: firstly, it should be recognized that the organizational work environment is very different from most other employees. Secondly, it is important to clearly define the primary job activities; and, thirdly, it is necessary to identify and counteract the factors which lead to a high labour turnover.

## Organizational work environment

Direct salesforces occupy a boundary-spanning role between their customers and their employers (Churchill, Ford and Walker, 1974; Winer and Schiff, 1980) and their unique position at the interface between the organization and customer requires them to be capable of fulfilling a wide range of roles. Such a position may give rise to the problems of role conflict, role ambiguity and physical and psychological isolation. Role conflict (Miles and Perreault, 1976) may arise as a result of salespeople being expected to work simultaneously in the best interests of their customers and their employers. This problem may be particularly acute with respect to financial services where customers place a high degree of importance on trusting both the individual and the organization supplying the product.

## Primary job activities

Selling 'intangible' services such as insurance, stocks and bonds requires a higher level of skill than that needed for many other selling jobs. Such selling is primarily, though not exclusively, to final consumers. Direct salesforces must be able to master basic sales activities of reaching the prospect and making the sale by converting the prospect's interest into buying intentions and actual purchase. In many instances, they also need to develop a continuing relationship with the customer after the first sale by encouraging additional purchases or continued loyalty.

The financial services marketplace, deregulated and increasingly technology driven, has become very competitive and changeable. In this changing environment, customer service has become a key factor in retaining and attracting customers and helping them differentiate between the various services on offer (Lewis and Smith, 1989). In this respect the direct salesforce plays a key role in determining the customers' assessment of the company and its service quality. As such their training and commitment to customer service is vital in influencing the current and future success of a company.

An important factor in ensuring quality of service is the ability to communicate. The salesforce must be able to:

- extract information, listen and express technical concepts in layman's language
- control situations by taking charge, instilling confidence and overcoming objections
- display good understanding of the full range of products and services on offer
- have full awareness of administrative procedures and policies within the organization and be capable of managing their own time effectively.

### Rewarding the salesforce – financial and non-monetary rewards

To a degree, the methods companies use to reward their direct sales personnel will affect the type of candidate they attract and their attitudes and behaviour. In practice, the method chosen is usually influenced by the service being offered and also by what is the norm for the financial services sector rather than an evaluation of the advantages and disadvantages of alternative options.

There are five main remuneration methods in the financial sector:

- Commission only – This is a highly cost-effective way of rewarding sales personnel as companies only have to pay on results. The attraction for the salesperson is that it offers unlimited income to those who are highly successful. Companies operating with a commission-only salesforce experience high levels of turnover. There are two main reasons for this: firstly, such companies tend to be less selective in who they employ and, secondly, working on a commission-only basis puts employees under a considerable strain.

  Apart from the problem of labour turnover, commission-only has other effects. Salespeople usually reach an income level with which they are satisfied and decide that the extra effort to earn more is not worth it. Many commission-only salespeople are self-employed. This can make it difficult for companies to gain commitment and control their agents. The career structure for commission-only sales personnel – particularly those who are self-employed – is often non-existent. In general, those operating commission-only schemes find that money alone is usually insufficient to motivate people to perform at a high level and stay with the company for long.

- *Quota-based systems* In contrast to straight commission which rewards all sales equally, quota-based systems provide sales personnel with an agreed target to aim for. Quota-based systems provide flexibility for structuring a range of incentives. Companies find this flexibility beneficial as they can adjust the emphasis they place on the promotion of products by the commission and reward system. The existence of an attractive, achievable target is likely to motivate and lead to high performance.
- *Small basic salary with high commission potential* This route provides people with a small degree of basic security and also limits the company's fixed costs. Nonetheless, many of the problems associated with commission only apply equally well to this category of employee.
- *High basic salary with low commission or bonus* With this situation, companies have to be far more selective in who they employ. It does provide people with security although if the commission is set too low it may not provide much of an incentive.
- *Salary only* It is hardly surprising that this is the remuneration system that employees usually prefer and employers like least. It provides security of income but employers have to be far more careful in their selection procedures and usually find that performance is not so high as under commission-only conditions.

In the later 1980s, efforts had been made by some of the traditional life offices to change remuneration packages, moving towards more commission and less salary, with the intention of making home service agents more sales conscious. By contrast, some of the unit-linked offices had switched away from remuneration packages which were almost entirely commission based, to include a more significant salary component. In part, the rationale for this move was to encourage more relationship building with clients. More recently, the changes in the regulatory framework described in Chapter 1 and the adverse publicity surrounding the mis-selling of personal pensions have encouraged a move back towards remuneration packages with a larger salary component. A number of life companies including Standard Life, Sun Life, Friends Provident, and Norwich Union have announced a switch towards salaries (plus bonuses) as the basis for rewarding their salesforces, although others such as Allied Dunbar have retained their faith in commission as the basis for salesforce remuneration.

*Salesforce motivation*

Within the overall field of motivation research, salesforce motivation has attracted a considerable amount of attention. This is because, unlike many other categories of employees, the performance of salespeople is easily measurable and there is a strong link between an individual's work efforts and performance. Moreover, high salesforce motivation is thought to lead to high sales performance (Walker, Churchhill and Ford, 1977). Despite the considerable volume of research in the area of motivation in general and that of salesforce motivation in particular, sales managers have found the task of motivating their salespeople to be a difficult one with no simple answers readily available (Doyle and Shapiro, 1980).

Organizations in the financial services sector have commonly assumed that what salespeople want most from a job is money. They have applied simple 'rational economic man' models of motivation to the salesforce and have then been surprised when salespeople have not worked as hard as they possibly can for more money. However, although money may be a major enticement into that type of work, once that need is satisfied other factors may become more important.

There are a variety of studies of salesforce motivations using a range of approaches (see, for example, Churchill, Ford and Walker 1979; Teas, 1981; Tyagi, 1982; Ford, Walker and Churchill, 1985; Hackman and Oldham, 1980). For purposes of illustration we will concentrate on one example of these studies; namely, the career stages framework suggested by Cron (1984).

Salespeople, like any other occupational group, pass through distinct career stages, which will influence their attitudes towards the job and their perceptions of what they need from work. The career stage framework of sales personnel developed by Cron (1984) identifies four distinct career stages: exploration; establishment; maintenance; and disengagement. This can be used to provide a framework for examining what salespeople are likely to look for in their work:

- *Exploration* Salespeople are concerned about whether or not they are in the right type of job. It is at this stage that appropriate training and support from managers is vital.
- *Establishment* Sales personnel have proved to themselves that they can sell. They now want more from their jobs than just money. The task of sales managers in conjunction with the reward mechanisms offered by the company, is to develop the importance sales personnel place on esteem and achievement needs. Sometimes this is achieved by various recognition procedures or awards such as exotic foreign travel for the top salespeople each year (Hastings, Kiely and Watkins, 1988).
- *Maintenance* Sales personnel become more committed to the organization and less inclined to leave. If management integrates sales personnel into the organization, they will become more committed.
- *Disengagement* This phase is likely to be relatively short. Sales personnel are likely to minimize the importance of both the mone-

tary and non-monetary rewards found in their work. Lower job performance is associated with disengagement which will have direct repercussions on income.

Irrespective of the precise analytical framework used in studying motivation, there are a number of key points which require consideration. Firstly, motivation is a dynamic process. Needs, values, expectations and views of fairness change over time. The career stage of sales personnel will affect what they want and need from work and their perception of their situation. Secondly, the sales manager plays a crucial role in determining and influencing salesforce motivation. The level of support and quality of training must be both appropriate to the needs of the individual and their career development stage. Thirdly, companies differ in the remuneration method being offered to direct sales personnel. The remuneration method being offered will attract different types of people with different needs.

*Training and support*

The earlier discussion of salesforce remuneration and motivation has emphasized the ways in which training and sales support systems assist retention and improve job performance. Effective training involves both a knowledge and a skills component and an important adjunct to such training is the provision of sales support to staff by management. A direct salesforce in financial services has to be fully familiar with all products and services offered by the company as well as understanding legislative requirements. One of the benefits of the Financial Services Act has been to increase the amount of training received by sales personnel.

The salesforce must also understand policies relevant to the selling function. This includes: salesforce compensation methods and evaluation; organization of the company and the relationships between functional areas; work organization and reporting mechanisms and procedures; competitors and their products and services. Most companies are extremely good at conveying the knowledge component of selling to their sales personnel or agents. Selling, though, is a skill which has to be learned, practised and developed. High performing salespeople have learnt and understood the requisite skills and are proficient at putting them into practice. Moreover, they are able to anticipate and plan so they can control sales situations.

## 8.5  Conclusion

Distribution channels represent a central issue in the future development of the financial services industry. Already the effects of electronic technology, deregulation, increased competition and heightened customer awareness have had a significant impact upon the delivery of financial products and services. In the basic bank markets, branch networks have already been modified by number, organization and function, but they will probably remain an important distribution channel in these markets. They will, nevertheless, increasingly be complemented and supplemented by new and emerging distribution systems. In the long term, the effects should produce financial institutions that are far more efficient and competitive, but in the process some of the fundamental aspects of their business may change. Home banking, for instance, will almost certainly provide a most substantive threat to the branch networks in the basic bank markets and introduce a fundamental change in the traditional banker–customer relationship. The traditional 'tied' salesforces of the life companies will constitute a similar threat to the branch network in the emerging private investment markets, especially with the more complicated products, which ideally need a more personalized service. In the final analysis, these and other considerations alluded to in the chapter will almost certainly undermine the branch networks' dominant position. The networks' importance in determining both organizational structure and competitive behaviour will, therefore, be reduced. Branches will, however, continue to form an important distribution channel, which, together with new and emerging distribution channels, will have to be managed in an endeavour to optimize performance. Indeed, the actual management of this mix of distribution channels will be of increasing importance in determining future competitiveness in the financial services market.

# 9  Customer care and service quality

Barbara R. Lewis

## 9.1  Introduction

In the financial services industry, the provision and delivery of services involves a variety of interactions between providers and their customers. In particular, personnel are instrumental in the creation and provision of service quality and, in so doing, they need to 'care' for the customer. The concept of 'customer care' is concerned with customer satisfaction: putting the customer first, anticipating needs and problems, tailoring products and services to meet needs, and being 'nice' to the customer. It also includes: service to the customer; delivery/operations; employee relationships with customers; and internal relationships between employees and management. In developing customer care strategies and programmes, financial services organizations are managing products and services, delivery systems, environment and people so as to provide an efficient and caring service, getting things right the first time, and maintaining standards. This process inevitably brings together marketing, operations management and human resource management. Further, customer care/service quality programmes may be integral to total quality management initiatives within these organizations.

In section 9.2, the reasons for developing customer care and service quality initiatives, and the ensuing benefits, are outlined. Attention is then focused in section 9.3 on the external customer: the elements of customer care are presented, followed by a review of conceptualizations of dimensions of customer care/service quality. The measurement of care/service quality and associated problems are also considered in section 9.4 and 9.5 respectively. Section 9.6 presents an overview of research concerning external customers in financial services. The chapter then moves onto a consideration of the internal customers' role in customer care and the need for internal marketing, in section 9.7, and of enlightened personnel policies to embrace recruitment, selection, training and rewards and recognition (see section 9.8). The penultimate section, on service delivery, highlights some of the issues pertaining to 'managing promises' to customers, namely service guarantees and service recovery procedures to handle customer problems and complaints.

## 9.2   The development of customer care

### 9.2.1  The need for customer care

The need for customer care is driven by customers, employees and a changing business environment. Customers, be they individuals, households or organizations, are increasingly aware of alternatives on offer, in relation to financial products/services and provider organizations, and also of rising standards of service. Consequently, expectations rise and consumers become more critical of the quality of service received, and so companies can never be complacent. In addition, knowledge of the costs and benefits of keeping existing customers relative to attracting new ones, draws companies' attention to looking after present customers, responding to their needs and problems, and developing long-term relationships. Companies realize that looking after customers does not conflict with profitability.

Looking after employees is also an opportunity for an organization. As organizations become larger they may also become anonymous and bureaucratic. Communications may deteriorate and relationships (between customers and customer contact personnel, between customer contact staff and backroom staff, and between staff and management) may suffer. Further, in a recessionary climate, cost-cutting exercises and re-organizations can impact on staff morale, motivation and performance. However, companies are realizing that commitment to employees brings rewards.

The business environment is characterized by economic, legal and technological changes. As Chapter 1 explained, recent deregulation in financial services has increased competition between providers and brought retailers into the industry, thus providing more choice for the consumer. In a competitive environment financial services organizations can react by emphasizing operations and financial efficiency, and/or more focused product and market strategies. Additionally, they can focus on customer care (service and quality) in their corporate and marketing strategies. Superior customer care may be seen as a mechanism to achieve differentiation and a competitive advantage, and so become integral to the overall direction and strategy of an organization. Service quality is such a pre-eminent issue that no major financial services provider can now stand still whilst others are enhancing service levels.

### 9.2.2  Benefits of customer care

Without a focus on customer care and service quality, financial service organizations may face problems and complaints from both employees and customers, and associated financial and other costs. Further, a proportion of dissatisfied customers will complain and tell a number of others, generating adverse word-of-mouth publicity and some may switch to competitors. However, with a focus on care/service an organization can expect a number of benefits:

*Customer loyalty through satisfaction.* Looking after present customers can generate repeat and increased business and may lead to attraction of new customers from positive word-of-mouth communication. Customer retention is more cost effective than trying to attract new customers (Reichheld and Sasser, 1990). Cost savings also accrue from 'getting things right the first time'.

*Increased opportunities for cross selling.* Comprehensive and up-to-date product knowledge and sales techniques among employees, combined with developing relationships and rapport with customers, enables staff to identify customer needs and suggest relevant products/services.

*Employee benefits.* These may be seen in terms of increased job satisfaction, morale and commitment to the company, successful employer–employee relationships and increased staff loyalty, which contribute to reducing the rate of staff turnover and the associated costs of recruitment, selection and training activities. Committed and competent employees will also make fewer mistakes (and in turn lead to fewer customer complaints), and so contribute to further cost savings.

In addition, good customer care/service enhances corporate image and may provide insulation from price competition; some customers may pay a premium for reliable service. Overall, successful service leads to reduced costs (of mistakes, operating, advertising and promotion), and increased productivity and sales, market shares, profitability and business performance.

## 9.3 The external customer

### 9.3.1 The elements of customer care

Customer care for the external customer requires an organization to pay attention to its products/services, delivery systems, delivery environment, technology and employees which are highly interdependent.

*Product/service range.* This will include both basic products and augmented service offerings (Gronroos, 1987). A basic or core financial service product, i.e. what the customer receives, might be a current account with associated services which are *required* to facilitate consumption of the core service (e.g. a cheque book), and supporting services which are not required but may enhance the service and differentiate it from competition (e.g. a cashpoint card). The augmented service offering includes how the service is delivered (process) and the interactions between a bank and its customers which can include: the accessibility of the service (e.g. number of bank clerks and their skills, branch layout); customer participation in the process (e.g. use of ATMs, the need to fill in forms); and the interactions between employees and customers, systems and customers, and the physical environment and customers.

*Delivery systems.* Delivery systems and procedures need to operate efficiently and effectively; they should be responsive and reliable, e.g. to avoid queuing in branches. Silvestro, Fitzgerald, Johnson and Voss, (1992) refer to three types of service process/delivery. Professional services are characterized by few transactions, highly customized services, a process orientation, relatively long contact time, with most value added in the front office. Mass services (e.g. banks, building societies and insurance companies) are typified by many customer interactions, limited contact time and customization, a product orientation, and with value being added in the back office. Service shops would come between the other two types. The extent of direct interaction between service providers and customers in the delivery process has been referred to as Service Encounters or Moments of Truth (e.g. see Albrecht and Zemke, 1985; Czepiel, Solomon and Surprenant, 1985), and may take varying forms. For example, a bank customer wishing to make an account enquiry may choose between an interaction with an ATM, or with a bank employee by telephone, letter or face-to-face in a branch. Every time the customer comes into contact with any aspect of the bank and its employees he or she has an opportunity to form an impression of the bank and its service. Service encounters also have an impact on employees in relation to their motivation, performance and job satisfaction, and their rewards. Recent perspectives and research activities relating to service encounters are reported by Bitner (1990), Bitner, Booms and Tetreault (1990) and Larsson (1990).

*The delivery environment.* The delivery environment includes both physical design and access aspects, and also emotional or atmospheric impact; and is experienced by both customers and employees. Physical design includes layout, signposting, furnishings, noise and music, space, colour, lighting, temperature and comfort; and is evidenced in recent redesign of branches – often more open-plan to eliminate the 'barriers' between customers and branch staff (Greenland, 1994). Access includes hours, availability, convenience of location and privacy. Tangible clues are integral in design of the service environment and may be essential/facilitating (e.g. information leaflets, computers) or peripheral and/or of no independent value (e.g. seats, decor, uniforms). Significant research relating to the physical environment has been carried out by Bitner (1990; 1992). She introduces the concept of 'servicescapes' which may involve customers only (e.g. in self-service), employees only (e.g. remote services), or customer-employee interactions – in most service delivery. She indicates that the physical environment needs to be conducive for both customer satisfaction and employees' ability to work and that perceptions of the environment lead to emotions, attitudes and subsequent behaviours. So, pleasurable environments lead to positive customer evaluations of service and a desire to spend more time and money there, whereas unpleasant servicescapes lead to avoidance.

*Technology.* Technology may be integral to a service product, its environment and delivery, and in financial services recent technological advances have made major contributions to facilitating customer–company exchanges and to increasing levels of service. For example, mechanization and computerization can increase speed, efficiency and accuracy of service (e.g. management and marketing information systems to include customer databases, the bankers' automated clearing system, direct debit facilities and security systems), but can also depersonalize service (e.g. ATMS, home banking). Depersonalized service can free staff either for other activities which may detract from customer contact and lead to less customer loyalty, or to concentrate on developing interactions and relationships to maintain customer loyalty. In all, technology will not replace people in the provision of financial services, and 'high tech' and 'high touch' go hand in hand, with enhanced use of technology acting as a basis for the provision of better personal service.

*Employees.* The role of employees in customer care cannot be overstated and includes their personal qualities, ability to understand and satisfy customer needs, and their skills and knowledge – including flexibility. In section 9.3.2 frameworks for identifying the dimensions of service are summarized, all of which include employee characteristics, which are again brought to light in the empirical research examples. Employees then become the focus of sections 9.7 and 9.8.

### 9.3.2 Dimensions of customer care

As the understanding of customer care and service quality has emerged, researchers have developed conceptualizations of the dimensions of care/ service quality. Lehtinen and Lehtinen (1982) refer to process quality, as judged by consumers during a service, and output quality judged after a service is performed. They also make a distinction between physical quality (products or support), interactive quality (where the dimensions of quality originate in the interaction between the customer and the service organization), and corporate quality (Lehtinen and Lehtinen, 1991).

Gronroos (1984a) discusses the technical (outcome) quality of service encounters, i.e. what is received by the customer, and the functional quality of the process, i.e. the way in which the service is delivered – in relation to staff in a financial services organization, this would include attitudes and behaviour, appearance and personality, service-mindedness, accessibility and approachability of customer contact personnel. In addition, there exists the corporate image dimension of service quality, which is the result of how customers perceive a service organization and is built up by the technical and functional quality of its services. Gummesson and Gronroos (1987) synthesized the Gronroos model with one from manufacturing and incorporated design, production, delivery and relational dimensions of quality. Edvardsson, Gustavsson and Riddle (1989) present four aspects of quality which affect customers' perceptions: technical, integrative, functional and outcome, while LeBlanc and Nguyen (1988) suggest that corporate image, internal organization, physical support of the service producing system, staff–customer interaction and degree of customer satisfaction, all contribute to service quality.

Parasuraman, Zeithaml and Berry (1985; 1988) suggested that the criteria used by consumers that are important in moulding their expectations and perceptions fit ten dimensions:

- Tangibles: physical evidence.
- Reliability: getting it right first time, honouring promises.
- Responsiveness: willingness, readiness to provide service.
- Communication: keeping customers informed in a language they can understand.
- Credibility: honesty, trustworthiness.
- Security: physical, financial and confidentiality, e.g. ATMs.
- Competence: possession of required skills and knowledge of *all* employees.
- Courtesy: politeness, respect, friendliness.
- Understanding/knowing the customer, his or her needs and requirements.
- Access: ease of approach and contact, e.g. opening hours, queues, phones.

Subsequent factor analysis and testing by Parasuraman et al. (1988) condensed these into five categories (tangibles, reliability, responsiveness, assurance and empathy) to which Gronroos (1988) added a sixth dimension – recovery.

Financial services organizations might also consider the contribution of Johnson, Silvestro, Fitzgerald and Voss (1990) and Silvestro and Johnson (1990), investigating service quality in UK organizations, who identified fifteen dimensions of service quality which they categorized as: *hygiene* factors – expected by the customer and where failure to deliver will cause dissatisfaction (e.g. carrying out instructions with respect to standing orders, confidentiality of financial affairs, lack of queues and return of telephone calls); *enhancing* factors – which lead to customer satisfaction but where failure to deliver will not necessarily cause dissatisfaction (e.g. bank clerk addressing you by name); and *dual threshold* factors – where failure to deliver will cause dissatisfaction and delivery above a certain level will enhance customers' perceptions of service and lead to satisfaction (e.g. explanation of a mortgage service – repayment level, interest charges, payback period, and other relevant conditions).

## 9.4 Measurement of customer care/service

Success with respect to customer care/service has traditionally been assessed by measurement of consumer satisfaction. However, as the research literature has evolved, customer service/quality has come to be defined in terms of the difference between consumer expectations and perceptions. Expectations are desires or wants, what people feel a service provider *should* offer, and are formed on the basis of previous experience of a company and all the elements of its marketing mix (including process, people and physical evidence, as suggested by Booms and Bitner, 1981), competition and word-of-mouth communication. Perceptions are consumer judgements about actual service performance/delivery by a company and if there is a shortfall in the comparison between predicted and perceived service then a service quality 'gap' exists which providers would wish to close. Definitions of service (quality) are offered by Gronroos (1984a; 1984b); Berry, Parasuraman and Zeithaml (1988); Berry, Zeithaml and Parasuraman (1985) and Parasuraman et al. (1985; 1988). The consumer service quality gap (i.e. the difference between consumers' expectations of the service and their perceptions of the actual service delivery by an organization) is influenced by four other gaps or shortfalls which were identified from the extensive research of Berry and his colleagues (Parasuraman et al., 1985; Zeithaml, Berry and Parasuraman, 1988):

*Consumer expectations – management perceptions of consumer expectations.* Managers do not necessarily know what customers (both internal and external) want from a company. If managers perceive customer expectations to be lower than they are, the result may be a lower level of delivered service. This gap may be remedied by market research activities, and better communication between management and personnel throughout the organization.

*Management perception of consumer expectations – service quality specifications actually set.* Even if customer needs are known, they may not be translated into appropriate service specifications, due to a lack of resources, organizational constraints or absence of management commitment to a service culture and service quality. Thus actual specifications for service may be below what management believes those specifications should be. The need for management commitment and resources for service quality cannot be over-stated.

*Service quality specifications – actual service delivery.* This gap is referred to as the service performance gap and occurs when the service that is delivered is different from management's specifications for service due to variations in the performance of service personnel. Where delivered service is below service specifications, this outcome may be a consequence of employees not being able or willing to perform at a desired level. It is also possible that highly motivated employees may deliver service in excess of specification which may mitigate the effects of gaps in the perceptions and specifications stages of service delivery.

*Actual service delivery – external communications about the service.* What is said about the service in external communications is different from the service that is delivered, i.e. advertising and promotion can influence consumers' expectations and perceptions of service. Therefore, it is important not to promise more than can be delivered, or fail to present relevant information. Success in this area requires appropriate and timely information/communications both internally and to external customers.

Researchers have developed increasingly sophisticated mechanisms to assess levels of consumers' expectations and perceptions of actual service delivered. Many use rating scales and are similar to, or are adapted from, the SERVQUAL instrument developed by Parasuraman et al. (1988). SERVQUAL has twenty-two pairs of Likert-type scales; the first twenty-two items are designed to measure customer expectations of service for a particular industry and the second twenty-two to measure the perceived level of service provided by a particular organization, e.g.:

Service Expectations:
'customers should be able to trust bank employees'
'customers should not have to queue'
'banks should tailor loans to customer requirements'
              strongly agree .................strongly disagree
                    1      2      3      4      5      6      7

and Perceptions:
'I can trust the employees of my bank'
'I do not have to queue at my bank'
'my bank tailored my loan to meet my needs'
              strongly agree .................strongly disagree
                    1      2      3      4      5      6      7

SERVQUAL provides an indication of the relative importance of Parasuraman et al.'s (1990) five dimensions which influence customers' service perceptions, but is limited to current and past customers as respondents need knowledge and experience of the company being assessed. SERVQUAL and other scales allow researchers and organizations not only to measure performance against customers' expectations but also to: track service quality trends over time; compare branches of a bank or building society; measure performance against competition (competitor mapping); measure the relative importance of service quality dimensions; compare service performance with customer service priorities; and categorize customers (see Parasuraman, Berry and Zeithaml, 1990; Berry et al., 1990). The relative importance of key customer care/service components may also be established from rankings, point allocations, and by trade-off analysis (Christopher and Yallop, 1990). Christopher and Yallop also provide examples of competitor mapping.

## 9.5  Measurement problems

The measurement of service dimensions is, however, fraught with methodological problems relating to the dimensions themselves, variations in customer expectations, and the nature of the measurement tools.

*Dimensions.* Companies need to be aware that some elements of service are easier to evaluate than others (Parasuraman et al., 1985; 1988). For example, tangibles and credibility are known in advance, but most elements are *experience* criteria and can only be evaluated during or after consumption. Some, such as competence and security, may be difficult or impossible to evaluate even after purchase and consumption. In general, consumers rely on experience properties when evaluating services.

*Customer expectations.* Customer expectations are usually reasonable, e.g. they expect ATMs to have sufficient cash and not to have to wait when they visit branches; and they expect basics from a bank with respect to security, cleanliness and being treated with respect. However, expectations vary depending on circumstances and experience, and experience with one service provider may influence expectations of others. In addition, consumers have what Parasuraman, Berry and Zeithaml (1991b) refer to as 'Zones of Tolerance', the difference between desired and adequate expectations. The desired level of service expectation is what they hope to receive, a blend of what 'can' and 'should' be, which is a function of past experience. The adequate level is what is acceptable, based on an assessment of what the service 'will be' – the 'predicted' service – and depends on the alternatives which are available. Tolerance zones vary between individuals and companies, service aspects, and with experience, and tend to be smaller for outcome features than for process dimensions. In addition, if options are limited, tolerance zones/levels may be higher than if many alternatives are available and it is easy to switch service providers. Further, expectations are higher in emergency situations (e.g. theft of a cheque book, loss of credit cards), and when something was not right the first time.

One also needs to realize that as customers are increasingly aware of the alternatives on offer and rising standards of service, expectations may change over time. Higher levels of performance lead to higher expectations. Also, over time, the dimensions of care/service may change and the relative importance of such factors. In addition, research and measurement usually focuses on routine service situations. Organizations also need to consider non-routine service encounters which may have a major impact on consumer (and employee) evaluations and satisfactions. An example would be service recovery situations, i.e. what happens when something goes wrong.

*Measurement tools.* Problems with SERVQUAL are highlighted by the authors themselves (Parasuraman, Berry and Zeithaml, 1991a) and in other research studies (Babakus and Boller, 1992; Carmen, 1990; Lewis and Mitchell, 1990; Smith, 1992; Lewis, 1993; Brown, Churchill and Peter, 1993; Lewis, Orledge and Mitchell, 1994). They relate to: respondent difficulties with negatively worded statements; using two lists of statements for the same items; the number of dimensions of service being assessed; ease of consumer assessment; and timing of measurement – before, during or after a service encounter. Parasuraman et al. (1991b; 1993) have addressed some of these issues and made amendments to SERVQUAL.

Rating scales in general raise questions with respect to: verbal labels and the use of extremes; interpretation of the mid-point of unlabelled scales; the propensity to indicate only positive or desirable answers; the number of scale points; and the measurement of desired as against adequate levels of care/service. Finally, researchers also need to be aware of cultural differences in attitudes and behaviour (of both internal and external customers – with respect to all the elements of customer care), and the cultural context of a rating scale assessment and consumer willingness to respond and if necessary criticize companies and service; both of which affect responses.

## 9.6   Customers: An overview of research findings

In the UK and Europe, there have been a number of consumer-based research projects that uncover the dimensions of care and service in financial services, relating to products/services, systems and technology, environment and employees. (There is also an extensive body of literature relating to the US experience which is not covered here due to space limitations. A useful introduction to this literature is contained in Rust and Oliver (1994)). Buswell (1983) identified five key service elements for a major British clearing bank: knowledge of staff, communications, expertise of staff, willingness to lend and branch design. Consumer attitudes towards these dimensions enabled the bank to develop benchmarks and a system which could reveal changes in service at a particular branch over time and to distinguish between branches at the same point in time.

Subsequent research has been carried out in the Financial Services Research Centre at the Manchester School of Management, to identify key dimensions of service and to assess service performance with respect to these dimensions for a number of major financial services providers – primarily banks and building societies in relation to both personal and small business customers. Lewis and Smith (1989) investigated the expectations and perceptions of bank and building society retail customers with regard to thirty-nine elements of service, grouped into four dimensions: physical features and facilities, reliability, characteristics of staff who customers come into contact with, and responsiveness to customer needs. Half the respondents had come to expect a better service from their banks and building societies in recent years, many believed that service had improved, and there was a great deal of satisfaction with the overall quality of service received. In particular, the organizations were successful with respect to elements of reliability (e.g. accuracy of transactions, ability to do things right, ability to keep promises, and competence of back-room staff); and responsiveness to needs (e.g. with respect to willingness of management and staff to help with problems and queries). In response to open-ended questions, particularly good aspects of service were found to relate to staff personal qualities. Nevertheless, a number of service quality gaps came to light; e.g. there were problems in relation to staff not knowing personal needs, insufficient individualized attention, lack of information about new services, perceptions of not enough staff available to serve – especially at peak times, and poor complaint handling – which could lead to account closure.

The responses from these retail bank customers were compared with a sample from the USA (Lewis, 1991). The international comparison provided evidence of cultural differences in attitudes and behaviour which impact on expectations and perceptions, e.g. the US customers visited their banks more frequently – largely explained by the practice of payment by cheque rather than by direct credit transfer to an account, or cash. Further, although they were more satisfied with the personal characteristics of staff and their banks' responsiveness to their needs, they appeared to be less satisfied with the overall quality of service they received, than their UK counterparts.

In addition, Smith (1989; 1990) investigated relationships between banks and their small business customers. She found, from in-depth interviews, that the key elements of service related to: bank personnel (do they understand the client and his or her potential needs?), organization and structure of banks (are they bureaucratic and are policymakers remote from local managers?), pricing policies (high interest charges and collateral requirements) and product offerings (sometimes seen as too complex). A total of fifty-five elements of service were then incorporated into structured rating questions for respondents to indicate expectations and perceptions/satisfactions. The most important elements were: accuracy or competence aspects; confidentiality and trustworthiness of the bank manager; promises being kept; reliability in the branch and at head office; and speed with regard to decision making, transactions and dealing with customers. In relation to perceptions of service, a number of problem areas emerged: for example, queuing with personal customers, charges, lack of explanations and collateral requirements.

A further study (Lewis, Orledge and Mitchell, 1994) took account of some of the problems associated with SERVQUAL and scaling techniques, and used a graphic positioning scale to assess the opinions of university students with respect to their banks' and building societies' provision of service in general, and loan and overdraft facilities and arrangements in particular. A typical question was:

Indicate how well you feel banks and building societies in general should perform by marking an 'E' on the scale. On the same scale,

please indicate with a 'P' how well your bank or building society performs.
smart and tidy appearance of employees......E.........P........untidy appearance of employees
up-to-date equipment.......E......P...........outdated equipment

Measuring expectations and perceptions at the same time enabled the students to visualize the distance between their bank and banks in general. Further, the gap scores were weighted by the expectation scores to reflect the importance of the factors and the magnitude of the gaps. Findings indicated that, overall, the banks and building societies were performing well in relation to their employees' personal characteristics, but could improve with respect to knowledge aspects, speed and efficiency, queuing and convenience. In relation to loan and overdraft facilities, a number of service shortfalls were identified mainly in relation to explanations of charges and conditions, approachability of managers, and privacy.

## 9.7 The internal customer

The role of an organization's employees in customer care has come increasingly to the forefront, and investment in people becomes integral to the service–profit chain as described by Schlesinger and Heskett (1991a):

Internal Service Quality → Employee Satisfaction → Employee Retention → External Service Quality → Customer Satisfaction → Customer Retention → Profit

Much of the given attention to employees relates to the concept of internal marketing. Internal marketing views employees as internal customers and jobs as internal products (Berry, 1980), and a company needs to sell its jobs to employees before selling its service(s) to external customers (Sasser and Arbeit, 1976), i.e. satisfying the needs of internal customers upgrades the capability to satisfy the needs of external customers. Gronroos (1981; 1985) referred to three objectives of internal marketing:

- Overall: to achieve motivated, customer conscious and care orientated personnel.
- Strategic: to create an internal environment which supports customer-consciousness and sales mindedness among personnel.
- Tactical: to sell service campaigns and marketing efforts to employees – the first marketplace of the company – via staff training programmes and seminars.

Internal marketing is primarily the province of human resource management within a company, who have responsibilities for developing enlightened personnel policies to include recruitment, selection and training, and also appraisal, rewards and recognition – for all employees, both customer contact and backroom staff in the branch, at region and at head office. Successful personnel policies include recruitment and selection of the 'right' people. Key characteristics for employees to perform effectively may relate to: process and technical skills; interpersonal and communication skills; teamwork skills; flexibility and adaptability; and empathy with the external customer. In general, employees must be able and willing to deliver desired levels of service in order to minimize gaps between service specifications and delivered service (Zeithaml et al., 1988). Employees' contributions in meeting customer needs cannot be over-emphasized.

Schlesinger and Heskett (1991b) stress that companies should realize that regardless of education levels people need training. Training needs will, however, vary as a function of the amount of contact (visible and non-visible) with customers, the skills and equipment/technology required, and the extent of relationships with customers and with other employees (Gronroos, 1990). Such needs, of both new and present employees, may be identified by a training audit, and translated into training activities.

Typically, training programmes cover: product, company and systems knowledge; awareness of employees' role in assessing and meeting customer needs; and the economic impact of everyone working together to support company goals. Critical to this is a focus on service encounters or relationships within organizations, at *all* levels and *between* levels (Lewis and Entwistle, 1990), which contribute to the service delivered to external customers. This includes relationships between: customer contact and backroom staff; operations and non-operations staff; and staff and management at all levels and locations – branch, region and head office. For example, customer contact personnel may want information and responsiveness from back-office or operations employees in the branch or head office – or from a management team to facilitate serving the customer. If these internal encounters are poor, the customer may be dissatisfied, complain and blame the customer contact personnel. Thus, a financial services organization needs to be aware of these relationships and manage them effectively.

In addition to product/technical knowledge and relationship management, personal skills and interpersonal communication skill development is vital. This allows organizations to *empower* employees to exercise judgement and creativity in responding to customer needs and problems (see Schlesinger and Heskett, 1991b). Empowerment should lead to better job performance and improved morale. It is a form of job enrichment, evidenced by increased commitment to jobs and reflected in attitudes towards customers. Knowing that management has confidence in employees helps create positive attitudes in the workplace and good relationships between employees, and between employees and customers.

Zeithaml et al. (1988) indicated that successful training programmes will lead to:

- Teamwork: evidenced by a caring management and involved and committed employees.
- Employee–job fit: the ability of employees to perform a job.

- Technology–job fit: are the 'tools' appropriate for the employee and the job?
- Perceived control: e.g. do employees have flexibility in dealing with customers? If not stress levels may rise and performance decrease.
- Supervisory control systems: based on behaviours rather than output quality.
- Avoidance of role conflict: for employees in satisfying employees' expectations of the company and expectations of customers.
- Avoidance of role ambiguity: employees should know what is expected of them and how performance will be evaluated.

Employee rewards were considered by Berry (1981) who discussed the associated possibilities for market research and segmentation. He suggested that organizations should carry out research among employees to identify their needs, wants and attitudes with respect to working conditions, benefits and company policies. Further, he indicated that people are as different as employees as consumers, and might be segmented in a number of ways, for example, with respect to flexible working hours which lead to increased job satisfaction, increased productivity and decreased absenteeism. In addition, 'cafeteria benefits' could be appropriate with respect to health insurance, pensions and holidays – the notion being that employees use 'credits' (a function of salary, service, age etc.) to choose their benefits. Berry was indicating a need for staff fringe benefits which embrace the heterogeneity of the labour force, and thus upgrade an organization's capacity to satisfy the needs of its external customers. Present-day staff benefits and facilities include restaurants, sports facilities, and crèches and nurseries. Koula (1992) also refers to pensions, mortgages, loans and insurance at reduced rates for financial services employees, and share options and profit sharing schemes. Recent attention of service companies is focused on issues of supervision, appraisal and performance evaluation together with performance related pay, recognition and reward schemes for excellent employees. Customer service awards may be financial or not, and may involve career development.

Financial services organizations were amongst the first major companies in the UK to invest significant amounts of money in customer care training programmes and were researched by Smith and Lewis (1988;1989) at an early stage of their development. Expenditure was viewed as long-term investment, and the programmes were designed to move a company to a service-oriented culture by breaking down barriers and improving internal communications, which necessitated changes in employee and management attitudes. Overall, the organizations wanted to: emphasize the need for high levels of service and the importance of the customer; train staff to deal effectively with customers; motivate staff through encouragement and rewards; and develop new styles of leadership and management. Consequently, they developed an array of management and staff training activities with variable success at that time. However, most, it not all, are now significantly further down the road in understanding the customer care concept and the principles which guide success.

Successful personnel policies require human resource managers to develop relationships not only with employees but also with marketing managers and operations management. Collins and Payne (1991) high-light some of the challenges and opportunities confronting inter-depart-mental organizational relationships. Success should also lead to appropriate service cultures to support relationships with external markets.

## 9.8   Employees: An overview of research findings

Lewis (1989) reported findings from leading UK banks and building socie-ties which had embarked on extensive and expensive customer care train-ing programmes. Employees, mainly those with customer contact, provided opinions with respect to: internal service encounters and rela-tionships; perceptions of customer service in their organizations; training for customer service; and areas for service improvement. At this time, there was evidence of a number of deficiencies with regard to personnel initiatives and customer care training activities resulting in: problems in meeting customer expectations and providing good service to all custo-mers, all of the time (e.g. insufficient product knowledge, dealing effec-tively with customers' queries and problems); and criticisms of internal interpersonal relationships, at all levels (e.g. attitudes of backroom staff to customer contact staff and customers, and between branch staff and head office employees).

More recently, Koula (1992) surveyed senior managers and other per-sonnel in a major Cyprus bank. Questions focused on: customer and service orientation of the bank; the role of personnel in service delivery; corporate objectives with regard to personnel; internal communications; recruitment and training procedures; interpersonal attitudes and beha-viour (e.g. relationships, teamwork and co-operation); employee commit-ment; and appraisal, rewards and benefits. Koula's findings showed that the senior managers realized the importance of a motivated workforce and of their personnel in the delivery of service, and the personnel appeared to have both the requisite capabilities and the confidence in themselves to perform well. There was also evidence of a good teamwork spirit and good interpersonal relationships and communications between customer contact and non-contact employees. Nevertheless, a number of shortfalls were evident between management and personnel perspectives which affected morale and motivation, quality of work and subsequently, the quality of service provided to the external customer. There was evi-dence of: role ambiguity – some staff being uncertain about what was expected of them; policies and procedures which limited the freedom of some employees to act in the delivery of service to external customers; role conflict – although they were confident in their ability to satisfy customers, some employees felt overworked; and differences of opinion with respect to the objectives of the control and reward systems – which again affect morale and performance.

Further research activity has focused on banks in Norway (Gabrielsen, 1993), where recent severe economic pressures have led to government intervention and control, and significant rationalization and restructuring (including layoffs) among the major banks. Even so, service quality initiatives and customer care training are a strategic priority. Gabrielsen interviewed senior managers and then developed a structured survey questionnaire completed by employees. He developed eighty-four attitude statements covering a number of key dimensions of organization, staffing and training to include: culture and environment; individual attitudes; attitudes towards management; role perception and training; organizational structure; evaluation and rewards; service recovery; and improvements which could be made. The findings again highlight the successes and potential failure points of internal marketing.

## 9.9  Service delivery

When an organization has assessed key variables of customer care/service, translated them into service standards and systems, and recruited and trained employees, it then has to 'manage its promises' so as to minimize any possible gap between the service promised to customers and the service delivered (Parasuraman et al., 1985; Zeithaml et al., 1988). What is said about the service in external communications should match the service that is delivered. Advertising and promotion can influence consumers' expectations and perceptions and, therefore, it is important not to promise more than can be delivered or fail to present relevant information. Realistic communications are needed so as not to increase expectations unnecessarily and decrease perceptions and satisfaction.

### 9.9.1  Service guarantees

As consumer expectations and company standards rise, service providers become competitive in the promises they make to consumers, and there is now increasing evidence of 'service guarantees' in both the public and private sectors. Examples of unconditional service guarantees include: Marriott hotels which offer cash compensation if difficulties are not resolved in thirty minutes; a pizza delivery which becomes free after a certain time delay; British Telecom promises with regard to waiting periods for telephone installations and repair of faults; the Royal Mail's compensation for late/lost delivery and damaged items; and Government Charters for health care and other public services. The use of such guarantees in financial services is not extensive although some banks including Co-operative and Midland do offer financial compensations for genuine mistakes. More generally, the UK banks and building societies now each have a Code of Practice in which they outline their commitment to customers, advise them of their rights and provide freephone (0800) telephone numbers for customer service, advice, queries and complaints.

Hart (1988) summarizes key considerations relating to service guarantees. Some aspects of service and customer satisfaction cannot be guaranteed, e.g. unconditional on-time arrival of planes, and so guarantees must be realistic. A good service guarantee should be unconditional, easy to understand and communicate, easy to invoke and easy to collect on. It should also be meaningful, in particular with respect to payout (which should be a function of the cost of the service), seriousness of failure and perception of what is fair. Ideally, a service guarantee should get everyone in a company to focus on good service, and to examine service delivery systems for possible failure points. However, inevitably, failures may occur and a proportion of customers will become dissatisfied, of whom only a small proportion will complain. The reasons why dissatisfied people keep quiet are discussed by Goodman, Marra and Brigham (1986) and Horovitz (1990) and include:

- fear of hassles or too much trouble to complain
- no one is available to complain to or there is no easy channel by which to communicate disquiet
- no one cares and it won't do any good
- do not know where to complain to
- customers attributing themselves as a source of service problems by their failure to perform in the creation of a service.

Hart, Heskett and Sasser (1990) discuss the additional costs of replacing customers over those of trying to retain customers who may be dissatisfied. They also refer to evidence of customers who complain and who then receive a satisfactory response subsequently being more loyal to an organization, more likely to buy other services/products, and more likely to engage in positive word-of-mouth communication. Reichheld and Sasser (1990) also refer to financial benefits of retaining customers and the need, if possible, to monitor defecting customers and their reasons for leaving a company. Consequently, financial services companies are encouraging dissatisfied customers to complain, in order to discourage negative word-of-mouth communication and to retain rather than replace customers. In so doing, they are managing service recovery.

### 9.9.2 Service recovery

The service recovery process is presented by Hart et al. (1990) and Mason (1993). Financial services organizations, typically, strive for zero defects in their service delivery, i.e. 100 per cent customer satisfaction, to get things right the first time. Consequently, they develop their service quality systems which tend to be rigid with sophisticated techniques and structured personnel policies – to try to provide consistent high quality service. But problems do occur (e.g. employees may be sick and absent), and mistakes will happen (e.g. a lost cheque book or incorrect statement). The challenge for banks and building societies is to recover the problem or mistake and get it very right the second time – to turn frustrated customers into loyal ones.

Service recovery has been defined as 'a planned process/strategy of returning an aggrieved/dissatisfied customer to a state of satisfaction with a company/service', making a special effort to put things right when something is wrong. This includes: focus on critical service encounters and anticipating and preventing possible failure points; identifying service problems; making it easy to complain (e.g. free telephone numbers); conducting research (e.g. phoning customers to check on services delivered); tracking and analysing failures; offering rewards for improvement suggestions; and measuring performance against standards.

When problems do occur, companies have to expedite service recovery to meet customers' recovery expectations – which may now be even higher than initial expectations. It is increasingly accepted that companies should first believe the customer, acknowledge the problem, take responsibility and avoid defensiveness. They should also apologize, and then fix the problem and recompense explicit and hidden costs if appropriate. Service recovery is 'emotional and physical repair'. Organizations need to deal with the customer first and then his or her problem (Hart et al., 1990). Service recovery strategies should be flexible and integral to this is the role of front-line employees and the extent to which they have been empowered to respond to the customer. Do they have the authority, responsibility and incentives/rewards to identify, care about and solve customer problems and complaints? Are they allowed to use their judgement and creative and communication skills to develop solutions to satisfy customers? Successful service recovery has economic benefits in terms of customer retention and loyalty. It is also a means to identify organizational problems with respect to all the dimensions of customer care, and to improve overall customer awareness and care.

## 9.10  Conclusion

In this chapter, the need for excellent customer care and service quality initiatives in financial services organizations has been highlighted, and has focused on both internal and external customers. Attention has been given to the elements and dimensions of customer care/service quality and how they might be measured. The concept of internal marketing and the need for appropriate personnel policies has also been presented. The final section has focused on increasingly important aspects of service delivery, namely service guarantees and service recovery.

Customer care programmes are high priorities in financial services organizations with expenditure viewed as long-term investment for future growth and profitability. To summarize, successful customer care strategies require substantial investments of time, money and the need to:

- Research and understand customer needs and expectations at all service encounters, i.e. at all stages in the service delivery process.

To identify the key components of customer care/service quality, and measure their importance.

- Develop enlightened personnel policies. Recruit the right people. Research and understand employee needs and expectations. Structure training programmes to: meet these needs; motivate employees towards commitment to the organization and its objectives; understand and respond to customer needs and the needs/wants of other employees; and provide product/service knowledge, personal and communication skills. Reward appropriately.
- Develop: products/services to meet customer needs; systems and procedures which are customer and employee focused, responsive, flexible and reliable; and a suitable delivery environment – including retail design.
- Make best use of technology in products/services, systems and environment – to ensure speed, accuracy and efficiency.
- Manage the delivery process. Pay attention to potential failure points, complaint handling and service recovery procedures, which become integral to employee training – i.e. empowering employees to exercise responsibility, judgement and creativity in responding to customers' problems.
- Monitor the customer care/service quality programme. Develop systems to research and evaluate customer satisfactions and dissatisfactions, and employee performance. Review customer care objectives.

Overall, financial services providers need to have a commitment to customer care and the creation of an appropriate culture. The organizational culture may require change, towards employee orientation to the company, and everyone's orientation to the external customer. This change starts at the top; the customer care process must begin with senior management commitment to employees and customers, hopefully with strong and visible leaders.

# 10 Bank marketing

Mike Wright and Barry Howcroft

## 10.1 Introduction

Banks were traditionally in the 'business of banking', namely borrowing from one market and lending to another. However, as seen in Chapter 1, since the early 1970s, their orientation has become the 'business of financial services', with a much wider focus in relation to consumer/market needs and consequent marketing strategies. This wider range of activities is expected to be maintained despite subsequent retrenchment from some product areas.

The UK banking system is dominated by the Big Four, Barclays, National Westminster, Midland and Lloyds (Table 10.1). After a lengthy period of stability in the structure of the industry, following notable mergers in the 1960s, further restructuring became more in evidence in the late 1980s and early 1990s. The TSB Group underwent substantial reorganization and stock market flotation. The Clydesdale Bank was sold by the Midland Bank to the National Australian Bank. Williams' and Glyn's Bank, which has long been a part of the Royal Bank of Scotland whilst maintaining its separate identity in England, became fully incorporated into the Scottish bank's corporate identity. In a further strategic development, reflecting some major non-UK banks' desires to extend their cross-border activities for the reasons outlined in Chapter 1, the Yorkshire Bank was acquired by National Australian Bank, who fought off competing bids from Deutsche Bank and BNP. The number of major banking groups was increased by the conversion of the Abbey National from a building society to a bank in 1989. The proposed merger between the Halifax and Leeds Permanent building societies announced in November 1994 was also linked to subsequent conversion of the new entity to bank status (see Chapters 1 and 12).

Perhaps most notable have been the developments in the 1990s involving the smaller of the Big Four banks, the Midland and Lloyds. As discussed in more detail below, the former was acquired by Hong Kong and Shangai Banking Corporation in 1993. Lloyds, having failed in its attempt to merge with Midland, became the first bank to acquire a major building society with its purchase in 1994 of Cheltenham and Gloucester. These developments have important implications for further diversification by banks beyond what has already taken place. To date, diversification has resulted in varying degrees of success as shown by the profits profile of the banks between 1983 and 1993 (Table 10.1). By extension, there are also implications for marketing strategies.

**Table 10.1** *Major banks' assets and profits (£m)*

| Bank | 1983 | | 1988 | | 1993 | |
|---|---|---|---|---|---|---|
| | Assets | Pre-tax profits | Assets | Pre-tax profits | Assets | Pre-tax profits |
| Barclays | 57 976 | 485 | 104 645 | 1391 | 166 008 | 664 |
| NatWest | 59 880 | 519 | 98 642 | 1407 | 152 862 | 989 |
| Midlands | 52 613 | 225 | 55 729 | 693 | 76 431 | 844 |
| Lloyds | 38 432 | 419 | 51 834 | 952 | 79 757 | 1031 |
| Standard Chartered | 28 917 | 268 | 23 692 | 313 | 31 883 | 401 |
| TSB | 9185 | 150 | 22 516 | 420 | 31 417 | 301 |
| Royal Bank of Scotland | 11 077 | 96 | 21 660 | 309 | 36 294 | 265 |
| Bank of Scotland | 5361 | 50 | 11 005 | 131 | 28 809 | 125 |
| Abbey National | 14 312 | 119 | 31 537 | 414 | 83 802 | 704 |
| Clydesdale Bank Group | 2254 | 18 | 3561 | 30 | 5562 | 89 |
| The Co-operative Bank Group | 1064 | 8 | 2228 | 23 | 3399 | 18 |
| Girobank | 904 | 16 | 1865 | 21 | 3265 | 75 |
| Yorkshire Bank Group | 1330 | 37 | 3185 | 100 | 3966 | 131 |

*Source: Annual Abstract of Banking Statistics, Vol. 11, 1994*

In this chapter, the focus is the marketing strategies and activities of the major UK banks in the provision of both personal and corporate services. The setting of marketing objectives and the design of marketing strategies are elements within the marketing planning process (see Chapter 3) whereby a bank will carry out, on an iterative basis: an audit of the company, its markets and environment; determine strengths and weaknesses, opportunities and threats; set objectives; develop strategies and tactics; and implement, evaluate and control the total marketing programme.

Initial attention is given, briefly, to aspects of the marketing audit, in particular the changing environment (section 10.2). This broad starting point is followed in section 10.3 by a review of the strategic considerations relating to market segments, including issues concerning banks' overall competitive strategies, as a precursor to analysis of the marketing mix. It is important to bear in mind that for such an approach to be effective requires a marketing-oriented internal culture within a bank where employees are fully attuned to why there is a need to serve customers better and how it is to be achieved. The AIB Group, for example (Bourke, 1992), in effecting a change from a traditional banking approach to a more marketing-oriented direction undertook a fundamental restructuring of activities in which the first five-year long implementation stage was based on strategy, information systems, leadership, professionalism, structure and technology. This stage was divided into four phases which involved creating awareness amongst staff, defining the change in management approach, involving staff in ideas for change in order to obtain commitment, and connecting change to the marketplace. This last phase consisted of five elements: building understanding of marketing principles and how to apply them; improving customer focus by practical action on the ground; focusing on the specific changes that are necessary in the way business is carried out; providing a bottom-up input into strategy development; and defining what the new customer-focused job role should be. Internal research after three years showed widespread support for the programme.

## 10.2 The marketing audit

The basis of the market audit is to review and analyse all the business conditions affecting a bank and its operations.

### 10.2.1 Environmental analysis

The major elements in the changing environment of the clearing banks, which impact on all elements of their marketing strategies are:

*Economic elements.* Inflation, interest rates and employment levels: demand for financial services is usually derived from the demand for other products and services which are affected by economic conditions.

*Demographics.* The changing age distribution of the population and how increasing education levels affect people's financial service needs.

*Social and cultural factors.* Changing lifestyles and public opinion have a number of effects, e.g. traditional values with respect to thrift and the stigma of credit are disappearing, with the emergence of a credit culture and the consequent changes in attitudes and behaviour with regard to spending and the use of a wide range of credit services. In addition, consumer attitudes towards technologically based bank services continue to become more favourable, and consumers are more discerning with respect to expectations of service quality and the quality of service actually received.

*Technological developments.* Technological developments are evident in the operations and management of banks and have emerged as important considerations in product design, delivery channels and promoting individual products and overall corporate image.

*Legal/political.* In a number of important respects government continues to play a major role. New patterns of consumer behaviour are encouraged in terms of home ownership, share ownership, pension planning, taxation etc. Furthermore, as seen in Chapter 1, de-regulatory legislation in the form of the Banking Act and the Building Societies Act has been designed to remove competitive barriers and create open and free markets, although this has been accompanied by regulatory supervision (i.e. the Financial Services Act).

*Competition.* The changing legislative environment of the late 1980s created both opportunities and threats for the banks in terms of the level of competition from existing bank competitors, new bank competitors (e.g. overseas banks in the light of the advent of the EC Single Market in 1992), and new market entrants to include building societies, retailers and other current and potential providers of financial services, e.g. American Express, estate agents, accountants and solicitors.

The building societies are developing growth and competitive strategies in a number of ways (see Chapter 12), in particular with respect to their branching and product policies. Retailers have few barriers to entry into financial services and can take advantage of their store networks and technological capabilities which are alternatives to the traditional bank branch. A number of retailers will eventually offer a wide range of financial services and one can pose the question as to whether or not companies like Marks & Spencer will follow the Sears Roebuck example and move beyond credit cards and loans, into insurance, mortgages and other financial services. To do so would enable them to focus on long-term relationships with households and to meet their changing financial service needs over time: an appropriate strategy might be to offer innovative products/services on the basis of superior value/quality, and to provide excellent customer service.

Competitor analysis will include not only identification of key organizations/sectors but also their position and coverage in the market, and their image.

*Market analysis.* The objectives of market analysis are to monitor trends relating to size and market share, competitive position and growth potential; to investigate customer profiles, needs and market segments; and to consider influences on the consumer decision-making process in relation to buying financial services.

### 10.2.2 Internal analysis

In conjunction with environmental and market analysis, a bank needs to audit its internal resources to include its people, production capacity, financial/investment capabilities, management expertise, together with its product range and branch network and delivery systems. As a result, the bank should be in a position to identify its internal strengths and weaknesses and to match its strengths to the opportunities in the environment and market. In the process the bank should also convert its weaknesses to strengths, thereby avoiding environmental/marketing threats, and move towards marketing planning, i.e. setting objectives and marketing strategies.

## 0.3   Growth and competitive strategies

The marketing strategies of banks follow from their broader strategies towards growth and competitiveness. Of particular relevance here is their product/market mix (see Chapter 4), from which the other elements of the marketing mix follow. The main growth strategies are via market penetration, market development, product development and diversification (see Ansoff, 1965 and the discussion in Chapter 4).

### 10.3.1 Market penetration

The focus of this strategy is to increase sales of present products/services in present markets, by means of increased and/or more effective positioning and targeting, delivery and promotional activities. Various penetration objectives and strategies prevail.

*Selling present services to new customers*

Within the framework of current customer segments (e.g. students, high net worth individuals, self-employed), the banks may wish to attract a higher share of the market which may be achieved via:

- new residents in an area, who may be 'persuaded' to switch banks and who may be targeted for a wide range of services
- new bank users (e.g. students or weekly cash-paid workers) – typically targeted for current accounts
- individuals who decide to become self-employed and need tax advice/planning, pension plans etc.
- competitors, in respect of any or all present markets or products.

When communicating with potential customers in these categories, a major emphasis will be to promote a competitive advantage or superiority over other banks and financial services providers with respect to products, price and delivery systems, and may include promotional gifts (to students and young people).

*Selling more service to present customers*

This involves trying to develop relationships with existing customers in order to cross-sell other services, e.g. promoting savings accounts to people with bank mortgages, investment/pensions plans/PEPs to professional customers. This is perhaps the most important growth strategy for banks but to achieve success they need to be efficient and effective with respect to:

- segmenting present markets and determining customers' needs for further services
- advertising and promotion including direct mail and telephone selling in order to reach customers
- personal selling, in the branch and/or via 'account representatives', a factor which has implications for continuing sales training for all customer contact employees.

*Encouraging increased product/service usage*

There is only limited analogy here between financial products and traditional product-based industries but customers might increase their savings/deposit levels if terms are sufficiently attractive, or if satisfied with a particular service – e.g. investment advice, share dealing.

## Discouraging account switching

A further means of increasing market shares is to maintain customer loyalty at a higher level compared to competitors, i.e. reduce customer dissatisfaction and switching behaviour to other organizations. This may be achieved by giving appropriate attention to customer service and service quality, i.e. by developing systems and training personnel to provide high levels of service quality and by establishing procedures to deal with customer problems and complaints, thus expediting 'recovery'.

### 10.3.2 Market development

Banks are concerned with developing sales of their present products/ services in new markets. This is perhaps a difficult route for UK banks which already have wide market coverage with respect to personal financial services, but examples of market development include:

- New segments within broadly defined existing markets, e.g. the targeting of working women, in particular those who have not previously been potential customers for mortgages/loans/ investment advice etc.
- New markets based on geographic factors. A number of opportunities prevail with regard to international market expansion following the abolition of exchange controls and the introduction of 'open' European markets from 1992. Additionally, some of the UK banks are already pursuing growth in North America, partly via merger and acquisition with US banks.

### 10.3.3 Product development

The objectives of product development are to introduce and develop sales of new products/services in present markets. This is most evident in all the UK banks and has resulted, primarily, from a combination of legislative, technological and competitive change. It is doubtful whether the banks would have envisaged, twenty years ago, the amount of change which would occur and the consequential need to develop and introduce new products/services in order to remain competitive and grow.

Product development may be, as already highlighted, a modification of existing banking products, e.g. interest on current accounts; advancements in delivery systems, e.g. home banking and remote ATMs; or expansion into financial services, e.g. life assurance, tax services, financial advice, travel related services.

### 10.3.4 Diversification

The fourth type of growth strategy, diversification, refers to attempts to grow by simultaneously focusing on new services and new markets, in an endeavour to pursue 'newness' outside the mainstream of present business, e.g. by offering an integrated house buying service to include conveyancing and estate agency, or agency business activities by linking with pension or insurance brokers, stockbrokers etc.

In addition to the various growth strategies banks might also consider 'competitive' strategies, i.e. the extent to which they wish to be one of the following:

- A market leader: with an emphasis on market share, economies of scale, a strong distribution network etc.
- A market challenger: also with an emphasis on market share but together with aggressive pricing, delivery and promotional tactics.
- A market follower: attempting to maintain or build a market share and profitability, and focusing on cautious marketing tactics.
- A market nicher: focusing on niches with respect to products and markets, i.e. NOT trying to offer all financial services to all markets.

At the time that widespread deregulation was beginning to affect the financial services sector in 1987, a survey by Ennew and Wright (1990b) found that over a third of UK banks were already highly diversified with a competitive advantage based on differentiation (Table 10.2). When asked where they expected to be in five years time, that is by 1992, of those banks pursuing strategies based on low cost over half expected to move towards differentiation strategies. Only one bank expected to move in the opposite direction. Note that a significant proportion of the banks expected to maintain their narrow niche-based strategies. However, with many banks intending to pursue similar broad-based strategies, at a time when other financial services firms were also doing the same (Ennew et al., 1989), questions were raised as to whether all could succeed unless overall demand increased quite dramatically. As shown in Chapter 1, major problems arose for many banks who pursued broad diversification strategies, which were often followed by subsequent divestment. Notable divestments by banks include the sale of its credit card operations by Chase Manhattan (acquired by Alliance and Leicester Building Society), the sale by Lloyds Bank of its Black Horse estate agency to Abbey Life and TSB's divestment of its Target Life insurance acquisition. It should be noted, however, that such divested assets may be purchased by other banks seeking to build on their skills base. For example, towards the end of 1994 Hambro Countrywide, the estate agency subsidiary of Hambros Bank, acquired the estate agencies of the Nationwide Building Society. Whilst the Nationwide decided to divest because of the failure of the estate agency chain to generate significant extra mortgage business and cross-sell other products, Hambro sought to focus on house sales, the core income generating activity of the chain.

**Table 10.2**  *Banks' corporate strategies*

|  | 1987 (%) | Expected 1992 (%) |
|---|---|---|
| Narrow product range to few market sectors | 27 | 14 |
| Narrow product range to many market sectors | 14 | 10 |
| Broad product range to few market sectors | 23 | 24 |
| Broad product range to many market sectors | 36 | 52 |

*Source:* Ennew and Wright (1990)

One of the most notable reversals of a broad-based differentiation strategy concerns the state-owned French bank Credit Lyonnais, which encountered severe problems in its strategy to become a major pan-European bank. In 1993 the bank reported a loss of FF6.9 billion after provisions against bad risks of FF17.8 billion, half of which was in respect of non-traditional banking activities. The bank's solvency ratio of 8.3 per cent was also weak. In order to strengthen its position the bank, under new senior management, has now embarked on a two-pronged strategy. First it aims to improve profitability and efficiency in its core banking business. To achieve this strategy measures taken by the bank include, in the UK, closure of some retail branches and a greater emphasis on corporate banking and market trading, new centralized management of European banking and the introduction of worldwide foreign exchange trading. The second element of the new strategy is to divest FF20 billion worth of non-core industrial shareholdings in 1994–95, including a part sale of its stake in the UAF life insurance company (*Financial Times*, 22.9.94, p.31).

Changing market conditions also raise issues which concern the continued independent existence of banks as well as the need to become larger in core activities if they are to survive. The takeover of Midland Bank by Hong Kong and Shanghai Banking Corporation (HSBC) is a prominent example (Stonham, 1994). Prior to the takeover, HSBC was a UK-based international banking group with little presence in European markets. The acquisition would enhance HSBCs' global capabilities and consolidate the group's position in the foreign exchange, trade finance and treasury markets. Growth was expected to come from a combination of higher market share and the cross-selling of fee-earning products and services. HSBC already owned 15 per cent of Midland which was the weakest of the big four clearers. Although Midland was undergoing major reorganization it was beginning to show signs of recovery and was aiming to increase its share of the UK market. It was, however, in a weak position largely because it was under-capitalized but the takeover by HSBC resolved this situation.

In contrast, Lloyds Bank, one of the most profitable clearing banks in the UK, after failing in its hostile attempt to merge with the Midland Bank sought to acquire a large building society. In June 1994, Lloyds made an agreed £1.8 billion bid for the Cheltenham and Gloucester Building Society, itself one of the most profitable and certainly recognized as the most efficient of the large building societies. This acquisition was designed to give the bank a larger more viable share of the retail financial services market, making it the fourth largest mortgage lender in the UK.

## 10.4 Marketing strategy

Instrumental to the marketing planning process is the need for a bank to set objectives with respect to products, markets and performance, and to develop strategies relating to markets, and the various elements of the marketing mix to include product, price, place, promotion and also people – i.e. all employees within the bank.

### 10.4 Market segments

Consideration of present and potential market segments for the bank cannot be separated from strategic issues relating to elements of the marketing mix. Nevertheless, a number of specific relevant issues relate to bases and approaches to segmentation.

Banks segment their markets on a number of bases, e.g. demographic, geographic, life cycle, psychographic, cognitive and behavioural. In so doing they aim to identify and respond to the particular needs, motives and expected benefits of customer groups.

*Personal customers*

Examples of traditional demographic segments are:

- Students: prime needs for deposit and overdraft facilities, cash/ATM cards.
- Working women: financial independence and, if 'single', buyers of a wide range of financial services.
- Self-employed: targets for loans, insurance, pension plans, tax advice.
- High net worth individuals: targets for Gold cards, investment management services, large mortgages and loans.
- Professionals (e.g. doctors, accountants, solicitors): high net worth customers with additional potential as small business clients.

Beyond demographics, the banks increasingly consider consumer lifestyles to include interests, opinions, attitudes and behaviour, when designing segmentation strategies. As such they are interested in:

- The image of/attitude towards banks and competitor institutions.
- Attitudes towards saving, credit and borrowing.

- Financial services behaviour: saving/spending/credit, bank accounts/products/usage/loyalty factors.
- Benefits required: convenience, security, service, professionalism, price, speed, technological sophistication.
- Knowledge and expertise with respect to financial services.
- Willingness to buy new financial services/innovativeness/perceptions of risk.
- Price sensitivity: willingness to compare interest rates and charges.
- Media habits.

Knowledge about consumer attitudes, behaviour and needs will allow banks to develop and enhance relationships with present customers and to consider the costs and benefits of new product and market development.

An interesting example of market segmentation is provided by the case of Credit Agricole in France which shows how it may be integrated strategically in pursuing profitability and competitiveness (Sturdy and Morgan, 1993). In recent years French banks have been forced to be more commercialized as there has been a growing realization that banks had been over-regulated and inefficient, with the result that many aspects of the domestic market were potentially vulnerable to entry by foreign competitors. Credit Agricole, one of the largest banks in France with a diffuse largely rural network, has sought to improve its profitability through identifying more profitable customers more accurately whilst retaining a differentiated strategy. The approach to segmentation is based partly on the identification of socio-styles. Six categories were identified which can be mapped onto two main axes of lifestyle (Figure 10.1). The behaviours and orientations of the different segments were then matched with ranges of risks types, available products, distribution channels/sales approaches, promotions media and appropriate messages. Using this approach, the socio-ambitieux group, for example, have been targeted through direct marketing with promotion taking place on the Minitel network.

The bank also changed its corporate logo to target more dynamic and younger segments rather than just its traditional conservative rural base. Other segmentation strategies are used together with socio-styles by the bank, such as family, banking and product lifecycles. Existing clients are also analysed in relation to their usage of bank services and the hierarchical classification of clients' profitability into stars, deadweights and leeches. Leeches, for example, are seen as conveying modest profitability, yielding benefits of cash flow and economies of scale but not requiring active targeted marketing. These approaches to segmentation have informed changes in product design, communications and distribution. The rationalization of distribution channels has produced three broad and segmented forms of distribution. Distribution of simple low added value products is being partly externalized through tele/home banking, mailing/phoning, mobile sales units and distribution alliances with, for example, local shops. The second level is for high profitability products sold by specialists in a made-to-measure service closely matched to individual

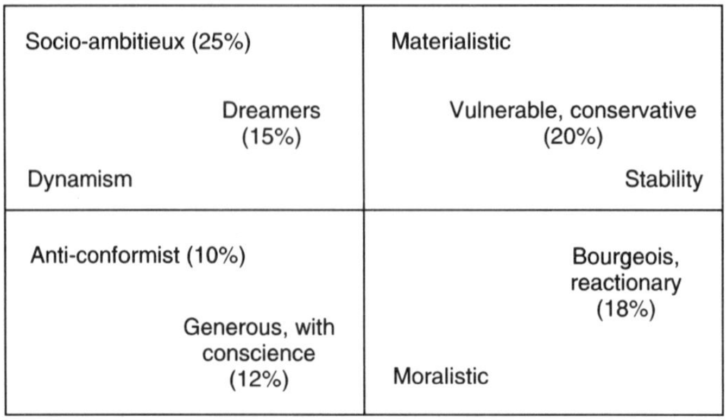

| Socio-ambitieux (25%) | Materialistic |
|---|---|
| Dreamers (15%) | Vulnerable, conservative (20%) |
| Dynamism | Stability |
| Anti-conformist (10%) | Bourgeois, reactionary (18%) |
| Generous, with conscience (12%) | Moralistic |

**Figure 10.1**   European social mentalities

*Source*: Sturdy and Morgan (1993)

needs. The third level involves the bank branch network which is used to sell the full product range, with products being packaged to appeal to different client groups.

## *Corporate customers*

General approaches to segmentation in respect of corporate customers were discussed in Chapter 2. Although there are a number of broad features which can describe the corporate customer, patterns of demand and the nature of services required will vary across sectors. Carey (1989) examines the demand characteristics by industry type for the banking sector and the implications for product type (see Table 10.3).

Thurman (1992) suggests that banks may need to differentiate their approaches to larger and smaller companies on the basis of a particular set of ties. Larger companies are likely to have a wider range of more advanced needs than is the case with smaller companies. He distinguishes five types of tie or bond between company and bank which help define the nature of the relationship: technical, organizational, knowledge, social and economic (price). Technical ties relate to routine services, e.g. money transmission, and are relevant to both large and small companies.

In some countries there may be ownership links between banks and firms. Such organizational ties may influence both the relationship and also the choice of bank for strategic and routine services. For smaller companies this relationship may arise from interlocking directorships; for larger companies it may be the consequence of historical connections. Mutual knowledge is important for both large and small firms in their relationships with banks. Some larger companies, however, may possess the requisite knowledge relating to certain activities, in which case price and social factors may be important in deciding the nature of a relationship.

**Table 10.3**  *Segmentation by parts of corporate financial sector*

| Sector | Fixed assets | Working capital | Product need |
|---|---|---|---|
| Primary | High | Medium | Long-term mainly non-bank debt at fixed rates. Interest rate exposure management. Limited demand for short-term bank debt and money transmission. |
| Manufacturing | High | High | Long-term, non-bank debt. Short- and medium-term bank debt. Interest rate and foreign currency management. Efficient money transmission service. Debtor collection and exposure management. |
| Services | Low | Medium | Relatively low usage of bank products. Greatest need probably understanding of business, due to low level of security available for borrowing. |
| Retail | Medium | Low | High cash flow requires efficient and cheap cash handling services and money transmission. Premises, if not rented, provide acceptable security for medium-term lending if required. |
| Wholesale | Low | Medium/high | Short-term and to a lesser extent medium-term bank loans, but access to short-term tradeable paper market an increasingly attractive source. |

*Source:* Carey (1989)

Price and social relationships may be important in respect of services conducted by specialized departments, especially for larger firms. For smaller firms, price and social relationships are more likely to be the only bonding functions, since they are less likely to make use of more specialized services.

## 10.4.2 Product decisions

The product offerings of the UK banks include:

- Current accounts: cheque books, standing orders, direct debits, bank giros, electronic funds transfer.
- Savings: deposit account, bonus saving, money market deposits.
- Loans: overdraft, house, car, home improvements etc.
- Card services: cheque card/cash/ATM, credit card operations.
- Advisory services: wills, trusts, executorships, tax planning, investment advice, money management etc.
- Financial service: pensions, personal equity plans, insurance products etc.
- Other: e.g. travel and foreign services.

Increasingly, the banks are being driven by a combination of internal and external forces to develop and offer new products and services. The internal pressures relate to growth opportunities, the need for increased earnings and market shares, whereas the external factors are concerned with competition from banks and non-banks offering banking and financial services, possible future entrants to the market, and technological advances. In particular, new products are needed to attract customers from untapped markets, to cross-sell to existing customers, to attract accounts from competitors, to sell to competitors' customers – independently of the core product, and to reduce the costs of service provision.

One may ask what is a 'new' or innovatory financial service product. Generally, one might suggest that innovative products are fundamentally new services which involve new technology, a sizeable investment, considerable risk, significant market potential and rewards. Examples of innovation include the first ATMs and bank credit cards, home banking, EFTPOS (see section 9.4.4 for a consideration of home banking and EFTPOs). However, in banking, innovation is not likely to lead to any significant amount of product differentiation due to the lack of protection by patents and copyrights for the innovating organization, in other words it is easy for competitors to imitate/copy product innovations.

At present, most of what is new in financial services is either in the form of product/service development (e.g. new facilities of ATMs, banking by mail, credit card insurance), or new product lines for particular banks, i.e. services which are new to the bank but not the market, whereby the bank enters a market in which other companies already compete – e.g. insurance, trust and travel services to compete with insurance companies, accounting firms and travel agents.

As an integral element of product range decision making, banks may carry out a product portfolio analysis in which products/services are classified as high, medium or low in respect of market attractiveness and competitive strength (Figure 10.2).

Competitive strength comprises components such as market share, size, customer loyalty, technology, personnel, image, management capabilities; and market attractiveness has components of market size, market growth, extent and type of competition, cross-selling potential, ease of customer switching etc. As a consequence some products will emerge as having greater potential (✓✓ in Figure 9.2), and marketing resources and management effort will be allocated accordingly.

As seen in Chapter 6, branding may be an important element of the product decision as it helps to convey information to customers and hopefully engender customer loyalty. Chapter 6 showed that there are various strategies for branding products, with financial services firms selecting the approach deemed most appropriate for a particular product. Although the association between a product and the name of the bank may be important in conveying notions of quality, there is now evidence of individual product branding.

**Market attractiveness**

| Competitive strength | High | Medium | Low |
|---|---|---|---|
| High | ✓✓ | ✓✓ | ✓ |
| Medium | ✓✓ | ✓ | x |
| Low | ✓ | x | x |

**Figure 10.2**  Product portfolio analysis

**Table 10.4** *First direct brand grid*

| Brand level/ brand strength | Prominent | Inferior | Endorsed | Disclosed | Undisclosed |
|---|---|---|---|---|---|
| Corporate | | | | | HSBC |
| Division | | | | Midland | |
| Super brand | First Direct | | | | |
| Brand | Visa | | | | |
| Variant | | | | | |
| Description | | | | Bank | |

*Source:* Saunders and Watters (1993)

An example in a banking context is provided by the case of the First Direct Visa Card (Table 10.4) (Saunders and Watters, 1993). At the corporate level, the identity of the owner, Hong Kong and Shangai Banking Corporation is undisclosed. This furtive approach to corporate branding may reflect the view that it would do little to help market the product in the UK despite the fact that the bank is very powerful and highly respected compared to the Midland. Divisional branding may be used where there are differences in segments served or differences in the associations of the brands involved. In the case of First Direct, divisional identity, i.e. Midland, is revealed but not in a manner that would help promote the brand. Indeed, at the time the product was launched there was little mention of Midland Bank, though the name is now more prominent.

### 10.4.3 Pricing

The UK banks have not, until recently, viewed price as a major element of marketing strategy because of government regulation with respect to price, the fact that banks have tended to operate as an oligopoly, particularly in relation to personal customers, and as the services offered are not standard. However, pricing is becoming more important as a result of deregulation, increasing competition and decreasing consumer loyalty to particular banks.

Pricing for banks takes a number of forms:

- Charge levels for different types of transaction, e.g. debits, cheque clearance, standing orders.
- Charge rates for overdrafts, loans.
- Fees for services, fixed or on a commission basis.
- Interest rates, on current/deposit/savings accounts.
- 'Free' banking.

In setting their fees, charges and interest rates, the banks are influenced (and to some extent controlled) by the Government/Bank of England/ legislation, competitor activities, cost structures, demand factors, benefit/

value to the customer of particular financial services, and their pricing objectives (e.g. profit maximization, market share leadership, return on investment) (see Chapter 7 for a more detailed discussion of pricing).

In relation to current accounts, the banks have been trying to maximize profits regardless of underlying costs, i.e. market rate pricing, and have been reluctant to pay interest on current accounts until competitive factors have forced them. Additionally, consumers are largely ignorant with respect to prevailing interest rates and the impact of notional interest on their current account balances. Consequently, there is little price sensitivity with respect to personal financial services.

Free banking services are traditionally offered to students and free advisory services may be offered to students and to established or potential customers: management needs to ask which products/services might be offered at no charge in order to attract and keep customers. New services may be offered at prices less than cost (accepted as very difficult to measure and allocate in banking) in order to build competitive advantage and market share, e.g. as with the first home-banking trials. Price 'discrimination' in the form of flexible pricing is evident in relation to both customers, i.e. varying prices for the same service or different packages for the same price (e.g. students vis-à-vis other customers) and place, e.g. ATM transactions may cost less than counter service.

Lastly, relationship pricing is becoming increasingly relevant as customer relationships become more complex. It will be possible and necessary to improve profits from client relationships by cross-selling high margin services, and at the same time offering relationship building services at a low margin or at a loss.

Pricing is also an important issue with respect to corporate customers. Banks may offer loans at low interest rate margins in order to attract or retain a customer with a view to developing a relationship which will yield more profitable business, such as securities issuing. If the loan is made to a customer who is a good credit risk and is well-secured, the fees from investment banking services might more than compensate for the low margin. Increasing competition may, however, mean that banks have to adopt less rigorous loan covenants in order to gain the loan business. An alternative, but related, problem arises where banks obtain highly profitable front-end fees for putting a transaction together (for example, in completing a leveraged buy-out or acquisition) but then syndicate most of the loan to other banks. In this way the relationship and the risk may be reduced, with the bank having little incentive to monitor the customer's progress. In both cases, whilst the banks' pricing strategy may enable them to gain market share, there may be question marks over the profitability of such activities, particularly if the loans which are made to more marginal customers default. Banks' lending to companies in the late 1980s, particularly to marginal highly leveraged transactions such as leveraged buy-outs which subsequently ran into trading difficulties, is a good example of these problems (Jensen, 1991). The difficulties experienced illustrate the need to consider pricing strategy within the overall strategy of the bank. They also highlight the need to design appropriate incentives for the banks' employees. If, for example as in the case of leveraged buy-outs, they are rewarded on the basis of the fees generated from new transactions completed, employees have the incentive to reduce price and/or to lend to more marginal transactions which may not be in the banks' long-term interest.

### 10.4.4 Distribution systems

Strategic decisions relating to the delivery of financial services concern the bank branch network and the increasing opportunities for the remote provision of financial services, via ATMs, EFTPOS and home banking, brought about by rapid and continuing technological advancements.

The full service bank branch has been the traditional means of distributing banking and financial services. It has been effective for collecting and delivering cash and deposits, making loans and providing a wide range of services. The history of the very extensive full service branch network is well-documented and has provided banks with a great deal of presence/visibility on the high street and customers with locational convenience. Until recently, there have not been any significant moves by the banks towards either rationalization of branches or towards limited service branches.

However, the rationale for an extensive network of full service branches is no longer justifiable, in the light of increasing costs, alternative distribution/transaction systems, changing consumer expectations with respect to convenience and availability, and competitive elements. The trends for the next decade and into the third millennium, which may be interpreted as having advantages and disadvantages to both the banks and their customers, are: branch closures, limited service branches, specialist branches.

There are now as many ATMs as bank branches and the trend is towards having them in remote locations (supermarkets, stores, airports, railway stations etc.) and for companies to have their 'own' ATM linked to all banks. This latter trend is possibly a result of the growth in shared ATM networks. At the time of writing there are two networks serving the seven main clearing banks in the UK, and a third network linking all the top building societies and five other major banks; in addition, there are also links between the banks and Access/Visa.

*Electronic Funds Transfer at Point of Sale (EFTPOS)*

'Smart Cards' were invented as recently as 1975, and may be used as either ATM cards or for electronic funds transfer at point of sale. The forces driving EFTPOS have been several: social, i.e. customer demand, competitive and technological. In the last few years a number of experiments have been ongoing in various shopping centres/petrol stations throughout the UK, involving banks and retail outlets. The main advantages and disadvantages of direct debit at the point of sale may be summarized as follows:

- Fully automated branches, with few staff – the appeal perhaps limited to younger/higher educated people.
- Remote banking (via ATMs, EFTPOS, home banking).
- The 'financial supermarket', whereby a very wide range of financial services are offered in one 'retail' outlet as a result of mergers/acquisitions between providers of financial services. At present, most consumers do not fully understand or appreciate the concept but the opportunity is there and the banks may move in this direction.

Following the delays in launching a national EFTPOS system it was essentially abandoned in favour of a more fragmented approach under the auspices of either Switch or Visa. The growth of these debit card payment systems has been given a boost by the changes taking place in the credit card market, particularly with respect to annual changes for credit cards and the possibility of retailers being able to charge a higher price to credit card users than to cash and debit card users.

## ATMs

ATMs, along with EFTPOS and home banking, may be considered to be 'product' developments or, perhaps more appropriately, as innovations in the delivery of financial services. ATMs have progressed from being merely cash dispensers to provide facilities for deposits, balance reporting and inter-account transactions, as discussed in more detail in Chapter 8. Consumer reactions to ATMs are well researched with perceptions of service improvements as a result of automated facilities generally outweighing criticisms (Table 10.5). The most advantageous features of ATMs are the twenty-four hour availability, time saving/convenience aspects, avoidance of queues and the perception that bank staff have more time to deal with counter customers. The features which attract criticism are computer breakdown; lack of cash, lack of certain facilities, personal safety when withdrawing cash, the possibility/liability of unauthorized use, mistakes, lack of privacy, impersonal nature (i.e. prefer counter service) and queues. Some of these criticisms are real and others merely perceived deficiencies. Either way, they are of concern to the banks and in the long term will be reduced through further technological developments, improved security and advertising and promotion.

## Home banking

A further area of technological advancement in service delivery is the provision of home banking facilities. The first commercial in-home banking system in the UK was launched by a building society in 1983 and was operated using British Telecom's Prestel videotext system as the standard interface, offering a two-way communication system to any subscriber. However, this and other early systems using a microcomputer or other terminals linked by telephone or videotext had limited appeal and success

**Table 10.5**  *Advantages and disadvantages of ATMs*

|            | Advantages | Disadvantages |
| --- | --- | --- |
| Banks | reduces paperwork/cheques<br>reduces costs<br>extends banking base via<br>   new accounts<br>provides a wider<br>   range of ATM style operations | competitive threats<br>installation costs<br>running costs<br>security<br>system fraud |
| Retailers | increased customer service<br>competitive edge with<br>   respect of technology<br>reduced time at the checkout<br>reduced cheque handling/<br>   cash security<br>store account credited<br>   more quickly | competitive threats<br>installation costs<br>running costs<br>customer privacy<br>customers without bank<br>   accounts<br>poor customer relations<br>   (resulting from<br>   non-authorization) |
| Customers | security<br>time saving<br>convenient<br>no need to visit a bank<br>fewer cash payments<br>simplicity<br>cheaper than cheques | too easy to overspend<br>instant debiting<br>possible technical error<br>loss/fraud<br>lack of privacy<br>cost passed on to consumer<br>monitoring of buying behaviour |

– due to the costs involved and the narrow range of services available: to some extent the rush to technology possibly preceded the search for market needs and consumer acceptance.

The first UK trials were in sharp contrast to French experience where a number of home banking systems participated in a national videotext network, Minitel, operated by the French post and telecoms industry which provide the basic equipment – a screen and a keyboard attachment for the phone – free to subscribers. Two-thirds of European banks now offer home banking systems which provide account interrogation, payment of bills, inter-account transactions, loan generation and other banking facilities. Consequently, the UK banks might be at a competitive disadvantage vis-à-vis the European banks. However, vital technological and strategic initiatives are advancing (including market trials), encompassing both screen-based videotext and also voice response systems whereby customers may talk to the banks' computers using only their telephone – with customers possibly having their voices pre-recorded and registered.

## Corporate electronic banking

Banks have established electronic based products for their corporate customers. For example, Hong Kong and Shangai Banking Corporation developed its Hexagon corporate electronic banking system in 1982 releasing it to selected customers in 1985, enabling it to deliver banking products to its corporate customers worldwide. By 1994 the system had 5000 corporate customers including one-third of the world's 200 largest corporations. The system provides customers with control over their finances twenty-four hours a day as well as a diverse range of market information and reporting. Corporate customers can dial into local access points in the data network through personal computers and modems. They are thus connected instantly to the group's mainframe system. Hexagon has two main product categories – banking products and management products. Three types of service are available. First the user can undertake a corporate accounts information enquiry, enabling it to retrieve information relating to its global portfolio with the group. Second, a market information inquiry can be undertaken to obtain real-time market information on a wide range of subjects about local and global security and commodity markets. Third, transactions can be initiated to transfer funds, apply for letters of credit etc. directly from the remote terminal.

### 10.4.5 Promotion

There are several objectives of banks' promotional activities: to build image and reputation; to differentiate each from their competitors; to generate interest and knowledge; to attract new customers; and to generate customer loyalty. To achieve these objectives the banks develop promotional strategies and tactics which utilize the usual mix of advertising, sales promotion, public relations and personal selling, with the number of methods becoming increasingly important and evident.

Bank advertising is carried out in many print and broadcast media, each with its own strengths and weaknesses, costs and benefits, and target audiences including financial service customers and also employees. In addition to attempting to make individual banks distinctive from the competition, a consistent theme in advertising by banks has been to convey an image of being caring, friendly and interesting to their customers. An advertising campaign may be designed to convey such a message but involve a series of variations designed to appeal to different market segments. For example, the Midland Bank designed and ran an advertising campaign with the message that it was able and willing to help with a number of clearly defined areas as identified by three different TV commercials aimed at the first-time buyer, those starting a business for the first time and those with rather more complicated personal finances. In an attempt to make these rather traditional messages appeal anew to customers, each commercial was in the form of a playlet constructed like rock videos with the actors mouthing their particular (sub-titled) financial problems to well-known popular songs.

Of special interest now and into the future is direct marketing or direct response marketing. The main contributor to the growth of direct marketing is the development of computer technology and databases of consumers and potential consumers, that allows prospects to be identified accurately, e.g. computers which have the capability to store data such as in-house databases containing customer profiles and services used, and produce mailing lists. Key characteristics of direct marketing are its selectivity with respect to segments, versatility (e.g. it provides unlimited space for offers), ability to generate leads, testability (of an approach or appeal with a clearly defined target segment), immediate and quantifiable feedback, and ease of control.

The channels used for direct marketing are both print and interactive media. For example, direct mail advertising may be sent out with a customer's statement, and may be a personal communication (including a letter from the bank or branch) which is not competing at the time with other advertising/promotion. Limited use has been made, so far, of reply cards and envelopes as customers are expected to be pro-active in getting in touch with the bank. Furthermore, the banks have by no means developed the potential of interactive media such as the telephone, which is still mainly used as an inbound device to respond to enquiries and complaints, and the emerging new technology on interactive television. This situation will no doubt change significantly in the coming years as banks begin to realize, more fully, the strategic implications of direct marketing.

Sales promotions comprise mainly short-term incentives, often used in conjunction with advertising campaigns and include: free banking for students to generate accounts; free home banking to create awareness; and generate publicity and consumer reaction; free cheque books and statement holders; gifts to children and students. Additionally, more recent activities include promotions among employees to encourage good performance and as a reward for achievement and quality service.

Public relations strategy among both internal and external publics is planned to publicize a bank and its services, so as to enhance and maintain favourable images. Most activities have high credibility and include:

- articles in magazines and journals
- press releases, annual reports, editorial comments
- talks to schools/community groups/prospective employees
- participation in Institute of Bankers affairs
- charitable donations
- fund raising with a charity
- sponsorship of the arts/sport/events on a national and local basis.

With sponsorship strategies, as with direct marketing, the banks are to some extent followers, compared with organizations in other product and service sectors (e.g. fast moving consumer goods, motor cars etc.). In consideration of sponsorship schemes, the banks wish to emphasize their social responsibility and their desire to provide assistance. However, at the same time they will want the bank to be presented favourably with respect to its target markets. In this respect the sponsorship will be used as a platform to promote the bank and its services, and thereby recoup a 'return on the investment'.

Public relations effected through sponsorship and the provision of articles in magazines may be particularly important in the corporate sphere. In this way it may be possible both to target marketing at specific types of customers and to demonstrate an expertise in a particular area. For example, the specialist magazine *Acquisitions Monthly*, read principally by finance directors and managers in similar positions, publishes an annual *Management Buy-out Supplement*. Such individuals are an attractive target segment for banks involved in funding management buy-outs since they may be involved in taking decisions to divest divisions to management or may be considering a buy-out of the division in which they are employed. The *Supplement* in 1994 had as lead sponsor Montagu Private Equity, with eighteen other sponsors, thirteen of whom were banks or other providers of finance to buy-outs. The *Supplement* carried a one-page profile of each sponsor, identifying key individuals in each, as well as a separate article written by a member of each sponsor on a particular aspect of management buy-outs in which they had particular strength. For example, the article by the representative of Barclays Development Capital emphasized developments in buy-outs in the regions of the UK reflecting their recently increased regional presence. Similarly the Bank of Scotland contributed an article on the pragmatic role of lenders in buy-outs. Potential problems of this approach are principally twofold. First, there are the familiar 'me-tooism' difficulties. Second, articles written to demonstrate a particular expertise may have to tread a fine line between blatant chest thumping and being genuinely informative if they are not to engender a negative reaction from relatively sophisticated readers.

Personal selling has only recently become evident with regard to personal financial services. Attitudes towards selling, among the banks, were well researched and documented in the 1970s and were largely negative – indeed, many managers equated selling with marketing. However, the present emphasis within banking is increasingly to change the corporate culture so that not only are all employees market oriented, i.e. everyone will have some influence on sales of the bank's products/services, but also that customer-contact personnel are sales oriented and can take advantage of situations and opportunities in order to cross-sell services.

Indeed, the banks are participating in relationship selling whereby customers are viewed as clients, and the emphasis is to retain, not just acquire, clients. Relationship selling may be defined as the attraction, maintenance and enhancement of client relationships. This is vital in an environment of decreasing customer loyalty, easy movement of accounts, a declining branch network, and access to bank services via plastic card and telephone. The rationale behind relationship banking is to transform single-service users into multi-service clients, and transform indifferent customers into loyal clients. Key ingredients for success are:

- Market segmentation and discovery of client needs.
- Identification of a core service, around which to build relationships.

- Incentives for clients, e.g. relationship pricing – 'free' investment advice/service if more than a certain amount of money on deposit.
- Account representatives, i.e. the liaison between the bank and the client, to include customer advisers in the branches and telesales staff.
- Training for relationship managers and other bank employees with respect to sales skills, either in-house or from outside consultants.

Personal relationships may be especially important in respect of corporate customers. First, extending loan finance to small and medium-sized firms is a particular marketing problem for banks, which may be eased by the development of relationships between banks and their clients. In particular, it is often argued that smaller firms have difficulty in obtaining finance because of banking practice in the UK which emphasizes asset-based security for loans (the so-called capital gearing approach) to the exclusion of consideration of a company's earnings potential (the income gearing approach) (Binks, Ennew and Reed, 1992). Edwards and Turnbull (1994) argue that in the small and medium-sized enterprise market, collaboration and partnering might fruitfully be directed towards reducing the problems of access to finance by such firms, by improving information transfer between client and bank. In a survey of 101 smaller firms they find that adequate forecast information, on which an income gearing approach might be based, is not available in most smaller firms and that the available information may often be cloaked in secrecy. However, it was also found that whilst smaller firms often have little motivation to provide better information and little awareness of the information that their bank would require in assessing a loan application, they would be prepared to change information provision if banks demanded it.

A second area where relationships may be particularly important is in investment banking. Ford (1980) provides a staged approach to relationship development which has been adopted by Turnbull and Moustakatos (1995) to show how an investment bank can design its marketing activities.

Breaking into existing early stage relationships may require the investment bank to emphasize a broad range of services it can offer. In approaching customers with more established relationships, the investment bank needs to determine the specific problems which the customer faces and provide a tailor-made product in response. In developing relationships, investment banks also need to be aware of the need to distinguish the strategic management and the operating management of relationships. A bank's structure must also follow the strategic objectives for the development of relationships. At the maintenance stage, an investment bank needs to detect and deal with problems of institutionalization. That is, the bank needs to re-examine its existing operations to see if they continue to be responsive and relevant to particular client relationships and market conditions, and the degree of resource allocation between different relationships according to their potential and stage of development.

### 10.4.6 People

Turning to an additional element of the marketing mix, people, the banks may be seen to participate in a number of internal strategic marketing initiatives which focus on the role of employees in the delivery of financial services, and subsequent consumer satisfactions and dissatisfactions.

A characteristic of most of the banks' service provision is simultaneous production and consumption, which generally necessitates interpersonal interactions between employees and customers. Thus, the banks' personnel are inevitably instrumental in the creation of quality in the service product, hence the phrase 'customer care'. Indeed, quality is a major contributory element to the effectiveness of service provision. Banks now regard customer care/quality as a key variable in strategic planning – and quality is seen as a means to achieve differential advantage and increase market share.

The banks are, therefore, developing and implementing customer care/quality programmes, with a pre-requisite for success being the total commitment of the organization from top management downward, with effective leadership driving a customer-oriented culture throughout the company. The banks consider their programmes to be a high priority with high expenditures, and view them as a long-term investment. They see the benefits in terms of improved customer service which leads to retention of existing customers and increased loyalty, attraction of new customers, and also improved staff morale and loyalty (see Chapter 9).

The programmes typically encompass activities related to staff attitudes and behaviour, and are concerned with staff training which may be one component of a total quality programme designed to enhance all aspects of service to the customer to include improvements in technology, retail design, systems and procedures. Programme objectives relate to:

- emphasizing the increasing need for high levels of service and the importance of the customer
- training staff with the skills and knowledge required to deal with customers effectively
- motivating staff through encouragement and reward
- developing a new style of leadership and management.

The implementation of quality programmes (incorporating special 'events', workshops, quality circles and in-house training) is already leading to some cultural changes: e.g. a more open management style; an environment where staff work together with shared goals and values; and an improvement in internal communications and staff relationships. The payoff is perceived in terms of a true market orientation, a better understanding of customer needs, improved service quality and increased customer satisfaction. However, in the final analysis, excellent levels of customer service or total quality may be described as a 'striving rather than an achieving process', and as a philosophy which needs to be ingrained into a bank's culture.

## 0.5   Conclusion

Returning to the marketing planning framework, it is necessary to comment on the need for the effective implementation, evaluation and control of the banks' marketing strategies. To achieve success, the banks need an appropriate marketing organization with leaders who are able to provide a true marketing orientation throughout their companies. Furthermore, they have to set standards for performance with respect to all aspects of their marketing activities to include: sales and profitability; efficiency of systems and operations, e.g. automated facilities; the impact of advertising and promotion; customer satisfaction and service quality; and staff performance. Additionally, the banks must establish methods to evaluate their actual performance in the marketplace. Instrumental to the process of evaluation and control is the increasingly vital role played by marketing research and marketing information systems. Once actual performance has been evaluated against standards and expectations, the banks will, typically, be modifying objectives and redesigning strategies and participating in a continuous marketing audit and planning process.

# 11 Insurance marketing

## Stephen Diacon and Trevor Watkins

## 11.1 Introduction

The most important feature of marketing can be simply stated as a customer-orientation which should pervade the entire insurance organization. Successful marketing requires firms to research the insurance requirements of their customers, to design products which meet those needs profitably, to decide how to distribute those products, and to persuade the customers to buy. However it is probably fair to say that many insurance companies are not well known for their market orientation, preferring a sales orientation instead:

> 'Faced with an increasingly competitive market, the natural reaction of some organizations has been to shout louder to attract customers to buy their products. No thought had yet gone into examining precisely what benefits a customer sought to obtain from buying a product – product policy was still driven by the desire to produce those products which the company felt it was good at making.' (Palmer, 1994, p.26).

Yet it is precisely this sales orientation which has given certain areas of the insurance industry such a bad name in the eyes of the public. High-pressure sales methods, allied with commission-based remuneration have led to a number of public relations disasters for the life and pensions industry particularly. These problems include the home-income plan debacle, the Securities and Investments Board criticisms of the mis-selling of personal pensions (in October 1994), the evidence that a substantial proportion of life and pensions contracts are terminated prematurely, and the revelations of the high costs of many long-term savings products. Concern is also being expressed that many of the low-cost endowments sold in conjunction with a mortgage will prove unable to meet the outstanding loan when the contracts mature. One way of avoiding similar mistakes in the future is to replace sales-orientated marketing with a customer orientation.

This chapter examines the contribution marketing can make in the various insurance markets. Section 11.2 provides a general overview of the role of insurance and highlights some key marketing issues. Sections 11.3 and 11.4 define insurance and explain why customers may wish to purchase insurance contracts. This is followed by a brief outline of the UK insurance market in section 11.5, describing the main providers, consumers and intermediaries. Section 11.6 discusses the main elements of the marketing mix as applied to the various insurance markets, while Section 11.7 uses insurance to illustrate the concept of the product life cycle in practice. A summary and conclusions are presented in section 11.8.

## 1.2  The role of insurance in financial services

Insurance plays two main roles in the provision of financial services to individual consumers and business corporations: risk taking and financial planning. The risk-taking role of insurance is perhaps the most familiar, since from the latest Family Expenditure Survey it appears that 63.5 per cent of UK households purchase insurance on their house structure, 74.5 per cent cover their house contents and 64.5 per cent have motor insurance (Central Statistical Office, 1994). Insurance is used in this context in order to provide compensation on the occurrence of a financial loss, or to deal with other problems that arise as a result of unexpected contingencies.

Long-term insurance, in the form of life insurance and pensions policies, is also a major tool in the process of financial planning, and it is in this respect that the insurance industry finds itself in active competition with other financial institutions such as banks, building societies, and unit and investment trusts. In making their personal financial plans, individual households will need to buy protection against disability and premature death, save for the future – particularly for retirement, and construct a portfolio of investments which achieves the right balance between short-term and long-term investments, net-of-tax income and capital growth, and risk and security. The 1993 Family Expenditure Survey shows that 65.7 per cent of households purchased some form of life insurance while 21.3 per cent had a personal pension. A breakdown of the gross financial wealth of the UK personal sector (for example, see Carter (1990) section 6) shows that typically almost half of personal sector wealth is invested in life insurance and pension funds, whereas the corresponding percentages for banks, building societies and unit trusts are around 13 per cent, 14 per cent and 2 per cent respectively. Similarly in the area of corporate financial management, life insurance and pension policies are used to facilitate employee benefit programmes (such as group life cover, and pensions for employees, executives and directors).

The insurance industry is an important part of the UK financial services sector in terms of turnover and employment. At the end of 1993, there were 828 insurance companies and 189 Lloyd's syndicates authorized to underwrite business in the United Kingdom. The whole industry – including insurers, brokers, Independent Financial Advisers (IFAs), loss adjusters, actuaries and other consultants – employed a total of 249,800 people. In 1993, the turnover of all UK insurance companies, Lloyd's syndicates, mutual clubs and associations and friendly societies (in terms of total worldwide premium income net of reinsurance written in the UK) exceeded £81,000 million (Association of British Insurers, 1994): of this almost 59 per cent involved long-term business (that is, life insurance and pensions). The UK insurance sector is also a major export earner, and almost 37 per cent of the general insurance premiums of UK insurance groups originates from overseas (the corresponding figure for long-term business is around 17 per cent). In practice, a significant proportion of the business transacted by UK insurance companies is purchased by corporate customers: although no accurate breakdown is available, it is thought that as much as 50 per cent of general insurance and 20 per cent of life and pensions business is commercial, rather than personal, business.

There are a number of aspects of the insurance business that raise particularly interesting problems from a marketing perspective. In the first place, insurance is scarcely ever purchased for positive reasons, since its main purpose is to protect the purchaser in the event of a highly undesirable accident or loss. Accordingly insurance is associated in people's minds with the worst (rather than the best) things in life: since individuals are loath to think about the things that can go wrong, they are reluctant to make preparations in advance. Although such perceptions are less applicable to corporate insurance purchases, it cannot be said that insurance is high on the agenda of many company finance directors. This is often used to justify the sales orientation of most insurance companies, and hence the old adage that insurance is 'sold and not bought'.

Secondly, the core service of insurance is highly intangible, since it comprises a promise by the insurer to pay a claim should a loss or accident occur at some time in the future. As the probability of a major house fire might be as little as 0.001 per cent, only one person out of 100 000 who purchased fire insurance is likely to utilize the main service provided by the insurer (namely the payment of a claim).

Finally, the whole insurance transaction is confused by a pronounced lack of information on the part of both the insurer and the customer. In general, many individual customers have wildly inaccurate perceptions of the risks they face, and little knowledge of the insurance products that are available. Furthermore, the UK insurance market has a large number of competing insurers so that all customers find it very difficult to make comparisons on price and quality. Similarly the insurers often have very little information about the risk or about the risk-taking behaviour of the customer – and, unless this information asymmetry is corrected, substantial distortions in the market for insurance can arise.

It is because of these many information asymmetries that insurance is often distributed by intermediaries, such as insurance brokers or independent financial advisers (IFAs), rather than via direct contact between the insurers and customers. The intermediaries serve as market makers by bringing buyers and sellers together and improve the amount of information available to the transacting parties. In 1993, around 60 per cent of general insurance business and just under half of new long-term premiums were obtained from independent intermediaries. Unfortunately the involvement of intermediaries in the market for insurance can lead to other problems arising from the conflict of interest between the intermediary and the customer. These conflicts were one of the major reasons for the introduction of consumer protection legislation in the UK financial services market in the 1980s, as described in Chapter 1.

## 1.3   What is insurance?

### 11.3.1  A definition

Insurance is a financial contract which transfers risk from the customer to the insurer. It has been defined as an arrangement by which one party, the insurer, promises to pay another party, the insured or policyholder, a sum of money if something happens which causes (or has the potential to cause) the insured to suffer a financial loss. The adverse effect of the loss on the insured is then mitigated to the extent that it is offset by the benefits received from the insurer. Thus the primary service provided by the insurer is a guarantee of payment of valid claims benefits on the occurrence of an accidental loss or event covered by the policy.

In practice there are hundreds of different types of insurance contract available, covering all aspects of risk as it affects individuals, partnerships, corporations, and local and national governments. The insurance industry is tremendously complex. Conventional descriptions itemize seven main types of insurance contract:

- Transportation, covering land vehicles, railway rolling stock, aircraft, ships, goods in transit, motor vehicle liability, aircraft liability and liability for ships.
- Property, covering damage to property including that by fire and natural forces (such as water, landslip, storm etc.) and loss by theft, breakdown, or accidental damage.
- Pecuniary, covering credit, suretyship, legal expenses, and business interruption.
- Liability, including general liability to third parties and liability to employees, customers, and users of professional services.
- Personal accident, sickness and health, covering sickness (short term) and ill-health (long term), accidental injury, and medical expenses.
- Life insurance, providing benefits associated with an individual's death.
- Pensions and annuities, which provide benefits so long as the individual survives.

The first five categories are generically known as general or non-life insurance; the latter two as long-term insurance (although long-term sickness cover – permanent health insurance – is normally included under the long-term category). There are two important differences between general and long-term insurance. In the first place, general insurance contracts are designed to offer protection in the event of an adverse contingency (such as a fire or motor accident) and normally provide cover for only one year, after which they must be renewed. On the other hand, life and pensions contracts are designed to be long-term (often extending over ten or twenty years) and normally have a major saving component, as well as offering some protection against life contingencies. This distinction means that most insurance consumers will buy general insurance on a regular basis but have rather less experience of long-term insurance purchase. It also means that the insurers have the opportunity to change the price or conditions of coverage for general insurance policies at the end of each year; whereas in long-term insurance, the price (that is the premium rate) is determined at the inception of the contract and remains fixed over the entire policy term.

The second major difference between general and long-term insurance relates to the regulation of marketing activities. Since life and pensions contracts are used extensively in personal financial management, their marketing is controlled primarily by the Financial Services Act 1986 and enforced by the self-regulating organizations (for further details see Chapter 1). The marketing of general insurance is regulated by the Insurance Companies Act 1982: the Act's conduct of business rules make it an offence to use false, misleading or deceptive statements in order to induce the purchase of (any type of) insurance. The financial operation and solvency of all types insurance companies is still regulated by the 1982 Act, and enforced by the Department of Trade and Industry. In most countries, individuals or companies are prohibited from carrying on insurance business unless they have previously obtained a licence to do so. In the United Kingdom the only bodies authorized to transact insurance are insurance companies, members of Lloyd's of London, friendly societies, and trade unions or employers' associations (in relation to the provision of strike or provident benefits for members).

### 11.3.2 The four insurance services

Although they may seem very different, all types of insurance contract have one key ingredient in common: they are all contingent contracts, in the sense that the insurer is only called upon to pay a claim if a random pre-specified event (such as a fire or illness) actually occurs. Thus in motor insurance, for example, although the insurer provides all its customers with a cover note or certificate of insurance at the start of the policy, only those policyholders who have suffered an accidental loss (as defined by the terms of the motor contract) are entitled to the payment of claims benefits. In the case of endowment life insurance contracts, the pre-specified event which triggers the payment of policy benefits may be the death of the policyholder (or his or her spouse) or survival for a given number of years.

In the absence of insurance, an individual or corporation exposed to risk may either have to take the chance that there will be insufficient resources to meet the loss, or make provision in advance by establishing a contingency reserve – that is, tie up capital on the off chance of a loss. In contrast, the contingent nature of insurance provides a major efficiency improvement since the benefits are only paid if the loss actually occurs, whereas money has to be tied up in a contingency reserve whether or not there is a loss.

The risk transfer role provided by the insurer is not the only service that the consumer gains from purchasing insurance, since in practice the insurer provides a package of additional services which consumers who are exposed to risk would otherwise have to provide for themselves. These other services have been characterized by Diacon and Carter (1992) as organization, investment and advice.

The main organizational work undertaken by the insurer is in the administration of the insurance pool so that the losses of the few can be shared by the many. The insurer gathers together a group of similar insureds and charges each a contribution (known as a premium) which is pooled in the insurer's technical reserves. Any claims benefits are then paid from this pool, although the insurer's free reserves and capital may be called upon if the technical reserves are insufficient.

If the consumer chooses not to buy a formal insurance contract, an alternative might be to collect together a group of similar insureds for the purpose of organizing their own mutual pool – in which case they would have to replicate the administrative work undertaken by an insurer including selection of pool members (i.e. underwriting), calculation and collection of premiums, assessment and payment of valid claims, and calculation of technical reserves. Such mutual pools are quite common in certain areas of business insurance (for example the protection and indemnity clubs in the marine insurance market). Many large corporations have taken the mutual pool one stage further and set up an insurance company for their own exclusive use – known as a captive insurance subsidiary. There have been other instances when large corporations have purchased insurance services unbundled from the risk transfer role: for example, following a major fire at one of MGMs hotel/casinos in Las Vegas in November 1980, MGM purchased insurance retroactively (i.e. back-dated to before the fire) with their insurer's consent – partly in order to utilize their insurer's claims management services.

All insurance contracts also involve the provision of an investment service since there is a time delay between the collection of premiums and the payment of claims. Any investment income earned on the insurer's technical reserves can then be returned to the insureds in the form of either lower premiums or improved benefits. The insurer's investment service is particularly important in insurance contracts whose principal use is as a form of long-term saving (such as life insurance and pensions).

Finally in the course of undertaking its business the insurer accumulates an expert knowledge about the risky activities involved, which is often passed on to the benefit of the insured. For example, insurers providing engineering insurance conduct a physical inspection of the insured's engineering plant and machinery which satisfies the obligation imposed on firms by health and safety legislation to undertake compulsory safety inspections.

The importance to the insured of these different services naturally varies between insurance contracts. Very large corporations, in particular, may be less interested in the protection afforded by the insurer's guarantee but may purchase the insurance to take advantage of the insurer's efficient administrative systems, expertise and advice.

## 11.4 Identifying and meeting customer needs for insurance services

In general the marketing process starts with an identification of customer needs, and then proceeds to develop products that will satisfy these needs in an efficient and profitable way. In considering the need for four insurance services (that is, risk transfer, administration, investment and advice), the starting point is to consider the customer's exposure to risk and the reaction to that risk.

### 11.4.1 Customer needs for insurance services

The adverse effect of risk on our lives scarcely needs emphasizing. Every individual person is exposed to the risk of financial loss and illness, injury or death, although some to a greater degree than others. The operation of business firms and public sector organizations also expose their stakeholders (such as owners, employees, managers, creditors etc.) to financial and even physical risk. However in many circumstances, it may not be straightforward to measure risk, particularly if an event occurs so rarely that it may be overlooked completely. Thus the first step in the process of marketing insurance is usually an assessment of the risks to which the customer is exposed.

In the case of insurance purchased by business corporations, risk assessment is normally undertaken by the company's insurance broker or risk manager (if it has one) utilizing various risk identification checklists. Once potential risks have been identified, the next stages of the risk management process are to measure the size of the problem (in an effort to quantify the probability distributions of loss frequency and loss size) and then to investigate the effectiveness of the many forms of physical and financial loss control – one of which is the purchase of various general insurance contracts. A similar procedure will need to be undertaken in relation to a company's employee benefit programme (pensions, health insurance etc.), and companies are major purchasers of long-term insurance as a result.

In the case of personal financial services such as life insurance, risk assessment is the first stage of personal financial management – which has been defined as 'the process of marshalling all of an individual's financial resources in the most efficient way towards achieving his or her personal objectives' (Carter, 1990). The main purposes of personal financial planning are first, to protect yourself, and your dependents, from the financial consequences of unpredictable events, and secondly to maximize the net-of-tax benefits that can be achieved from the investment of your financial assets.

There is another very important reason why the insurer needs to make an assessment of the risks to which the customer is exposed. In practice there are substantial differences between the insurer and the insured in the amount of information that the insurer has about the risk itself and about the behaviour of the insured in relation to that risk. A failure on the part of the insurer to charge a price which adequately reflects the risk will encourage insurance purchases by high risk customers, since they are effectively getting their insurance at a discount: this is known as adverse selection. Similarly a failure by insurers to observe any behaviour by customers which might increase the risk after the purchase of insurance (for example by taking less care in looking after their property) may lead to the problems of moral hazard.

## 11.4.2 An individual's demand for insurance services

Even if an exposure to risk, and hence the (passive) need for insurance can be demonstrated, customers will not necessarily demand insurance services unless those needs can be turned into active wants, backed by a willingness and ability to pay. Customers will only want to buy insurance services on a voluntary basis if it can be demonstrated that the purchase enhances their welfare, by either controlling risk or by providing cost-effective organizational, investment, or advisory services. There are substantial differences between personal and corporate customers in the reasons why they might want to purchase insurance. In the case of long-term insurance, an individual's purchase of life insurance and pensions is also motivated by the need to redistribute income from the present to the future (in order to finance future expenditures), to maximize the net-of-tax return on investments, and also by the desire to make a bequest to dependents.

In practice, the purchase of insurance cover is often enforced by law or by contractual provision. Thus third-party motor insurance is compulsory for all drivers under the conditions of the Road Traffic Acts, while the Employers' Liability (Compulsory Insurance) Act 1969 makes it compulsory for all employers carrying out business in the UK to acquire employers' liability insurance. The purchase of fire insurance on private property is usually a contractual requirement before lenders will advance a mortgage or bank loan, especially if the property is being used as security for the loan.

Individuals who do not worry about risk to themselves, or others, will have little need for the primary risk transfer service provided by insurers (although they may still make a purchase if they value the insurer's other services). The extent to which people may worry about exposure to the risk of financial loss and/or physical injury depends on their risk aversion and on their altruism towards others who may also be affected. It is generally believed that, when fully appraised of the risk, most individuals would behave in a risk averse manner (that is, they prefer a guaranteed certain outcome to an uncertain one with the same average result). It is this risk aversion which motivates an individual's demand for the risk-transfer service provided by insurance and greater degrees of risk aversion generally increase the demand for insurance. Some of the television and media advertising undertaken by insurance companies' attempts to increase customer risk aversion by dramatic representation of disasters (such as the well-known series by the Commercial Union, which tries not to make a drama out of a crisis). In the past, the Advertising Standards Authority has been critical of some insurance advertisements which have the capacity to cause unnecessary distress to viewers.

### 11.4.3 A corporation's demand for insurance services

It is not generally possible to argue that corporations purchase insurance because they are risk averse. This is because worry or concern about risk is a human attribute, and companies are not human beings. So we have to assert that a corporation's insurance purchases are motivated either by the risk aversion of a substantial number of the company's (human) stakeholders – such as owners, managers or employees – or by real-service efficiency gains in the firm's own operations. A very well-argued case study of corporate insurance demand is provided by Doherty and Smith (1993), who examine the decision by British Petroleum in 1990 to insure against small property losses (under $10 million) while remaining uninsured for losses exceeding $10 million, even though the destruction of one of their North Sea oil platforms could cost BP over $2000 million.

Of course, in the case of a small owner-managed firm, variations in the trading results of the business have a direct effect on the only substantial stakeholder (the owner). It is not surprising therefore that insurance purchases by such firms should be motivated by the owner's risk aversion. What is less clear however is why the owners of large publicly quoted companies should be worried about the risk of fluctuations in the company's trading results. The argument is reasonably straightforward: because of risk aversion, the shareholders of large quoted companies normally hold their shares as part of a diversified share portfolio. They do this because the cost of holding a diversified portfolio is not significantly higher than that of owning the same number of shares in just one or two companies. If the portfolio is large enough, the shareholder is able to diversify away all of the risk which is specific to an individual share (known as specific or unsystematic risk): the only risk that remains is that which is common to almost all the companies represented in the portfolio, and which therefore cannot be diversified away (known as systematic risk).

Thus widely diversified shareholders do not normally need to purchase insurance against firm-specific risk (such as property damage, liability, pecuniary loss etc.) because the effect on them of this risk has already been reduced to zero. The only exception to this rule arises if firms are able to purchase insurance at a price which is equal to, or even below the average cost of losses, since firms will then be able to make a profit out of their insurers: this situation may arise if competition in the insurance market is particularly intense or if insurers underestimate the risk.

In their discussion of the corporate demand for insurance, Mayers and Smith, (1982) advance four ways in which a large quoted company can increase its profits by making discretionary insurance purchases:

*Controlling the costs associated with financial distress or bankruptcy.* The owners of a limited company may not worry too much about the risk of company bankruptcy because of their limited liability and diversified portfolios. However the possibility of bankruptcy (or of financial distress – which describes the cash-flow problems that a firm may experience as a prelude to insolvency) may impose additional costs on the firm, and owners will be keen to control these. There are two main costs associated with financial distress or bankruptcy. First, other stakeholders (such as employees, banks, suppliers) may be concerned that the firm will be unable, by virtue of its limited liability, to pay its debts in the event of bankruptcy or cash-flow problems and they will therefore charge the firm more for their services (in terms of higher wages, interest rates, or input prices). The purchase of insurance ensures that additional resources are available to meet these debts, and may therefore produce cost savings for the firm. Secondly, the actual occurrence of bankruptcy imposes additional costs on the firm which will reduce the residual paid out to owners. These 'bankruptcy costs' include the professional services of accountants and lawyers, the sale of fixed assets below cost price, and the loss of tax credits and goodwill. Any insurance which can reduce the chance of bankruptcy may be of value if the premium is small in comparison with the expected value of the bankruptcy costs saved.

*Real-service efficiencies.* Part of the corporate demand for insurance is explained by the insurer's efficiency in providing low-cost services, such as risk assessment, claims negotiation and management and administration, which arises from the insurer's specialization and economies of scale.

*Reducing the costs of agency problems.* Agency problems arise because of the conflicts of interest that exist between the firm's various stakeholders (that is, owners, managers, employees, bankers etc.). These conflicts mean that one group of stakeholders may take actions which are detrimental to the interests of others. For example, managers who are keen to improve short-term profitability may undertake opportunist behaviour (in postponing maintenance, cutting research and development costs, or trimming on employee safety, say) which has an immediate reduction in costs, but may well decrease the value of the firm to shareholders. The costs involved in such agency problems occur because stakeholders will need to monitor each other's behaviour (thus owners will need to monitor managers) and will also want to bond themselves to a particular set of actions.

Insurance can be used to reduce a firm's monitoring and bonding costs in a number of ways. First insurance companies have an interest in making sure that managers do not postpone any expenditure on risk-reduction devices, and will therefore implement their own monitoring by regular inspections of the company's premises and machinery. Secondly insurers will require the company to undertake certain actions which reduce risk (such as conducting regular cleaning of the premises and maintaining the fire and safety systems) and failure to do so will invalidate the insurance (see Diacon and Carter, (1992) Chapter 4 for a discussion of insurance warranties). Thirdly insurance provides the funds for reinvestment following a property loss, and hence reduces the incentive by shareholders not to put new resources into the business following a loss (the so-called 'under-investment problem').

*Reductions in profits or corporation tax.* Most tax codes give a number of implicit or even explicit tax advantages to firms which purchase insurance. Such advantages are not normally available to self-insured contingency reserves, and thus enable companies which purchase insurance to minimize the net-of-tax impact of any losses. The tax breaks given to insurance are a major reason why many large companies have established their own captive insurance subsidiaries – in order to have the benefits of self-insurance as well as the tax advantages of insurance.

## 11.5   A brief overview of the UK insurance market

The modern United Kingdom insurance industry has grown up largely free from government interference, and is widely acknowledged to be the most developed and complex in Europe. Although new entrants to the industry must fulfil the licensing requirements of the Insurance Companies Act 1981, these are not particularly onerous and do not act as a substantial barrier to entry (evidenced by the fact that between ten and twenty new insurance companies are licensed each year). In addition since July 1994, companies with head offices in other European Union and European Economic Area member states have been able to operate under the terms of a licence issued by their home country supervisory authority.

The relatively free entry to and exit from some quarters of insurance business means that existing firms face competition not only from within the industry but also from potential entrants, thus effectively making these sectors a contestable market. Under such circumstances, the hit-and-run behaviour of potential entrants is sufficient to deter existing firms from making excessive profits. Similarly existing firms which are inefficient (through the use of out-of-date technology, which leads to either higher costs or poor underwriting decisions) are vulnerable to profitable hit-and-run entry by new competitors (as has been evidenced by the emergence of direct writers like Direct Line in the UK motor insurance market).

The UK insurance market is heavily involved in both reinsurance (that is, a 'wholesale' insurance contract between one insurance company and another) and direct insurance, which covers transactions between insurers and the rest of the world. The direct and reinsurance markets in the UK have three main components:

- Buyers, including individuals, companies, and local and national governments.
- Insurers, including stock and mutual insurance companies, friendly and collecting societies, and individual names organized into the syndicates at Lloyd's of London.
- Independent intermediaries, including insurance brokers licensed by the Insurance Brokers' Registration Council and/or by Lloyd's of London, and independent financial advisers which are registered with the Personal Investment Authority (and previously with FIMBRA).

The UK insurance market is a complex one, and is involved in an enormous number of different types of insurance contracts; it is a mistake to think that insurance is just one homogeneous market. It is possible to divide the market into two broad, but overlapping, categories: the so-called 'London Market' (which is mainly involved in international insurance business) and the national markets (which cater for the long-term and general insurance needs of UK-resident individuals and companies).

### 11.5.1 The London insurance market

Carter and Falush (1994) note that, whilst there is no watertight definition of the London insurance market, there is a general agreement that the core of its activity is the conduct of internationally traded insurance and reinsurance business. It comprises a large number of Lloyd's syndicates and other insurers and intermediaries located in the City of London which are active in placing and accepting mainly marine and non-marine general insurance and reinsurance business. Many of the insurers and brokers operating in London are specialists, and do not trade insurance business outside the market. The majority of insurance contracts written in the London market are transacted on subscription basis whereby insurers share their coverage by subscribing to a 'slip' prepared by an insurance broker which contains details of the risk. The price and terms of the contract are set by a lead underwriter and other insurers follow by indicating on the slip the share of the risk that they are prepared to accept. The market is linked electronically by the London Insurance Market network (LIMNET) which provides the basis for electronic trading and communication. The London insurance market is the world's most important international insurance market.

### 11.5.2 The national insurance markets

The UK national insurance markets provide general insurance and life and pensions policies to UK-resident individuals and companies. Figures provided by the Swiss Reinsurance Company (1994) show that, in 1992, the UK was the fourth largest market in the world in terms of expenditure on premiums (after the USA, Japan and Germany), and UK residents spent an average of £950 and £1730 per capita on general and long-term insurance respectively. A measure of insurance penetration can be obtained by expressing premium expenditure as a percentage of Gross Domestic Product: in 1992, UK residents (including the corporate sector) spent 4.0 per cent of GDP on general insurance and a further 7.3 per cent on long-term business. Out of the world's sixty-six largest countries, the insurance penetration in the UK was exceeded by only the USA in general insurance (with a figure of 5.1 per cent) and by South Korea (9.8 per cent) and South Africa (10.3 per cent) in life and pensions business.

Although there were 828 insurers licensed to transact business in the UK at the end of 1993, the national market is dominated by a small number of large insurance groups transacting both general and long-term business. Many of the DTI licensed insurers are subsidiaries of larger insurance groups, others are not trading or are specialist insurers not active in the open market, and a substantial number operate only in the London market. In fact, the main classes of insurance in the UK are often dominated by the same insurers: the figures in Table 11.1 illustrate the share of UK business of the largest companies in 1992. For many reasons, the UK long-term insurance market has been becoming increasingly competitive, and it is widely believed that there may be a sharp reduction in the number of competing life offices by the year 2000.

The largest insurers in the UK are independent stock companies, quoted on the London Stock Exchange, and selling a wide range of both general and long-term insurance products, including such well-known names as Prudential, Commercial Union, General Accident, Royal, Sun Alliance, Guardian, Legal and General, and London and Manchester. On the other hand, there are also a number of large independent mutual companies in the market (including Norwich Union,

**Table 11.1** *The largest insurers, and their market share, in the UK insurance market (1992)*

| | |
|---|---|
| Motor | Eagle Star (9.3%), Norwich Union (7.9%), General Accident (7.7%), Royal (7.4%), Sun Alliance (6.8%) |
| Property | Sun Alliance (14.0%), Royal (13.2%), Commercial Union (9.4%), General Accident (8.7%), Eagle Star (8.1%) |
| Liability | Sun Alliance (12.1%), Eagle Star (12.0%), Commercial Union (9.3%), Guardian (9.2%), General Accident (8.1%) |
| Pecuniary | Sun Alliance (9.6%), General Accident (9.2%), Eagle Star (8.3%), Royal (6.6%), Financial (4.1%) |
| Accident and health | BUPA (26.1%), Private Patients Plan (15.4%), Sun Alliance (6.5%), General Accident (3.6%), Norwich Union (3.4%) |
| Life | Prudential (11.4%), Standard Life (6.9%), Norwich Union (6.3%), Sun Life (5.7%), Legal and General (3.9%) |
| Pensions | Prudential (7.9%), Standard Life (7.6%), Equitable (7.2%), Legal and General (6.4%), Scottish Widows (6.0%) |
| Permanent health | Standard Life (14.7%), UNUM (13.0%), Medical Sickness (11.5%), Norwich Union (6.2%), Allied Dunbar (5.4%) |

*Source:* UNIC 1994

Standard Life, Equitable, Scottish Widows, Clerical Medical, Friends Provident, Scottish Amicable, Scottish Equitable and NPI – all but Norwich Union being specialist life offices) which are owned by a sub-section of their life insurance policyholders. Most of the remaining large companies operating in the UK insurance market are wholly owned sub-sidiaries, including Eagle Star and Allied Dunbar (which are owned by BAT Industries), Pearl (owned by the Australian Mutual Provident insurance company), AXA Equity and Law (owned by the French AXA Group), Cornhill (owned by the German insurer Allianz), and London and Edinburgh (owned by the American ITT Company).

Among the UK insurers which are subsidiaries, there is a growing number of specialist life offices which are owned by UK banks and building societies (the so-called bancassurers) including: Barclays Life (Barclays Bank), Abbey National Life and Scottish Mutual (Abbey National Bank), Lloyds Abbey Life and Black Horse Life (Lloyds Bank), Nationwide Life (Nationwide Building Society) and Woolwich Life (Woolwich Building Society). Most bancassurers sell partly through their branch networks and partly through dedicated salesforces, and specialize in unit-linked savings and investment products. It is widely believed that bancassurance companies enjoy a cost advantage in comparison with more traditional life insurers, which results from more efficient sales and an ability to spread overheads and other costs across a wide range of financial services products.

A key feature of the national UK insurance market is the involvement of independent intermediaries (including brokers and IFAs, and other independents such as accountants and solicitors) in placing general and long-term insurance with companies. Although most insurers now gain their business from a variety of sources, not so long ago it was common-place to find major insurers which obtained virtually all their business via independent intermediaries. A breakdown of the sources of general (split between individual and corporate business) and long-term insurance is provided in Table 11.2.

Table 11.2 shows that the share of the market controlled by brokers (or IFAs in the case of life and pensions business) varies by class of business and market. In the case of corporate general insurance business and marine, aviation and transit (which is virtually all from corporate customers), the market is dominated by brokers and other independent intermediaries. One reason is that business transacted on the London market can only be placed by brokers: only Lloyd's brokers have rights of access to the trading floor at Lloyd's of London. However the dominance of brokers in the market with the best-informed customers demonstrates that independent intermediaries can play a valuable role in designing and placing corporate insurance programmes and in improving the efficiency and effectiveness of the insurance market.

In the case of individual general and long-term insurance however, the share of the market controlled by brokers/IFAs and other independents is decreasing. In the life and pensions market, the main reasons are the increased market share obtained by the bancassurers (which do not use IFAs), and the simultaneous contraction in the number of IFAs arising

**Table 11.2** *The sources of UK insurance business 1990 and 1993*

| | Independent intermediaries | | Company agents | | Direct |
|---|---|---|---|---|---|
| | Brokers/IFAs | Other | Staff | Other | |
| **Individual (personal lines) general insurance** | | | | | |
| 1990 | 41 | 30 | 6 | 12 | 11 |
| 1993 | 32 | 25 | 11 | 8 | 21 |
| **Corporate (commercial lines) general insurance** | | | | | |
| 1990 | 70 | 11 | 3 | 5 | 11 |
| 1993 | 71 | 10 | 4 | 4 | 9 |
| **Marine, aviation and transit insurance** | | | | | |
| 1990 | 94 | 1 | 0 | 2 | 3 |
| 1993 | 97 | 1 | 0 | 1 | 2 |
| **Total new long-term annual premiums** | | | | | |
| 1990 | 23 | 9 | 47 | 19 | 2 |
| 1993 | 23 | 5 | 50 | 19 | 3 |
| **Total long-term single premiums** | | | | | |
| 1990 | 40 | 12 | 38 | 9 | 1 |
| 1993 | 39 | 11 | 34 | 14 | 1 |

*Source:* Association of British Insurers 1994

from the onerous requirements of the Financial Services Act 1986. For example, at the end of 1988, the regulatory body charged with licensing IFAs (FIMBRA) had a membership of 9300, but this subsequently fell to 7700 in mid-1990 and around 5000 in early 1995.

The main reason for the declining share of independent intermediaries in the general personal lines market (such as household property and motor) is the substantial rise in direct writing by insurers such as Direct Line (owned by the Royal Bank of Scotland), Churchill, Guardian Direct, and The Insurance Service (owned by Royal). Most of the major insurance groups now operate direct writing subsidiaries in order to by-pass the independent intermediary. Direct writing motor and household insurance offers a number of advantages to the insurer over more conventional distribution methods, such as:

- It is more convenient for customers since they can purchase, change or update their insurance cover by telephone.
- It is cheaper for insurers (and hence for customers) because no commission has to be paid to an intermediary.
- It allows the insurer to obtain efficiency improvements through the use of new technology.
- It does not expose insurers to the bargaining power exerted by intermediaries (in forcing up commissions, in reducing price and in persuading insurers to accept high-risk business).

- It does not allow customers to make easy price comparisons.
- It allows the insurer greater flexibility in underwriting and pricing, as prices and terms and conditions can be changed almost instantaneously.

## 1.6 The marketing mix for insurance companies

A general introduction to the concept of the marketing mix was provided in Chapter 4. The types of marketing activities which make up the marketing mix in insurance will be discussed under the traditional headings of product, pricing, promotion and place.

### 11.6.1 Product

The earlier discussion of the demand for insurance services has highlighted the role of insurance in transferring risk and in providing real-service efficiencies to customers. However, because of the complexity of insurance products and the lack of advance information about their performance, it is often difficult for consumers to evaluate product quality. It is for this reason that the regulatory authorities have frequently intervened to improve the information available (as in the case of personal financial services) and take responsibility for monitoring insurer solvency.

In the provision of its risk-transfer service, the insurer is selling a promise of future performance: that is, its guarantee that future valid claims will be paid. An insurer's ability to deliver this promise largely depends on its financial strength and solvency. The time-lag between the inception of the contract and the eventual payment of the claim may be several decades: this is obvious in life insurance and pensions policies, but is equally the case in many classes of general business too – for example, many UK employers' liability insurers are still paying claims in the 1990s on policies that were sold in the 1940s and 1950s as a result of the exposure of workers to asbestos dust. Thus a key feature of the insurer's risk transfer product is the continuity and future survival of the insurer. It is for this reason that much effort is expended by brokers and corporate customers particularly in trying to assess the solvency of different insurers. It is also quite common to see advertisements by insurers selling personal lines general business and long-term insurance which advertise their current financial strength.

Insurers in a weak financial position will offer a poor-quality risk transfer service. There is always the possibility that an insurer will be unable to pay claims as a result of its deteriorating financial position (and eventual bankruptcy) and there have been several instances of insolvency in the UK insurance market in recent years. For example, in early 1992 the collapse of Trinity Insurance and Bryanston Insurance (both of which specialized in reinsurance business) meant that the claims of many of their policyholders were not paid. In May 1992 the Municipal Mutual (which at the time was the UK's eleventh largest general insurer) announced that it was technically insolvent and ceased trading: its subsidiary Municipal General was subsequently put into provisional liquidation and over 6000 personal lines claims (totalling in excess of £24 million) remained unpaid. Insurers in a poor financial position are also likely to dispute and delay the payment of valid claims. In their discussion of British Petroleum's decision not to insure against large losses, Doherty and Smith (1993) explain that a major factor was the difficulty that BP had experienced in extracting valid claims payments from its insurers.

The quality of an insurer's employees is a vital ingredient in the provision of non-risk transfer services to customers. The attitudes, skills, knowledge and behaviour of employees can have a critical impact on the levels of satisfaction the user derives from service product consumption. Of particular importance in the quality of insurance services are the ethical standards and behaviour of insurance personnel, since customers who do not trust their insurers will not be customers for very long. Many of the surveys of consumers and independent intermediaries which ask about customer satisfaction and choice of insurer highlight the quality of service as the most important factor. Insurers are able to improve the quality of the service they provide by continually investing in training for their staff, and by employing more staff with professional and/or academic qualifications. Service quality is also an issue of concern to regulators (particularly in view of widespread evidence of mis-selling of life insurance and pensions products in the late 1980s) and, in the market for personal financial services, the Personal Investment Authority has taken a number of steps to monitor and improve service quality, including imposing minimum standards of staff training competence, implementing a system of mystery shopping to check on the quality of advice that customers receive, and fining those insurers which are found to be in breach of its guidelines.

For life insurance and pensions policies, the key factor in product quality is the future investment performance and liquidity of the monies invested in the contract. Since performance cannot be guaranteed, customers can only make judgements of product quality based on the past performance of similar contracts using the numerous league tables that appear in journals such as *Planned Savings*, *Money Management*, *Pensions Management*, *Investors Chronicle* and *Money Marketing*. However, extrapolation of past performance into the future is fraught with difficulties. As a result of the drive to improve product information, the regulatory authorities (in the shape of the Securities and Investments Board) have implemented new disclosure requirements to ensure that customers are better informed about the investment strategies, costs, and early termination rates of the insurers than they were before. Since January 1995, life insurance companies, and other providers of personal financial services, have had to provide the client at the point of sale with the following key features of the contract:

- All administrative charges associated with the policy;
- Surrender values and maturity values based on the life office's own intended surrender value practices;

- Projected product investment performance, based on the office's own recent experience (and not on industry benchmark figures, as had previously been the case);
- Written information on commissions payable (or their equivalent), by all sellers – both IFAs and company salesagents, including allowances for additional benefits; and
- A 'reason why' letter which explains why a particular contract has been recommended or why cancellation has been advised.

## 11.6.2 Pricing

Pricing is an intensely difficult issue in many classes of insurance. The basic concern for insurers is to set a price that covers the average claims and other costs which are expected to arise from the contract. But of course, the insurer never knows in advance what the customer's claims costs are going to be, and may not even know what claims can be expected from a large group of identical customers (if such a group exists). In those cases where the insurer has a choice of distribution channels (see the discussion of Place in Section 11.6.4) the price charged to the final consumer may differ between channels – known as 'differential pricing'. These price differences may arise because of the channels differ in the costs they impose on insurers (using a direct salesforce is normally more expensive than either direct writing, or even independent intermediaries, for example) or because of attempts by insurers to enforce an element of price discrimination by charging a higher price to less price-sensitive customers.

Insurers which fail to charge a price that adequately reflects the risk involved will expose themselves to the problems of adverse selection. Thus most insurance contracts are priced on a customer-specific basis, so that the premium rate is determined according to the individual circumstances of the customer. In motor insurance, for example, the premium rate depends on a number of underwriting factors including the type of car, the age of the driver and driving experience, type of use, area of use, garaging etc. Similarly in household property insurance, the premium depends on the house's address (i.e. post-code) because weather, ground conditions and crime rate vary between regions.

Insurance premium rates can be determined in many different ways (for example, see Diacon, (1990) Chapters 11 and 12) but a broad distinction may be made depending on the amount of information that the insurer has about the risk involved. In many classes of insurance, the insurers have a mass of statistical detail on previous claims experience of similar policies in that class, so that there is little ambiguity about the risk. This is typically the case in most personal general business (such as household fire or motor) and life and pensions insurance. The insurer will therefore be able to make an accurate assessment of the probability distributions of loss frequency and loss size for a typical customer, and compute a premium which reflects the risk. On the other hand, many other classes of insurance (particularly those relevant to corporate customers) are characterized by considerable levels of ambiguity in that insurers have little objective information on which to compute an accurate premium. In these circumstances insurers have to resort to a number of strategies if the risk is to be insurable, including the imposition of conditions and warranties on the customer which have the effect of improving the information and changing the risk to meet the specifications assumed by the insurer (as discussed by Heimer, (1985) in an interesting case study on insuring the first North Sea oil platforms). It is also quite common to find that the insurance prices on ambiguous risks are computed as a moving average of the insured's own previous claims experience (say over the preceding three years).

Another feature of the insurance of ambiguous risks is the quite dramatic fluctuations in price and insurer profitability from one year to another. In the mid-1980s for example, the premium rates on some classes of US corporate liability insurance reputedly increased tenfold in a single year. The generic term for the fluctuation in prices and profits is the 'underwriting cycle', although there is often little of a regular cycle involved. The causes of the underwriting cycle are unclear, although recent researchers have suggested that it may be due to the need by insurers to finance major losses retrospectively by putting up premiums following a loss. Insurers need to do this because the capital markets may be reluctant to provide external finance which will be used solely to pay claims. Unfortunately fluctuations in insurance prices can detract from the stabilization service that insurance is meant to provide to its customers.

Customized products drawing from a wide range of options means that customers' price comparisons can be extremely complex. In general insurance, the infrequent nature of insurance losses makes it very difficult for the customer to make value-for-money judgments and it is not uncommon to find instances in which, over an extended period of time, customers have paid out many times the amount that they have received back in claims. In some classes of life insurance and pensions, the whole concept of price is meaningless because it is so confused with the investment performance of the contract. In order to improve customer information on the factors that affect the true price of life insurance and pensions products, and to encourage competition among providers to reduce costs and hence prices, the Securities and Investments Board has required the full disclosure of the provider's costs and charges since January 1995. A typical illustration of the impact of such charges on a twenty-year endowment policy is provided in Table 11.3. The table shows that, on maturity, a typical customer might have paid premiums of £24 000 and received benefits of £43 200: the total incurred charges of £6130 then represent 25.5 per cent of total premiums and 14.2 per cent of benefits.

### 11.6.3 Promotion

Promotion is the third of the conventional 4Ps. Once a suitable product has been designed, promotion must be used to contact potential

**Table 11.3** *An illustration of the impact on life office charges*

The figures relate to a man aged 39 paying £1200 per annum for a twenty-year endowment with sum assured of £40,000. Investment yield assumed to be 7.5 per cent per annum

| Year | Total premiums paid (£) | Surrender value (SV) (£) | Total charges | | |
|---|---|---|---|---|---|
| | | | £ | % premiums | % SV |
| 1 | 1200 | 1040 | 200 | 16.6 | 19.2 |
| 2 | 2400 | 2320 | 247 | 10.3 | 10.6 |
| 3 | 3600 | 3620 | 370 | 10.3 | 10.2 |
| 4 | 4800 | 4960 | 556 | 11.6 | 11.2 |
| 5 | 6000 | 6390 | 744 | 12.4 | 11.6 |
| 10 | 12 000 | 15 200 | 1760 | 14.7 | 11.6 |
| 15 | 18 000 | 27 200 | 3430 | 19.1 | 12.6 |
| 20 | 24 000 | 43 200* | 6130 | 25.5 | 14.2 |

*Maturity value

customers and to persuade them to by it. The promotion mix includes advertising, selling, sales promotion, direct selling and direct mail, sponsorship, merchandising and public relations. Jones (1989) notes that these techniques are used in communications intended to influence the buying process by achieving cognitive (learning), affective (feeling) or behavioural (doing) outcomes in target audiences. A company's promotion policy must harmonize with the other elements of the marketing mix in order to produce a composite brand company image.

Although the media advertising budget of most insurance companies is small compared with other financial services firms, it is none the less an important form of promotion. Some of the insurers' advertising is directed at independent intermediaries (via the specialist insurance trade press in journals such as *Post Magazine*, *The Review*, *Business Risk* and *Corporate Cover*) but an increasing proportion is being targeted at the final consumers, particularly by the direct writers of motor insurance such as Direct Line. In 1993, seventeen insurance companies spent over £45 million on TV advertising alone – but many commentators have wondered whether this is really effective in view of the continuing poor reputation of the industry as a whole. Media advertising by insurance companies is undertaken for a number of reasons including name awareness, product promotion, and the creation of a brand or company image. This last reason is particularly important in an industry with so many competing companies which provide a fairly homogeneous product as far as most (uninformed) consumers are concerned. Numerous research studies have shown that when consumers are presented with a choice of companies (perhaps by an independent intermediary) they will invariably go for the one they have already heard of.

Because of the intangibility of insurance services, insurers are often concerned to be associated with a physical representation which simultaneously communicates the services provided, and the security and trustworthiness of the provider. Thus in recent years, UK television audiences have been exposed to widows (linking the visual image of a widow to a company's name – Scottish Widows Assurance), umbrellas (representing protection provided by the Legal and General), squirrels (emphasizing the savings capabilities of NPI), dancing clerics and doctors (in the case of Clerical Medical Investment Group), and cheeky little red telephones on wheels (which reinforce the ease with which one can use a hot-line contact direct to the direct-writing motor insurer Direct Line).

Watkins and Diacon (in Diacon, 1990, Chapter 13) note that commercial sponsorship of sporting and cultural events has grown very rapidly in recent years, with the insurance companies often at the forefront by sponsoring cricket, swimming, table tennis, horse racing and a host of other sports and arts events. Although it is unrealistic to expect a direct link between sponsorship and increased sales, sponsorship does increase company name awareness. Perhaps the best example is still provided by the sponsorship by Cornhill Insurance (which is owned by a German company) of international test cricket in England.

### 11.6.4 Place

Place decisions are concerned with the physical distribution of insurance services, making these available to customers when and where they are wanted. Place decisions in services marketing are concerned with location and distribution channel. In many aspects of insurance the location decisions of the insurance company head office may not have a significant impact on marketing performance since consumers do not really care where Direct Line's telephone sales staff are situated (for example) or where their policy documents are processed. For many years it was thought that it was vital for insurers selling to individual customers to have a physical location on the high street. It was for this reason that Commercial Union experimented with insurance shops in the 1970s, and many of the major insurers acquired estate agency chains in the 1980s. One of the main marketing advantages of the bancassurers (such as Halifax Life, NatWest Life, and Midland Life) is supposed to be their widespread network of retail outlets. In practice, it is doubtful whether people want to buy their insurance or make their financial decisions while sitting in a shop window, and most face-to-face contact with an insurance salesagent (even those employed by bancassurers) is made in the privacy of people's homes.

There are however two instances where an insurer's location decision may be more important. In the first place, general insurers wishing to participate in the London Insurance Market must have an underwriting office in the City of London. In October 1993, the London Underwriting Centre was opened to provide specialist facilities to insurers which wanted to trade in the London market, and there were soon over twenty companies based in the building. Secondly, insurers which obtain much of their business from independent intermediaries need to have regional branches around the country (although not normally in high street locations) in order to service the needs of their intermediaries – which in turn tend to be geographically dispersed. However in both cases, the development of Electronic Data Interchange (EDI) networks is reducing the need for physical proximity.

When considering decisions on distribution channel, there are two related issues that must be considered: the type of channel to be used, and the sales incentives to be adopted to maximize the firm's profits. Insurance companies are faced with a number of strategies to market their products to final consumers, and nowadays most use a mixture of distribution channels including:

- Independent intermediaries, full-time brokers and independent financial advisers and part-time independents such as accountants and solicitors. The distinguishing feature of independent interme- diaries is that they are not tied to any one provider, and have to be able to recommend products from a wide range of providers in the industry. The customers serviced by intermediaries are therefore likely to be fairly price-sensitive. The main intermediaries involved in the corporate insurance market (including reinsurance broking) tend to be very large multinational companies such as the Sedgwick Group and Willis Corroon: these offer clients a wide range of con- sultancy as well as broking services. There are also large broking firms operating in the financial services market (such as Sedgwick Noble Lowndes, Frizzell, and Bradford and Bingley Insurance Brokers), as well as franchising companies (so-called umbrella groups or broker/IFA networks) which provide centralized admin- istrative support for individual brokers. Networks like DBS, Countrywide and Burns Anderson are thought to have total mem- bership exceeding 2000 firms of independent intermediaries.
- Appointed representatives (ARs), which are non-insurance organi- zations such as estate agency chains and bank and building society branch networks that act as tied agents for just one product provi- der under the polarization requirements of the Financial Services Act 1986. A full updated list of the polarization decisions of the major institutions is provided in Chapter 8. Although ARs are often separate from the product providers in organizational terms, the provider is responsible for the training and behaviour of the sales staff involved.
- Own salesforces, which can be employed directly by the insurer or work as self-employed agents (for companies like Lloyds Abbey Life and Allied Dunbar for example).
- Direct selling, using telesales techniques combined with intensive media advertising. Direct writing was initially confined to personal lines motor and household business, but insurers are likely to build on the successes of companies like Direct Line by extending direct selling into other classes of business.
- Other methods such as direct mail and direct response advertising.

Table 11.2 provided a breakdown of sales by distribution channel for 1990 and 1993.

The traditional method of rewarding the sale of insurance (via both independent and non-independent channels) is by the payment of commission – normally calculated as a percentage of premium expenditure. In the UK there are no controls on the level of commission that can be paid, although since January 1995 all commissions received on the sale of life and pensions products must be disclosed to the client by the sales person in cash terms at the point of sale (so-called 'hard disclosure'). The difficulty for insurers is that although commission provides an ideal incentive to sales agents to maximize sales revenue, it can produce a conflict of interest between the interests of the sales agent and those of the client which can lead to biased advice, high-pressure sales and mis-selling (for example, see Gravelle, 1994). The fines levied on insurers as a result of mis-selling of personal pensions by the Personal Investment Authority also illustrate that incentives which maximize sales revenue may not always maximize profitability.

In order to correct the conflict of interest problem (and also to reduce the apparent commission that has to be disclosed), several life insurers (such as TSB Life and Friends Provident) have attempted to reduce their reliance on commissions as a method of remuneration, both for independent intermediaries, and for tied agents and salesforces. Unlike direct salespeople, intermediaries cannot be paid by a fixed salary because they are not employed directly by the insurer. It is therefore increasingly common for brokers and IFAs to charge their clients a fee for the advice and either rebate any commission (received from the insurer) back to the client or use one of the insurer's non-commission products (which will have enhanced benefits).

## 11.7   The product life cycle

The concept of the product life cycle may be a useful tool in analysing the suitability of the existing range of an insurance company's products, and is illustrated in Chapter 3. The product life cycle provides a framework for analysing the company's product range: from a profit and a cash-flow basis, the range should include a sufficient number of profitable contracts in the growth and maturity stages in order to enable the development of new products to be financed. The concept separates the life cycle of a product into five main phases: new product development, introduction, growth, mature and decline.

*Development stage*

An overview of the process of new product development is provided in Chapter 5 and most of the generic issues relating to financial services are relevant for insurance. In general it is difficult to use market research effectively in developing brand new insurance products because of their long-term and contingent nature. Since services cannot be patented, most new product development is undertaken by copying a competitor's ideas, or borrowing from another market. Dread disease insurance, for example, was introduced in the UK after first being developed in South Africa.

The main features of a new product that need to be worked through are the actuarial aspects of pricing, the tax position if it is to be a 'qualifying' life or pensions contract, the documentation required by the regulatory authorities (for example, the fact find to be used by sales staff, and the key features document and 'reason why' letter that must be given to clients) and the computer systems.

## Introduction

Once the product has been developed and launched, the introductory phase involves intensive training for direct sales staff and broker-support staff. This training is important because the sales approach must not only persuade the customers to buy, but also satisfy the regulatory authorities (in the case of a life and pensions product) that the process conforms with the PIA's requirements for best advice. Given the nature of the insurance industry it very difficult to make a 'splash' and to create an impact with a new product launch. As it is difficult to test-market new products, companies will often have little idea in advance of which sub-set of customers will be most responsive.

If not already alerted, competitors will closely monitor the success of the new product, and may copy it with a version of their own, since insurance products cannot be patented. However, the incumbent firm may be able to gain first-mover advantages if the product requires particularly onerous training or computer-systems development.

The aspect of the product's success which is most difficult to monitor (even for the producer) is whether the actual claims experience is in line with that assumed in the pricing process. Thus during the introductory phase, the insurer's statistical and actuarial advisers will monitor claims experience closely and may insist on changes in pricing or underwriting if claims appear to be too high.

The possibility of adverse selection against a new product is of particular concern. For example, in the rush to expand sales of endowment mortgages in the mid-1980s, several UK life offices introduced policies with 'streamlined' application forms which asked no questions about the customer's medical history. The insurers assumed that customers who were well enough to take out a mortgage presented no extra mortality risk. Unfortunately these contracts were purchased by a large number of people who were too ill to obtain a normal endowment policy (assisted by their relatives, who often met the mortgage repayments), and the insurers suffered exceptionally high claims experience as these customers often died much earlier than had been anticipated.

## Growth

If the product is successful it will reach the growth stage, where sales increase at their most rapid rate and the product becomes established.

Customers who are followers rather than leaders buy the product during the growth stage, and sales agents can refer to others who have already bought the product. As the distribution of the product becomes established, sales agents and independent intermediaries become more effective at selling it. The company must also implement strategies for dealing with competing products, since competitors will probably have introduced these by now. For example, in 1987 only three UK life offices were selling dread disease (or critical illness insurance), but within four years, the number had increased to over forty. The usual method of enhancing an insurance product in its growth stage is to widen the cover (to include a wider range of risks): this is easier for an established provider to do because it can be more certain of the claims experience involved.

## Maturity

The mature stage is reached as sales cease to grow faster than the underlying growth in the economy. Typically for insurance products this stage can last a long time (for over one hundred years in the case of traditional with-profit endowment policies, for example) and these traditional profitable products will form the mainstay of a company's sales income. However it is still possible to boost sales in the usual ways by seeking new distribution channels, adding further new features, making special promotional offers (especially to existing clients), and improved promotion.

## Decline

For many insurance products there is never a decline stage, since the product continues to service customer wants. Thus marine insurance which was first introduced into the world three thousand years ago will still be needed in the future: although the nature and design of ships may change, the perils of the sea will not. Similarly, other basic protection-based insurance products (such as fire/property insurance, motor, life etc.) are unlikely to decline substantially. All that happens in these cases is that products are periodically given a facelift (with a new name and new literature), but with no fundamental changes to their basic design.

Sales of other insurance products, however, may decline as the contracts become outmoded and superseded. Sometimes this may occur because of tax or regulatory changes (which accounted for the disappearance of a vast array of life single premium bonds in the early 1980s), although the same influences often generate a market for a new contract. Sometimes, technical improvements in the insurer's administrative systems necessitate a radical redesign of an established product (which is illustrated by the gradual replacement of conventional reversionary bonus endowment policies by the so-called unitized – not unit-linked – with-profit endowments). Finally, many insurance contracts can be redundant because of changes in economic circumstances, thus in an era of low inflation, contracts which involve index-linking (in both general and long-term insurance) have little real relevance.

Perhaps the best example of a product in its decline stage is industrial branch (IB) life insurance. These contracts are simple life policies, often for extremely low premiums paid to collectors in cash, which are sold on a door-to-door 'home service' basis. The archetypal salesman was the 'Man from the Pru' characterized by his bicycle and bicycle clips. Door-to-door sales and collection of premiums has become increasingly expensive, and the costs of industrial life offices are often much higher than their ordinary branch competitors. Early in 1994, the main industrial branch provider, the Prudential, announced that it was to cease transacting such business – marking the end of an era for IB business.

## 1.8 Conclusion

This chapter has attempted to identify the specific marketing features of the UK insurance sector, starting first with an analysis of why insurance is purchased, and then going on to consider the marketing mix as it applies to insurance. Marketing is usually defined as a management process devoted to identifying and satisfying customer wants in a profitable manner. In the marketing manager's Nirvana, product providers would understand their customers so well that the products virtually sell themselves: all the company has to do is to make the product available. Unfortunately, the difficulties in marketing insurance products – which include the consumers' reluctance to think about risk, and the problems of asymmetric information between buyers and sellers of insurance – mean that traditionally the insurance industry has been sales oriented rather than customer oriented.

It is questionable whether the sales orientation of many sectors of the UK insurance industry is very effective at increasing insurance company profitability, since it merely encourages companies to ignore the costs involved in mis-selling insurance products in favour of maximizing premium income and market share. These costs can include a higher-than-expected claims experience, bad publicity from consumer groups, distrust of the advice of commission-driven salesforces, fines and compensation payments imposed by regulators, and increasing disenchantment with insurance. What is needed in insurance marketing is a proper appreciation of consumer wants and needs, and the design and delivery of services which meet these needs in a way which maximizes long-term company profitability rather than short-term sales.

# 12 Building society marketing

## Donald W. Cowell

## 12.1 Introduction

The UK personal financial services sector has experienced major change in recent years. Once a highly fragmented market, the traditional boundaries betweeen financial institutions have now become blurred. In response to more intensive competition, advancing technology and greater consumer sophistication, financial institutions have expanded into areas once the traditional preserve of competitors. In recent years for example, building societies have broadened their activities to include unsecured loans, overdrafts, credit cards, travellers cheques and house insurance, all traditionally associated with financial institutions like banks and insurance companies. Furthermore an increasing number of societies have established or are considering the establishment of an insurance subsidiary. As shown in detail in Chapter 1, diversification opportunities for building societies were relatively limited until 1986 and the enactment of the Building Societies Act. This provided them with powers to engage in a wide range of new services essentially covering all personal financial services, investment, banking and housing. Within two years the Act was reformed, extending the powers of societies in the areas of investment and insurance services, trusteeship, executorship and land services.

As a direct result of the new legislation, and its subsequent reform, societies were able to revise their strategies with greater freedom. However, while the legislation provided societies with greater opportunities, the new highly competitive environment in which they now operated also posed considerable threats. Building societies had little previous experience of the turbulent market conditions they now faced. Previous competition had been intra type (i.e. between societies) and controlled by the Building Societies Association. In addition, consumers had been relatively unsophisticated and comparatively loyal. In response building society strategies were largely supply driven (i.e. by cost and technology) rather than demand driven (i.e. by consumer needs). Such strategies were inappropriate to the new situation they faced.

The major environmental changes which had such an impact upon building societies have been coupled with moves to adopt and implement the marketing concept. An essentially conservative and traditional set of institutions has become much more market driven, though some societies may have done too little too late according to Thwaites and Lynch (1992). Recent empirical evidence suggests that financial services organizations in general have shifted from the operations centred and finance dominated emphasis that was common a few years ago towards a more market-driven approach (Ennew, Wright and Thwaites 1993). Indeed, growing experience of strategic marketing and of marketing mix tools has seen a number of the major players in the building society industry rapidly moving up the marketing learning curve. Some have achieved considerable marketing sophistication in a short space of time. This chapter examines the nature and practice of marketing in building societies. Section 12.2 examines competitive marketing strategies using the concepts of differentiation, cost leadership and focus. section 12.3 reviews the marketing mix and section 12.4 presents a summary and conclusions.

## 2.2 Competitive strategies and building societies

All competitive strategies are long term though they require continuous reworking in response to environmental changes. Building societies like any other organizations must monitor these changes and select appropriate strategies to meet the challenges of the new market environment. Within the strategic management literature a variety of strategic options exist though the current orthodoxy is that there are three major generic strategic alternatives. Further detail on these strategic options is contained in Chapter 3. These strategies of 'differentiation', 'focus' and 'cost leadership' are considered and may be applied to building societies as follows.

### 12.2.1 Differentiation

A differentiation strategy is based on consumer perceived unique or superior distinguishing features perhaps through, for example, the range of services available, the image created or the quality of service. Effective differentiation strategies can increase customer loyalty and reduce price sensitivity and the risk of substitution. Differentiation poses a unique challenge for building societies as they are service organizations. The intangible nature of services means that the features of services can be replicated very quickly by competitors. To ensure success, the means of differentiation must have a real effect on customers' choice of building society and be difficult to replicate. Societies basing strategies on differentiation need to be creative and innovative to stay ahead of competitors.

In the past, many societies attempted to differentiate themselves using television advertising, (e.g. 'We're with the Woolwich'). Such advertisements increased awareness of societies but failed to create meaningful differences. More recently, the Bradford and Bingley and the Halifax Building Societies have successfully pursued a strategy of differentiation, the former creating an image of the traditional society and the latter highlighting its size as the largest society.

Research findings suggest that a differentiation strategy is particularly applicable to the medium-sized societies (Robson, 1989). Associations of size provide large and small societies with distinct images, however the images of medium-sized societies are less clearly defined. In addition, medium-sized societies are sometimes too small to convert to PLC status and thus diversify into all areas of personal finance, and too large to become niche players, i.e. focus on one market segment. Differentiation thus offers a particularly viable strategy to medium-sized societies.

Differentiation, however, can only be classed as a successful strategy when the means of differentiation corresponds with actual consumer wants and needs. The attributes which have a real effect on consumer choice of building society, the determinant attributes, must take into account both the importance of the attribute and the individual's ability to differentiate between societies on the basis of that attribute. Societies must address this area if they are successfully to pursue a differentiation policy. It is known that suitable attributes for differentiation in service businesses are often those connected with staff and service, and societies attempt to improve the quality of their service, the personalization of the service or the helpfulness of staff through investing considerable effort in training and in customer care (e.g. National and Provincial). The current vogue is to base differentiation not on the service itself but on the service delivery system harnessing technology, service quality and customer care as key discriminating features.

Previous research has also established that image is 'learnt', and each exposure (e.g. visit to the society or advertisement) reinforces the image held making it more vivid. Attempts to dramatically change a society's image can cause consumer confusion and may undermine the collective attributes upon which image is formed. Societies should assess their current image profile before selecting a means of differentiation. In recent research, the National and Provincial Building Society was perceived by consumers to have a good service, and the Alliance and Leicester was perceived to have up-to-date products. Such images could be strengthened and used to differentiate these societies even further.

Legislation has provided societies with the ability to exploit differences between them. The polarization rule (Financial Services Act 1986) allows societies (and banks) to differentiate themselves according to whether they are, or are not tied agents. The significance and patterns of polarization decisions are discussed in greater detail in Chapter 8. Few societies have retained their independent status with respect to insurance companies, though among the top ten societies the Bradford and Bingley has emphasized its continuing independent status as a source of differentiation.

The Building Societies Act also provides societies with a means of differentiation by enabling certain societies to convert to PLC status, thus becoming a new type of financial institution. This option is however only available to the larger societies who meet the specified asset requirements. To date the Abbey National has been the only society to pursue this option; others have received substantial publicity as they decide upon whether or not to convert and most recently the Halifax and Leeds have announced the intention to convert provided their proposed merger is successful. Whilst differentiation may be achieved for those societies who are amongst the first to convert, little recognition may be given to those subsequently converting.

## 12.2.2 Focus

A focus strategy involves offering a product/service which meets the needs of a well-defined group of customers. Such groups, or segments, are sometimes too small or specialized to attract large competitors. Whilst this strategy is commonly associated with small organizations, larger building societies can adopt a focus strategy by pursuing several segments. An interesting phenomenon of the mid-1990s is that a number of building societies such as Cheltenham and Gloucester have been re-examining earlier strategies pursued in the late 1980s and are refocusing again on their core activities. They appear to have learned the lesson successful retailers have long known that it is impossible (and costly) to try to be all things to all people. Efficient and effective marketing involves knowing who are your target market customers as well as who are not your target market customers.

Previously, societies segmented the consumer market by geographically targeting the local areas in which they operated. For example, the West of England Building Society conducted a series of campaigns to encourage people residing in the southern and western parts of England to identify the society as 'their' society and thus build customer loyalty. More recently some societies have attempted to segment the market using other factors (e.g. age). Research suggests that consumers can be segmented in a number of ways using demographics and savings behaviour (see Chapter 2). An attractive segment for societies to target is high net worth individuals. Consumers with high net incomes prefer a society which is modern, and bank-like, makes quicker decisions and has shorter waiting times. Also attributes of flexibility and safety are particularly appealing to this group.

Studies in the US found that high net worth individuals choose their financial institutions on the basis of 'ego-enhancement' (i.e. according to the use of names, personal attention, access to the managers etc.). Also research conducted by the Leeds Building Society identified speed as an important factor in choice behaviour. It could be concluded from these findings that a society wishing to target high net worth individuals should focus upon the speed and quality of service offered to them. Some smaller societies are perhaps already suitably positioned to target this segment as associations of size suggest that small societies provide a more personal service. In addition, a number of societies (e.g. the Chelsea) are perceived as 'up-market' societies and thus may have the image of exclusiveness which could pander to the desire for ego-enhancement.

Another attractive segment of the consumer market is the fifty-plus age group. Members of this group often have considerable disposable income, resulting from paid-up mortgages and the absence of dependent children. In addition, it is this group which is most likely to benefit from substantial inheritances. A number of smaller regional societies already have a high proportion of fifty-plus consumers due to their location in traditional retirement areas. Such societies could use these characteristics to their advantage. By maintaining a traditional image, and by providing additional services specific to this group (e.g. advice on wills and inheritance), the societies could develop their share of this market.

### 12.2.3 Cost leadership

A cost leadership strategy is based on lowest costs and hence greatest profit margins, though it should not be confused with a low price strategy. There are numerous ways in which a society can attempt to achieve cost reduction, and the major options of diversification, merger and rationalization are now considered.

*Diversification*

Diversified organizations achieve cost reductions by spreading the fixed costs of operating over a larger number of units. Diversification can take a number of forms. At its simplest, it may involve the introduction of new products in areas related to the base activity. Alternatively, it may involve diversifying into product markets in which the society has no previous experience. A diversification strategy may encompass both these aspects and can be accompanied by a departure from existing areas.

To date a substantial proportion of societies have diversified to varying degrees. Most have introduced new products into areas related to the base activity, e.g. home contents insurance (Bristol and West, Leeds Permanent), whilst others have entered new markets, e.g. travel and car insurance (Britannia). Societies will continue to diversify both within related and non-related areas, as the majority have now obtained their members' permission to do so. However, two interesting trends are now apparent. First, some societies have re-examined earlier strategic moves with divestments being made of recent acquisitions (e.g. estate agencies). Second, some markets are reaching saturation level through the 'me too' strategies adopted in the past. The choise of a diversification strategy is not however available to all societies. Whilst the larger, national societies have sufficient assets to allow them to become major providers of personal financial services, the smaller societies are confined by the 1986 Building Societies Act to areas with minimal risk association.

The appropriateness of a diversification strategy to individual building societies can be considered from two aspects: expected cost reductions and consumer response. While economic theory suggests that diversification generally results in cost reduction, this association may not occur in all industries. For example, building societies currently operate in areas of low risk, requiring little provision for bad debts. The majority of the new areas available to societies (e.g. unsecured loans) are comparatively high risk. Entrance into these areas requires increased expenditure on staffing and provision for bad debts. Costs can be particularly high during the introduction of the new services; specialized and skilled staff are required to supervise the new areas of operations and current staff require training. Whilst these costs will reduce as the society gains experience in producing the service, such additional costs could offset any economies of scale.

In addition, potential benefits associated with entry into new areas may be minimal due to over-capacity. All financial institutions are currently evaluating the markets of their competitors, markets from which they were previously prohibited entry. Some of these markets are generally mature markets and the prospects for growth are limited. The entrance of new players into the mortgage market is a prime example of over-capacity. Many new providers have gained market share by accepting lower returns. New players may find it both expensive to stay and expensive to withdraw from this market. The current account market is another example. Interest-bearing accounts were offered by societies to gain market share, and by banks to defend their market. Whilst such accounts may have cross-selling opportunities their cost can make them an unattractive alternative to the traditional building society savings account.

Consumer response to the pursuit of a diversification strategy by societies is not always favourable. For example, the Building Society Members Association campaigned to retain housing, rather than banking, as the main concern of societies. In addition, several surveys have repeatedly identified the resistance of the consumer to use services from those financial institutions with which they are not traditionally associated.

Though consumers are increasingly sophisticated about financial matters, current research would also appear not to support building society diversification. Some consumers possess a low level of knowledge and awareness of financial institutions and their services; they are still learning about personal finance and often find the subject difficult. The introduction of a variety of new services by the building societies can result in consumer confusion.

Research also suggests that the response of UK consumers to building society diversification is largely determined by the type of diversification pursued. Whilst diversification in related areas adds to the specialist nature of societies and thus enhances their image (e.g. societies could offer a complete housing package with estate agency services, conveyancing, mortgage, anti-gazumping insurance, home contents and structure insurance and unsecured loans for home improvements), diversification into new and different areas alters the very nature of societies. For example, societies extending their portfolios to include products traditionally associated with the clearing banks, (e.g. cash cards, cheque books) could acquire a more 'bank-like' image – which may be unwise given the poor image associated with some banks.

Clearly adoption of a diversification strategy is appropriate to only a very small number of societies, and even then must be implemented with great care. Individual societies need to consider their current image profile and adopt a diversification strategy which takes account of current consumer perceptions. For example, the Alliance and Leicester and Nationwide are currently perceived as modern, bank-like societies, with a wide range of services. A diversification strategy therefore may be appropriate for these societies, provided adequate consideration is given to the quality of staff and service.

*Mergers*

The building society industry has been characterized by mergers (transfer of engagements) throughout its development. Since 1900 the number of societies has reduced from 2286 to around 80 in 1995. This number is expected to reduce further to 35 by the year 2000. In addition to the range of recent and proposed mergers (such as the Halifax and Leeds) it is apparent that building societies are also potentially attractive acquisition targets as illustrated by the Lloyds takeover of Cheltenham and Gloucester.

While economic theory suggests that an increase in size results in economies of scale, there exists some doubt as to whether or not building society mergers actually achieve economies of scale. Assuming that societies can achieve some economies of scale, what are the likely responses of consumers to continued mergers? The effects of merger on the image of the participant societies can be viewed from two perspectives – increase in size and change in identity.

The perceived size of a society is an important attribute. Many associations are formed with size; for example a large society is associated with financial soundness, a wide range of services, better chance of obtaining a mortgage, efficiency and preferential interest rates. A small society is associated with a limited range of services, but a more personal service. It is the medium-sized societies whose images are least defined. Whilst the growth of medium-sized and large societies could have a positive effect on image resulting from the associations of size, growth of smaller societies, via merger, could damage consumer perceptions of their personal service.

As for change in identity in the event of a merger either one or both participating societies adopt a new identity. Three options are available to societies following merger.

1. Retention of one name – the name of one of the participating societies (usually the larger) is retained. For example, following the mergers of the Paddington/West of England, and the Property Owners/Woolwich, the names of the second societies in each case – the larger ones – were retained.
2. Combination of names – the names of both participating societies are retained. This usually occurs where societies of an equal or similar size merge. For example, following the merger of the Alliance and Leicester building societies and the Nationwide and Anglia building societies, a combination of the names was used – though in the latter case only the name Nationwide is now used. While a new name is created, the identities of each society are retained. Societies involved in several mergers are however unable to continue this practice.
3. Creation of a new name – new names are usually adopted when societies have been involved in several mergers, e.g. the Britannia Building Society was originally the Leek and Moorlands Building Society.

The response of consumers to building society mergers will largely depend upon the nature of the merger. Research suggests that new (and hence unfamiliar) names are associated with a new society despite participating societies having been in existence for many years. For example, the Nationwide Anglia merger involved two old societies, the Anglia (established in 1848), and the Nationwide (established in 1884). Knowledge of a society and familiarity with its name are important attributes, indicative of stability and security. A newly merged society has to invest heavily in promotion to increase name awareness, which can offset initial economies of scale.

An alternative strategy for societies wishing to achieve economies of scale is to enter joint ventures with other societies and/or financial institutions. For example, societies joined together to form the Link and Matrix ATM networks. Reciprocal use of the machines allowed societies to provide their consumers with a near-national network, the cost of which most individual societies would have been unable to meet. Also though the 1986 Building Societies Act enables societies to offer unsecured loans, the majority who do so operate through links with banks (e.g. the Co-operative Bank) for finance companies. Some building societies have chosen to go it alone in overseas markets (e.g. Halifax). However the cost benefits of joint ventures in international markets have been highlighted and others have developed relationships with partners to provide opportunities to evaluate such relationships in advance of a complete joint venture (e.g. Bradford and Bingley involvement in EGFI, European Group of Financial Institutions, cited in Glaister and Thwaites, 1992).

## Rationalization

This focuses upon cost reduction either by improving branch productivity and product mix or by deleting unprofitable products or branches. For example, branch productivity may be improved by reducing branch costs and increasing consumer 'sales', i.e. the level of consumer transactions. In a service organization staffing usually accounts for a higher proportion of costs and as such it is a prime area for cost reduction. The number or quality of staff may be lowered to raise the overall profit to cost ratio. Reduction in the number of staff could lead to longer waiting times, both within societies for counter service, and at a managerial level, in decision making. Speed in both these areas is important to consumers. Consumers prefer a society with a short waiting time and quick decisions. A number of societies are currently perceived by consumers to be deficient in these areas, suggesting a need to increase levels and/or invest in training.

Branch productivity may also be improved by closing unprofitable branches. Research suggests that branch location is more important than absolute numbers of branches. Branches with high operating costs to profits could be relocated in areas more convenient to the consumer thus increasing consumer flow through branches. Research is, of course, required at local branch level to determine which locations are perceived by the consumer to be convenient.

The introduction of postal accounts in recent years has been an important development for some of the smaller and medium-sized societies enabling them to extend their geographic marketplaces through a relatively low cost service. Postal accounts have not yet been embraced by the larger societies.

It is suggested that building societies may build their success through the use of the above competitive strategies. However, leading societies are not necessarily differentiators, focused or cost leaders. They may be cost leaders and differentiators (e.g. Cheltenham and Gloucester). Some of the smaller societies owe their success to combining differentiation with a clear focus (e.g. on particular well-defined customer groups). What is of fundamental importance for marketing effectiveness is that societies must build marketing programmes around viable competitive strategies and tactics and not only upon markets. The ability of a society to evaluate its weaknesses and strengths compared with the competition and to choose an appropriate core strategy has become of major importance to market success in the current highly competitive climate.

## 12.3    Building society marketing mix

The marketing mix for a building society service is, in practice, little different from that for a product. What differences do exist arise from:

1. The general distinctions between services and products which include features like intangibility of services, heterogeneity of service quality, perishability and the complexities these features sometimes pose for building societies.
2. The recognition amongst building society marketers of the importance, in what are often undifferentiated product markets, of features like customer care and service, branch atmosphere, smooth operational and transaction performance and image.

The planning of an efficient and effective marketing mix is facilitated through marketing research. The building societies have become major users of market research in recent years contributing to the overall expansion of financial services research expenditures, both in-house and among Association of Market Survey Organisations members. The aim of a building society's marketing mix is to create a differential advantage to make the society and its services better than those of its competitors so that a particular group of customers (the target market) prefers its services. Differential advantage may occur fortuitously. It is, however, much more likely to occur when it is based on an effective marketing strategy and the detailed planning and implementation of marketing programmes to meet the needs of the society's target market customers. A society's differential advantage may result from one or more parts of its marketing programme including service quality, interest rates, branch ambience, ease of transaction processing, location, and psychological benefits created through skilful promotion.

The marketing mix consists of the principal variables with which building society marketing managers are concerned in their attempts to manage demand for their services. The process of marketing mix formulation and balancing is unique to each society and service. There are different specifications for the services marketing mix, as described in Chapter 4; however, a traditional framework which can provide a guide for building societies is:

(a) services (i.e. products)
(b) price
(c) promotion
(d) place
(e) people.

### 12.3.1 Services

Building society customers derive satisfaction and benefits from the services they are offered and use (e.g. high interest accounts; financial advice). Thus the decisions therefore that are associated with the planning, development and offering of a society's range of services are central to its success. Marketing concepts like the product life cycle, systematic new service development and deletion procedures, service concept testing, blueprinting and design, branding, after-sale customer care procedures and processes, which are common in product markets have just as much importance to building societies. The characteristics of the services offered (e.g. intangibility, heterogeneity, perishability) mean that conventional marketing ideas may require adaptation and refinement in building society contexts. For example, services cannot be patented and it is thus difficult to prevent competitors from copying new types of accounts (e.g. for children) or new kinds of mortgage arrangements (e.g. based on PEPs). On the other hand, service product warranties can be important in marketing certain kinds of accounts like those which guarantee a high rate of interest for a fixed period of time or which guarantee a certain rate of interest above normal rates for a fixed period of time (e.g. guaranteed bonds – both fixed rate and escalator). Expanding the number of features associated with a service is a common practice, so too is adding additional service product lines (e.g. West Bromwich budget account); or linking services with other organizations and schemes (e.g. Norwich and Peterborough link with BUPA).

There is evidence that some societies are taking a much more systematic and rigorous approach to the profitability and contribution of their services. For example, a number of societies have dropped their share-dealing services and have rationalized their children's savings accounts (e.g. Cheltenham and Gloucester). Also there is some evidence that more attention is now being devoted to improving the scrutiny of new service ideas through more systematic product development schemes. Such schemes are much needed as recent evidence suggests that many societies need to improve the approaches used for developing new services (Edgett, 1993).

There have been considerable innovations amongst building society services in recent years and this process is likely to continue. However there is also evidence to suggest that some societies have rushed into introducing new services without thinking through the implications on other elements of the marketing mix (e.g. staff training) as well as upon the range of services on offer. One outline set of questions societies can use in their planning and integration of this element of the marketing mix is:

1. What benefits will the customer derive from this service? How clear are we that these benefits are needed?
2. What is the service formula? What is the bundle of elements of the service both functional and psychological; tangible and intangible?
3. What service levels are involved? What quality and quantity of service is associated with the service operation and marketing?
4. What service delivery system is needed to ensure successful service operation and marketing? How clear are we about the linkages between the service features and its delivery including systems and staff?

Central to the success of building society services policies is continuing focus on the benefits the customer derives from them, and whether the services offered are desired and relevant. In addition, the service range and its development must be part of an overall marketing and institutional strategy. There is no doubt that the range of services offered by building societies will continue to expand as they search for new opportunities in the UK and in Europe. While mortgages will remain the core business for some societies, the sheer number of players in the market will mean that alternative services will need to be introduced if some of the societies are to remain viable. Large societies through their branch and estate agent networks are likely to offer a wider range of financial services including insurance and in some cases banking. For example, at present a number of major societies are deciding whether to start lending to small companies now they have the freedom to do so. Others are cautious about entering a field of corporate finance that has caused the banks so much anguish in recent years. In addition, Europe provides a major opportunity for some institutions in the traditional mortgage markets. Service innovation will be a major feature of the societies' portfolios for the remainder of the 1990s.

## 12.3.2 Price

The notion of 'price' in a building society environment can take a number of forms. It is concerned for example with 'interest' rates which may apply to a mortgage; with a 'fee' that may be payable for a house survey; with a 'premium' that may be due on an insurance policy or with a 'charge' that may be levied on a particular kind of account. Though the terms used to describe building society prices may be different, the traditional forces influencing price (i.e. costs, competition, demand and customers' perceptions of value) are similar.

An integrated marketing strategy implies that the various elements of the marketing mix – including price – are formulated and implemented in the light of the objectives underlying that strategy. For building societies the pricing decision must take account of a number of factors including:

1. How the 'price' set will influence the customer's perception of the service in relation to other competitive sources (i.e. perceptual position). In the current competitive mortgage market, interest rate differences of only a few percentage points are of considerable significance.
2. The building society's views of where the service is in its 'product life cycle'. A new service, like a low cost mortgage aimed at young couples, may be very competitively priced to gain market share and obtain maximum penetration. Alternatively, rather higher rates could be charged to high earning couples to 'skim' the mortgage market. The effectiveness of either policy would be determined by the elasticity of demand – that is the responsiveness of demand to price changes. In some building society markets (e.g. deposit accounts) there is much depositor inertia. However, customers are growing in sophistication and are increasingly prepared to shop around for the cheapest loan or switch deposits for a higher interest rate elsewhere. Societies cannot assume continuing customer inertia to switch accounts in the future.
3. The competitive situation is currently a major influence. Usually 'price ranges' operate in even the most competitive of markets. Some societies because of reputation may have more room for manoeuvre than others in a particular market and may be price 'makers' as opposed to price 'takers'. Nevertheless there is rarely scope to be positioned significantly differently from market norms on price. This single factor (i.e. competition) is a major influence on the price discretion available to building society marketing managers. Even so, the variations in interest rates on 'short notice' accounts reflect the opportunities available for setting different 'prices' across different values of deposits through the interest rates offered.
4. Government policies, like interest rate policies, also influence building society prices. However, they more often influence the general level of prices rather than the discretionary range or band around which a particular price may be set.
5. Finally, many of the tactical price techniques used in other markets are relevant to some kinds of building society services. They include 'differential pricing', 'discount pricing', 'guaranteed pricing' and 'loss leader pricing'. Recent special offers on mortgage rates by various building societies, targeted at different customer groups, reflect the use of some of these tactical price techniques.

Thus price is an important element in marketing mix strategies of building societies in their competition for business.

### 12.3.3 Promotion

The aim of a building society's promotional efforts is to communicate with its customers, employees and other relevant audiences. The main goals of promotion are to inform, to persuade and remind audiences about the society and its services. An informative promotion might, for example, advise customers of interest rate changes; a persuasive promotion might, for example, try to encourage non-users to open an account or take out a mortgage; while a reminder promotion might seek to maintain a society's position and presence in the market through, say, major sponsorship of a sporting event. There are a large number of promotional tools available to the building society marketer. Astutely used, whether singly or in carefully integrated combination, these tools constitute a powerful set of instruments for communication and influence. The key consideration is to ensure that specific communications campaigns are designed for particular marketing situations to achieve the desired emphasis and impact.

Some building societies have shown a readiness to experiment with many of the available tools. Examples of some of the direct promotional tools currently used include the following:

*Press advertising*. Press advertising is an important medium for all societies, large and small. It attracts a major share of all building society advertising appropriations. The large number of national, regional and local publications available together with the array of specialist publications on offer in the UK provide major opportunities for coverage and flexibility. All societies advertise in the national and financial press with their expenditures tending to reflect asset size from the Halifax and Nationwide at one extreme to smaller societies like the Shepshed at the other.

*TV advertising*. Television advertising is more expensive than press advertising (as much due to the costs of production as of media costs) and national TV campaigns tend to be undertaken mainly by the larger societies. However, satellite broadcasting and the single European market may have an impact on the costs of existing TV advertising through opening up new opportunities for innovative societies.

*Cinema advertising*. Cinema advertising, whilst constituting a very small portion of total advertising, is nevertheless a most potent medium for reaching cinemagoers who tend generally to be young adults. Low cost starter mortgages and regular savings schemes can often be targeted at viable target market segments using this medium. Radio advertising too is useful in reaching certain target groups.

*Direct marketing*. Building societies have made growing use of direct marketing since the late 1980s along with other financial institutions (Thwaites and Lee, 1994). Skilfully managed and controlled, direct marketing is a powerful tool to complement other advertising and promotional activities. However, direct marketing also performs a distributive role as well as a promotional function and these two roles suggest it will become an even more widely used activity in the next few years.

*Sales promotion.* Sales promotion is a major element in general marketing practice yet still appears to play a modest role in the marketing activities of building societies. While some price-based promotions are inappropriate for such services, there are nevertheless opportunities to use 'value adding' promotions (e.g. free gifts; 'piggy backing' a complementary service) more widely as a recent study of the use of competitions in financial services has illustrated (Peattie and Peattie, 1994).

*Exhibitions.* Exhibitions provide opportunities to widen the exposure of a building society's services to existing and new customers.

*Public relations.* Public relations activities are undertaken increasingly by building societies. They have included involvement in community projects (e.g. restoring older properties); special events for young people, the elderly or the disabled; providing educational opportunities (e.g. through prizes and grants); and through sponsorship of the arts and cultural events. Such activities provide a potent way of enhancing corporate image and involvement within the community and with worthwhile causes.

*Point of sale.* Point of sale materials in the form of brochures and leaflets are used by nearly all building societies. Such materials can perform a range of functions (e.g. cross-sell services) and raise awareness of levels of services available. In recent years, greater attention has been devoted to co-ordinating the design of such material as part of an integrated total promotional effort.

*Personal selling.* Personal selling and the role of counter service staff is increasingly recognized by the societies as a most persuasive form of promotion. Great importance is now attached to customer-focused staff training; staff appearance; staff availability; 'internal' marketing and customer care in general. Some societies have made major investments in these areas as it is recognized that the relationship between staff and customer can be a major determining influence upon patronage decisions.

*Other promotion methods.* Other less direct methods of promotion which building societies seek to develop and harness include 'image', standards of service, logos and the use of brand names. These are seen as valuable means of differentiation in markets where the distinctions between one core service and another are minimal.

There have been major changes in the promotional efforts of building societies in the last few years. The effect of competition has been a major influence upon the greater sophistication of promotional tools now employed.

## 12.3.4 Place

The place element of the marketing mix, concerned with how to make services available and accessible to customers, has always been of importance to building societies, although in the past attention was mostly focused upon building up branch and agency networks in convenient locations to serve customers' needs. Such policies have been justified by consumer surveys of building society customers which reveal the importance of location and accessibility in society choice and patronage. Branch expansion and agency expansion remain important strategies for some societies.

However, societies have begun to take a critical look at the profitability of their branch and agency systems and some societies have closed branches (e.g. Nationwide) or dropped agencies (e.g. Alliance and Leicester). Also major refurbishment programmes and branch redesign have been put into operation (e.g. Bradford and Bingley) to improve both the image projected and facilities available to customers. The societies are learning from other high street retailers and have recognized the importance of 'atmosphere' and 'ambience' in branch design and their contribution to the creation of a distinctive overall 'personality'. This feature will continue to be of importance.

Of particular interest in recent years has been the adoption by a number of the major societies of 'alternative channels' which permit service access and service use. New technology in the form of automated telling machines (ATMs) and automatic cash dispensers has been increasingly applied in the industry. In addition mailed services have been developed to overcome restricted branch presence in certain locations (e.g. Nottingham Building Society) and direct mailing itself is growing in use as a method of selling and distributing services.

Nevertheless the branch, its location, design and operation is likely to remain a key element in the marketing mix programmes of many building societies. A significant recent trend has been the application of operations management tools and techniques to the management of branch service operations in conjunction with marketing tools and techniques. The main roles of the operations manager, the efficient and effective management of resources and the provision of customer service, are often more complex in service operations. This is because of variations in customer needs, conflicts between different kinds of customer needs, problems of specifying and delivering service 'quality', and the involvement of the customer in service operations. Customer service in building society operations increasingly demands motivating the customer to play a role in service delivery (e.g. queuing systems, ATMs), as the traditional role of motivating branch staff to deliver quality service. The effectiveness of a building society's delivery systems provides a potentially powerful means of differentiation in the more competitive climate in the sector.

### 12.3.5 People

People are essential in the production and delivery of most building society services. They are the critical element linking other marketing mix elements. They so often contribute fundamentally to the effectiveness and efficiency with which services are delivered and the overall 'quality' of service. Ranging from branch managers to specialist investment providers; from receptionists to counter service staff, these people may perform a 'production' or 'operational' role but they crucially have 'contact' with customers and potential customers. Their behaviour is a central influence upon the quality of service received and perceived by the customer. It is recognized by all building societies today that all personnel in contact with customers are involved in marketing their services. Such contacts and relationships cannot be left to chance. Therefore a major development by the societies in recent years has been the emphasis on staff training, staff development and customer care programmes as it has been recognized that staff are the most effective means of differentiating one society from another in the competitive market conditions of the 1990s. The process of delivering customer care and managing service quality is discussed in greater detail in Chapter 9.

## 2.4  Conclusion

Building societies will continue the development and use of appropriate marketing tools both for offensive and defensive reasons. Rationalization through merger, together with likely further changes in the status of societies will mean that there are likely to be around thirty to forty societies left by the year 2000. Many smaller societies will have disappeared, though there is no reason why some of the smaller societies will not still be around provided they can: focus their marketing efforts on distinctive regions or services; effect alternative organizational arrangements to maintain independence through some form of federation; and, most importantly, offer valued services through their knowledge of local markets and outstanding service care for their customers.

While there is likely to be more diversity between societies in terms of their range of services, methods of operation and managerial sophistication, the underlying principles of marketing apply. In essence customers seek solutions to their problems and expect services to fulfil their needs and provide the benefits they seek. The key to the successful marketing of building society services is people. Most services are provided by people (though they may be performed by equipment) but all services are provided for people. It is vital, then, that building societies extend their understanding of their customers and consumers, why they behave as they do and how they make their decisions and choices. The centrality of the customer reminds us that in the most fundamental sense, marketing building society services is no different to any other kind of marketing. If customers do not receive what they want from a particular society, then the changed competitive environment gives them opportunities to take their business elsewhere.

# 13 The marketing of unit and investment trusts

Paul Draper

## 13.1 Introduction

Unit and investment trusts are collective investment vehicles for pooling subscribers' contributions and investing them in a variety of transferable assets such as ordinary shares and bonds. They are run by investment managers who use their knowledge and experience to select individual securities which are aggregated to form portfolios that meet predetermined objectives and criteria. These portfolios are then sold to the public and offer investors three main services: portfolio diversification and the reduction of unsystematic risk, portfolio management in the form of specialist investment knowledge and administrative services; and financial intermediation by creating a new financial asset which may be more easily marketable than the underlying securities in the portfolio.

These services provide the basis around which the marketing manager must work. Existing and potential investors must be convinced of the expertise and skill of the portfolio manager and persuaded: to save rather than spend; to invest through a financial intermediary in preference to investing directly; to choose risky securities and not fixed interest deposits such as a building society account; to select unit or investment trusts instead of life assurance or increased pension contributions; and finally to identify the appropriate investment manager and objective. The marketing manager must identify strategies and target promotion efforts that will reach investors at each of these crucial decision stages and must do so within constraints on expenditure in an environment of vigorous competition and increasingly tight regulatory supervision of sales.

This chapter sets out the environment in which the marketing manager must operate. Section 13.2 explores the nature of unit and investment trusts paying particular attention to their structure and organization, the creation and valuation of their securities, product differentiation, remuneration and profitability, and performance comparisons. Section 13.3 examines the market for unit and investment trusts with emphasis on the impact of regulation on marketing decisions while section 13.4 considers some of the opportunities that exist for expanding the sales of investment products. It explores three areas of interest: increasing the variety of securities available; improving channels of distribution so as to make investment products easier to acquire; and possible alterations to the investment packages on offer with a view to making them more flexible and useful to investors. Section 13.5 presents conclusions.

## 13.2 The nature of unit and investment trusts

### 13.2.1 Structure and organization

Investment and unit trusts offer the same services to investors despite having different legal forms and origins. The investment trust industry has a long history, with the first trust – Foreign and Colonial – established in 1868. The industry suffered a long period of decline from the 1960s to the late 1980s (Table 13.1) with a substantial decline in both the number of trusts and market value as a proportion of the total UK equity market. In the last five years the industry has seen something of a renaissance with twenty-eight new trusts issued in 1993 and twenty-two new trusts issued up to May 1994. Unit trusts were first introduced into the UK before the Second World War and after a slow start have grown enormously in importance and popularity. Since 1981 the number of unit trusts has almost tripled and their value increased more than fifteenfold (Table 13.2).

The legal form of the two investment vehicles is quite different and may result in differences in value, marketing, advertising and distribution. Investment trusts are companies regulated by the Companies Acts with their business activity that of investing in the securities of other companies. The object of investment trusts is to raise capital from investors by the issue of their own ordinary shares and invest the proceeds, together with any capital they may have raised from the issue of fixed interest securities such as debentures or loan stock, in the securities, both equity and debt, of other enterprises. Some constraints exist on the extent and the scope of their investments, the precise terms depend on the Company's Memorandum and Articles of Association, but in general they are free to invest in a wider range of assets than unit trusts and

**Table 13.1** *Investment trust statistics, 1981–91*

| | No. | Total assets (£m) | Market value of shares (£m) | Investment trust value as per cent of total market value |
|---|---|---|---|---|
| 1981 | 202 | 9335 | 6123.2 | 6.2 |
| 1982 | 191 | 10 506 | 7322.3 | 6.0 |
| 1983 | 184 | 13 888 | 9670.0 | 6.2 |
| 1984 | 164 | 15 998 | 10 991.1 | 5.4 |
| 1985 | 166 | 18 125 | 12 264.6 | 5.0 |
| 1986 | 156 | 21 172 | 15 806.4 | 4.9 |
| 1987 | 159 | 20 959 | 13 934.2 | 3.7 |
| 1988 | 162 | 20 275 | 15 790.9 | 3.9 |
| 1989 | 158 | 24 840 | 20 918.8 | 4.0 |
| 1990 | 200 | 20 618 | 19 273.2 | 4.1 |
| 1991 | 215 | 23 919 | 19 144.2 | 3.5 |
| 1992 | 159 | 29 363 | 20 817.1 | 3.3 |
| 1993 | 267 | 40 151 | 31 772.6 | 3.9 |

*Source:* AITC Publications

**Table 13.2** *Unit trust statistics 1981–93*

| Period | Value of fund | Gross sales (£m) | Repurchase (£m) | Net invest. (£m) | Unit holder accounts | Number of trusts |
|--------|---------------|------------------|-----------------|------------------|----------------------|------------------|
| 1981 | 5902 | 955.6 | 428.0 | 527.6 | 1.79 | 529 |
| 1982 | 7768 | 1157.6 | 567.2 | 590.3 | 1.80 | 553 |
| 1983 | 11 689 | 2459.8 | 960.2 | 1499.6 | 2.04 | 630 |
| 1984 | 15 099 | 2918.2 | 1476.7 | 1441.5 | 2.20 | 687 |
| 1985 | 20 308 | 4487.7 | 1949.1 | 2538.6 | 2.55 | 806 |
| 1986 | 32 131 | 8416.7 | 3482.1 | 5234.6 | 3.41 | 964 |
| 1987 | 36 330 | 14 545.1 | 8214.3 | 6330.8 | 5.05 | 1137 |
| 1988 | 41 574 | 7675.7 | 5880.4 | 1795.3 | 4.89 | 1255 |
| 1989 | 58 159 | 10 606.0 | 6774.0 | 3835.0 | 4.85 | 1116 |
| 1990 | 46 342 | 8612.0 | 8219.0 | 393.0 | 4.63 | 1187 |
| 1991 | 55 145 | 10 483.0 | 7715.0 | 2768.0 | 4.46 | 1306 |
| 1992 | 63 874 | 9562.0 | 8915.0 | 647.0 | 4.35 | 1379 |
| 1993 | 95 518 | 18 740.0 | 9606.0 | 9134.0 | 5.04 | 1474 |

*Source:* Unit Trust Association, Central Statistical Office Financial Statistics

historically have had strong overseas links as well as a variety of specialisms including the provision of venture capital. Possibly the most important constraints on their activities arise from the desire of most investment trusts to secure 'Approved' status which carries with it significant tax benefits but requires the trusts to meet a number of conditions with regard to the size and spread of their holding and distribution of dividends. Unlike a unit trust it is not necessary for a UK-based investment trust to secure approved status. However, such status is fiscally advantageous so most trusts endeavour to secure and retain this status. Investment trusts are taxed like other companies and for this reason are in a position to issue fixed interest debt, the interest on which is deducted from profits before the calculation and payment of tax. The existence of debt allows the trusts to gear up their activities by borrowing and to invest the proceeds in equities. Provided the return on equities is greater than the cost of borrowing the investment trust benefits. The ability to borrow is not, in general, available to unit trusts and potentially enables investment trusts to offer investors a wider spectrum of risk-return investment products since increases in gearing provide a simple means of increasing the risk and hence the return on a trust.

In contrast to the company structure of investment trusts, unit trusts are legal trusts governed by a trust deed. The trust deed is an agreement between the trustees and the managers of the fund which covers the main aspects of the running of the trust, sets out the rights and responsibilities of all concerned and includes the maximum charges that can be levied, provisions for new members, the pricing of new units, and the investment aims of the trust including restrictions on the proportions of equity held in any one company and on the proportion of the portfolio invested in any asset. Investment management is in the hands of the managers of the fund but the trustees issue and redeem unit trust certificates and handle the cash and securities. The role of the trustees, typically a major bank, is to ensure that the trust is managed within the terms of the trust deed and so protect the owners of the unit trust from fraud and malpractice.

## 13.2.2 The creation and valuation of securities

The portfolio of securities owned by a unit trust is divided into a number of equal portions called units which are held by investors (unitholders). Each unit represents a specific proportion of the portfolio and has a value that is exactly tied to the value of the underlying assets in the portfolio. In purchasing a unit a unitholder is purchasing an exact entitlement to part of the portfolio and as such must bear all the costs associated with creating that portfolio including brokerage fees and taxes. If the value of the portfolio rises then so also will the price of the unit. If the value of the portfolio falls then the price of a unit will fall. This correspondence between asset values and unit prices is an important factor in the sale of units since investors can be confident that a rise in the share prices of the underlying investments will be reflected in the price of the units. Units can be bought or sold at any time as the managers of the unit trust will buy back or create units to meet demand. If necessary, units bought back can be destroyed by selling assets from the underlying portfolio. In practice, however, most trusts have been expanding and the bought back units are simply sold to new unitholders. If demand for units is greater than the supply of bought back units the manager simply creates new units which must be of equal value to the existing units. There is an infinitely elastic supply curve; the manager will always be ready to create units so long as there is a demand for them. The unit trust manager has no control over price as such. The price of units is a direct function of the value of the trust's assets. This effectively precludes the use of price as a marketing tool. Managers cannot promote sales by reducing prices and in general must look for other ways of competing and promoting sales. By reducing their own charges unit trust managers can and do offer small discounts to investors. The scope for such discounts is, however, very small.

The capital of an investment trust is fixed and can only be increased with the approval of the shareholders. The return on its equity arises from the investments of the trust. The value of these investments go up or down as does the value of the investment trust's own ordinary shares but there is no one-to-one relationship between the change in value of their assets and the change in value of their own shares. The value of an investment trust's own ordinary shares depends on the forces of supply and demand which in turn reflect relative risks and yields and the abilities of the managers to secure above average returns. At times the value of the investment trust's own shares may exceed the net value of its assets. The abilities of its investment managers to secure above average returns may be recognized so that its shares are in demand and trade at a premium. More commonly in the past, however, the net value of the investment

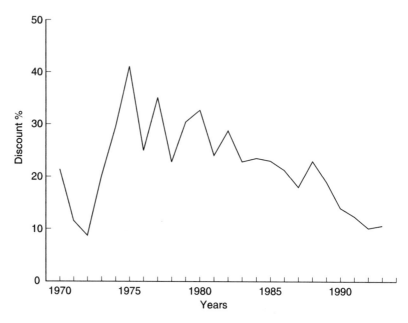

**Figure 13.1**   Average discount on investment trusts, 1969–1993

trust's assets exceeded the value of its ordinary shares and the equity traded at a discount. Figure 13.1 provides an illustration of the size of the discount on investment trusts over the last thirty years. It has been persistent, and until recently, often large, and a major factor affecting the freedom of action of investment trust managers.

Growth of an investment trust occurs either by the increase in value of its own assets or by the issue of new shares to new and existing investors. Increases in asset value have been a notable feature of the share market in recent years but such growth is restricted since it fails to provide access to the pool of new consumer savings in the economy. To tap this pool the investment trust must issue new shares. In the past such issues have been severely hindered by the existence of the discount since there is no incentive to subscribe for new investment trust shares if their price falls once trading begins. More recently, however, with the narrowing of the discount there has been a flood of new issues both of additional equity by existing investment trust and of equity for new trusts. The new trusts have been oriented particularly towards investment areas requiring specialist knowledge and managerial skills. Single country funds, smaller companies, privatizations, mining and emerging markets have all been popular areas of activity.

## Product differentiation and promotion

Unit trusts make extensive use of advertising to sell their products. In the early years of the industry it was common to advertise in the national press inviting subscriptions. In recent years the importance of block offers, the offer of a large number of units for sale to the public, and off-the-page sales has declined but unit trusts continue to advertise heavily to reinforce brand loyalty and product differentiation. Sales are typically made through financial intermediaries, particularly insurance brokers, as well as through accountants, solicitors, stockbrokers and other financial advisers. Direct mail and sales representatives also play their part so that unit trusts can be purchased through a broad spectrum of marketing channels.

Investment trusts are also marketed through financial intermediaries but the inability of the managers to buy and sell securities in the trusts they manage and the need to acquire the investment trust equity through the stock market makes investment less easy and precludes off-the-page selling. Existing investment trusts are marketed much less aggressively than unit trusts and for many years investment trusts undertook little promotional activity. The problem, as the industry perceived it, was the Prevention of Fraud (Investments) Act, now the Financial Services Act, which prohibited a company from promoting its own shares. More recently, the prohibition has been interpreted less strictly so that investment trusts have engaged in more promotional activity than previously. This has been particularly true of new investment trusts which in some cases have been quite heavily advertised. The ability of unit trusts to advertise extensively remains, however, an important advantage of unit trusts over investment trusts and has resulted in a level of consumer awareness and knowledge of unit trusts that far surpasses that for investment trusts. In recent years the Association of Investment Trusts (AITC) has devoted considerable effort marketing the industry as a whole but its activities are necessarily limited. A survey by London Weekend Television in the late 1980s of London investors found that only 14 per cent of their total sample had not heard of unit trusts but 32 per cent had not heard of investment trusts (6 per cent and 19 per cent respectively of those with over £10 000 of savings). More worrying perhaps for the investment trusts was that of savers with over £10 000, 44 per cent claimed to know a considerable amount about unit trusts but only 27 per cent to have a similar knowledge of investment trusts. In the past the better-off private investors were the main market for investment trust shares. Despite this survey, Philip Worland, Director of the Association of Unit Trusts and Investment Funds, has commented that 'the average person in the street cannot distinguish between a unit trust, an investment trust, a unit linked insurance policy, a unitized insurance policy and, I guess, unit 8 at their local industrial park' (*Unit Trust Year Book*, 1994).

As part of their marketing campaigns unit and investment trusts compete by differentiating their investment portfolio. They offer investors a wide range of alternative investment objectives in the hope of exciting a potential investor's interest. Table 13.3 provides a summary of the main investment objectives offered by each. The variety is extensive and even then obscures some of the more unusual objectives such as investment in precious metals or investment in small country funds. Increased specialization and greater product differentiation has been a pronounced feature of recent years with both investment trust and unit trust groups starting new trusts to fill gaps in their marketing profile. The incentive for further differentiation of portfolios is the prospect of increased sales but the dis-

**Table 13.3** *Portfolio and product differentiation*

| Investment trusts | Unit trusts |
| --- | --- |
| International general | International growth |
| International capital growth | International equity income |
| International income growth | International balanced |
| UK general | UK growth |
| UK capital growth | UK general |
| UK income growth | UK equity income |
| High income | UK balanced |
| North America | UK smaller companies |
| Far East including Japan | |
| Far East excluding Japan (general) | |
| Far East excluding Japan (single country) | UK gilt and fixed interest |
| Japan | International fixed interest |
| Europe (general) | North America |
| Europe (single country) | Japan |
| Emerging markets (general) | Far East including Japan |
| Emerging markets (single country) | Far East excluding Japan |
| Property | Australasia |
| Closed-end funds | Europe |
| Commodity and energy | Investment trust units |
| Smaller companies | Financial and property |
| Venture and development capital | Commodity and energy |
| Split capital trust | Funds of funds |
| | Money market funds |
| | Convertibles |

*Source: Unit Trust Yearbook, Investment Trust Index*

covery of new, previously uncatered for objectives and the launch of a successful new fund is not without problems. Products in the financial sector are easily replicated so that it is difficult to differentiate purely on the strength of the investment objectives of the trust.

In addition to increasing their appeal to investors by specialization, both unit and investment trusts employ a variety and range of marketing schemes to achieve wider sales. The unit trust movement pioneered repackaging techniques that enabled unit trusts to appeal to a wider market. Of particular significance was the sale of unit trusts with life assurance, an investment portfolio with insurance added in, which reduces risks. By linking unit trusts to life assurance the unit trust management companies were able to tap a new market and benefit from favourable tax treatment since prior to 1984 tax relief was granted on premiums so boosting the investment input from the policyholder. Insurance linking was much slower to arrive in the investment trust industry although a number of schemes now exist.

Other schemes that exist for both unit and investment trusts include personal pensions, personal equity plans (PEPs) and regular savings schemes. The aim of the schemes is to use the investment portfolios of unit and investment trusts as the savings element of any plan that requires regular savings contributions. PEPs, for example, offer tax advantages to encourage personal sector investment in UK shares and are ideally suited to being linked to unit and investment trusts.

### 13.2.4 Remuneration and profitability

Unit trust managers are rewarded by the levy of two different charges on unitholders; an initial charge and an annual management fee. The initial charge is normally around 5 per cent and is included in the price payable to the managers on purchase. It is used to meet the advertising and promotional costs of the unit trust including the payment of commission to independent intermediaries. Newman (1984) indicates that advertising expenses have been falling and were 0.5 per cent of sales in 1982 and 0.3 per cent of sales in 1983. However, she also notes that advertising has been very variable and is much higher when the stock market is booming. The maximum rate of commission currently agreed by the majority of firms in the industry is 3 per cent. By altering the initial charge the managers can alter their competitive position and strategy. In the short run, high initial charges will fund high promotional expenditures. In the long run they are likely to affect performance adversely.

If current proposals become law it is possible that some trusts will replace initial charges with graduated exit charges. These charges might be 5 per cent for investors holding the units for less than a year, declining perhaps to zero if held for five years or more. Such charges have an appeal in that they reward investor loyalty but they may also lock investors into poorly performing trusts.

The annual charge is usually levied half yearly and amounts to around 1 per cent of the total value of the fund on average although it can, for some specialist trusts, be very much higher. The charge is deducted from the income earned by the unit trust and is intended to reward the managers for their expertise. As with the initial charge, alteration of the annual charge provides the managers with some control over value. A number of other small charges such as trustee fees may also be levied on the fund.

Unlike unit trusts, investment trusts generally impose no initial fee on purchasing their shares since purchasing through the stock market provides no mechanism for such a fee although commission and taxes are payable. The requirement to purchase through the stock market reduces the appeal of promoting investment trusts for many financial intermediaries since the commission from such sales is small although, in a bid to win sales, a number of investment trusts do now pay fees to intermediaries, funded by initial charges on investors. Such initial charges are not the norm since most investment is not through the managers but directly between investors using the Stock Exchange. Although no initial fee is typically payable annual management charges are levied. These charges may either represent the actual costs incurred or represent a charge based on the fee payable to the investment management group that undertakes the investment for the company. The annual management charges are generally considerably lower than for unit trusts. Scope for competition between unit and investment trusts would appear to exist on the basis of low management fees and charges. Experience to date, however, suggests that competition on the basis of price is unusual and does not appear to be very successful except possibly for a few niche players. The reasons for this are presumably a result of the investor's belief in being able to pick successful trusts in which the increase in returns from the manager's abilities can greatly outweigh the higher costs. Unfortunately there is little reason to believe this to be true.

### 13.2.5 Performance comparisons

Performance comparisons are a source of interest to investors and an important tool in the marketing of portfolios. However, the abilities of the portfolio manager to influence the performance of a trust is much less than is commonly accepted. Some gloss can be added by appropriate comparisons although the regulatory bodies make specific provision for information disclosure with respect to the performance of investments and requires comparisons to be fair so that the possibilities for massaging performance figures are strictly limited.

Portfolio performance is the sum of the change in price of the portfolio over a period, the capital gains, and the dividends received on securities over the same period. The dividend element is generally stable and small, but in contrast, changes in price are largely unpredictable and may be swiftly reversed. Share prices are a result of competitive pressures. At any moment of time the share price of a company impounds all available information, since any information that is available that investors can use to improve their predictions of future share prices is immediately acted upon. The result is that a firm's share price reflects what is currently known about the company and the environment in which it operates. Changes in price come about only when new information reaches the market and since the arrival of new information is likely to be unpredictable, share prices also move in an unpredictable fashion. This is known as the Efficient Market Hypothesis. Share prices impound all publicly available information. Studies of the reaction of the stock market to new information consistently show that it reacts rapidly once the information becomes publicly available. Elton and Gruber (1987) provide a good introduction to the topic and, a recent survey is provided by Fama (1991). Changes in share values can be sudden and dramatic. By chance, some investors will earn very large profits from these changes but it is unlikely that they can earn such profits with any degree of consistency. A variety of empirical tests including analysing the buy and sell recommendations of investment analysts, financial journalists and market tipsters have all suggested that it is impossible consistently to make abnormally large returns. Such a conclusion has implications for the management of investment portfolios since if share price changes are unpredictable, portfolio performance must also be unpredictable. Information arriving at the market that is favourable for the securities in which the fund is invested will result in good investment performance for the fund whilst the arrival of information that is less auspicious will result in poor performance. In the long run the chance factors will largely balance out and the investment funds will earn the return for the risk they assume, no more and no less.

Once we accept that consistent superior investment performance is difficult to achieve it becomes apparent that there is an asymmetry in investment performance. On average, investment portfolios will secure the return for the risk they assume but this return will be reduced by management costs so that the lower the management costs the better the funds' performance. Evidence for this position is provided by numerous empirical studies of portfolio performance and, more persuasively perhaps for practitioners, by the move of many large, informed investors into index funds which follow a passive strategy of imitating the market index and keeping management costs low. There is, however, no evidence to suggest that the majority of investors either know or believe in such concepts and it appears true that many investors are apparently insensitive to changes in management charges.

## 13.3 The market for unit and investment trusts

### 13.3.1 Competition

Unit and investment trusts do not operate in isolation. They must sell to investors who have the choice of a wide spectrum of financial products as well as the option of additional consumption. It is convenient to assume that individuals make decisions on how much to save and then decide on the distribution between alternative investments but in reality the decision process is certainly more complex. Attractive investment products may be able both to increase the trusts' share of the total market for savings and to increase the size of that market.

The very term 'market' is ambiguous. We portray the trusts as competing against the entire spectrum of financial assets from bank and building society fixed interest deposits through pensions, life assurance and the direct purchase of equity and debt and even property. In reality, by no means all savings are free to move. Many are contractual, particularly pensions and existing life assurance policies, whilst individuals may have preferences for property or safe fixed interest deposits that are almost immovable. However, it is clear that at the margin investors do switch between products and that investors can be persuaded to invest in one product rather than another. Little is known about how investors make such decisions. Financial theory presents the choice as one of risk and return. Investors wishing for low risk should invest in fixed interest deposits and those wanting more risk should invest in equities, but whilst such trade-offs may be an appropriate guide to action for the informed investors utilizing the stock market it is difficult to believe that it is a useful guide for the less sophisticated consumer. Indeed, the relative unpopularity of the investment trust over the unit trust despite lower charges cannot be explained by poorer performance and suggests that advertising and information, ease and convenience of purchasing, availability of 'advice' and sales effort and innovation are all important determinants of sales. In short, sales of financial products respond to marketing efforts and despite a wide spectrum of alternatives investors can be persuaded to choose particular products. The market for financial products is not entirely free however. Regulatory agencies supervise most aspects of the market and impose considerable constraints on the activities of the companies.

### 13.3.2 Impact of regulation on marketing

The regulatory framework administered by the Securities and Investments Board (SIB) has imposed considerable costs on both unit and investment trusts. The regulator's rulebooks have forced changes in investment practice particularly with regard to the marketing of investments. Two issues stand out as having particularly important consequences for unit and investment trusts; the disclosure of life assurance commissions which effectively puts life assurance on the same footing as other collective investments, and the requirement of advisers to provide 'best advice'.

The nature of life assurance business with the issue of life policies which are frequently for ten years or more and require annual payments throughout their life means that the costs of selling a policy are incurred at the beginning of its life whilst the revenues to the company flow in over an extended period of years. The result is that the initial premiums received from the policies are swallowed up in expenses and do not go into the investment fund. Fearing perhaps that new policyholders will be deterred by the size of the expenses, the insurance companies have been reluctant to disclose the size of commission and other initial costs. After much argument the life offices have been forced to reveal the effect of expenses on the yield of a policy so that from 1995 it will be much easier to compare the expenses of with-profits life assurance with unit-linked life policies and indeed with unit and investment trusts. Over the longer term there may be moves to reduce expenses by the use of fee-based advisers where commissions are not paid to intermediaries but instead a fee is charged to clients for advice so that advisers are not persuaded to sell particular products as a result of the commissions offered.

The result of disclosure is to make the costs of alternative investments more transparent. In so far as many life policies have heavier expenses than unit or investment trusts there could be significant shifts in consumer choice from life policies to unit and investment trusts. The benefits from disclosure to the investment and unit trusts should not be over-emphasized however. It is of interest that, despite the disclosure of commission and publication of unit trust charges which have doubled since controls were lifted, unit trust sales have gone from strength to strength. Higher charges do not appear to have deterred investors. 'Best advice' is a cardinal principle of the regulatory authorities but its meaning is not as clear-cut as might be hoped. The regulatory framework has as one of its major tenets the concept of polarization. Intermediaries who advise on investments must either be fully independent or the 'tied' representative of just one company. The requirements for each are different. All sales agents of investment products are required to give the client best advice on the type of investment which is best suited to his or her needs. For the tied representative this will be the appropriate product from the company's range and in the absence of any suitable product from within the company's own range tied sales agents must refrain from recommending any. For independent intermediaries the requirements are more stringent and they must believe that no other 'investment of which the member is or ought reasonably to be aware' would be likely to better meet the clients' needs. This has been interpreted by many industry observers to mean that independent intermediaries should have knowledge of other investment products than life assurance and unit trusts. To ignore the merits of investment trusts, for example, in making recommendations would be in breach of the independent intermediary's duty. The requirement for best advice will affect independent intermediaries and sales agents' recommendations. The marketing manager must be aware of the implications of the current regulatory system and any changes in regulation for their sales strategies.

## 3.4 New directions in product differentiation and distribution

The problem for the marketing manager is to determine how unit and investment trusts can be made more attractive to both existing and new investors. What improvements must be made to the products and the marketing and distribution channels to make them more easily saleable? Three areas for improvement are of particular interest: increasing the choices open to investors; improving the channels of distribution and making the sale and administration of funds easier; and extending the usefulness of the investment product to give investors greater flexibility. We do not explore here the possibilities of increased advertising, the choice between advertising media and the benefits of direct sales by company salesmen over sales by financial intermediaries since these are essentially empirical matters which require market research and estimation of marginal costs and benefits so that advertising and promotion expenditure can be directed to equate marginal returns. Instead, we assume that investment trusts will extend their advertising in so far as they are allowed and examine ways in which the products of both unit and investment trusts can be made more saleable.

### 13.4.1 Wider product choice

Increasing the choice open to investors investing in unit and investment trusts is, in part, simply a continuation of existing trends. As investing becomes easier and cheaper with an ever increasing range of alternative financial products the trusts must continually ask what they can do that investors cannot easily do for themselves. Increased specialization, both geographic, with a greater variety of one-country funds, and by industry, with a wider range of industries and assets, is an obvious area of development which the trusts have been particularly active in pursuing in the last five years, although progress is hampered by the availability of expertise and market liquidity on the supply side, and investor sophistication on the demand side. Geographic and industry sector specializations are simply two of many possible methods of differentiating trusts. Other alternatives include differentiating funds by risk and by management strategy. The advent of new financial instruments, particularly options and futures, has opened up the possibility of portfolio insurance strategies which can be used to determine the risk and return of a fund in advance. However, the recent scandals surrounding the collapse of Barings may result in many investors being wary of products associated with such investments. By suitable use of futures the minimum performance of a fund can be set and the fund's performance guaranteed. It is possible to offer investors a range of risk and minimum returns over a period with far greater certainty than is possible by using all equity portfolios. Such funds have enabled the trusts to tap new market segments and attract investors away from other savings media such as building society and bank deposit accounts at one end of the risk spectrum and from high leveraged funds at the other end of the investment spectrum.

Portfolio insurance strategies imply a disciplined approach to fund management. At present, investors purchase fund management with little differentiation between management styles apart from that conveyed by brand and management names which may imply respectability, caution or even excitement. An area of opportunity lies in exploring much more carefully the role and nature of fund management and differentiating products by exploiting differences in management. Active and passive management are popular terms in the investment industry but these do not adequately encompass the range of styles and possibilities. Active managers vary from the rule based who may, in the extreme, follow the recommendations of a computer programme to those who invest on the basis of the most recent 'hot' tips. Passive management styles may be reflected in index funds, low turnover or long-term buy and hold and cost minimization strategies. Theoretical support for passive management styles is manifest in the earlier discussion of portfolio performance and given the emphasis on reducing costs could lead to the emergence of the 'plain vanilla' investment or unit trust with no initial fee and low annual management fees although such an approach may lack appeal since it restricts the investment managers' opportunities to charge premium fees for their services. The index fund is one response to demands for passive, low cost management and is aimed at the sophisticated investor who recognizes the difficulty of securing above average performance. Further possibilities for emphasizing differences in management include targeting particular groups of investors who may either be uninformed, or informed believing that by specialized investing they can secure additional returns. Targeting the uninformed has been a popular method of promoting sales in the past using as justification the past performance of a trust, and offering the opportunity of untold wealth and riches. However, if best advice is to be meaningful we would expect advisers in the future to be more aware of the evidence on performance and to be under a duty to look less favourably on high cost general funds.

The targeting of investors interested in specialized funds is more acceptable. By their nature specialized funds are either aimed at exploiting some perceived anomaly such as investing in small firms or represent funds that are deliberately imperfectly diversified. Investing in particular industries is one example of such specialization; in particular countries is another. Such specialist funds allow investors to follow their own hunches and preferences by forming a portfolio which itself consists of specialist trusts investing in particular countries, sectors or securities. International diversification has been shown to reduce portfolio risk below that available by investing in UK equities alone but changes in exchange rates can introduce a considerable extra dimension to risk, particularly for shorter time horizons. Progress in providing more specialized portfolios has been held back in part by regulatory and taxation problems, or by a wait-and-see attitude as other managers experiment. Possibilities, however, include immunized and fixed duration portfolios as well as portfolios that specialize in particular financial instruments searching for mispriced and other attractive securities (for a discussion of immunization and duration see Elton and Gruber, 1990).

Our discussion so far has centred on the possibilities of providing more specialized investment portfolios for investors. Investment trusts also have the opportunity of providing specialized securities more directly through the direct issue of equity, debt or hybrid securities in the investment trust company. Warrants are now a common feature of the capital structure of investment trusts but other securities on offer include zero coupon and stepped preference shares, split capital and income shares and in a few cases the issue of equity index loan stock which represents a pure index fund free of dealing and management costs. Such securities provide a range of risk and repayment provisions and enable investors to better construct portfolios that meet their requirements.

### 13.4.2 Improved channels of distribution

Increasing the choice open to investors makes unit and investment trusts more attractive to new consumers and may attract further savers into the industry. Improved choice may not, however, be sufficient. It is also necessary to improve the distribution of funds. There are two areas of particular concern, the purchase procedures and the methods of alerting consumers of the benefits of the trusts. The purchase of unit trusts is already a simple procedure and transactions can take place with the minimum of delay. The same is not always true of investment trusts which as stock exchange securities cannot be bought directly from the managers but must be acquired in the market. Once learned the procedure is no more difficult than for unit trusts but to the new investor may appear cumbersome and offputting. Efforts are in progress to simplify the purchase of investment trusts. Some of the largest investment trust management groups introduced schemes to sell investment trust shares through intermediaries such as insurance brokers, accountants and solicitors and offer commissions much like the unit trusts. Many of the trusts have also introduced savings schemes which allow for cheap and easy purchase of investment trust shares. Such schemes have brought the purchase of investment trusts more in line with the procedures for unit trusts but there still remains areas of improvement.

A more fundamental problem is the method by which consumers can learn of the benefits of the trusts and be encouraged to invest. Traditionally investment trusts have relied on stockbrokers and press comment. The result has been slow growth and a lack of knowledge of the trusts outside the traditional stock market investors. Unit trusts have appealed to a wider public with the use of extensive advertising, financial intermediaries and direct marketing and sales. Expansion of sales through building societies and banks is a possibility although there is the essential difficulty that equity savings may be at the expense of their fixed interest deposits. What is required is a greater expansion of sales using other purchase and sale mechanisms such as credit cards, bill payment and retail sales. There is no reason to believe that investments cannot be sold along with other household items although regulatory requirements for cooling-off periods, knowing your client and best advice may restrict some of the possibilities. Newman (1984) notes that M & G at the end of the 1960s distributed a sixteen-page promotional magazine through branches of Tesco, but she doesn't comment on its success. Whilst it demonstrates the possibilities of attracting new investors such advertising doesn't significantly make payment easier, an area where improvements might be made. The sale of unit trusts by Marks & Spencer shows the possibilities of using the retail payments network for sales but as yet progress is relatively slow. Regular accumulation of savings followed by periodic investment in units or shares, or loans for investment followed by periodic repayment are ideally suited to existing retail sales payment mechanisms and properly promoted could lead to a considerable expansion of sales. The recent growth in telephone sales of insurance, and a number of experiments currently underway in selling financial products by telephone, suggest that considerable changes in the way savings products are sold and paid for, might be expected in the next few years.

### 13.4.3 Improved product flexibility and usefulness

The linking of unit and investment trusts to life assurance, personal pension and PEP schemes has already been noted but we must also ask whether there are any other financial services which investors might like which could be linked to unit or investment trusts. Wilcox and Rosen (1988) provide a list of consumer needs which they term transactional, coping/planning and interpersonal needs and suggest that these needs should be addressed in developing and promoting financial products. A number of authors have identified the key characteristics of financial products as including money transmission and payment; savings and investment; insurance; lending, and information and advice, and have suggested that the ability to evolve products which embody more of these characteristics is a useful and profitable institutional strategy since it provides customers with increased flexibility and enables the financial institution to sell clients a wider range of services. The ability to borrow is possibly the main financial service that is lacking from the majority of unit and investment trust packages on offer and some thought could be given to borrowing facilities which allow individuals to borrow against their accumulated units or shares at lower interest rates to reflect the security, or even to borrow to invest in units or shares. Such an approach highlights a life-cycle approach to investment, recognizing that individuals' requirements vary over the years so that borrowing is heavier and saving smaller for families with young children than it is for the couple shortly before retirement. Completely integrated financial planning is unlikely given the uncertainty in employment and income that faces most individuals but for specific and targeted groups, middle class professionals for example, realistic forecasts of borrowing and saving may be possible. Carefully targeted marketing together with new product innovations that extend the range and variety of the savings/investment packages could provide a useful extension of the market.

## 3.5 Conclusion

Kotler (1994) argues that for service organizations their marketing mix consists of five Ps – product, price, place, promotion, people. Unit and investment trusts exercise little control over price and, except through direct sales, little over people. Their problem is, within the existing regulatory and institutional constraints, to differentiate their products and depending on the particular trust, whether it is specialized or general, independent or part of a large group, to choose a segment of the market to which it can most appeal and by suitable promotion in the appropriate place attract investors. The services they provide are far from unique and for the most part easily reproducible. There is competition from other products and institutions and the difficulty is to identify new market opportunities and target potential investors more accurately. Extensive advertising is unlikely to be successful in cost-benefit terms. Unit and investment trusts need to develop marketing strategies that build on their strengths and appeal more widely. A wider choice of products, more extensive distribution network and more flexible products are all possible areas for building a competitive advantage.

# 14 Credit cards

Steve Worthington

## 14.1 Introduction

Imagine the scene; you are in New York for a business meeting, having flown in from your home in Iowa. You take your business colleagues to a restaurant in the evening and following the meal you seek to settle the bill by paying with a cheque drawn on your Iowa account. The restaurant refuses to accept this as they have never heard of your bank in Iowa and, as you do not have enough cash, you have to face the embarrassment of asking your business colleagues for contributions to the meal you were hosting for them.

In such circumstances the credit card as we now know it was born, when in 1950 an American entrepreneur created the Diners Club and issued its members with a plastic card that had a line of credit attached to it. By proffering this card in restaurants that agreed to accept it as a means of payment, a Diners Club cardholder could settle bills against the line of credit and then pay the entire debt off at the end of a nominated account period. Diners Club charged an annual fee for the issuance of the card to its members and also charged the restaurants a Merchant Service Charge (MSC), for guaranteeing and facilitating the payment of the members' bills. The restaurants, provided they followed the agreed procedures, had a guaranteed payment and by advertising that they accepted payment by this method, they stood to gain additional business from Diners Club cardholders. The cardholders themselves were prepared to pay the annual fees because of the convenience of being able to pay by plastic card anywhere they saw the acceptance sign and because the line of credit enabled them to manage their cash better and delay payment of the credit outstanding until the end of their account period.

These same principles underpin today's credit cards, although the plastic card product has become internationalized, issued by a wide variety of banks, building societies and retailers and held by many millions of cardholders. The card itself has matured into several different types of product. The Diners Club card was always a charge card, in that the total amount of credit taken by the cardholder on the card had to be paid off in full at the end of each account period. Sometimes also called Travel and Entertainment (T&E) cards, Diners was quickly joined by American Express, and these two cards are now available worldwide as charge cards. The credit card itself is distinguished from the charge card by its offering of revolving credit. Here the cardholder has the option of either repaying the credit taken in full or of repaying only part of the amount advanced by the card issuer and paying interest on the balance outstanding. Cardholders who take credit and pay interest are called 'revolvers', whilst those who settle their account in full are 'full payers'.

There are a number of variants of the basic credit card product. The Gold Credit Card is targeted at the higher income groups and is offered as a competing product to the charge cards, in that it has larger lines of credit than the basic credit card. Usually requiring a higher annual fee, the gold cards also offer better insurance and cardholder support than the standard credit card. Another variant is the Affinity Credit Card, offered to members/supporters of various charities, clubs and causes, as a credit card which will carry the name of their affinity group as well as that of the card issuer and by the use of which, affinity credit card holders can donate some of their spending power to their chosen affinity group. Worthington and Horne (1993) discuss the marketing synergy for both charities and affinity credit card issuers. A variant of affinity cards are those issued by banks on behalf of non-bank organizations who wish to enter the credit card market and these are sometimes called co-branded cards. Car manufacturers have recently been active in this market and here the credit card carries the marque of the car manufacturer as well as that of the bank and the international card association, i.e. either Visa or MasterCard. Some proportion of the amount spent on these cards goes into a rebate account for that cardholder, which can then be used against the purchase of a new car from the manufacturer which promoted the credit card. Thus these cards rely on the same principles as other affinity cards, except in this case the recipient of the donation from the issuing bank is an individual rather than a group. Worthington (1994c) discusses the rationale and the economics of the credit cards provided by the car manufacturers.

Retailers have also entered the market for credit cards; indeed the origins of the credit card (as opposed to the charge card), are to be found in the United States, where at the beginning of the century retailers offered credit accounts, as an alternative to cash payments, although those were restricted at that time to use in the issuing retailers' own outlets. Today, many retailers offer their own 'store cards' and use these as a means of offering their customers a line of credit and of communicating with them on a regular basis, via the monthly statement. Some retailers e.g. Marks & Spencer will only accept their own credit cards as a means of payment by plastic (see Worthington 1994b), but most accept all types of plastic card, although they encourage use of their own 'store cards'.

The plastic card payment market can be divided into three basic types of card. The pay-later card where credit is taken, to be paid off, in part or in full, at some time in the future. Into this category fall the various types of credit card and the charge cards. The 'pay-now' plastic card is the debit card, where the amount paid to a merchant via a debit card transaction, is immediately debited to the cardholder's account held at a financial institution. Finally there is the 'pay-before' plastic card, often called the pre-paid card, where value is held on the card and used up when the card is activated. Examples of pre-paid cards are telephone and travel cards, although technological developments with the integrated chip (IC) have made possible the so-called electronic-purse/wallet where value can be held in many places on the chip, to be used in a wide variety of payment situations. An example of this, Mondex, is described in Chapter 1. This chapter however will look at the credit card product in particular and having outlined its history and development in section 14.2, will examine the current market and the attraction of the credit card as a key to the marketing of a wide range of financial services to cardholders in section 14.3.

Section 14.4 discusses the role of new entrants and the importance of building relationships with customers is examined in section 14.5. The future of the credit/plastic card market is examined in section 14.6 and a summary and conclusions are presented in section 14.7.

## 14.2  History

By the late 1950s, a number of American banks were operating credit card services which offered a revolving credit facility. One of the most successful of these early issuers was the Bank of America and in 1966 it offered to license its blue, white and gold Bank Americard to other banks. Barclays Bank was the first overseas licensee of the Bank Americard (the forerunner of the Visa card scheme) and the first British bank to launch a credit card, the Barclaycard, in 1966. The success of Barclaycard prompted the other three major British banks, NatWest, Lloyds and Midland, together with the Royal Bank of Scotland to form the Joint Credit Card Company (JCCC) in 1972. The JCCC was to provide the marketing service and the joint processing capacity to launch a rival credit card under the brand name of Access, providing direct competition to Barclaycard. Both Access and Barclaycard were brought within an international framework, when at the end of the 1970s they joined MasterCard and Visa respectively. These international card associations had been formed by rival groups of banks to enable cards branded with their marques, to be used internationally.

The credit card proved to be a very successful product and during the 1980s, the volume of credit card transactions grew on average by 20 per cent per annum, and by the end of 1990 there were thirty million credit cards on issue and some £30 billion was spent using credit cards during 1990. Many other banks and some building societies subsequently became credit card issuers under the Visa or Access marques, as they too sought a share of what was a growth market. By 1990 there were seventy-six separate cards on issue and the credit card market was becoming a mature market, with most potential cardholders holding at least one credit card and with most of the card issuers associated with either Visa or MasterCard/Access. Indeed by 1990 the major card issuers had opted for 'duality' in that they were issuing both Visa and Access cards, the latter now increasingly marketed under the MasterCard marque. This was one of the factors that had brought to an end the 'cosy cartel' of the credit card issuers, whereby interest rates and other terms and conditions were not competitive issues in the credit card market (see Chapter 1). The Monopolies and Mergers Commission Report (1989), *Credit Card Services* was a further factor in raising the level of competitive activity, when it issued its recommendation that greater competition would remove excess levels of profitability in the industry. By the end of the 1980s the market was beginning to be much more competitive, as the potential of the credit card for establishing and building relationships with customers was realized and as the changing economics of the industry had forced card issuers to differentiate their offering to attract different segments of a now fragmenting market.

## 4.3   The current market

The size of the market for consumer credit in the United Kingdom has increased substantially since 1982 (HMSO, 1994). Table 14.1 shows the sources of consumer credit excluding mortgages and demonstrates that the total of credit outstanding at the end of the year had risen from £15.9 billion in 1982 to £52.9 billion by the end of 1992. Bank loans still remain the main source of consumer credit, although their overall share continues to stand at just under 63 per cent in 1992. Credit card lending by banks and all other institutions authorized to take deposits under the Banking Act 1987, continues to rise steadily and accounted for just under 19 per cent of outstanding credit in 1992. Retailers accounted for only 5 per cent of consumer credit in 1992, half the proportion of ten years earlier, although some retailer credit cards are now run and funded by the Finance Houses.

Consumers can choose to pay for goods and services by a variety of methods of payment. Table 14.2 reveals how the methods have changed since 1976 (HMSO 1994). The table combines regular payments, such as those for gas, electricity and telephone bills, with spontaneous payments which are made face to face at retail outlets, to other individuals and for such items as entertainment and mail order goods. Between 1976 and 1992, there was a swing of seventeen percentage points from cash pay-

**Table 14.1** *Composition of United Kingdom consumer credit (%)*

|                                                | 1982 | 1987 | 1991 | 1992 |
|------------------------------------------------|------|------|------|------|
| Bank credit card lending                       | 12.7 | 16.7 | 18.2 | 18.7 |
| Bank loans[1]                                  | 66.5 | 62.7 | 62.8 | 62.6 |
| Finance houses[2]                              | 8.3  | 11.9 | 10.2 | 9.5  |
| Insurance companies                            | 2.0  | 2.5  | 2.8  | 2.9  |
| Retailers                                      | 10.5 | 6.0  | 4.7  | 4.9  |
| Building society loans[3]                      | 0.0  | 0.2  | 1.3  | 1.4  |
| Credit outstanding at end of year (= 100%)(£billion) | 15.9 | 36.2 | 53.8 | 52.9 |

[1]   Banks and all other institutions authorized to take deposits under the Banking Act, 1987.

[2]   Finance houses and other credit companies (excluding institutions authorized to take deposits under the Banking Act, 1987).

[3]   Building Society unsecured loans to individuals or companies (i.e. Class 3 loans as defined in the Building Societies Act, 1986).

**Table 14.2** *Consumer payment (Great Britain): By method*

|                                          | 1976 | 1981 | 1984 | 1989 | 1990 | 1991 | 1992 |
|------------------------------------------|------|------|------|------|------|------|------|
| **All payments**                         |      |      |      |      |      |      |      |
| Cash[1]                                  | 93   | 88   | 86   | 80   | 78   | 78   | 76   |
| Non-cash                                 | 7    | 12   | 14   | 20   | 22   | 22   | 24   |
| **Non-cash payments**                    |      |      |      |      |      |      |      |
| Cheque                                   | 68   | 68   | 64   | 55   | 52   | 50   | 46   |
| Standing order/direct debit              | 21   | 20   | 22   | 23   | 23   | 24   | 25   |
| All plastic payments cards of which:     |      |      |      |      |      |      |      |
| Credit/charge card                       | 6    | 8    | 12   | 15   | 15   | 14   | 14   |
| Retailer card                            | –    | 1    | –    | 1    | 1    | 1    | 1    |
| Debit card                               | 0    | 0    | 0    | 2    | 4    | 8    | 11   |
| Other[2]                                 |      |      |      |      |      |      |      |

[1]  Cash payments under fifty pence in 1976, and £1 from 1981 onwards, are excluded.
[2]  Includes deductions made directly from wages and salaries, and payments made by postal order.
*Source*: Research Surveys of Great Britain Ltd for Association of Payment Clearing Services.

ments to non-cash payments. Of the non-cash payments, cheques accounted for the largest proportion throughout the period, although overall the number of payments by this method fell by a third. Conversely, over the same period, the proportion of payments by credit and charge cards more than doubled. Those by debit cards increased more than fivefold in the three years from 1989 to 1992. Worthington (1993) discusses the rationale and the launch of a debit card product. Spending via retailer credit cards has remained static throughout the 1980s and 1990s. Pre-paid cards continue to grow in usage and are included in the other category.

More recent evidence of the growth in use of credit cards as a means of payment, comes from the Credit Card Research Group, established in 1991, by all the major issuers of Visa, Access and MasterCard credit cards. Their figures for 1993 show the total value of credit card expenditure to be £31 659 000, an increase of 5 per cent over the preceding year. This spending took place on the twenty-seven million credit cards on issue in the United Kingdom, held by twenty million cardholders, a decline from the peak of issuance in 1990, attributable to the introduction by the major card issuers of annual fees, which has reduced multi- and inactive ownership of credit cards.

The number of opportunities to use a credit card as a means of payment in the UK continues to grow, as more merchants agree to accept payment by this means. Acceptance points for Access/MasterCard rose by 11 000 to 483 000 at the end of 1993, whilst merchants displaying the Visa logo went up by 25 000 to 421 000. Table 14.3 breaks down credit card expenditure into ten categories, ranging from food retailers to hotels

**Table 14.3** *Credit card expenditure by retail sector, 1993*

| Sector | Total (£m) | Average transaction value (£) |
|---|---|---|
| Food and drink | 3668 | 34.82 |
| Mixed business | 2525 | 39.14 |
| Clothing | 2227 | 40.29 |
| Household | 3590 | 61.90 |
| Other retailers | 3254 | 32.99 |
| Motoring | 4862 | 23.75 |
| Entertainment | 2259 | 39.25 |
| Hotels | 1699 | 103.29 |
| Travel | 4688 | 143.59 |
| Services | 2887 | 64.62 |
| Total | 31 659 | Overall average 42.90 |

*Source:* Credit Card Research Group

and shows actual spending by cardholders, including visitors to the UK. Table 14.3 also reveals the average transaction value by sector.

Whilst the use of credit cards as a means of payment continues to grow, there is no equivalent growth in the amount of actual borrowing undertaken on such cards. The figures in Table 14.1 for bank credit card lending include outstanding balances which are paid off in full at the end of each account period. The actual amount of credit outstanding at the end of 1993 was £9.4 billion (an increase of only 1.5 per cent on 1992) of which approximately two-thirds were held in interest-bearing balances. An increasing number of United Kingdom credit cardholders display the tendency to pay off their credit card account in full, and industry sources put this at over 50 per cent and growing. This means that these cardholders rarely, if ever, take credit on their cards and they in effect use their credit card as a deferred payment card. For these people the interest rate charged by the card issuer on credit taken, the so-called Annualized Percentage Rate (APR), is something of an irrelevance. These interest rates are expressed both as a monthly percentage and as an annual percentage rate, which includes where relevant the annual fee.

The variety of approaches by United Kingdom credit cardholders to the taking of credit on their credit cards is one of the reasons why the market has in recent years become more competitive, as card issuers have begun to segment the market, according to perceived cardholder demands. Some card issuers have for example chosen not to introduce an annual fee, using this as a point of differentiation within the market. To compensate for the loss of the annual fee as an income stream, some issuers have then reduced the length of the interest-free period, so that their cardholders have a reduced number of days to pay, following the issuing of their monthly statement. Other issuers have devised card products with low APRs, but no interest-free period and these are targeted at those cardholders (estimated to number ten million) who always carry credit outstanding and who would therefore benefit most from a lower APR.

**Table 14.4** *UK credit cards as of May 1994*

| Card issuer | Monthly interest (£) | Annual fee | Purchase APR(%) | Interest free days | Usage incentives |
|---|---|---|---|---|---|
| Bank of Scotland | 1.57 | £10.00 waived first year | 21.7 | 50 | Prize draw of 2 cars per month |
| Barclaycard | 1.585 | Nil | 22.42 | 46 | Profiles scheme – 1 point for every £10 charged to the card |
| Co-operative Bank | 1.70 | Nil | 22.42 | 46 | No annual fee if the card is used 10 times p.a., if not fee is £12 |
| Ford Barclaycard | 1.585 | £10.00 waived first year | 20.7 | 56 | Profiles points can also be used for discounts on new Ford cars/vans; 200 points gives £100 rebate, £600 p.a. £1.8K over 3 years |
| HFC Bank/GM Card | 1.53 | Nil | 19.9 | 52 | Rebate points worth 5% of every purchase, accumulate to max. £500 p.a. (2.5K over 5 years) for discount off new Vauxhall car |
| Lloyds Bank | 1.5 | £12.00 | 21.0 | 56 | – |
| MBNA | 1.39 | £10.00 waived first year | 17.9 | 56 | Annual fee rebate – spend over £1.5K during the preceding year and pay no fee |
| Midland Bank | 1.595 | £12.00 | 22.3 | 56 | For every £10 spent, 1 point is awarded which can be exchanged for goods and services. 220 points pays off the £12 annual fee |
| National Provincial | 1.53 | Nil | 19.9 | 51 | Photocard available to help combat fraud |
| NatWest Bank | 1.6 | £12.00 | 22.4 | 56 | Air miles earned at the rate of 1 mile per £20 charged to card |
| Royal Bank of Scotland Master Card | 1.25 | Nil | 16.0 | 0 | – |
| Save & Prosper | 0.95 | £12.00 | 13.9 | 56 | – |

*Source:* Steve Worthington, Staffordshire University Business School

Recognition by card issuers that spending on credit cards is increasing and that the economics of the credit card mean that such spending alone can provide an income stream to the card issuer, has prompted some card issuers to introduce usage motivation schemes into their card products, where the more you spend on the credit card, the more you earn in rebate value. These schemes are based on similar principles to those of the affinity cards mentioned earlier, the economics of which are discussed by Worthington and Horne (1992). Table 14.4 demonstrates the variables of some of the various credit card products, as of May 1994 and some of the usage motivation schemes introduced by the card issuers.

## 4.4  New entrants

Whilst for many banks and some building societies, issuing credit cards was something of a 'rite of passage' in the 1970s and 1980s, the early 1990s saw profitability on credit cards decline, as the recession caused bad debts and fraud to increase. With most of the banks and the major building societies already in the credit card market, there was however little change in the 'players' in the marketplace. One consequence of the recession however was a realization by many organizations that the key to survival in the 1990s would be the 3Rs: Retention of existing customers, Recruitment of new customers wherever possible, and the building of deeper and wider Relationships with all customers. This led many of the existing players in the credit card market, to reappraise the position of their credit cards in their portfolio of products and to see them not just as profit streams in isolation, but as one of the keys to establishing and building relationships with both existing and new customers, in pursuit of the 3Rs of survival. The same thought processes also brought a number of new entrants to the United Kingdom credit card market, as they realized the potential of the credit card in fulfilling their aspirations to be major players in world markets and the necessity of establishing continuing relationships with customers, in order to facilitate their strategic ambitions.

A good example of the latter is the General Motors credit card, launched in October 1993 in the United Kingdom, following its success in the USA during the preceding year. The rationale for this and the other car-based credit card schemes is described in Worthington (1994a), but essentially they are rebate-based loyalty schemes that use a credit card product issued by a bank to retain existing customers, attract new ones and build relationships. The General Motors credit card is issued both in the USA and the UK, by Household Finance Corporation (HFC) and whilst they are in a subservient position vis-à-vis the power of General Motors, HFC also stand to gain new customers via the distinctive General Motors credit card.

This card is an added value credit card, that offers benefits to the individual card holder, based on the formula that the more you spend on the card, the more you benefit. The General Motors card was followed in December 1993 by the launch of the Ford Barclaycard and both of these cards offer rebates earned at the rate of 5 per cent of the value of each transaction carried out on their credit cards. These rebates accumulate and can then be used in part payment for the purchase of a new General Motors (Vauxhall) or Ford car. In this way the car manufacturer sponsoring the credit card hopes to retain existing customers, recruit new ones via the credit card schemes and use the credit card and its accompanying monthly statement to build relationships with customers, both old and new.

Another recent new entrant into the United Kingdom credit card market is the American bank, Maryland Bank of North America (MBNA), which is primarily a credit card issuing bank. Their proposition is based essentially on the affinity credit card market, where they are the leading exponents in the USA. Their rationale for entering the United Kingdom is to establish a base here, as a prelude to entering the European market, because their opportunities for further expansion in the USA are limited. MBNA's strategic decision is underpinned by their appreciation of the importance of customer retention and of relationship building. Reichheld and Sasser (1990) and Reichheld (1993) have used MBNA as an example of an organization that has been successful in customer retention, because it has designed its entire business system around the concept of customer loyalty. MBNA have found that their loyal customers are the most profitable ones, as they tend to spend more and they may even act as unpaid ambassadors through positive word of mouth communication with other potential customers. Also the cost of acquiring new customers is, on average, eight times that of retaining an existing one. The success of MBNA in the USA, in using an added value credit card to establish initial relationships with customers, prior to developing other financial service relationships with them, has prompted many of its now United Kingdom based competitors, to re-examine their credit card products, to see if they can use the popularity of the credit card as a means of payment, to establish and develop relationships with customers they might otherwise not come into contact with.

## 14.5   Relationship building

The attractions of the credit card as a means of payment are many. The card is a compact size and easily carried, especially when compared to a cheque book. It offers a convenient and permanent line of short-term credit, with more flexibility in repayment than a personal loan and, if used astutely, at a lower cost than an overdraft. The holding and use of a credit card can also convey a certain status, as a line of credit is seen nowadays as more of a social status than a social stigma. As a result of the above attractions the credit card remains a popular means of payment and as more card issuers add value to their credit cards in the form of usage motivators, then it is likely that the number of credit cards on issue will increase in numbers and the value of spending carried on via credit cards will continue to rise.

Conversely the number of cheques written will fall, as payment by plastic, be it via credit, debit or pre-paid cards, continues to rise. The number of cheques written between 1992 and 1993 fell by 9 per cent and whilst the cheque book remains the physical representation of the current account, it is no longer the primary link between the consumer and the provider of personal financial services. Credit cards were of course originally offered by the card issuers to the customers who held current accounts with them. This enabled the card issuer to better ascertain the credit worthiness of those customers and to control the repayment of the debt incurred when credit was taken on the card. By virtue of being first in the market and of having a large market share of current account holders, Barclays were able to gain a large share of the credit card market and Barclaycard, with just over nine million cards on issue, remains the market share leader in the United Kingdom credit card market.

There is of course no obligation on current account holders to take their credit card from the bank or building society with whom they hold their primary account. Indeed evidence of 'switching' behaviour by consumers between credit card issuers has become much more commonplace in recent years, as cardholders seek out the best credit card for their circumstances. The General Motors credit card in the first three months of its launch in the United Kingdom was issued to 300 000 card holders. As their credit scoring was as rigorous as the existing issuers, these would not have been customers new to the credit card product, but the vast majority must have switched to the General Motors card from a previous relationship with another credit card issuer.

Most United Kingdom credit cards are issued by a bank or building society which also has a current account relationship with the cardholder. Barclaycard, because of its early entry into the market, is the exception to the rule, as a third of its credit cards are issued to non-Barclays current account holders. The current account is however still believed to be the primary relationship, with other products and services sold as add-ons, either via the branch or via the current account's monthly statement. In the United States the importance of a primary relationship based on a current account is less relevant and the credit card relationship is often viewed as more important than the current account relationship. With the entry of new players into the United Kingdom market and with new versions of added value credit cards, it seems possible that future trends is the domestic market may follow developments in the United States, with a weakening of the bank–customer relationship and a greater degree of shopping around by customers for the best deals relevant to their individual circumstances.

In this situation the credit card can be seen as the key to relationship building with those segments of the market able to pass the credit scoring criteria. If customers can be attracted to a particular credit card by its distinctive features and if they can be 'locked in' to that card, and encouraged to use it to the exclusion of all others, then the card issuer can build a relationship on the back of an accepted regular communication and a constant flow of information. The monthly statement of spending and debt outstanding provides a justified reason for a monthly communication with all cardholders. This communication can be used to widen the relationship by offering other products and services via the use of inserts in the mailing. It can also be used to deepen the relationship by reminding the cardholders what a good choice they made in choosing a particular issuer and by the use of rebate schemes, where value is held on the card by the issuer on behalf of the cardholder. Such techniques will also encourage longer relationships, for to walk away from that card issuer will result in a cardholder forfeiting opportunities to further build up that value.

The motivation schemes that encourage cardholders to use their credit card to the exclusion of all others and to possibly transfer spending from cash, cheques and debit cards to their chosen credit card, also provide a continuing stream of information about the cardholder and their spending patterns. When added to the information disclosed by the cardholder when completing the application form for the credit card, this is a very powerful file of real data about customers that can be used to design and target further products and services, to a known and active database.

Of particular concern to the traditional credit card issuers, is the fact that the new added value credit cards are being issued by the so-called 'non-traditional' suppliers and it is these non-traditionals who therefore stand to gain relationships based on the credit card product, to the detriment of the traditional issuers. If credit card customers can be lured away, will other financial services relationships be similarly vulnerable? The current level of competition and the transparency of the costs of the credit card product (see Table 14.4), have helped to raise the level of financial literacy amongst the United Kingdom population. As customers begin to demand more from their financial services providers and if the variety of potential suppliers continues to proliferate, then 'switching' by customers between suppliers will increase and the 'inertia' factor which has sustained the viability of many of the traditional suppliers will no longer be as much comfort.

Such a development can only be for the good both of all customers and ultimately of suppliers of financial services and it will have been the credit card product that provided the impetus for change. 'Non-traditional' issuers have entered the credit card market, because of their appreciation of the value of the 3Rs of Retention, Recruitment and Relationship building. Unless traditional issuers respond effectively, they stand to lose customers to the new issuers for whom the credit card is the key to a continuing and mutually beneficial relationship.

## 14.6  The future

Forecasting is always difficult, particularly as far as the future is concerned! Nevertheless there are some interesting possibilities for the credit card. The first is that with the continued increase in international trade and travel and with the continuing penetration of the credit card product in countries hitherto resistant to payment by plastic (e.g. Germany), then the utility of the credit card will increase. The international card associations, MasterCard and Visa, have a major role to play here in both promoting and facilitating payment by plastic card throughout the world. The convenience and relative security of payment by credit card, plus the prospect of either a deferred payment in full or of taking revolving credit on an instantly available line of credit, will continue to make the credit card an attractive proposition to those who feel able to handle the taking and repayment of credit. The functionality of the credit card may also be increased by the introduction of the integrated chip (IC) onto the credit card. Such a move would enable the use of the card in either a pay later, pay now or pay before form, as well as further enhance security. The tantalizing prospect of a single piece of plastic with which all financial transactions could be carried out is not that far removed from reality.

A second possibility sees financial institutions beginning seriously to address the issue of costing and charging for the services they offer. The credit card offers a useful indicator of the way things should evolve. With the growth of the number of cardholders who pay off in full and therefore use their credit card as a deferred payment card, there has been (and still is in many instances) a considerable degree of cross-subsidization between various types of cardholders. Those who were able or inclined to pay in full were in effect not paying any interest charges on their outstanding balances and their use of those funds during their interest-free period was being subsidized by those who did take credit and therefore did pay interest charges. Those charges were necessarily higher than the true cost of credit to compensate the card issuer for the losses they made on the full payer accounts. In the late 1980s the major card issuers attempted to redress this imbalance, by imposing annual fees on credit cards, so that all cardholders made at least some contribution to the costs associated with the operation of their credit card account. This development has reduced, although not eradicated the cross-subsidization of full payers by those who revolve their credit accounts and has resulted in both a reduction of interest rates and in a wider variety of rates, annual fees and interest-free periods. Eventually the major financial institutions will have to address the issue of cross-subsidization on their other financial services products in order more accurately to reflect the costs of operation in the charging structure. When applied to current accounts such a structure could result in annual fees for current accounts or in a charge per cheque issued above a certain minimum per account period. When and if charges are applied to current accounts the effects will be considerable and wide ranging. Amongst them will be a further decline in the number of cheques written, a further increase in both the value and volume of plastic card transactions and a further weakening of the current account as the primary relationship between a customer and his or her financial institution. Under such a scenario, the credit card will become even more a key to the establishment and continuance of the relationship between customer and financial institution.

A third possibility is that with the continued growth of full payer behaviour the credit card becomes a marginally profitable product, because only a minority proportion of the credit outstanding is actually interest bearing. In these circumstances credit card issuers may seek to reduce the interest-free period so as to lessen the costs of funding the credit taken and by so doing they may encourage full payer holders of credit cards to transfer their expenditure to debit cards, whilst only offering credit to those who revolve and therefore pay interest charges. Such a development would see a reduction in the number of credit cards on issue and a reduction in the amount of expenditure carried out on credit cards.

By comparison the usage of debit cards as a payment mechanism would increase.

## 14.7  Conclusion

From its development in the 1950s, the credit card market has undergone considerable change and development. Although there are a number of possible directions for the future, what is certain is that at the time of writing the credit card market is a textbook example of a maturing market. The previously dominant players are in danger of being outflanked on price and premium by the newcomers to the market. These new entrants have announced their arrival with reduced interest rates and added value offerings and the major players have to decide whether to match the value proposition, whilst watching their margins squeezed as they seek to respond by cutting their interest rates. Whilst at a tactical level it is a very dynamic market with new offers and price changes frequently seen, it is at the strategic level where the real battle is being fought and this concerns who should have the credit card relationship with the customer and to what extent can this be the key to establishing other financial services relationships with those cardholders. The bottom line for all suppliers is which cards will the consumer carry in their purse or wallet, which ones will they use the most and what will this mean for their relationship with customers?

# 15 Case studies

---

## Case 1 Dominion Insurance

---

*Axel Johne and Robert Davis*
City University Business School and Dominion Insurance

# Part A: Initiating change

### Introduction

The year 1990 was a turning point for Dominion Insurance. The general manager, who had held the post for some eight years, retired in mid year and his successor, Alberto Alfa, who had been joint general manager with him in the months preceding the official retirement date, 31 July, took full control.

Alfa had been a member of the board for ten years and had had thirty years' experience in the insurance industry (spanning some fifteen companies). He was concerned about Dominion's future and was determined to make the company more innovative and pro-active in a market undergoing rapid changes. 'For the company to survive, we must become market orientated and must be in a position to deal with the market. My interest is in the future because I am going to spend the rest of my life here.' Alfa was keen to create an action-orientated company. Another of Alfa's sayings would ring in the ears of Dominion's managers – 'five years is not a plan, it is a lifetime'.

Alfa's analysis of the situation was that although the insurance market was going through a trough in its traditional cycle, this phenomenon was only a smokescreen: there were in fact great competitive drives for market share and control of distribution channels taking place which could squeeze smaller companies like Dominion out of existence. Something had to be done urgently.

Towards the end of 1989 it was found that the company's ten-year-old IT systems needed replacement. Alfa asked Robert Davies, an MBA graduate who was then assistant manager of the UK Division, to write a report on Dominion's IT requirements with recommendations as to how to replace the outdated system. Working on the assumption that the choice of IT systems should be made with reference to competitive strategy, Davies included market trends and an analysis of Dominion's position in the market in his report, which is summarized in Appendix 11.1.

**The company**

Dominion Insurance sells non-life insurance products solely in the UK. It was founded in the early 1900s and in 1985 became a wholly owned subsidiary of La Fondiaria, one of Italy's largest insurers. Dominion is a small company with a UK market share in 1989 of about 0.2 per cent in terms of gross premium income. Its largest product line was private motor insurance but even in this area it has a market share of only 0.5 per cent, insuring some 70,000 cars. Direct Line, a new direct dealing motor insurer established in 1985, had in its first five years built a private car customer base four times the size of Dominion's. Dominion sold its products to both commercial and personal end-users, mainly through the traditional brokers and intermediaries. All but 3 per cent of Dominion's business was sold in this way. Dominion's 2,700 intermediaries were all independent (i.e., the company had no tied or sole agency agreements). Most were small or medium-sized brokers trading from High Street locations.

From the mid-1980s onwards more and more insurance companies were turning to direct writing in an attempt to gain market share. Against this background, Dominion was considered to be a broker-friendly company. Dominion's distribution strategy in relation to its competitors is shown in Figure C1.1. This breaks suppliers into four strategic groups – Dominion belonged to Group D, a shrinking group of small companies selling only through brokers. Within Group D the use of information technology (IT) was

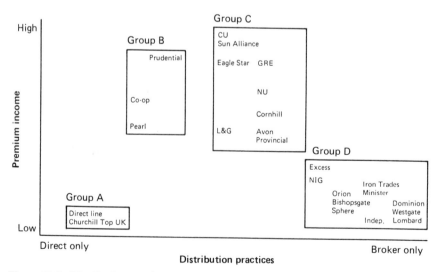

**Figure C1.1** Distribution practices

not in an advanced state and companies did not engage in rigorous planning.

At the time of his research (1989), Davies concluded that the larger companies in Groups A, B and C were gaining business through direct marketing operations (particularly in personal lines) and that the smaller companies in Group D were faced with a 'grow or go' option. At the same time as growing there was an urgent need simultaneously to replace outdated IT systems and also to adopt more sophisticated marketing strategies. The broker industry was set to shrink from 24,000 brokers in the UK to approximately 15,000–18,000. Davies concluded that, lacking critical size economies, Group D companies faced costs which were rising faster than in larger companies. Group D companies were particularly vulnerable to takeovers by larger companies. There were a number of large powerful groups of insurers operating in the UK. The top ten companies had a combined market share of over 50 per cent in 1987 (Table C1.1).

*Table C1.1   UK net written general premium of top UK companies, 1987*

|  | £m | % share |
|---|---|---|
| Sun Alliance | 1,180 | 9.0 |
| Royal Insurance | 1,040 | 7.9 |
| General Accident | 880 | 6.7 |
| Eagle Star | 835 | 6.4 |
| Commercial Union | 795 | 6.1 |
| Guardian Royal Exchange | 615 | 4.7 |
| Norwich Union | 605 | 4.6 |
| BUPA | 410 | 3.1 |
| Prudential | 410 | 3.1 |
| Co-operative | 370 | 2.8 |
| Cornhill | 250 | 1.9 |
| Legal & General Assurance | 225 | 1.7 |
| Excess | 190 | 1.5 |
| Private Patients Plan | 180 | 1.4 |
| Zurich | 180 | 1.4 |
| Provincial | 170 | 1.3 |
| Municipal Mutual | 165 | 1.3 |
| Municipal General | 150 | 1.1 |
| National Farmers | 145 | 1.1 |
|  | 8,795 | 67.1 |
| All others (excl. Lloyd's) | 4,305 | 32.9 |
| Total | 13,100 | 100.0 |

Figures have been grossed up to 100 per cent from the 95 per cent coverage claimed by the ABI.
*Source*: DTI returns/IFT analysis. In IFT Marketing Research Survey, *Non-Life Insurance Market in the UK* (1989).

## Company organization

Until 1990 Dominion was organized according to geographical area, as can be seen in Figure C1.2, with two main divisions:

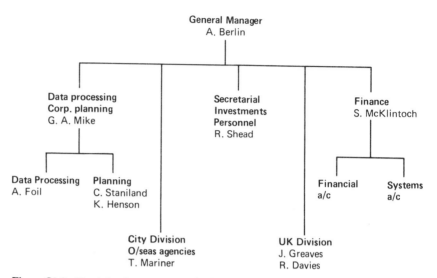

**Figure C1.2**  Dominion Insurance organizational chart – pre-1990. (Source: company records)

- The City Division, which earned a quarter of Dominion's income and was responsible for the Company's losses in 1989. This division operated in the Lloyd's insurance market.
- The UK Domestic Division, which made an underwriting profit in 1989. This division had a network of nine regional underwriting and claims processing centres and employed 250 employees out of a total of 500.

Within each division the company was further divided into a number of business areas, as shown in Figure C1.3. New product development was undertaken in traditional fashion by underwriters at the head office in London. Underwriters had little contact with a newly created marketing department or with end-users of the products. Product development was essentially reactive. New products were copied from innovations made by competitors such as Norwich Union and Royal Insurance. There were no guidelines for product development. Cooperation between the business areas (motor, fire and accident etc.) was on an *ad hoc* basis.

Davies's proposal was to change to a more market-based structure by dividing the company according to commercial and personal lines. For commercial business, Dominion was to maintain a distributed structure for underwriting and development, but the autonomous regional offices would become interrelated. They would form a connected series of development centres where underwriting staff attention would be focused on commercial business only. Administration support to intermediaries would be provided locally with the use of IT. The former regional managers would perform the role of development managers.

In respect of personal lines, insurance processing was to be concentrated on one or two regional development centres. Standard underwriting routines would be automated through advanced IT systems so that only a very small team of underwriting staff would be required to administer cases falling outside the criteria programmed into the computer system.

Davies argued that with a new organizational structure the company would:

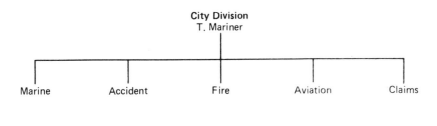

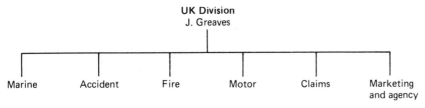

**Figure C1.3**  Dominion Insurance organizational chart – 1990. (Source: company records)

1 Be encouraged to adopt a market focus which would encourage better product development.
2 Limit the duplication of resources.
3 Introduce some standardization in the processing systems.
4 Gain economies of expertise by focusing the activities of senior underwriting staff.
5 Best serve the intermediaries (Dominion's suppliers of business) by providing local representation for commercial lines and centralized dedicated processing centres for personal lines.

## The planning process

It soon became clear to a small group of people within Dominion, including Alfa and Davies, that the effectiveness of these proposed changes would depend upon how they were implemented. In particular, it would take a long time to gain acceptance of the new organization because Dominion had not seen fundamental changes in the past twenty years. The City and UK Divisions never worked properly together. On their own the new IT systems and a redrawn organization chart could not solve the problems now facing the company.

Dominion had had a negative growth rate in recent years when allowance was made for inflation and had also suffered financial problems as a consequence of US liability business written as early as 1945. Claims from this business increased rapidly in the late 1980s and Dominion desperately needed a sound domestic business to finance this increase in costs. (Table C1.2 provides an overview of Dominion's accounts). The broker industry upon which Dominion was dependent was shrinking as a result of new competition. Figures C1.4 and C1.5 show major strengths and weaknesses of Dominion as perceived by their brokers. Both Alfa and Davies saw systematic business planning together with a market-orientated new product development strategy to be essential for developing a new competitive edge.

Table C1.2  Dominion Insurance: five-year view of accounts

| | 1985 £'000 | 1986 £'000 | 1987 £'000 | 1988 £'000 | 1989 £'000 |
|---|---|---|---|---|---|
| Written premiums | | | 60,535 | 63,909 | 69,967 |
| Reinsurance premiums | | | 24,717 | 16,415 | 11,799 |
| Net premium income (PI) | 36,726 | 40,594 | 35,818 | 47,494 | 58,168 |
| Profit before taxation | (4,287) | (2,113) | 2,113 | 1,010 | (8,451) |
| Percentage to net PI | (11.7%) | (5.2%) | 5.9% | 5.2% | (14.5%) |
| Profit after taxation | (3,037) | (1,454) | 1,459 | 411 | (8,501) |
| Retained profit | (3,037) | 546 | 1,459 | 411 | 470 |
| Capital | 8,250 | 8,250 | 13,000 | 18,000 | 18,000 |
| Reserves | 5,614 | 6,160 | 2,869 | 3,280 | 3,750 |
| Net assets | 13,864 | 14,410 | 15,869 | 21,280 | 21,750 |
| Percentage to net PI | 37.7% | 35.5% | 39.3% | 44.8% | 37.4% |
| Insurance funds | | | | | |
| Non-marine | 84,311 | 90,457 | 79,106 | 88,611 | 113,602 |
| Marine and Aviation | 4,203 | 5,032 | 4,737 | 5,059 | 5,729 |
| | 88,514 | 95,489 | 83,843 | 93,670 | 119,331 |
| Percentage to net PI | 241.0% | 235.2% | 207.6% | 197.2% | 205.1% |
| Total Assets | 115,557 | 127,578 | 116,145 | 136,173 | 164,085 |
| Actual net assets at market value | 21,417 | 20,652 | 18,734 | 23,418 | 23,484 |
| Percentage to net PI | 58.3% | 50.95% | 46.4% | 49.3% | 40.4% |

Notes
Early in 1989 La Fondiaria announced that it would provide £20 m for further capital (£5 m were injected in 1988).
During 1989 the company adopted a new accounting policy of discounting certain 'long-tail' liability business underwritten in the City Division Accident account. These are expected to be paid during the period 1990–2006. Discount rates: between 5 per cent and 7 per cent.
Breakdown of turnover:

| | 1988 | 1989 |
|---|---|---|
| Fire and Accident | £29 m | £30 m |
| Motor | £28 m | £33 m |
| Marine, Aviation, Transport | £6 m | £7 m |

Percentage to net PI in 1987 relates to net PI of £40,389,000 before deduction of the premium paid for aggregate excess of loss reinsurance.
Retained profit is stated after transfers from contingency reserve and prior year adjustments.
Source: Company Reports, 1988 and 1989.

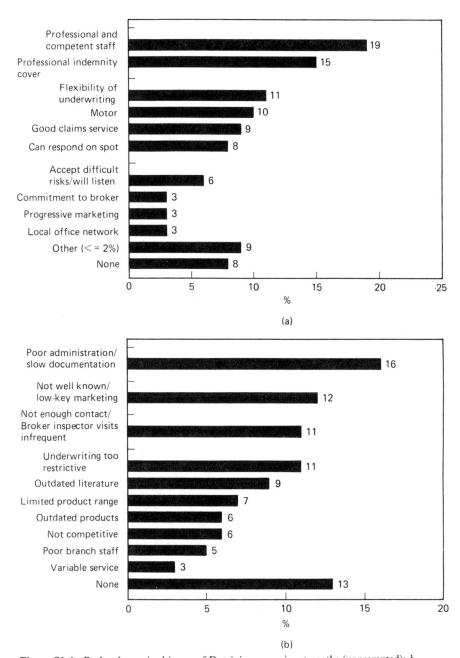

**Figure C1.4** Brokers' perceived image of Dominion: *a*, major strengths (unprompted); *b*, major weaknesses (unprompted). Base = all (200). (Source: financial marketing consultancy)

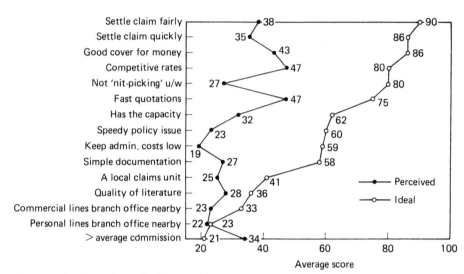

**Figure C1.5** Brokers' perceived image of Dominion: ideal image versus perceived image. Base = all (200). (Source: financial marketing consultancy)

Further, Alfa and Davies believed strongly in a bottom-up planning process. Alfa stressed 'Planning is for the people. Those who will have to implement the plans are those who will have to construct the mission statement, the strategy and the supporting operational plans.' Davies saw his job as providing guidance and quantitative support for managers to produce their own business plans; however, this would be the first time that underwriters and managers in Dominion were to go through systematic business planning. It would be necessary first to convince them of the need for such planning and then guide them through the process.

It was decided that the best way forward would be to organize a 'planning conference' with the following objectives:

- To produce a share of business scenario.
- To finalize underwriters' proposals to meet stated growth objectives.
- To develop greater liaison between the UK and London market operations.
- To generate ideas to gain competitive advantage.

Davies, who was responsible for running the planning conference, had several objectives in mind. He believed that the key to success was to create greater awareness of market trends and to develop a mission statement of strategic intent. His aim was to overcome the following three weaknesses at Dominion:

- Lack of communication between the City and UK divisions.
- Lack of market awareness.
- Reactive and esoteric new product development based on copying innovations made by competitors.

He hoped that within one year the following would be achieved:

1 Breaking down traditional functional boundaries.
2 Creation of a greater awareness of customer requirements.
3 Creation of new ways of thinking on new products development.

In the second year he aimed to achieve a level of awareness such that managers could produce their own business plans based on market analysis and likely competitive rivalry. The foundation for achieving these objectives would be the planning conference held on the 30/31 July 1990 for senior managers of the company (see Figure C1.7). As a background to the conference Davies prepared and circulated a review of the UK insurance market and trend extrapolations for the years 1990–5.

## The planning conference

The conference was the first of its kind to take place at Dominion. It was also the first time that managers from the City and UK Divisions came together. The first day of the planning conference consisted of a series of introductory speeches given by Alfa and Davies, and a series of presentations from staff with responsibilities in the areas of IT, human resources, marketing, accounts and statistics. A further presentation was given by an outside speaker on the subject of innovation and product development. These were followed by workshops in which small groups of managers discussed possible business strategies for particular product lines.

A small group of 'idea generators' including Alfa, Davies and the outside speaker, provided assistance to each working group. On the second day each group would be asked to give a forty-five minute presentation. The group presentations are summarized below.

*Presentation 1   Motor (Commercial)*
Commercial motor insurance covered everything from motor fleets to coach insurance. The working group explained that as brokers come to Dominion automatically with *volume* business they had decided to focus on how to get business that does not come automatically, i.e. mini fleets and smaller risk business. The group identified with small businesses, particularly those just starting up in regional development areas. It was suggested that service industries and franchise holders might be possible targets. Two ways of bringing attractive business to this segment might be: (1) to offer premium instalment facilities and (2) to offer a helpline facility for private and commercial vehicles. The group noted that Dominion would have to make the following changes to become really successful in this segment of the market:

- Provide more help to proposers than at present.
- Use direct marketing techniques (hand-in-hand with brokers).
- Have a highly trained field force.
- Encourage brokers to improve their local marketing.
- Set aside funds to create brand awareness amongst the target customer groups.
- Simplify Dominion's documentation.

*Audience response*  The response to these proposals was mixed. Some, including Davies, were keen to carry these ideas forward and develop them as embryonic business proposals. Others were reticent, particularly about the idea of direct marketing. Some pointed out that the increased administration costs might make this proposal too expensive to carry on. In the course of the discussion the group had another idea: to offer discounted insurance policies to staff in participating companies. This was the first time in the recent history of Dominion that any form of cross-selling had been formally suggested.

Davies was concerned about who among the team would champion product development and carry these ideas forward. Addressing all the teams Davies said he would provide organizational focus and coordination to help groups develop their ideas. 'It is important at an early stage that groups decide which products are viable and how to effectively make a case for additional resources.'

*Presentation 2  Liability*
This group divided their presentation into three areas – the Lloyd's market, UK professional indemnity and UK liability.

> The Lloyd's market.  The group envisaged that price would continue to be a major competitive feature. Future strategy must be to present Dominion as a specialist niche underwriter. A suggestion was made that underwriters within the London market should share their skills with their regional colleagues to enable the regional operation to quote for larger liability risks.

> UK professional indemnity.  The group anticipated no real growth here until 1991. It commented that market conditions were difficult and that Dominion had to fight to maintain its position until conditions recovered and competition became less severe. The new products that were suggested were directors' and officers' liability and VAT investigation cover.

> UK liability insurance.  This group focused on insurance for smaller business and came up with three ideas: a small package liability cover for the building trade, extended warranty insurance and holiday travel insurance.

*Audience response*  Several respondents felt that they had heard these ideas before but that little progress had ever been made with these in the past.

*Presentation 3  Property*
This group decided to split their presentation along traditional lines. The first to present covered the UK property market. The group started by noting the difficult economic conditions. However, the following ideas were put forward:

- A policy for the motor trade combining traditionally separate fire and motor insurance covers.
- To add legal expenses insurance to Dominion home insurance and other property policies.

- To boost direct marketing operations.
- To enter the travel insurance sector.

The group went on to present the Lloyd's property market. Two ideas were put forward. First to cover electronic equipment breakdown and, second, to provide banks with contingency policies covering properties on which losses were quoted.

*Audience response* Davies expressed his frustration because he had heard all these ideas before. 'We must aim to generate new ideas. The purpose of this conference is to give you a mechanism to generate new ideas. We must become market-orientated. Look and keep looking for opportunities.' The outside speaker recommended the groups look to the future rather than reviewing the past.

*Presentation 4  Marine and Aviation*
Members of this group were noticeably more nervous than others. Past results had been poor and perhaps they were concerned that their jobs might be threatened. Ideas concentrated on cost leadership, although one idea was put forward which involved insuring pilots against loss of licence through physical disability.

*Audience response* The outside speaker noted that driving costs down has limitations as a sustainable competitive strategy in a small company – 'one must first find a truly defendable niche with barriers to entry or, eventually, one will get beaten by larger competitors'. To this one senior manager retorted: 'You are alluding to segments of the market, we, however, are talking about product lines.'

*Presentation 5  Personal Lines Insurance*
This had been the most active team and it was difficult for it to present all ideas in the time available. The following potential markets were identified:

- Life
- Motor – focusing on the minibus, caravan and lady driver market
- Household – focusing on the higher socio-economic groups for contents insurance
- Healthcare – again focusing on identified socio-economic groups and the female market in particular
- Extended warranty
- Legal expenses
- Travel insurance – cross-selling to previously identified socio-economic groups

*Presentation 6  Agency strategy*
This group first identified the fact that only 10 per cent of Dominion's brokers provided the company with volume business. There was a need, therefore, to focus on key brokers to build up a nucleus of large profitable accounts. It was considered pointless to align with banks, building societies or to go direct, as Dominion would be entering these sectors too late.

The group went on to state that Dominion must improve its relationship with intermediaries and improve the selling techniques employed by field staff. Dominion's brokers frequently complained that inspectors lack underwriting authority and that visits were infrequent. These were identified as factors which needed to be put right first. Figure C1.6 details market research findings in respect of insurance company salesforces. The group identified a changing role for the traditional insurance salesperson. What was seen as needed were field underwriters who could visit brokers and quote on the spot. An embryonic management structure to support such a field force was put forward.

*Audience response*   The response was divided – half the audience could not see the need for salespersons to take on the traditional role of underwriter. The group quickly made the point that to survive the salesperson of tomorrow needs authority to solve clients' problems on the spot. One member of the audience asked rhetorically 'Who is our customer? The customer is the broker. He needs decisions and our problem is to solve his problems. In this way we can satisfy our customers' needs best.'

*Closing remarks: Robert Davies*
'We have recognized at this conference the need to be market led, the need for change and the need to interpret environmental changes more accurately. There have been many excellent suggestions for new product development and improved channel marketing. What we must do now is to form a small group of people to manage product development and distribution policy for the company as a whole.' Accordingly, Davies called for volunteers to form a 'product development group'. After some hesitation, seven members of the audience volunteered.

*Closing remarks: Alfonso Alfa*
'I have been impressed today with the professionalism shown. As you know, my main job is to identify talent and to put the right people in the right

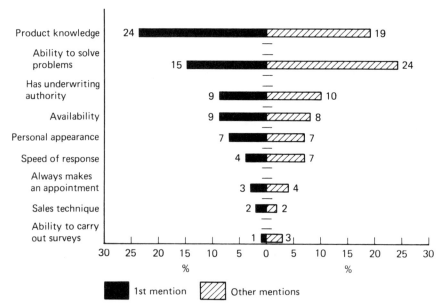

**Figure C1.6**  Brokers' perception of Dominion broker inspectors, i.e. factors setting them apart. Base = all (200). (Source: financial marketing consultancy)

place. I have seen plenty of talent but not enough places. Through the planning conference we have identified about fifty possible projects. These projects will provide the job opportunities of tomorrow.'

## After the conference

Both Davies and Alfa were very pleased with the responses obtained at the conference. Over a two-day period a number of managers had changed their outlook completely and had become convinced that a market orientation was crucial to Dominion's survival. There were still a number of disbelievers, but on the whole the objectives of the conference had been met. Each working group was accordingly requested to submit preliminary written outline planning proposals based on their presentations at the conference. Figure C1.7 provided details of the envisaged planning timetable.

By 30 August Davies had read all the preliminary planning proposals. His reaction was one of utter disappointment. All but one were far below standard. Working teams seemed to have ignored the guidance given for presenting proposals and the numerous new product ideas that had been suggested at the conference had obviously got lost. Enthusiasm for change had apparently evaporated. Managers seemed unwilling or unable to take up the new challenge.

After discussions with Alfa, it was agreed to tighten the original timetable. The market was changing far faster than anticipated back in January 1990. Alfa stated categorically that he expected to see complete plans by December 1990. Davies felt he had a serious problem. There was no lack of talent. The conference had shown this. The problem was how to energize this talent.

| | |
|---|---|
| 5 July | Plan instructions issued to divisional managers, underwriters, claims managers, human resources, investment, marketing and DP functions |
| 9–14 July | Briefing groups<br>Issue plan instructions to regional managers |
| 30–31 July | Planning conference |
| 6 August | Final deadline for preliminary submissions to planning department |
| 25 August | Regional managers' planning submission deadline |
| 3–14 September | Full review of preliminary submissions to agree<br>– base strategies<br>– key action plan requirements for business areas include one-day review with regional managers |
| 1 October-2 November | Final action plans submitted by underwriters and operational managers |
| 24 November | Final general management appraisal of action plans |
| 10 December | Budget 1991 finalization |

**Figure C1.7** Dominion 1990 planning cycle

## Questions: Part A

1 Analyse the main threats and opportunities facing Dominion. Distinguish clearly between external market and competitive factors on the one hand and internal operating factors on the other.
2 Explain 'bottom-up planning'. Is this type of planning suitable for a company like Dominion? What other mechanisms apart from a conference might have been used to introduce formal planning within the company?

### Appendix C1.1 Summary of Davies's report on IT

In terms of the popular three-stage life cycle used to describe IT developments (1, to increase efficiency; 2, to increase quality of service; 3, to provide new and more flexible products and distribution methods), it is anticipated that UK insurance companies will enter stage 3 during the period 1990–5.

1 Insurers are developing customer-based relational databases which offer strategic advantages particularly in the areas of marketing and new product development. As they come to realize that existing customers need to be regarded as major assets, they will build a reservoir of information about them which can be manipulated and retrieved in new ways to maximize business opportunities. A market survey carried out in 1988 reported that insurers' two highest priorities were the development of client- not policy- based systems and the need for rapid new product development. Relational databases can enhance decision-making in this area and reduce development lead time.

2 The use of networking (Electronic Data Interchange) as a means to improve communication with intermediaries is increasing. The AA Insurance Services goes so far as to stipulate the use of the Brokernet network system by intermediaries representing them. There is, however, some resistance to these systems on the part of smaller independent intermediaries, probably based on ignorance of benefits, cost barriers and the absence of long-term planning.
Networking can reduce processing delays and offer considerable cost reductions. It is expected to be a prerequisite on the part of new entrants. Though less than 2 per cent of all UK personal lines was handled through networking in 1989, it is estimated that by 1994, this percentage will increase to at least 50 per cent. In commercial lines, it is likely to be around 30–40 per cent.

3 Reduced hardware costs, increased use of hardware flexibility and fourth generation languages, and the availability of software packages are lowering technology cost barriers and allowing insurers to implement information technology as a central part of their strategies. (e.g. London & Edinburgh and Economic).

4 The use of expert systems (e.g. Minster Insurance, Direct Line, London & Edinburgh) is providing cost savings and opportunities for differentiation. Their benefits include reducing staff numbers, broadening underwriting areas into specialist products, enhancing training and the distribution of scarce knowledge within the company, and raising service levels.

5 Image processing is also being used to cut costs and improve service. The Prudential reported cost savings of 25 per cent, and a 50 per cent improvement in the turnaround of replies to customers because documents

and data can be displayed simultaneously in computer processing procedures.

It is hoped that IT will provide more sophisticated methods for pricing, such as contribution analysis, instead of traditional 'cost-plus' methods. IT decisions now faced by insurance companies will become central to their future survival. In particular, the IT system chosen will have to allow long-term flexibility in the choice of distribution channels.

# PART B: Introducing a Planning Process (1 September 1990 to 31 March 1991)

If, on 29 August 1990, Davies thought he faced problems, then he was in for a nasty surprise. For in the coming five months things were to deteriorate. Two weeks earlier Davies had passed to Alfa copies of the underwriters' proposals following the planning conference. The contents were the same as they had always been. Present trends were simply extrapolated. Growth rates were indicated a little above inflationary trends. None of the strategic problems identified at the planning conference was explicitly addressed. Alfa immediately called for a meeting of all underwriters and senior managers. At this meeting Alfa was in no mood to hear excuses. He asked: 'Why are we as businessmen merely satisfied to go for inflationary growth? Why have none of the issues identified at the planning conference been explicitly tackled in any of the plans?'

One underwriter who was in control of one of Dominion's largest accounts, quickly intervened. 'It is because we have always done it this way. I have worked for Dominion for many years and I have always been held back in planning. The message that I have always worked to, and I am working to now is: keep on going as you are, don't do anything dramatic.' Alfa quickly intervened: 'Isn't it obvious that doing what we have always done in the past will get us nowhere, the company will merely decline into oblivion.' The room fell into silence. Another manager intervened. 'Perhaps managers within Dominion haven't been used to a formal planning process and they need more time to understand it.' Alfa retorted: 'This isn't a difficult process, it is, after all, taught as part of any business management course.' The room again fell into silence. Alfa then turned to Davies and said: 'You must take each underwriter through an education process in the art of strategic planning. It is imperative that attitudes and perceptions change. We cannot continue as we are.'

At this point Davies felt as if all his previous work had been wasted. Outside the meeting Alfa made it clear to Davies that he must succeed in changing the attitudes of the underwriters. This was such an important process that all work that Davies was undertaking in examining the future structure of the company was to cease. Alfa made it clear that the fundamental problems had to be addressed first.

Gathering his thoughts Davies decided to tackle this job in phases. He just did not have the time or resources to take all underwriters, in both the UK provincial market and the London market, through the planning process on an individual basis. Alfa suggested that he should concentrate initially on motor insurance. Davies, however, felt that many business areas were interrelated, so he decided to tackle the company's UK provincial business, covering fire, accident and motor classes, first. Davies drew on all his past MBA experience and structured a rational step-by-step planning process shown in Figure C1.8 Basically, this consisted of five steps:

Step I      Define the main market trends and prioritize these.
Step II     Define company strengths, weaknesses, opportunities and threats.
Step III    Armed with the above information, produce a product portfolio analysis.
Step IV     Define the company's mission and long-term strategic objectives.
Step V      Produce supporting short-term action plans.

Not all was gloom, however. The product development group met for the first time two weeks after the planning conference. Staniland (the company's statistician) and Henson (Davies's assistant) were eager to look at private medical insurance, a new area for Dominion. Brearton (a regional manager) and Grant (marketing manager) took on small business package development as well as a broker package to encourage business from a selected group of brokers. Another regional manager travelled from Manchester for the meeting and had already researched the private car insurance market for new niches. At least something was happening. Davies eagerly presented this information at the next monthly management meeting attended by all of Dominion's top managers.

After the management meeting Mariner, the deputy general manager, explicitly stated that the product development group was not to examine any area without his personal prior approval. In addition, the leadership of the group was to come under the company's underwriting management structure. Not surprisingly meetings dried up. However, Henson, Staniland, Brearton and Grant continued their work in a low key fashion. In fact, Davies found a close ally in Grant, the newly appointed marketing manager. When Grant joined Dominion he found that most managers just did not understand the purpose of marketing. Most felt that marketing should be limited to PR, advertising and general promotion activities. Davies and Grant found their attitudes in creating strategic plans and marketing plans ran along parallel lines. Time was, however, ticking on. It was already the end of September and Alfa had requested that corporate plans be finalized by the middle of December 1990. There just was not time to agree major market trends and to undertake a SWOT analysis (the first two steps in Davies's planning process) with individual underwriters and business managers. Davies and Grant therefore decided to do this work independently and present their conclusions to a core management group – Alfa, Mariner, Greaves (UK Division) and McKlintoch (finance) – in an attempt to gain support for a general strategic direction and mission before reopening discussions with underwriters and other business managers.

Grant had some experience of using product portfolio analysis techniques with a previous employer. Davies thought that this would provide the sort of analysis needed. It would enable underwriters to visualize their product strategies without producing volumes of words. Therefore, Davies decided to operationalize the Directional Policy Matrix, having learnt this concept during his MBA course. Figure C1.9 gives an example of the product portfolio analysis for motor insurance.

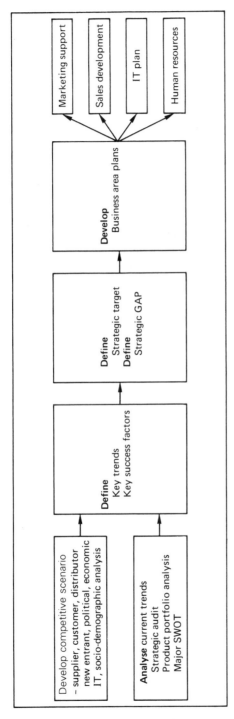

**Figure C1.8** Davies's planning process for Dominion's UK provincial division

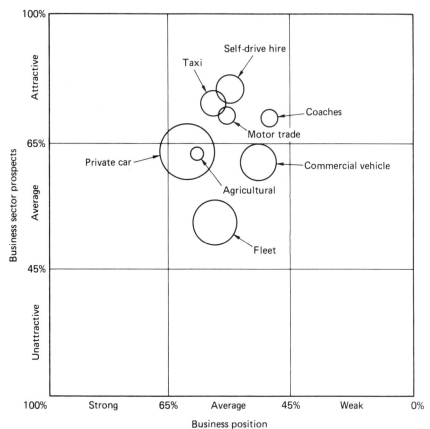

**Figure C1.9**  Examples of a portfolio analysis: motor insurance

Grant and Davies presented their recommendations at the October 1990 management meeting and general approval was received. Throughout November 1990 Grant and Davies continued work with the three UK underwriters, taking each through the planning process. This method worked well with the Motor underwriter. He enthusiastically embraced the process and accepted the challenge of relatively rapid expansion with relish. It was the first time that he had been allowed 'off the reins'. He added that it was a pity he was so near retirement. If only he had been given this opportunity twenty years earlier! The fire underwriter (Cooper) readily agreed with Grant and Davies's conclusions regarding market trends and the company's strengths, weaknesses, opportunities and threats. However, he simply did not know what to do. In his view Dominion's competitors had already done everything there was to do! Grant and Davies guided Cooper using the Directional Policy Matrix through a possible product strategy and outlined the distribution alternatives that were open to him. At this point Davies decided to write Cooper's five-year strategic plan for him. In the same way, Weekins, the accident underwriter, also agreed with the broader vision that Grant and Davies introduced, although he was very cautious regarding account expansion.

Because planning within Dominion had been financially (budget) based, the supporting commentaries had traditionally been short on recommendations

---

° *Strategic Unit*:
Motor – Provision of insurance services to fleet vehicle and commercial vehicle owners

*Key Objectives*:
1 Self-drive hire, motor trade and fleet product development
2 Research 'high-risk' facility
3 Systems improvement
4 Regional training

*New Product Development/Old Product Improvement*:
1 To develop a new self-drive hire contract. Target launch date September 1991
2 In conjunction with the Fire & Accident departments, to develop a new motor trade contract. Target implementation date April 1991
3 To develop a separate fleet contract. Target implementation date September 1991
4 To research, with sales and marketing, the creation of a 'high-risk' insurance facility, possibly embracing self-drive hire, taxi and coach risks. Target implementation date March to September 1992

*Reinsurance*:
This area is currently under review, but at this time it is intended to continue the present arrangements for 1991

*Distribution (including sales/marketing support)*:
1 To identify, in conjunction with the sales/marketing and statistical functions, key geographic areas for future development
2 The attainment of planned growth rates will depend heavily on an efficient sales strategy focused on the development of key brokers and the targeting of inspectors for new business development
3 The marketing and planning functions will provide key data on competitor and environmental trends. Marketing will also provide market price position data where possible

*Systems/capacity planning/resourcing*:
1 Networking, it is anticipated, will become a prerequisite to participation in this sector. Such facilities will be required at the latest by mid-1992

*Training*:
1 Regional new product training to support new product lines
2 Development of regional training programmes

---

**Figure C1.10**  Dominion motor insurance action plan: 1991

for action. Davies devised a new 'achievement-orientated' action type of planning. An example of this for motor insurance is shown in Figure C1.10. Grant and Davies presented the new action plans to the management meeting on the last working day before Christmas 1990. Through the absence of any objections they assumed that the action plans were agreed. It now remained for them to tackle the London market business area that they were not quite so experienced in.

Alfa, on his return from Italy after Christmas 1990, offered Davies some advice. 'Remember that your job isn't to *produce* the plans. What you have really got to do is recommend to managers how they should plan and format their views about the future. Don't go any further . . . ' With these words in mind, Davies decided to provide underwriters in the London market with a framework for a recommended process. This time Grant and Davies did not intervene heavily. It took six weeks to gather these managers' views and March 1991 loomed – the date by which Alfa wanted to see final plans. The London market plans did not directly reflect Grant and Davies's views. Davies knew that they did not really look a lot different from those originally proposed back in August 1990. The plans were circulated to the senior management team to be reviewed at the March 1991 monthly management meeting.

Davies knew that he faced trouble on two fronts. It was likely that the London market plans would not receive Alfa's approval as they did not tackle any fundamental strategic issues. It was now early March 1991. Little progress had been made in moving to implement any of the action plans, most notably in the area of product development and improvement. It was as if more systematic planning did not exist in Dominion. Managers appeared to be carrying on as they always had done.

### Questions: Part B

1  What are the principal components of a SWOT analysis? Is such an analysis adequate on its own for strategic planning purposes?
2  Critically evaluate the managerial methods used by Davies and Grant to gain support and cooperation for the more formal approach to action planning.

# PART C: Restructuring the Company (1 April 1991 to 15 April 1991)

Immediately after the March 1991 management meeting Alfa called Davies into his office. Alfa opened: 'From all your analysis we can draw one conclusion. That is that any successful insurance company must have an organization structure that will both allow it to achieve a low cost position and to offer quality products. I now look to you to design such an organization for the company.' To tackle the restructuring process, Davies, who had by now been promoted to Planning Manager, decided to embark upon the following five-step process:

1  Identify key trends in the UK insurance market.
2  Analyse the categories of likely future demand. For this process Davies used the concept of strategic business area (SBA) segmentation.
3  Use the demands of different SBAs to carry out a SWOT analysis of Dominion's current position.
4  Drawing upon the analysis in Step 2, determine the structure of the strategic business units (SBUs) that might be used as the delivery vehicles to meet the needs of SBAs.
5  Present a definition of the needed SBUs and the accompanying organization structure.

Before he started his work Davies knew that all insurance companies faced an apparent paradox. On the one hand it was likely that the efficiency or cost base of insurance companies would deteriorate. On the other hand, insurance companies would have to face new threats, particularly in the distribution sector, that would require innovative thinking. Any new structure had simultaneously to address these issues. Davies was concerned that the attainment of a lower cost base might overshadow the need for innovation. He did not want to fall into the trap that he felt most of Dominion's competitors would do – of creating a highly efficient machine bureaucracy. What was really required, Davies thought, was an organization that simultaneously displayed characteristics of a machine bureaucracy and that of an adhocracy.

## Step 1: analysis of future trends

*Customer demand analysis*

Davies knew that the demand for all general insurance products would grow at a fairly slow rate, averaging about 7 per cent per annum. Insurance spending as a proportion of GDP would only show a nominal increase. The corollary seemed to be that current levels of excess competition would remain. However, Davies knew that the UK insurance market could not be treated as one product market. He therefore turned his attention first to the personal insurance market.

In respect of the personal insurance market, with some exceptions he concluded that it would remain a price-driven commodity market. This reinforced Davies's view that the provision of insurance products in respect of the personal market from a leading low cost base would be a prerequisite to successful participation. Davies then looked at different segments of the personal insurance market and concluded that certain age groups and socio-economic groups would show above average growth rates and that there would be an increase in demand for 'social insurance' (health insurance, legal expenses insurance and employment insurance) that would lead to a greying of the traditional boundaries between life and non-life companies.

From this structural perspective Davies concluded that:

- There was a need to establish a leading low cost process base.
- Increasing competition would lead to sophistication in risk premium assessment methods.
- It would be necessary to provide specially designed products targeted at specific customer groups. Dominion should not continue to rely on single products to serve entire market areas.
- A defined product development mechanism was needed.
- It was necessary to create the ability to provide products across traditional boundaries, such as fire, accident and motor insurance.

Davies then considered the commercial insurance market, noting that demand fell into three main groups – small package commercial risks (shops etc.), larger industrial risks, and the more esoteric risks placed in the Lloyd's market. In both the latter categories Davies noted that an organizational structure would have to be flexible enough to meet the demands of individual customers.

*Distribution*

Davies then moved on to examine structural changes in the distribution side of the industry. His views here were already well known within Dominion. He was worried that 97 per cent of Dominion's business came through smaller, independent intermediaries and brokers. This was the group that would be under threat from direct writing strategies and from acquisition strategies by large national brokers. Dominion had historically poor relations with such large national brokerages. Davies was adamant that the absence of a long-term distribution strategy was one of Dominion's greatest weaknesses. The ability to support multi-channel operations would therefore be a feature of Davies's structural design to provide a last resort fallback should the broker market collapse.

*Competitor analysis*

Davies felt that it was important to try to predict how Dominion's competitors would react to the emerging competitive environment. He was on good personal terms with corporate planners within other broker-supporting companies. A typical reaction amongst this group of peers was to attempt to differentiate company offerings on the customer, in addition to developing closer associations with intermediaries through incentives and increased commissions, as well as establishing links with the bulk retail providers (AA, Swintons etc.). Few companies seemed to have consistent customer support systems. Dominion was, however, falling behind the competition in terms of productivity. Davies was able to gain information on the operations of a number of companies to provide estimates of productivity. The results of this analysis are shown in Table C1.3 in relation to Dominion's productivity base of 100 (competitors' names are disguised). Davies knew that Church had plans to increase productivity by a further factor of 50 per cent. Dominion was a fourth quartile productivity performer and had a considerable amount of catching up to do. If it was to attain a leading market position in terms of productivity and thereby attain low cost competitive advantage, it would have to increase productivity by a factor of five.

In terms of proposing structural design changes within Dominion, Davies moved forward on the basis of the following assumptions:

- A leading low cost base can only be achieved through a hybrid combination of structure, systems and skills for each product market. Davies planned to develop this idea by dividing product markets into strategic business areas.
- The current organization was too complex. Policy processing must be centralized to achieve economies of scale.
- Organization design must be based on main customer groups and not on internal operations – to encourage product development.
- Both commodity and differentiated products must be capable of being provided to selected markets.
- The new organization must be capable of multi-channel distribution.
- Organizational layers should be limited to no more than five to encourage information flows.

*Table C1.3  Productivity measures*

| Company | Productivity index |
| --- | --- |
| Dominion | 100 |
| Nationwide | 208 |
| Galaxy | 225 |
| Morning Star | 200 |
| Church | 340 |

Table C1.4 Examples of strategic business areas

| SBA | Customer group | Distribution method | Product/services requirement | Key organizational issues | Geography |
|---|---|---|---|---|---|
| 1 | Domestic standard | UK provincial broker | Predesigned product. Price remains a key 'purchase' factor. Rapid claims, query and documentation facilities. Differentiation will centre upon features of predesigned product, e.g. product segmentation for different demand groups | Physical: dedicated bulk processing IT: high use of automated underwriting and documentation. EDI facilities will emerge in mid-1992 onwards. Skills: low under intermediate supervision. | UK |
| 2 | Domestic standard | Retail broker chain | Predesigned product to meet distributors' requirements and/or defined customer segment. Distributor will demand dedicated processing response and EDI facilities | Physical: dedicated unit providing predefined service levels IT: as SBA 1 but greater emphasis upon EDI Skills: high in scheme negotiation phase, otherwise as SBA 1 | UK |
| 3 | Domestic standard | Specialist broker scheme providers | As SBA 2, but as broker's resources may be more limited greater marketing support may be requested. Pricing will be key negotiating feature | Physical: dedicated unit desirable IT: as SBA 2 with ability to support direct mailing to agreed client list Skills: high in negotiation phase, otherwise as SBA 1. | UK |
| 4 | Domestic standard | Financial institutions and FMCG retail stores (grouped for convenience) | Complete 'branded' facility, including provision of advice under distributor's brand name, therefore dedicated unit. Predesigned product envisaged. 'On-line' advice/documentation as SBA 5 | Physical: dedicated unit IT: as SBA 3 including dedicated telecoms. Skills: intermediate in view of higher direct customer interaction than in cases of SBA 1–3 | UK |

Table C1.5  Determination of strategic business units (SBUs)

| SBA | Customer classification | Distributor | Generic strategy | Skill level | SBU |
|---|---|---|---|---|---|
| 1 | Domestic standard | Provincial broker | Price | Low | ⎫ |
| 2 | Domestic standard | Retail chain broker | Price | Low | ⎬ 1 |
| 3 | Domestic standard | Scheme broker | Price | Low | ⎭ |
| 4 | Domestic standard | Banks etc. | Price or differentiation | Intermediate | 2 |
| 5 | Domestic standard | Direct | Price | Intermediate | 3 |
| 6 | Domestic non-standard | Provincial broker | Differentiation | Intermediate | ⎫ |
| 7 | Domestic non-standard | Retail chain broker | Differentiation | Intermediate | ⎬ 4 |
| 8 | Domestic non-standard | Scheme broker | Differentiation | Intermediate | ⎭ |
| 9 | Domestic non-standard | Direct | Differentiation | Intermediate | 3 |
| 10 | Commercial small–medium | Provincial broker | Price | Low | ⎫ 5 |
| 11 | Commercial small–medium | Scheme broker | Price | Low | ⎭ |
| 12 | Commercial small–medium | Banks etc. | Price of differentiation | Low | 6 |
| 13 | Commercial large | UK Provincial broker | Differentiation | High | ⎫ |
| 14 | Commercial large | Banks etc. | Differentiation | High | ⎬ 7 |
| 15 | Commercial large | Direct | Differentiation | High | ⎭ |
| 16 | Commercial large (London market) | London market | Differentiation | High | 8 |

## Step 2: determination of strategic business areas (SBAs)

Davies decided to define SBAs by (a) customer type, (b) distributor type, (c) the service offering requirements demanded by insureds and distributors and (d) the geographic areas in which the offering would be consumed. For each SBA Davies added a heading dealing with the key organizational issues. He identified a total of 16 SBAs. An example of four of these SBAs is presented in Table C1.4.

## Step 3: SWOT analysis

Working back from the demands of the different SBAs, Davies rated the current organization structure on a scale of 1–10 examining production and system issues, sales issues and marketing/planning activities. This analysis revealed poor utilization of current skills, lack of responsiveness to environmental changes, particularly in terms of distribution changes, and finally, declining efficiency.

## Step 4: determination of strategic business units (SBUs)

From his analysis in Step 2, Davies identified sixteen SBAs. He now reflected upon the supply strategies appropriate for each. For this purpose eight supplying SBUs would be needed. Within business units Davies looked for commonality in (a) customer group, (b) the most appropriate generic business strategy and (c) the required skill level of employees within each SBU. Table C1.5 shows the rationale behind this process.

## Step 5: SBUs within the broader organizational structure

The next step was to attempt to classify SBUs into business groups. For this purpose three supplying businesses were proposed, each reporting as a profit and loss centre to the Chief Executive Officer.

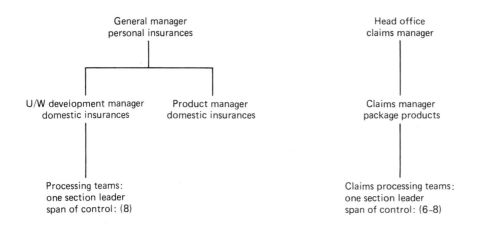

Processing teams will be specialized in either motor or non-motor, but staff will be rotated on a 6-9-month basis

**Figure C1.11** Physical structure

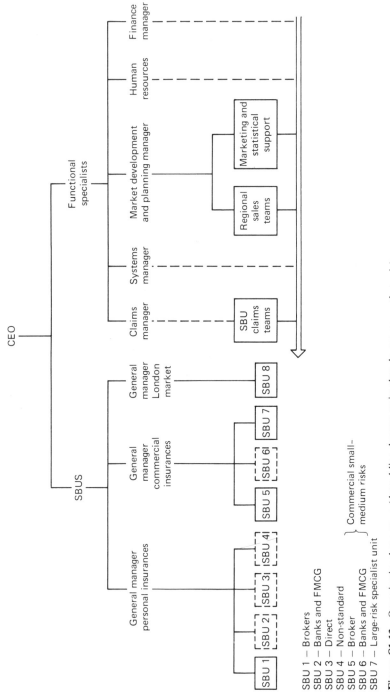

CEO

SBUS

Functional
specialists

General manager
personal insurances

General
manager
commercial
insurances

General
manager
London
market

Claims
manager

Systems
manager

Market development
and planning manager

Human
resources

Finance
manager

SBU 1
[SBU 2]
[SBU 3]
[SBU 4]

SBU 5
[SBU 6]
SBU 7

SBU 8

SBU
claims
teams

Regional
sales
teams

Marketing and
statistical
support

} Commercial small–
medium risks

SBU 1 — Brokers
SBU 2 — Banks and FMCG
SBU 3 — Direct
SBU 4 — Non-standard
SBU 5 — Broker
SBU 6 — Banks and FMCG
SBU 7 — Large-risk specialist unit

**Figure C1.12**  Organizational structure (dotted line denotes units that do not currently trade)

1 Personal insurance services would be responsible for coordinating SBUs 1, 2, 3 and 4.
2 Commercial insurance services would cover SBUs 5, 6 and 7.
3 London Market would cover SBU 8.

Each supplying business was to have its own general manager. Davies saw functional specialisms such as human resources, marketing etc. as providing consultancy services to each supplying business. The idea was that the general manager of supplying businesses would choose either to buy their required services from the functional specialists within Dominion or from outside. The rationale behind this organization structure is shown in Figures C1.11 and C1.12.

As far as each of the three supplying businesses was concerned, Davies proceeded to design their internal workings on the following basis:

● Keep layers of management as flat as possible – no more than three in each supplying business.
● Encourage focus upon product development and systems development.
● Encourage matrix working with functional specialists for new product development purposes.

## Questions: Part C

1 How can a company like Dominion aim to become *both* a low cost supplier *and* a supplier of high quality insurance products?
2 Companies require to update existing products and also to develop completely new products. It has been suggested that these two activities require quite different managerial skills which are best kept separated organizationally. Do you agree with this statement in the context of Dominion's operations?
3 Evaluate the analytical methods invoked by Davies (particularly the concepts of SBAs *and* SBUs) to restructure the company for meeting future competitive challenges. What managerial problems are likely to occur in operationalizing these two concepts and how might they be overcome?

## Further reading

Ansoff, H.I. and MacDonald, E.J. (1990) *Implanting Strategic Management*, Prentice Hall, Englewood Cliffs, NJ
Dyer, N. and Watkins, T., (eds) (1988) *Marketing Insurance* (2nd edn), Kluwer, London
Ennew, C. T. (1990) Marketing strategy and planning. In Ennew, Watkins and Wright (1990)
Ennew, C. T., Watkins, T, and Wright, M. (1990) *Marketing Financial Services*. Heinemann, Oxford
McDonald, M.H.B. (1989) *Marketing Plans: How to prepare them; how to use them*, Heinemann, Oxford
Ohmae, K. (1988) *The Mind of the Strategist*, Penguin, London
Scheuing, L.E. and Johnson, E.M. (1989) New product development and management in financial institutions. *International Journal of Bank Marketing*, 7(2), 17–22
Watkins, T. (1990) Insurance marketing. In Ennew, Watkins and Wright (1990)

# Case 2 The distribution of collective investments in France

Mike Wright and Laurence Major
University of Nottingham

## Introduction

The term collective investment refers to any type of investment scheme where investors place their funds in the hands of professional managers who manage a portfolio of funds so as to provide a return to investors. Such schemes have grown rapidly in the past five years. With the development of the European Community's Single Market, there is increasing interest in selling collective investment products from one country in another member country. Harmonization of the structure of collective investment schemes throughout the European Community (EC) has been introduced in the directive on Undertakings for Collective Investment in Transferable Securities (UCITS) which came into force in October 1989. The UCITS directive defines common procedures for the authorization and supervision of UCITS schemes. As long as a scheme meets the requirements of UCITS it can be marketed in other EC member states and be subject to the marketing regulations which apply to financial service in each country. In principle, this directive eased the cross-border marketing of collective investment schemes. In practice, even following the directive, very few cross-border schemes are marketed. The alternative approach is for a foreign-based firm with expertise in collective investment schemes to enter the market in another country by establishing a physical presence and to sell the kind of products traditionally found in those markets.

## French market characteristics

France has the third largest market in the world for collective investments and is the largest in the EC (Table C2.1). Organisms de Placement Collectif en Valeurs Mobilières (OPCVMs) is the French term for UCITS. In France, OPCVMs consist of investment companies with variable share capital or open-ended share capital (Societes d'Investissement à Capital Variable – SICAV) and the strict equivalent of unit trusts (Fonds Communs de Placement – FCP). Although there are about four times as many FCPs as SICAVs, the asset value of the latter at about FF1200 bn considerably exceeds that for FCPs at approximately FF 450 bn. Private individuals account for more than half of the ownership of the French OPCVMs. In 1986, OPCVMs accounted for some 10.5 per cent of personal sector assets in France. By 1989, this proportion had risen to 13 per cent.

*Table C2.1  Evolution of Collective Investments in Different Countries* (ECVs bn)

|         | 1986   | 1987  | 1988   | 1989   | 1990   |
|---------|--------|-------|--------|--------|--------|
| EEC     | 304    | 328.7 | 423.05 | 519.8  | 531.5  |
| France  | 142    | 157.4 | 202.9  | 247.7  | 278.6  |
| UK      | 44     | 52    | 64.2   | 79.8   | 65.1   |
| OUT EEC | 877.2  | 888.7 | 1088.4 | 1214.2 | 1127.9 |
| USA     | 670    | 590.4 | 692.1  | 827.6  | 790.9  |
| Japan   | 185.5  | 271   | 360.9  | 343.2  | 250.9  |

Source: ASFFI.

*Table C2.2  Volume and value growth of SICAVs*

|              | 1986  | 1987  | 1988    | 1989    | 1990    | July 1991 |
|--------------|-------|-------|---------|---------|---------|-----------|
| Number       | 500   | 625   | 758     | 862     | 898     | 896       |
| Value (FF bn)| 706.4 | 819.7 | 1,072.6 | 1,266.2 | 1,428.3 | 1,561.7   |

*Source*: Europerformance.

Between 1986 and 1991, the number of SICAVs increased by almost 80 per cent (Table C2.2). The fastest growth in terms of numbers and values has been experienced by Money Market SICAVs. The bond SICAV increased by almost a third over this period whilst the equities SICAV stayed almost constant in nominal terms over the five years.

## Market structure

In contrast to the UK, but in common with Germany and Spain, the vast majority of OPCVMs (90 per cent) are distributed through the banks (Table C2.3). In the UK only 10 per cent of similar products are sold through bank branch networks. As a result, very little distribution is carried out in France through insurance company sales networks, independent brokers and direct marketing. Only 3 per cent of products are sold by independents. Three French firms have been created since 1989 with the aim of distributing OPCVMs products. In the UK, some 70 per cent of products are sold by insurance companies and direct marketing, in equal proportions, with the balance of 20 per cent being sold by independent brokers.

Within the French market, the ten largest bank networks accounted in 1990 for almost 80 per cent of the market. Among these ten banks, the five most important groups represent about 55 per cent of the total market (Table C2.4). A number of non-French institutions have entered the market. These institutions are mostly from the UK, but also from Holland and the United States. Entry has either been by creating a network, using an existing one or by buying a small French bank (Barclays bought the Lafitte network of Européenne de Banque).

The structure of distribution channels is changing with the appearance of new entrants such as insurance companies and other financial intermediaries. The role of direct marketing is increasing. Between 1986 and 1990 two firms,

*Table C2.3   Distribution channels for collective investments in different European countries (%)*

|          | Banks | Insurance companies | Independents | Direct marketing |
|----------|-------|---------------------|--------------|------------------|
| Germany  | 70    | –                   | 20           | 10               |
| Spain    | 90    | 5                   | –            | 5                |
| France   | 90    | 5                   | 3            | 2                |
| UK       | 10    | 35                  | 20           | 35               |
| Italy    | 30    | –                   | 70           | –                |

*Source*: ASFFI.

Cortal and Robeco, attained a market share of 2 per cent from nothing through the use of direct marketing. However, there remains some customer resistance to this approach because of concerns about the safety of the investments proposed in this way.

French banks have traditionally offered only their own products to customers. If a customer wants to buy a SICAV from another bank through her own bank, the bank cannot refuse to sell the product but it is likely to delay the process, charge increased fees and generally offer as little service as possible. Thus buying the alternative product will not normally be advantageous. Moreover, banks frequently try to ensure that their customers associate their SICAV products with the banks' name, which is usually incorporated into that of the product. Some of the largest banks (such as BNP and CIC) have, however, developed agreements with major insurance companies (e.g. UAP and GAN) to sell the latter's SICAVs through the bank branch network.

The various methods of distribution in France are illustrated by the following examples, which include large bank networks and French and UK intermediaries:

● BNP is the third largest provider of SICAVs in France. With twenty years' experience in the market, BNP has a range of 21 SICAVs and twenty FCPs. BNP has a network of some 2,000 branches in France and abroad. When a new product is launched, a major element in the marketing effort is to inform staff in the branch network about the product attributes, sales conditions and the target customer groups through circular letters and detailed internal documentation. This information is distributed prior to the promotion of the product in the press. To reinforce the impact of a new product launch, a specific booklet is produced and distributed to the sales staff and to the targeted customers. In addition, documentation on the whole product range is produced twice a year and distributed to customers on request. Advertising in the national newspapers and specialist financial press began only at the beginning of 1990, being strongly influenced by the need to follow competitors who had already begun to advertise. However, it is considered that the branch network is a more efficient place to promote products. Customers are segmented into four star categories on the basis of incomes, savings possibilities, socio-economic groupings etc. The level of targeting varies across the range of star categories. At the bottom of the range, one and two star customers with lower wealth and income are targeted solely through the branch counter. At the top of the range a small number of specialist managers, advisers in property management, are responsible for customer

*Table C2.4  Funds invested and market shares of the main networks of SICAV providers*

| Network | Dec. 1986 | Dec. 1987 | Dec. 1988 | Dec. 1989 | Dec. 1990 | Jun. 1991 | Jul. 1991 |
|---|---|---|---|---|---|---|---|
| CDC–CE–Poste | | | | | | | |
| Funds invested | 77.8 | 88.4 | 116.6 | 151.8 | 198.8 | 241.3 | 251.3 |
| Rank | 3 | 3 | 3 | 2 | 2 | 1 | 1 |
| Market share (%) | 11.0 | 10.8 | 10.9 | 12.0 | 13.9 | 15.7 | 16.1 |
| Credit Agricole | | | | | | | |
| Funds invested | 106.7 | 136.4 | 176.3 | 211.1 | 216.7 | 240.9 | 243.4 |
| Rank | 1 | 1 | 1 | 1 | 1 | 2 | 2 |
| Market share | 15.1 | 16.6 | 16.4 | 16.7 | 15.2 | 15.6 | 15.6 |
| BNP | | | | | | | |
| Funds invested | 82.5 | 91.6 | 127.1 | 138.9 | 155.8 | 152.8 | 149.6 |
| Rank | 2 | 2 | 2 | 3 | 3 | 3 | 3 |
| Market share | 11.7 | 11.2 | 11.8 | 11.0 | 10.9 | 9.9 | 9.6 |
| Credit Lyonnais | | | | | | | |
| Funds invested | 56.9 | 66.1 | 87.0 | 115.2 | 135.9 | 138.9 | 139.7 |
| Rank | 5 | 4 | 4 | 4 | 4 | 4 | 4 |
| Market share | 8.1 | 8.1 | 8.1 | 9.1 | 9.5 | 9.0 | 8.9 |
| Société Générale | | | | | | | |
| Funds invested | 69.3 | 62.6 | 74.3 | 84.7 | 110.6 | 121.2 | 122.9 |
| Rank | 4 | 5 | 5 | 5 | 5 | 5 | 5 |
| Market share | 9.8 | 7.6 | 6.9 | 6.7 | 7.7 | 7.9 | 7.9 |
| Groupe Parisbas | | | | | | | |
| Funds invested | 19.0 | 21.0 | 26.2 | 64.2 | 73.7 | 81.3 | 81.5 |
| Rank | 10 | 10 | 9 | 6 | 6 | 6 | 6 |
| Market share | 2.7 | 2.6 | 2.4 | 5.1 | 5.2 | 5.3 | 5.2 |
| Banques Populaires | | | | | | | |
| Funds invested | 29.5 | 35.6 | 44.9 | 52.8 | 63.6 | 66.8 | 69.0 |
| Rank | 6 | 6 | 6 | 7 | 7 | 7 | 7 |
| Market share | 4.2 | 4.3 | 4.2 | 4.2 | 4.5 | 4.3 | 4.4 |
| Groupe CIC–UE | | | | | | | |
| Funds invested | 24.5 | 28.9 | 39.9 | 45.3 | 53.1 | 66.4 | 67.5 |
| Rank | 7 | 7 | 7 | 8 | 8 | 8 | 8 |
| Market sharte | 3.5 | 3.5 | 3.7 | 3.6 | 3.7 | 4.3 | 4.3 |
| Groupe Suez | | | | | | | |
| Funds invested | 23.8 | 22.7 | 23.4 | 44.7 | 46.0 | 50.5 | 52.4 |
| Rank | 8 | 9 | 10 | 9 | 10 | 9 | 9 |
| Market share | 3.4 | 2.8 | 2.2 | 3.5 | 3.2 | 3.3 | 3.4 |
| Groupe CCF | | | | | | | |
| Funds invested | 20.1 | 23.1 | 28.8 | 40.9 | 46.3 | 38.8 | 38.7 |
| Rank | 9 | 8 | 8 | 10 | 9 | 10 | 10 |
| Market share | 2.8 | 2.8 | 2.7 | 3.2 | 3.2 | 2.5 | 2.5 |
| Total 10 networks | | | | | | | |
| Funds invested | 510.1 | 576.4 | 744.5 | 949.6 | 1,100.5 | 1,198.9 | 1,216.0 |
| Market share | 72.2 | 70.3 | 69.4 | 75.0 | 77.0 | 77.8 | 77.9 |
| Total SICAV | 706.4 | 819.7 | 1,072.6 | 1,266.2 | 1,428.3 | 1,540.8 | 1,561.7 |

*Source*: Europerformance.

service. Each branch has its own customer database, linked to a centralized information system.

● Crédit du Nord, part of the Paribas group, is the sixth largest provider of OPCVMs and has been established in the market for twenty-five years. As with BNP, distribution is essentially carried out throughout the branch network and customer advisers. Attempts at direct mail targeting of prospective customers, with a follow-up telephone call, have been tried but the results were not considered to be encouraging. Crédit du Nord sells five different types of packages comprised of a few products. The bottom end of the market is served by direct advisers. The top end of the market is targeted through special financial advisers responsible for developing a portfolio made from a package of transferable securities allocated by countries and sectors. The Minitel system is also used as a marketing tool. This system allows customers to both buy and sell OPCVMs. While this approach has the benefits of time and cost savings there is a risk of losing contact with customers. As a result, Crédit du Nord maintains contact with customers through mail shots and telephone canvassing.

● The financial intermediary AFFIDIA was created in 1989 as part of Compagnie du Midi, itself part of AXA since 1988. AFFIDIA was bought by Norwich Union in 1990 but is autonomous from its new parent in terms of choosing the best products available on the market for its clients. AFFIDIAs network comprises 111 financial advisers in thirty branches spread across twenty-five towns and cities. AFFIDIA aims to provide an asset management service for personal clients who have financial assets of between FF2 m and FF 20 m. Promotion is achieved partly through direct mail contact with potential clients followed by a telephone call to arrange a personal interview and partly through professional exhibitions, chartered accountants etc. AFFIDIA also holds information seminars on asset management in various professional fields in order to obtain new contacts. The company also operates through recommendations in order to establish a strong trust relationship between the customer and the adviser and to develop the notion of an AFFIDIA Circle. They also sponsor events such as golf competitions or art exhibitions.

● Barclays Bank has sold French OPVCMs in France for over ten years. OPVCMs management is conducted from two regional centres in Paris and Nice. The bank recently merged with the stockbroker Puget-Mahe and has thirty-four branches in France together with a further sixteen branches of the recently acquired Européenne de Banque. Barclays has a range of 16 FCPs and seven SICAVs and with a less than 1 per cent share is ranked about twentieth in the market. The branch network is a key distribution outlet. Products are targeted at the top end of the market to individuals with an annual income in excess of FF 300,000. As a result, while some use is made of press advertising and leaflets in the branches, the main promotional effort is through the targeting of individual customers by specialist customer advisers who are aiming to sell a service offering a solution to a particular financial situation. Customer prospecting is also done through referrals and direct marketing through highly focused mail shots.

● INVESCO MIM France is a subsidiary of INVESCO MIM PLC and was established in France in 1988 and has developed a similar marketing approach to its parent. Target customers are personal customers via financial intermediaries, and financial institutions who can integrate MIMs products in their own trusts. Small provincial banks with no international financial management expertise may be attracted by the possibility of offering MIMs products to their customers. From its Paris office, MIM promotes only the group's products through financial advisers and stockbrokers and does not make direct contact with final customers. The target market comprises less than 10 per cent of the whole OPCVM market in France. The minimum investment is FF 60,000. MIM aims to provide a quality service to customers, which extends to training and monitoring intermediaries who sell its products and the provision of detailed market documentation and sell/not sell advice to its customers. MIM offers a range of seventeen products to French investors, segmented on four international regions. The main product is a Luxemburg fund with eleven elements, four other Luxemburg trusts, a British unit trust and a French FCP.

## Questions

1 Analyse the likely effects on the distribution of collective (managed) investments in France of entry by UK providers.
2 Analyse the problems faced by UK entrants into the French market for collective investments.
3 What problems are likely to arise in the cross-border marketing of collective investments?

## Further reading

Diacon, S. (1990) European integration: strategic implications for the marketing of long term insurance. *International Journal of Bank Marketing*, **8**(3), 29–36

Dixon, R. (1991) *Banking in Europe: The Single Market*, Routledge, London

Howcroft, J.B. and Whitehead, M. (1990) The Single European Market: the challenge to commercial banking. *International Journal of Bank Marketing*, **8**(3), 11–16

Metais, J. (1991) The situation and outlook for funds and portfolio management institutions in France. In *Funds and Portfolio Management Institutions: An international Survey* (ed. S. Preda). North-Holland, Amsterdam

Preda, S. (1991) The situation and outlook for funds and portfolio management institutions in Italy. In *Funds and Portfolio Management Institutions: An International Survey* (ed. S. Preda), North-Holland, Amsterdam

# Case 3 Allied Irish Banks

*Kate Stewart*
University of Ulster

## Introduction

Allied Irish Banks, as its name suggests, was formed when three of Ireland's established banks merged in 1966. Each of these banks had strengths in different markets. The Munster and Leinster Bank had the largest bank network in the country and was seen as the bank of 'the plain people of Ireland'. The Provincial Bank of Ireland's prosperity was closely tied to that of the linen industry which flourished in many parts of the country. The Royal Bank of Ireland was a mercantile bank. At the time of the merger, Allied Irish Banks had 430 branches with 2,600 staff. With the exception of an office in London and another in Birkenhead, the bank was based exclusively in Ireland. Assets totalled IR£270 m.

## Company development

Within twenty years Allied Irish Banks was much changed from these humble beginnings. Britain was a natural choice for the bank's international expansion in the early 1970s because of its proximity and the size of the market. By 1988, Allied Irish Banks was one of the largest non-indigenous banking groups in Britain, though with sixty branches it was obviously a small player. A marketing strategy focusing on selected niches was developed. These niches tended to be drawn from the business market and the young professional market. In Britain the bank also attracted the ex-patriot market, though not in a deliberate manner.

Different approaches were taken in the business, personal and corporate markets. A proliferation of subsidiaries developed through the years with specialist products geared to specialist financial markets. Some of the subsidiaries making up the Allied Irish Banks Group included Allied Combined Trust Ltd and Allied Irish Leasing Ltd. The bank also had developed a presence in capital markets, offering customers services in treasury, international banking and investment banking. Services are operated by subsidiaries within Allied Irish Banks Group PLC such as Allied Irish Fund Management Ltd, Grofund Managers Ltd and similar offshore companies.

In 1983, Allied Irish Banks took a substantial minority interest in First Maryland Bancorp in the United States of America. After six years, the bank acquired full ownership. This gives the Irish bank a significant presence in the greater Maryland marketplace which extends into the neighbouring areas of southern Pennsylvannia, the West Virginia panhandle and, most importantly, the nation's capital, Washington DC. These changes could be described as company-initiated, but externally focused.

The author wishes to thank the staff of Allied Irish Banks PLC, particularly Donal Delahunt, for their cooperation in the development of this case study.

## External change

Allied Irish Banks faced the same changes in its external environment as confronted many, if not all, banks in Britain and Ireland. The decade of the 1980s saw many of the certainties which had characterized the banking industry become much less secure. Deregulation and liberalization in the financial services industry introduced new competitors such as building societies, the Post Office and large retailers offering credit. Technology led to greater efficiency in back office operations, a greatly enhanced ability to develop new products and more sophisticated marketing information systems.

Contemporaneously, markets were changing. Customers of retail bank services had a greater choice of products and would-be suppliers. Declining customer loyalty and the holding of accounts in a number of banks/building societies became a feature of many markets. Market research showed Allied Irish Banks that the proportion of their customers who held savings or investments outside Allied Irish Banks had significantly increased in the mid-1980s. These changes forced the banking industry to adopt the concept and techniques of marketing. Allied Irish Banks was, in many respects, typical of any bank confronting, and having to adapt to, change in the 1980s. Possibly the only significant difference was that Allied Irish Banks as an entity had a shorter history, having only been established in 1966.

## Adapting to change: the Marketing Action Programme

In 1987, Allied Irish Banks embarked on a programme designed to address marketing issues. The Marketing Action Programme was of a long-term nature and aimed to change staff attitudes and the general corporate culture. Both were to become more participative and more market-focused. Facilitated by consultants, the programme was designed to question every area of the company's business, even the mission statement which read:

> to be the premier Irish financial services organization capable of competing worldwide by consistently delivering high quality service on a competitive basis to our customers in Ireland and throughout the world.

The Marketing Action Programme had to address marketing strategies, marketing information systems, the marketing professionalism of all employees, marketing structures in terms of job roles and business units and marketing technology which embraced delivery systems, physical facilities and procedures. All were to reflect a 'total customer orientation'. This examination led to many initiatives. All staff were trained in customer care. Some sixteen units were established throughout Ireland, comprising local branch managers. These 'think-tanks' were given a remit to develop recommendations on how the bank could market more effectively on both local and national levels.

By the end of 1988, implementation of the Marketing Action Programme was well under way. Strategies were being refined, the Action Learning Programme for staff was being progressed and re-designed structures were being agreed. The new structure divided the company into three main areas of interest: Ireland, Britain and the United States of America. While this may not seem too radical, the significant point is that the three regions were now seen as of equal consequence to the bank. This was a departure from the traditional view of Ireland as the mainstay of the bank's operations and source of business.

The growth of Allied Irish Banks over its first twenty-five years can be illustrated as follows:

|              | 1966       | 1991          |
|--------------|------------|---------------|
| Assets       | IR£270 m   | IR£16,000 m   |
| Employees    | 2,600      | 14,000        |
| Bank branches| 430        | 650           |

In the Republic of Ireland, the bank could justifiably claim to be the 'number one' bank, with a 'bank' market share of some 40 to 45 per cent, its closest rival being the Bank of Ireland. In Northern Ireland the situation was somewhat different: Allied Irish Banks held only 12 per cent of the market, a similar figure to the Bank of Ireland. The major players in this market were the Northern Bank (formerly a Midland Bank subsidiary but now owned by National Australia Bank) and the Ulster Bank (a subsidiary of National Westminster Bank).

## Corporate identity

*From 1966*

As already stated, each of the three banks which merged in 1966 had its own strengths and identity. The new entity adopted a new visual identity and corporate house style which reflected its origins. The various subsidiary companies which developed through the subsequent years adopted the same colours, logo, typefaces, signage and so on.

*Corporate identity review*

Given so many changes inside and outside the organization, the bank decided to examine its corporate identity in 1989. The review was to consider all the factors which contribute to or influence the constituents of corporate identity. This, by implication, necessitated looking at these factors from the past, present and future perspectives.

A two-pronged approach was used, to collect both primary and secondary information. Primary information was collected through in-depth interviews with selected Allied Irish Banks' executives, the bank's own advertising agency, marketing research consultants and financial journalists. Secondary information was collected through a review of Allied Irish Banks' strategy papers, desk research into the banking and financial sector and a detailed audit of how Allied Irish Banks communicates itself visually through its publications and brochures, its advertising and the physical design and layout of its offices, in particular its branch bank offices.

*Corporate identity review findings*

The review identified the following issues:

*Character and personality*

The privileged position enjoyed by banks had changed. National legislation and the ending of cartels served to make banks more business-like, with an emphasis on shareholder scrutiny, competition and market performance. This contrasts with traditional banking where success was primarily related to size.

Internally this new order necessitated profound changes while externally it led to an increased importance in being perceived as a business and an attractive one.

The nature of the business is also changing. Banks of all sizes are forced to question just what business they are in. The trend has been to adopt the enhanced label of being in the business of the profitable provision of financial services and for very large banks this may indeed be true. For smaller banks, however, and on an international scale this is the more accurate description of Allied Irish Banks, this may be a rather exaggerated boast. One question to be resolved is that of emphasis: should the focus be on banking with financial services or on financial services including the traditional banking services?

Allied Irish Banks, as a consequence of these industry changes, has moved towards a market-focused, customer orientation. While advertising copy and the slogan 'you bring out the best in us' bring this to the public's attention, the organization as a whole needs to project this in everything which it does. The Marketing Action Programme has, to a degree, changed internal attitudes from being those of a 'bureaucratic juggernaut' to those of a more flexible business.

While these substantive changes were developing, so was the personality of the bank, that is, what makes it different, particularly in how it feels to do business with it. Part of this personality change concerned new markets, especially the expansion in Britain and the United States. What had been purely an Irish bank now was substantially more than Irish and more than a bank.

In periods of profound organizational change, internal conflict is often experienced by both staff and customers. In this case some differences did emerge, primarily between the different cultures operating in the different companies and between head office and branches. This could best be summarized as a lack of cohesiveness, or the feeling that not everyone was playing in the same team. That said, a distinctive friendliness was found in staff throughout the organization.

*Nomenclature*
As has been explained, the company name relates directly to its origins as a merger between three Irish banks. The parent company is Allied Irish Banks PLC, while its principal operating subsidiary is Allied Irish Bank. In the Irish market it was found that customers often used the terms 'AIB' or 'the Allied Irish' and that there was often some confusion as to whether it was the parent or the bank to which one was referring. Furthermore, First Maryland Bancorp kept is original name despite having been purchased outright by Allied Irish Banks PLC. The other subsidiaries already mentioned were referred to by either their full titles or an abbreviated form: for example, Allied Irish Finance or AIF. Little consistency in the usage of names was found.

The corporate identity review also focused on the use of the term 'Irish'. The local market hardly needed reminding that the bank was Irish since it was such a ubiquitous part of commerce and society in Ireland. In Britain and, it has to be said, in parts of Northern Ireland, things Irish can have either positive or negative connotations.

*Visual identity*
Visual identity covers the areas of corporate print, including promotional material, the logo and typeface, corporate advertising and bank branch design.

The review found the corporate print to be of reasonable quality, but not distinctive. A three-spoked roundel whose hub encapsulated the letter 'A', as in Allied, formed the corporate logo. The corporate colour, royal blue, as used in signage and stationery was also used for the logo. Apart from looking very similar to the logo used by Daimler Benz, the three-spoked roundel appears bland and somewhat anonymous. The use of corporate blue in the logo and typeface exacerbates the distinctiveness problem in two ways. First, blue is acknowledged to be a cold colour and, secondly, it is perhaps the most widely used colour in banking. It should not be assumed that this is the image to which the bank wishes to aspire.

The television advertising campaign of the early 1990s used the imagery of a butterfly emerging from its chrysalis. Again, the end-line stated 'you bring out the best in us'. The imagery was designed to signify the metamorphosis to the 'new' customer caring organization. Print advertisements also featured the butterfly and copy promoted the new corporate mission and the ambition to 'be the best' by recognizing that 'our customers are the most important people in our organization and to fully satisfy their needs, nothing less than the best will do'. While these advertisements were visually striking, there was some question as to whether they were understood and appreciated by both the personal and business markets. It could also be argued that the advertising was making substantial promises while the process of change was continuing.

*Bank branch design*

For the most part branch banking takes place in the High Street, whether that be in a small provincial town or a busy city. In some cases the branch building was old, in others it had either been modernized or was a new building. The overall appearance was somewhat bland, especially when viewed alongside the specialist High Street retailers who had invested heavily in store design. Internally the same situation was found. The coldness of the colour blue was, in some cases, exacerbated by the choice of furnishings and finishes in the modernized branches. To an extent, branches had also adopted their own 'visual style', in the absence of detailed corporate guidelines.

As a consequence of this review, AIB was now in a position to identify strategies to create an appropriate corporate identity.

## Questions

1 Bearing in mind the role of corporate identity, outline the key corporate identity problems pertaining to Allied Irish Banks.
2 What solutions to these problems would you recommend to the bank? Your solutions should, in the first instance, be of a strategic nature. Thereafter, make recommendations regarding names, colours, logos, branch design and so on.

## Further reading

Howcroft, J. B. and Lavis, J. (1987) Image in retail banking. *International Journal of Bank Marketing*, **4**(4), 3–13

Smith, D., and Harbisher, A. (1989) Building societies as retail banks: the importance of customer service and corporate image. *International Journal of Bank Marketing*, **7**(1) 22–27

Stewart, K. (1991) Corporate identity: a strategic marketing issue. *International Journal of Bank Marketing*, **9**(1) pp 32–29

# Case 4 Lloyds Bank and professional introducers

*Jim Devlin*
University of Nottingham

## Introduction

Lloyds Bank PLC is a major UK clearing bank which has developed a strategy of concentrating on those market segments in which it feels that it can achieve a strong competitive position, resulting in market leadership where possible. To complement its niche market approach the bank has attempted to differentiate itself from its fellow clearing banks by aiming to create an image of quality and exclusivity. Market research has shown that the bank has achieved some success in this respect.

The bank has, when necessary, withdrawn from certain operations such as UK gilt market-making, owing to insufficient return on capital. Some overseas subsidiaries have also been sold to provide funds for growing the business elsewhere. In this way Lloyds Bank has avoided the need to call on its shareholders for extra funds in recent years, unlike other major clearing banks. Part of the overall strategy of selling to profitable niches has been the targeting of high net worth individuals (HNWIs)

## Lloyds Private Banking

Lloyds Private Banking is, as the name suggests, the 'private banking' company owned by Lloyds Bank PLC, specializing in the provision of a comprehensive range of financial services. Its target market is the 'High Net Worth Sector' which comprises individuals with a large amount of personal wealth (typically £100,000+) in the form of cash and marketable securities. Clients are serviced through regional centres ensuring local delivery and increased personal contact with clients. Through the strength of the relationship which results the bank aims to maximize its earnings from the High Net Worth market by meeting clients' financial needs, hence increasing its fee and commission income. This complements Lloyds Bank's strategy of reducing its dependence on lending-related profits where margins are under pressure.

## The product

The main product which Lloyds Private Banking markets is the asset management service which combines a flexible investment management option with complete financial planning and enhanced banking arrangements.

Each client is allocated a Private Banking Executive who is responsible for delivering advice as required. A fee is paid by the client which is based on the amount of funds under management.

The concept is best illustrated by way of an example. Suppose a couple in their fifties inherit £300,000. An initial interview with Lloyds Private Banking is arranged to discuss the needs of the clients. They are both working and do not need to produce an income from the funds until they retire. There are plans to spend approximately £50,000 and a further £25,000 is required as a cash reserve. The couple are financially naive but do appreciate that in order to protect the real value of their funds they need to consider investing in growth orientated investments. A portfolio will then be constructed for the remaining £225,000, including Government Securities, shares in various sectors of the stock market and overseas investment by way of unit or investment trusts. This portfolio will be monitored constantly and changes made as appropriate. The couple also require advice on re-writing their wills, which is part of the service, as well as a policy to cover their potential inheritance tax liability. Finally, Lloyds Private Banking also completes the couples' tax return at the end of each financial year.

### The market

Lloyds Private Banking is a major competitor within its chosen niche with almost 23,000 customers and £3.5 bn under its control. The company gained a competitive advantage when it introduced the Asset Management Service in 1985. The service is still one of the most comprehensive on the market and client numbers are expanding rapidly. However, more competition emerged at the beginning of the 1990s and the company can no longer claim it has a unique service. Many more companies have targeted the HNWIs market as a growth area in recent years, which is not surprising given the potential which exists. Traditionally the main competition has been stockbrokers' and merchant banks' private client departments based primarily in the City of London. Other major banks also have departments specializing in fund management. Increasingly, competition is emerging from building societies, many of whom have entered into joint ventures with insurance companies. Although not as comprehensive as the private banking services offered by those mentioned above, insurance-based investment products, such as with profits and unit linked investment bonds are alternatives to an equity portfolio. Many more companies are now using Direct Sales Forces to market their products aggressively, adding to the competition provided by commission-driven independent financial advisers. There may also be entry into the market by European firms post 1992. Taken in this context the stated aim of the Chairman of Lloyds Private Banking, that the company will more than double its assets in three years, appears demanding.

### Marketing issues

At present the vast majority of the clients who use Lloyds Private Banking are Lloyds Bank PLC customers who have been introduced through the banking branch network, which has been the source of new business that Lloyds Private Banking has relied upon. Representatives from Lloyds Private Banking visit branches regularly to educate staff and to help market the service to existing pools of wealth. This process was very effective in the early stages of product marketing as much personal wealth was kept at banking branches and potential clients could be identified and approached. At present, it is still the main source of new clients. However, it is becoming increasingly difficult to attract new business in this manner as most wealthy customers have now been approached a number of times and have either joined the service or declined the invitation. To compound the problem, the bank now has a direct salesforce which is partly commission-driven and dedicated to selling the products of the bank's in-house insurance company. The direct salesforce also relies on the bank branch network for introductions which results in customers being approached more frequently and by different parts of the same organization, often resulting in confusion. Although there are guidelines imposed to prevent this happening, they are often ignored by managers and staff who are under pressure to produce fee income for their branch.

Lloyds Private Banking now relies increasingly on 'opportunist' situations, i.e. an individual inheriting wealth, to provide new clients. However, if the company is to achieve its aim of increasing its assets by over 100 per cent in three years it must find alternative sources of business and more particularly succeed in attracting quality clients who do not at present maintain their personal banking arrangements with Lloyds Bank PLC. This has proved difficult in the past as individuals tend to exhibit much loyalty to their chosen bank. The problem which Lloyds Private Banking has is that it must find an alternative source of new business which will provide a consistently high level of quality introductions, thus enabling demanding growth targets to be met.

## Lloyds Private Banking marketing response

Lloyds Private Banking has attempted to address the problem by marketing its service, the Asset Management Service, through the professional introducer sector. Solicitors and accountants were approached at a local level with presentations to the senior partners to encourage them to refer clients to the bank for financial advice. Although both solicitors and accountants can obtain authorization to offer independent financial advice to their clients, they are often wary of so doing because it is not cost effective for them to acquire the necessary information. An advertising campaign was initiated in the relevant professional journals to complement a mail shot of about 10,000 firms.

Apart from the promised quality of service, the main inducement which Lloyds Private Banking offered was financial, with a lump sum being paid to any firm who introduced an individual who subsequently became a client. This approach did not inspire a large number of introductions as most solicitors and accountants offset fee and commission earnings of this nature against clients' fee accounts thus leaving their total revenue unchanged. To date the series of one-off presentations has proved unsuccessful in generating any significant new business, although £12m was introduced in this way in 1991.

## Conclusions

Lloyds Private Banking has achieved a strong position in its target market by utilizing the vast potential of Lloyds Bank PLC's customer base. In order to maintain that position alternative sources of consistent introductions of new business must continue to be evaluated and explored. Its professional introducer initiative must be reviewed and amended and further marketing strategies developed to ensure continued success.

**Questions**

1 Lloyds Private Banking employed a 'bottom-up' strategy when it decided to approach firms' local offices. Do you think this was the correct approach to take? Discuss alternative approaches to this strategy.
2 What other opportunities exist for Lloyds Private Banking?

**Further reading**

Ennew, C. T. (1990) Product strategy. In Ennew, Watkins and Wright (1990)
Ennew, C. T., Watkins, T, and Wright, M. (1990) *Marketing Financial Services.* Heinemann, Oxford
Marsh, J. R. (1988) *Managing Financial Services Marketing*, Pitman, London
Watkins, T. (1990) The demand for financial services. In Ennew, Watkins and Wright (1990)

# Case 5 Regional Bank of Northern England

*Barry Howcroft*
Loughborough University Banking Centre

## Introduction

The Regional Bank of Northern England (RBNE) is a major UK regional bank with a network of branches extending throughout Lancashire and the North Midlands. It employs some 7,000 people and has pursued an aggressive policy in opening new branches, the branch network having grown from 135 branches in 1965 to 300 at present. Less ambitious has been its policy towards automated teller machines (ATMs): at present it only has 16 ATMs and is not associated with either Link of Matrix.

Although the bank has adopted an aggressive policy towards expanding its branch network, it has been less successful in expanding its personal business portfolio than some of its main competitors, especially some of the main building societies. The bank's incursions into small business finance have also been tentative: the mix of asset business on the books reveals that 68 per cent of all overdraft business is still associated with personal borrowing. The bank has not attempted to diversify into international banking, investment banking or large-scale corporation lending and has maintained a policy of keeping the core business simple. There is concern, however, about the possibility of a takeover from either a UK non-bank financial institution or from a European bank seeking a foothold in the UK market. The full range of personal and business services provided by the bank is shown in Table C5.1 and Table C5.2 shows the demographic profile of RBNE's personal customers.

Last year the bank made a pre-tax profit of £65 m, slightly down on the previous year's profit. Table C5.3 compares RBNE's profitability with its main competitors, namely, a major UK clearing bank and a building society. RBNE's sources of income over the five years to 1991 are shown in Table C5.4.

## Evolution of pricing policy in UK banking

The banking industry's approach to pricing could best be described as 'implicit' and 'irrational', being characterized by a policy of cross-subsidization. This cross-subsidization can be detected at three district levels:

*Table C5.1   RBNE's personal and business banking portfolio*

| Personal banking | Business banking |
|---|---|
| Current account, including interest-bearing current accounts | Business current accounts |
| Savings accounts, available on a variety of terms | Advances |
| Advances – overdraft facilities | Deposit taking |
| Instalment loans | Business loans |
| Residential mortgages | |
| Credit card | |
| Foreign travel facilities | |
| Executor and trustee services | |
| Safe custody and nightsafe facilities | |

*Table C5.2   Demographic profile of RBNE's personal customers*

| Age | % | Social class | % |
|---|---|---|---|
| 16–20 | 5.7 | AB | 21.1 |
| 21–24 | 6.5 | C1 | 28.8 |
| 25–34 | 16.9 | C2 | 28.4 |
| 35–44 | 19.6 | DE | 21.7 |
| 45–54 | 18.3 | | |
| 55–64 | 18.0 | | |
| 65+ | 15.0 | | |

*Table C5.3   Profitability analysis (%)*

| | RBNE | Clearing bank | Building society |
|---|---|---|---|
| Gross profit margin | 35.6 | 43.9 | 19.6 |
| Expense ratio (overheads) | 24.6 | 34.1 | 8.9 |
| Net profit margin (before tax) | 9.0 | 9.8 | 10.6 |

The gross profit for the building society is based on total income less interest paid on shares, deposits and loans. The net profit for the building society is based on the gross profit (as derived), less management expenses, depreciation and mortgage losses.

*Table C5.4   RBNE's sources of income (%)*

| | 1987 | 1988 | 1989 | 1990 | 1991 |
|---|---|---|---|---|---|
| Net interest | 65.9 | 67.2 | 66.4 | 68.7 | 70.2 |
| Foreign exchange | 3.2 | 2.6 | 2.7 | 2.1 | 2.4 |
| Fees and commission | 26.2 | 25.9 | 26.5 | 26.0 | 22.6 |
| Other | 4.7 | 4.3 | 4.4 | 3.2 | 4.8 |
| Total | 100 | 100 | 100 | 100 | 100 |

1 The strategic level, in the cross-subsidization of sectors, arguably, the corporate sector at the expense of the personal sector.
2 The business level, in the cross-subsidization of borrowers at the expense of depositors.
3 At the marketing level, in the cross-subsidization of products within a given sector.

These distortions in pricing policy not surprisingly affected and determined both business structure and its direction. Following the line of least resistance, retail banking has had a tendency to concentrate on asset formation in the corporate sector rather than pursue the higher margin but rather more diffuse personal sector business.

The logic behind this distortion derived directly from the London Clearing Bank's traditional cartel and oligopoly in the money transmission mechanism which focused attention on the collection of deposits and expansion of the retail branch network. This focus of attention also provided an opportunity to provide personal customer services. However, the cost of providing such services has always, to some extent, been discounted in the lower rate of return offered to depositors, relative to other less attractive forms of investment. The cartel with its emphasis on similar business styles, philosophies and cost structures also prevented explicit pricing of personal customer services.

The price for deposits and the tariff for payment systems were, therefore, pre-set and competition emerged in the form of 'non-price competition'. More accurately it could be described as implicit price competition, as factors such as convenience and the quality, speed and efficiency of service became significant features of competition. The nature of interbank competition judged on this basis was more intense than might have been thought and provided a very effective barrier to entry for other industrial groups.

With the eventual fragmentation of the oligopoly and the inevitable emergence of new competitor groups, pricing mechanisms based on oligopolistic principles became less tenable. Principles of cross-subsidization become unsound when competition is extended beyond an oligopolistic group as price then becomes the competitive norm. Even if price does not reflect the cost characteristics of an individual product, it should reflect the costs and profitability of customer and business segments. This partly explains the moves by most retail banks to reorganize their business along lines that reflect broad business segments.

The retail banking industry faces several major problems in deriving an appropriate pricing policy that are not present in other individual sectors. Profitability is still essentially based on interest income which is determined to an extent by efficient gap management, maturity transformation and the underlying quality of assets, etc. Trends in the absolute level of interest rates are, however, beyond the control of banks, being largely determined by government policy. Moreover, retail banks are essentially price takers, *ceteris paribus*, any increase in price by one bank leads to a reduction in its customer base and any decrease in its prices are usually met by its competitors. Furthermore, the scope for interest competition is further restricted by the cost structure of retail banking compared with new competitors entering the market. The downward pressure on interest margins has to an extent been offset by the increase in nominal interest rates with the result that interest margins have in fact remained fairly constant. However, the emergence of even more competition, combined with an easing in nominal interest rates, suggest that interest margins will be under even greater pressure in future.

**Pricing issues**

Pricing is an important element in the marketing mix because it is the only one which produces revenue – all the other parts being cost driven. Despite being so critical to profitability, aggressive pricing strategies have seldom been adopted by the banks, although in recent years, since the abolition of the interest rate cartel, price competition among the banks has grown. The best example of this trend was the advent of 'free banking' for personal current account holders who remained in credit. More recently the question whether or not to pay interest on current account credit balances has become a serious discussion point. This is, after all, another form of pricing, although a general move to pay interest on all current account funds could be very damaging to retail bank earnings. It is also interesting to note how the purchase of deposits by paying competitive rates of interest is both a pricing mechanism and a cost, as the interest paid for deposits reduces profit. However, if the price paid to account holders for deposits is lower than the cost of gaining funds in some other way (in the wholesale money markets for example) then there is a cost saving. Moreover, if the interest rates paid increase deposits and this enables lending to be increased, there will be a profit based on the margin between what is paid for deposits and what is earned from lending these funds.

When considering the unusual trading nature of a retail bank which buys in funds and relends them it should not be overlooked that costs are both fixed and variable. Where variable costs are involved, their impact is affected by volume. Fixed costs need to be recovered irrespective of sales by means of an appropriate pricing policy. Variable costs that are volume-related need controlling.

Finally, it is worth noting the difficulties most banks have in assessing true direct and indirect costs for each service or related range of services. If pricing is based on cost recovery, then knowing the cost is normally an essential prerequisite. In the case of the retail banks, great strides are being made to identify and apportion direct costs to individual services but indirect cost allocation is very much more arbitrary. This is not surprising in an organization with 300–400 separate services sold through a network of over 3,000 High Street branches. Progress is being made to make each separate unit of a bank either a cost or a profit centre, and this is improving the knowledge about pricing generally. This should result in more concise pricing policies and strategies, and ultimately result in more effective use of pricing as a marketing tool.

Perhaps the major problem associated with pricing practice in banking is that of the 'production cost' for an individual service. The difficulty is that in an organization like RBNE, there are high overheads (in people, premises and so on) and relatively low variable costs. The way in which those overheads are allocated between the services has a major effect on the 'cost' of an individual service. A new service can look very profitable, marginally profitable or distinctly unprofitable, depending on the decision as to whether to allocate its share of overheads on the basis of variable costs, proportion of turnover, or estimated load on executive time, space etc. It may be useful to differentiate between those services for which prices are fixed centrally, singly or in the form of a range of prices; and those for which prices are negotiated with the particular customer concerned. Centrally fixed services usually include: personal current accounts, deposit accounts, trustee and taxation services, factoring, leasing and personal fixed-term loans. On the other hand, services that may be negotiated individually include: business current accounts, overdrafts, merchant banking, international services and loans (fixed rate or base rate plus).

There are many products offered by RBNE for which there is no centrally fixed price or pricing system. In such cases, the bank manager has to negotiate a fee or a charge more or less on the spot. There are some guidelines or precedents for the manager to use, but there is still room for the manager concerned to decide on the appropriate price within the various parameters laid down by the bank. The actual prices charged by RBNE should attempt to exploit different price sensitivities in different market segments. However, in order to do this, RBNE must ensure that there is no intersegment leakage. Otherwise, customers will merely bypass the higher priced segment and obtain cheaper services by moving into a different market segment.

Future trends in the development of pricing policies will probably be based on the attempt to measure more accurately the costs involved in a particular product or group of products and thus tend to derive some sort of cost plus pricing system. One basic problem facing the banks is that they have relatively little control over the magnitude of their revenue. The government's ability to determine the minimum lending rate means banks may find themselves in a situation of high profits one year and potential loss another. As a result, pricing policies that shield at least some of RBNE's activities from external variables are very important.

## Questions

1 Assess the performance of RBNE and make general recommendations aimed at strengthening the bank's position and increasing overall profitability. In particular, consider:
   ● which existing markets and activities the bank ought to expand;
   ● which existing markets and activities the bank ought to reduce;
   ● which new markets and activities the bank ought to consider entering.
2 Outline the sort of motives the bank ought to consider in arriving at a product pricing strategy. Apply this approach to:
   ● those existing markets and activities (identified in Question 1) which the bank ought to expand;
   ● those new markets and activities (identified in Question 1) which the bank ought to consider entering.
3 Consider the implications for future pricing policy in RBNE of the development of closer bank–customer relationships.

## Further reading

Ennew, C.T., Watkins, T, and Wright, M. (1990) *Marketing Financial Services.* Heineman, Oxford

Howcroft, J.B. and Lavis, J. (1989) Pricing in retail banking. *International Journal of Bank Marketing,* **4**(4), 3–13

Hughes, T. (1990) Pricing. In Ennew, Watkins and Wright (1990)

Kimball, R.C. (1990) Relationship versus product in retail banking. *Journal of Retail Banking,* **12**(1), 13–25

Lawson, R.W., Watt, A.W. and Netherton, D.R. (1981) Marketing orientated pricing in UK banking. *Proceedings of European Academy for Advanced Research in Marketing,* March

Revell, J.R.S. (1980) *Costs and Margins in Banking.* OECD Report, Paris

# Case 6  Preston and Lancaster Building Society

*Tim Hughes*
Bristol and West Building Society

## Introduction

UK building societies are relatively late entrants into the use of sophisticated marketing techniques partly because, until 1987, they were severely constrained in their activities by legislation. However, the potential to benefit from consumer marketing in the new competitive environment is considerable, given that building societies have large customer databases and control over their own distribution networks. These two aspects in particular lend themselves to quantification of the results of campaigns, using techniques which have been applied in direct mail on the one hand and in measuring retail sales on the other. The Preston and Lancaster Building Society, a major regional building society, attempted to use these techniques in judging, controlling and developing a campaign in support of a new product.

## The product and the strategy

The product involved was an investment bond, supplied by a major insurance company, which was freely available from other intermediaries but which the building society wished to sell as an own label product. The product required a minimum investment of £2,000 and gave particular benefits to higher rate tax payers. The gross profit on the product derived from a 5 per cent commission on sales. Any marketing costs incurred had to come out of this 5 per cent. At the time of the launch, no building society had marketed this type of product before and therefore there were no existing data on the possible take-up of a bond, which while it held the possibility of capital growth, also held the possibility of decline. This feature could be very alienating for the traditional building society investor. As a result of this it was crucial to keep the 'up-front' marketing costs as low as possible and 'feel the way' as the campaign progressed, with more promotional money progressively being made available if it was shown to be cost effective. The issue for the marketing department was how much to promote the product in the first place and how to measure the success of the campaign quickly and effectively to take the decisions that needed to be made on further activities.

In view of this need to keep up-front expenses low, and because the product was essentially up-market, the promotional activities were confined to in-branch display, targeted direct mail to the customer base, black and white advertising in the national press and PR.

## The promotional activities

The promotion of the product in the branches was obviously very important, as for any company with expensive retail networks the success or failure of mainstream products will often be determined by the effort put behind the product by the branch staff. Special attention was given to training for everybody, including part-timers, both in understanding the product and sales opportunities and also in setting up procedures to monitor the number of applications from each branch. The sales material used in the branches was strongly branded and the same basic leaflet was used both in the branches and through direct mail to give a consistency in presentation. However, the application forms were colour coded so that it would be possible to identify how many investments were the result of customers picking up the leaflet in the branch, as opposed to how many had been received through a mail shot and then brought into the branch.

The direct mail campaign was confined to the customer base and limited to particular sections of it. The success of any direct mail campaign will be mainly dependent on how well it is targeted. It was therefore important to code the application forms which went to the different target groups to make it possible to assess which groups responded in terms of numbers and amount invested. The targeting on this occasion was based on savings account balances with the society, so that the mail shots were confined to only those customers with a balance of over £2,000. The value of identifying the response rates from different sections of the customer base was that three months later a second mail shot could be directed to the best target groups on the basis of the response rates so far.

To attract investments from new customers, direct response 'off the page' advertising was also tested. This was designed to get investments through the branches and also through the post to a special unit in head office. The view was taken that, as long as the advertising brought in money through the post, cost effectively (advertising costing less than 5 per cent of the value of funds coming in) it could be successful. An added benefit was that it would also bring in new customers through the branches. Decisions on advertising expenditure were made very simple on this basis as responsiveness to each newspaper could be monitored weekly and judgements made on how much it was worth paying for advertising in each newspaper. The campaign continued for about eight months and was very cost effective. It should be noted that setting up the response mechanisms to the advertising involved a great deal of time and effort. Because of the complexity of the product it had to be done through a two-stage sell with customers responding to the advertisement being sent more details and an application form. This meant it was necessary to code each application by hand so that the subsequent investment could be attributed to a particular newspaper advertisement. In addition a follow-up letter was sent out, if no investment was forthcoming within the month following the sending out of the application. Telesales was also tested as a way of converting inquirers into investors.

## Outcomes

The overall campaign was considered to be tremendously successful with net profits on the product contributing significantly to overall profits for the year. Undoubtedly the success of the campaign owed a fair degree to having the right product at the right time, but also to the amount of planning that was done in the first place, so that throughout the period the marketing department had access to information on the most important and quantifiable elements, which were essential to controlling and developing the campaign. The ability to achieve this came from the marketing department deciding at the outset what it would need to know to develop the campaign. This aim in turn depended on the administrative and sales staff, who were handling responses, being willing to take on the very time-consuming extra work that was necessary to produce the information, which was from their point of view unnecessary. Therefore the value of collating the information had to be communicated throughout the organization to ensure that resources were made available. Having the relevant information regularly available then made decision-making relatively easy and allowed the marketing department to extend the campaign to maximum effect.

## Questions

1 What pro formas would you set up to analyse different marketing activities within a campaign and with what frequency would you expect to receive the different pieces of information?
2 What are the similarities and differences in the problems that need to be overcome in setting up analyses of different marketing and sales activities?

## Further reading

Ennew, C. T. (1990) Advertising and promotion. In Ennew, Watkins and Wright (1990)

Ennew, C. T., Watkins, T, and Wright, M. (1990) *Marketing Financial Services.* Heinemann, Oxford

Martin, T. (1991) *Financial Services Direct Marketing*, McGraw Hill, Maidenhead

Simmonds, D. (1988) Direct marketing – direct mail. In *Insurance Marketing* (N. Dyer and T. Watkins eds) Kluwer, London

# Case 7  Borders Investment Managers

*Paul Draper and David Cook*
Universities of Strathclyde and Bradford

## Introduction

Borders Investment Managers (BIM) is an old established firm of investment managers. Founded during the 1920s to launch and manage an investment trust, the English and Scottish Borders trust (ESB), the firm has operated as a partnership managing in recent years a limited range of investment trusts. The investment managers have a reputation for prudence and conservatism and BIM is operated by a small but high quality investment staff almost all of whom either have a degree or a professional qualification (accounting or actuarial). The partnership has in the past managed portfolios for a variety of clients but is now almost totally concerned with managing investment trusts. The value of funds under management is in excess of £800 m. A small number of private client portfolios are also managed by the firm, predominantly for rich individuals and charities together with four pension fund portfolios but these activities represent less than 10 per cent of the total funds under management. Investment trust portfolios are the main source of interest and revenue for the partnership. BIM has in fact totally missed out on the management of unit trusts and in truth has little experience in the pension fund field.

## The investment trust industry

The investment trust industry has suffered significant attrition during the past twenty-five years. Membership of the Association of Investment Trusts fell from 273 trusts in 1965 to 164 trusts in 1984 and while there was a resurgence in the second half of the 1980s, until very recently the new trusts launched have almost all been small and highly specialized. Like many other managers, BIM has in recent years lost two of its trusts with a consequent loss of income to the partnership. Investment trusts are companies that while legally separate from their investment managers are, in practice, very closely related. The investment managers (in this case BIM) are remunerated by the trust (for example, the ESB) for their services by payment of a fee based on the percentage of assets that the investment trust controls. This percentage fee has been rising since 1964 as also has the total value of assets (largely a consequence of the rise in the stock market over the period). However, with the reduction in the number of trusts it manages the partnership income accruing to BIM has not grown significantly. The causes of the decline in the relative size of the investment trust market are many and varied but of particular consequence is the existence of a discount which has made it difficult over most of the past twenty-five years either to launch new trusts, or to protect existing trusts from predators. Investment trusts invest predominantly in marketable securities such as in the equity shares of industrial, commercial and financial companies quoted on the Stock Exchange. In consequence the value of their assets is known with a considerable degree of precision. There is, however, no necessary one-to-one relationship between the value of their assets and the value of the investment trust's own equity shares quoted on the Stock Exchange. In general, the value of the trust's assets have been worth more than the value investors have placed on the trust's own shares. The difference between the two is known as the discount and it has generally been positive (see Figure C7.1). The existence of the discount makes it attractive to take over the trusts and break them up. In effect an acquiror may be able to acquire £1.20 worth of assets for every £1.00 invested.[1] The prospect is enticing and has contributed to the decline of the sector. Opinions vary on the cause of the discount but whatever the cause, attempts to reduce it both by the investment trust sector as a whole, and by individual trusts have been far from successful.

At the same time as the investment trust sector as a whole has been suffering attack and growing relatively slowly, other sectors of the investment market have been growing much more rapidly. Table C7.1 shows the growth in the major portfolio institutions since 1965. Of particular note is the growth in unit trusts over the period from one-sixth of the size of the investment trust sector (measured in terms of assets under management) to about the same total size. The growth of pension fund schemes is also impressive.[2] It is clear from the table that investment trusts have been the slowest growing major sector of the portfolio investment market.

There has been a tendency in the past for many of the investment trust portfolio managers to stand back, shake their heads and to predict doom for the more explosive growth sectors of the investment management market such as unit trusts. However, it became clear by the mid-1980s that unit trusts were, in fact, here to stay, that investors generally found them easier to buy, sell and understand, and the growth was going to continue to be faster than in the investment trust market. Comparisons of unit and investment trust performance might show that investment trusts performed better[3] (although comparisons of performance are notoriously difficult to do accurately and often depend on the particular assumptions involved) but the ability to sell

---

[1]To be more specific, imagine an investment trust that invested only in BP and ICI. If the numbers of shares held by the trust in each company is known, then the exact value of the investment trust's portfolio can be calculated. There is, however, no reason why the share in the investment trust company itself should be worth in total exactly the same as the value of the portfolio in BP and ICI. If the BP and ICI shares are worth more than the trust's own shares can be bought for on the stock market, then a discount exists.

[2]Note that the classification of these schemes in Table 5.1 relates to the ultimate ownership of these assets and not to the investment management of the schemes. Local authority schemes, for example, are primarily managed by private investment managers.

[3]Each £1 invested in an investment trust grew more rapidly on average than £1 invested in a unit trust for the same period.

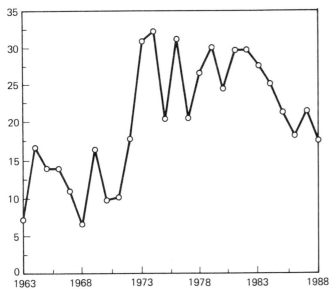

**Figure C7.1**  Average discount (December 1963–1988), calculated for forty-five largest trusts (data from *Datastream*). (Source: Draper, 1989)

*Table C7.1  Assets of UK investment institutions (£m)*

| End of: | 1965 | 1969 | 1974 | 1979 | 1984 | 1987 |
|---|---|---|---|---|---|---|
| Unit trusts (MV plus cost of buying securities, initial charge, etc.) | 522 | 1,412 | 1,310 | 3,937 | 15,099 | 36,330 |
| Investment trusts (MV of holdings) | 3,143 | 4,902 | 3,739 | 5,752 | 15,251 | 14,410 |
| Superannuation funds* | | | | | | |
|   Public sector (MV of funded schemes) | 1,148 | 1,699 | 2,517 | 12,302 | 36,186 | 40,191 |
|   Local authority** (MV & holdings) | 838 | 1,246 | 1,644 | 5,361 | 17,815 | 26,470 |
|   Private (MV & holdings) | 3,293 | 4,468 | 5,108 | 16,711 | 79,324 | 129,621 |
| Total superannuation | 5,279 | 7,413 | 9,269 | 34,374 | 133,325 | 196,282 |
| Insurance companies (book value) | 9,866 | 14,201 | 24,357 | 52,797 | 131,038 | 207,900 |

*Source: CSO Financial Statistics.* Insurance company statistics embrace their investment portfolios only.
* The pension fund information has been temporarily withdrawn due to the data problems. This makes updating of the table prothematic at the moment (December 1991).
** 1969–70 figures relate to 31 March of the following year. Frequent changes in sample coverage and methods of compilation imply that the figures are only suggestive. The pension fund information has been temporarily withdrawn due to data problems. This makes updating of the table problematic at the moment (December 1991).

unit trusts more or less over the counter or even off-the-page[4] without having to go through a stockbroker was an advantage that was difficult to beat.

[4]Investors could be invited to clip the coupon in a newspaper advert and invest immediately in a unit trust.

Investment trusts might appeal to the more sophisticated investor[5] but the mass market was with the small saver who wanted something more exciting than a building society. The downside, of course, is that if the stock market fell then unit trusts could be redeemed by investors with potentially serious consequences for the investment manager and the unit trust.

### Borders Investment Managers

The growth of the unit trust market has been well known to the partners of BIM but despite the growth they have displayed a certain reluctance to become involved in the unit trust market. It is difficult to identify the precise cause of this reluctance but conservatism, prudence and lack of resources all play their part. The partnership has no doubt that it could handle the investment side of unit trusts although even here there might be some difficulties. It is unusual in the unit trust market to offer just one unit trust to the public. The norm is to offer a whole range of units. Cynics argue that it is to make sure that at least one unit trust performs well for advertising purposes, but whatever the reason BIM would have to offer a whole range of both general and specialized trusts, sometimes in areas in which it had little investment expertise. One suggestion, for example, is for a Hong Kong and Far East (excluding Japan) fund, areas in which the partnership invests but on the advice of others rather than through its own analysis. The main fears of BIM, however, relate not to possible difficulties in investment but to its lack of experience in marketing and the absence of a distribution network for selling the unit trusts to the public. In the early days of the industry it had been easy to sell unit trusts. Unit trust managers simply had to advertise in the financial pages of the newspapers pointing out their superlative investment performance, and money from investors would flood in to the managers. By mid-1980s, however, sales of units were often through financial intermediaries, typically insurance brokers, or through a direct sales force working on behalf of the unit trust managers. The latter form of distribution is out of the question for BIM; the resources are simply not available. However, if BIM were to go for the financial intermediary market how would it attract the attention of intermediaries? Competition is intense and the ability to pay high commission limited, but if BIM is to be successful in unit trusts it has to secure some sort of distributional network.

The partners are worried about the cost of such initiatives but on the plus side feel that the partnership has a history of successful fund management in the investment trust sector. Several of the partners are not only aware of the Efficient Market Hypothesis (EMH) but also largely subscribe to its conclusions. From their own experience they recognize the difficulty of outperforming the market as a whole without taking on excessive risk, and hence the problems of offering investors outstanding performance. However, they have several reasons to be optimistic. The partnership has tended to invest for the long term in a diversified portfolio of small to medium-sized international companies. Turnover and hence management expenses have been low suggesting that if the EMH is correct then, over the long run, they should outperform their competitors many of whom trade much more frequently and, according to BIM partners, often on the basis of little information at all. The diversified, international nature of BIM portfolios is

---

[5]But if they were sophisticated they could perform the services offered by the trusts for themselves.

felt to offer investors the possibility of securing lower risk than from just investing in UK securities while the traditional concentration on small- and medium-sized companies appears to exploit one of the apparent anomalies not explained by the EMH, the small firm effect[6]. Unfortunately it is not entirely clear how these advantages can be properly exploited. The sale of a general unit trust is unlikely to be sufficiently exciting to attract investors in the numbers wanted. BIM would have to offer a number of different specialized portfolios and in some of these areas their skills are very limited.

Not all of the partners of BIM are enthusiastic about unit trusts. The senior partner is particularly dismissive of unit trust investment management although if it could be shown to be profitable, he would consider any possibility. The senior partner and several other members of the firm believe that the pension fund market is much more attractive. They argue that all that is required is for the firm to use its investment skills on behalf of pension funds instead of investment trusts. Some marketing skills are still needed but the marketing required is more limited and more subtle.

Pension funds are established by companies (or other organizations) to benefit their employees. The companies themselves rarely have the expertise to manage the assets of the fund that builds up as individuals (and the company) contribute to the pension scheme. Instead, the companies hire professional fund managers to manage the investment of the assets. The process by which managers are selected is known as a beauty parade. The consulting actuary to the fund draws up a short list of investment managers who are allowed to present their philosophy and proposals for investing the assets of the pension fund to the pension scheme trustees. Five or six managers might make a presentation to the trustees and one, or occasionally more, is selected. The pension fund market has been growing rapidly and provided BIM can convince consulting actuaries of their skills it should be possible to pick up some investment business fairly quickly. Thereafter, progress is likely to be slow unless investment performance is really spectacular[7] but the business is reasonably stable,[8] not too cost conscious (trustees do not tend to force down expenses to rock-bottom costs) and should be cheap to enter.

BIM is not alone in looking for new investment products to sell. A significant number of investment trusts continue to be run by small investment managers who are in the process of diversifying, usually into pension fund business, but occasionally into unit trusts or other investment vehicles. Competition has been becoming increasingly fierce as insurance companies, stockbrokers and banks amongst other financial institutions have sought to secure a foothold in the fast-growing investment market and offer a variety of products including insurance, unit trusts and pensions (Table C7.2). These institutions are able to secure substantial economies of scale and frequently have access to a ready-made distribution channel through their

[6]The small firm effect refers to the additonal return over and above that explained by asset pricing models that has been found to be associated with the shares of very small companies.

[7]The partners know on the basis of past experience and the predictions of the EMH that spectacular performance is only likely to occur by chance. While they hope for a run of luck they do not place undue faith in their ability to deliver spectacular performance to order.

[8]Pension fund investment managers may be dismissed immediately but in practice a four- or five-year spell of managing a fund is common and much longer periods reasonably frequent.

*Table C7.2   Pension fund managers (selected)*

|                                                | Total funds (£ bn) |
|------------------------------------------------|--------------------|
| Baillie Gifford                                | 1.9                |
| Baring Investment Management                   | 7.3                |
| BZW Investment Management                      | 14.6               |
| CIN Management Ltd                             | 12.7               |
| County Nat West Investment Management          | 14.0               |
| Dunedin Fund Managers                          | 3.0                |
| Fleming Asset Management                       | 9.4                |
| Hambros Bank Investment Management             | 2.6                |
| Henderson Fund Management                      | 5.3                |
| Kleinwort Benson Investment Management         | 2.9                |
| M & G Investment                               | 1.6                |
| Mercury Asset Management                       | 25.1               |
| Martin Curry Investment Management             | 1.4                |
| Murray Johnstone Investment Management         | 3.0                |
| Phillips and Drew Fund Management              | 16.1               |
| Prudential Portfolio Manager                   | 10.4               |
| Schroder Investment Management                 | 16.9               |
| Scottish Amicable                              | 3.1                |

*Source*: *Institutional Investor*, November 1990 (British Pension Directory).

branch networks. BIM is tiny in comparison with many of these institutions. It owes its continued existence primarily to its historical connection with the English and Scottish Borders trust and to its relatively low costs as a result of its location outside of London.

BIM does very little to promote its own investment trusts. It belongs to the Association of Investment Trust Companies and largely relies on promotion by the Association for the investment trust industry as a whole. It has introduced low cost purchase (and sale) schemes for small investors and is promoting a savings scheme but it has not, as yet, started paying commission to intermediaries for introducing business. Advertising is minimal largely because it is illegal for a company to promote its own shares. However, scope almost certainly exists to design strategies that appeal to reasonably well-off individuals who are attracted by the lower costs of investment trusts relative to unit trusts. The need is either to attract relatively knowledgeable individuals who are prepared to use the stock market to buy and sell rather than transact through an intermediary, or to make the purchase process for investment trusts as painless as it is for unit trusts.

BIM then is faced with three choices. Stick to its present market segment, investment trusts, and hope that the current upsurge is permanent and that the decline in the market is largely over; diversify into the retail investment market by selling unit trusts; and/or move into pension fund investment management. The first choice is felt by most partners to have been followed for far too long with the result that BIM has grown only slowly and profit growth has been negligible. Movement into unit trusts is the high-risk, high-reward option. If they could get it right potential profits could be very large but the firm lacks marketing skills and a satisfactory distribution network. The third possibility, movement into pension fund investment management, appears relatively safe but the profits would not be vast. There is still a marketing problem, in particular, selling BIM's investment philosophy to both the consulting actuaries and the trustees, but at least they would not have to cope with the exigencies of the retail market.

## Questions

1 Advise BIM as to whether or not they should enter the unit trust market and if so outline the proposed marketing plan, paying particular attention to the target market, the product range, distribution methods and commission rates paid to intermediaries.
2 Advise BIM as to whether or not they should enter the pension fund investment management market and in particular, how the partners might approach consulting actuaries and trustees and the overall marketing mix which might be adopted.
3 Bearing in mind the legal difficulties of companies promoting their own shares, evaluate how BIM currently sell their present range of investment trusts.

In the preparation of your advice you might find it useful to study the competitive offerings and advertising messages in the appropriate trade journals and magazines, such as: *Investors Chronicle; Money Management; Financial Adviser; Pension World; Pensions and Employee Benefits.*

4 What market research would be useful to enhance the market knowledge of the partners and enable them to improve their marketing decision-making?

## Further reading

Draper, P. (1989) *The Investment Trust Industry in the UK*, Avebury, Aldershot

Draper, P. (1990) The marketing of investment and unit trusts. In Ennew, Watkins and Wright (1990)

Ennew, C. T., Watkins, T. and Wright, M. (1990) *Marketing Financial Services*, Heinemann, Oxford

# Case 8 Munich Reinsurance

*Trevor Watkins, Christine Ennew and Desmond Le Gruys*
South Bank University, University of Nottingham and Munich Reinsurance

## Introductions

Recent years have witnessed a substantial growth in the market for permanent health insurance (PHI) in the UK. PHI provides a mechanism for individuals or groups to insure against the loss of income and poverty which can be associated with long-term illness or disability. The policy holder, once accepted, pays a specified premium which does not change, on a regular basis. Should they become disabled by sickness or accident, the policy will provide compensation (in the form of weekly or monthly payments) for the period of the disablement (after a specified waiting period, usually between one and three months) or until recovery, retirement or death.

## Disability claims management

When a claim is made against a PHI policy, the insurer must investigate all aspects pertaining to the validity of the claim. This investigation will normally include:

1 Evaluating the existence and implications of a particular medical condition.
2 Evaluating the amount payable.
3 Ensuring that the claim is valid.

Since many aspects of the claims procedure require specialist knowledge (often medical), a number of insurers employ an independent claims management service to handle at least some of their claims. For this product, like any other form of insurance, profitability is dependent on minimizing the payment of claims, subject to behaving equitably towards clients who are suffering from some genuine disability. For any company, this is a difficult balance to maintain. Claims management is concerned with maintaining this balance by ensuring that all claims are genuine.

The two main UK suppliers of disability claims management services are Victory and M & G who are both reinsurers. There is some evidence to suggest that Victory have the larger market share of the two. In 1989, some insurers seemed concerned about the extent to which the two services could cope with an increase in business. Munich Reinsurance, a well-established reinsurance company in the UK market, has identified disability claims management as an extra service which it could offer to the UK market. Two potential markets were identified. First, among UK insurers offering personal or groups PHI policies and second, among pension funds who were liable for claims against the pension fund in cases of long-term disability. Market research was used to analyse the potential of both target markets.

## Market research

All insurance offices currently offering or planning to offer personal or group PHI policies along with a sample of pensions funds were contacted by questionnaire. The postal survey produced a 23 per cent response rate with twenty-five returns from insurance offices and twenty-eight returns from pension funds. Among insurance offices 82 per cent used external agencies for aspects of disability claims management, and the most common pattern was to use two agencies. This contrasts sharply with the pension funds where only one fund reported using external agencies. Some 45 per cent of insurance offices anticipated that their use of outside agencies would increase, but pension funds expected no change in the future. Tables C8.1 and C8.2 outline respondents' assessment of the relative popularity of different features of a disability claims management service.

The ownership status of an external agency was seen by many respondents as an important feature in guiding their choice. Among insurance offices ownership by a reinsurer or by an independent company was attractive while ownership by either a competing insurer or a pension consultant met with some resistance. Pension funds were favourable to external agencies owned by an independent company or a pension consultant but were resistant to ownership by a reinsurer or by another pension fund. As far as other service features were concerned, fixed pricing was seen as popular by both groups of respondents as was the ability to handle blocks of work and work to previously agreed timescales. The availability of experienced PHI claims managers and specialized medical staff through the claims management service was also seen as a particularly attractive feature.

In-depth discussion with around five insurance offices revealed that in most cases outside claims management was not used on a regular basis and that it was not used for all claims. The more straightforward claims were dealt with in-house with an external specialist being called in to deal with the more

Table C8.1  *Popular features of disability claims management (insurance offices)*

| Ranking | Feature | Score |
|---|---|---|
| 1 | Ongoing check after payments have been initiated | 1.17 |
| 2 | Rehabilitation advice to claimants | 1.04 |
| 3 | Prognosis report by specialist adviser | 1.00 |
| 4= | State benefits advice | 0.92 |
| 4= | Confidential check | 0.92 |
| 6 | Initial check before payments are initiated | 0.83 |
| 7 | Termination advice to company on claims that should no longer be paid because claimant has recovered | 0.67 |
| 8 | Analysis of experience | 0.57 |
| 9 | Analysis of claims handling | 0.54 |
| 10 | Legal advice | 0.42 |
| 11 | Employer representation | 0.36 |
| 12 | Legal representation | 0.26 |
| 13= | Computer system to handle claims | 0.25 |
| 13= | Complete system | 0.25 |

Score based on: Never use = 0; may use = 1; regular use = 2; always use = 3.

*Table C8.2   Popular features of disability claims management (pension funds)*

| Ranking | Feature | Score |
|---------|---------|-------|
| 1 | State benefit advice | 1.00 |
| 2 | Rehabilitation advice | 0.96 |
| 3 | Ongoing check | 0.92 |
| 4 | Prognosis report | 0.78 |
| 5 | Initial check | 0.74 |
| 6 | Termination advice | 0.61 |
| 7 | Confidential check | 0.54 |
| 8 | Analysis of claims handling | 0.43 |
| 9 | Complete system | 0.40 |
| 10 | Legal advice | 0.39 |
| 11 | Legal representation | 0.35 |
| 12 | Analysis of experience | 0.33 |
| 13= | Negotiations for fund | 0.30 |
| 13= | Computer systems | 0.30 |

Scores as calculated in Table C8.1

difficult claims. Since these external agencies would be acting on behalf of the insurance office it was generally felt that all staff dealing with the claimant should be credible and professional. In particular the staff should be familiar with the insurer's claims philosophies. Ideally the agency should have both medical and insurance specialists.

## Questions

1 Advise Munich Reinsurance on the prospects for providing a disability claims management service. What further research should be undertaken before any such product is launched?
2 What services should be offered and how should they be marked?

## Further reading

Dyer, N. and Watkins, T., (eds) (1988) *Marketing Insurance* (2nd edn), Kluwer, London
Stevenson, B. D. (1990) *Marketing Financial Services to Corporate Clients*, Woodhead-Faulkner, Cambridge

# Case 9  West of England Bank

*Barry Howcroft and Ian Morison*
University of Loughborough Banking Centre

## Introduction

The West of England Bank (WEB) was established in 1875 and for most of its 116 years has concentrated upon the personal and small business customer, though latterly it has developed a modest corporate banking capability. Until 1989 it was owned by a consortium of insurance companies and investment banks, most of whom had been shareholders since 1920 when, at the insistence of the Bank of England, WEB was properly capitalized for the first time. Subsequently, it experienced a long record of expansion, financed exclusively since 1956 from retained earnings. The Board of Directors comprised representatives of the shareholders; however, management was given a relatively free hand in conducting the affairs of the bank.

In 1989 the shareholding institutions decided to sell WEB: most of them felt that it was no longer appropriate to retain strategically significant investments in a company over which they did not enjoy management control, and which in some instances gave rise to commercial conflicts of interest. Particulars of WEB were circulated to a number of potentially interested UK and overseas institutions and it was in the event sold to a leading French bank, Crédit Commercial Toulousain (CCT). CCT is a long-established institution with a broad range of both personal and corporate banking activities. It employs about 55,000 staff in France, where it has 2,400 branches, and a further 14,000 in its 450 overseas outlets. Its end-1989 balance sheet footings amounted to £151 bn in sterling terms, of which shareholders' funds represented £4.4 bn, subordinated debt £1.3 bn and other medium- and long-term debt £7.5 bn. It made pre-tax profits of £1.22 bn, up from £1.18 bn in 1988.

## The business of WEB

Traditionally WEB's business was confined to the South West of England, but in the mid-1970s management decided to expand the bank's geographical coverage. As a consequence, the business has been expanded into South Wales and the Midlands, and has made more recent limited inroads into the South East. In the South West the bank's proportion of total personal current accounts is 20 per cent, though very much less in its areas of more recent expansion.

In pursuing its expansion strategy, the intitial objective was to open ten branches a year, but this proved a little optimistic. Nevertheless, the branch network has expanded from 198 in 1960 to 300 in 1989, with an annual increase of approximately six per year since the mid-1970s, supported by 250 ATMs.

The main customer base continues to be personal account holders. WEB now has over 1 million current account holders – an increase of 25 per cent over the past five years. The growth of current account balances over the same period was 71 per cent. The age and social class complexion of the account base is not greatly different from the national average, to wit:

| Age    | %    |
|--------|------|
| 16–20  | 6.7  |
| 21–24  | 8.5  |
| 25–34  | 19.9 |
| 35–44  | 21.6 |
| 45–54  | 15.3 |
| 55–64  | 13.0 |
| 65+    | 15.0 |

| Social class | %    |
|--------------|------|
| AB           | 21.1 |
| C1           | 28.8 |
| C2           | 28.4 |
| DE           | 21.7 |

The bank's subsidiaries in recent years have contributed between 4 and 10 per cent of operating profits and management sees them as an important source of future growth. The major operating subsidiaries are described below.

- *WEB Finance* provides hire purchase and rental services. It operates out of thirteen area offices, with customer service also available through the bank's branch network. Outstandings have grown from £83 m in 1984 to £155 m in 1988. The range of products has also been extended significantly over the past five years.
- *WEB Retail Services* provides point-of-sale instalment credit, mainly through large retail chains. It administers credit cards on behalf of such retailers and also manages a Visa 'Budget' account facility (ClientCard) on behalf of WEB itself.
- *Dean Vehicle Rentals* is a long-established vehicle contract hire business. WEB acquired 75 per cent of the company in October 1986 and its busines has since grown substantially with a fleet of nearly 9,500 vehicles.
- *WEB Home Loans*  This company was set up in 1986 to operate the MIRAS home loans business which, for regulatory reasons, is not carried on the books of the bank. It is run as if it were a department of the bank.
- *WEB Development Capital* was established in March 1989 to carry out venture capital business. It had a fund of £25 m available and in its first two months of operation had already arranged a management buy-out worth some £4 m. It is expected to obtain a large part of its business from the bank's branch network.
- *WEB Insurance Services* was recently established to operate an insurance broking business. (WEB is an independent intermediary under the Financial Services Act.)

The bank has made full use of computer technology in its business. Its systems are based on Unisys machines and it is in the process of developing a major new computer centre. It has recently developed a new computerized account management system which it believes will generate significant marketing opportunities. Thanks largely to computerization, transactions handled have expanded by over 60 per cent since 1983 while staff have increased at barely a third of this rate.

The bank has a relatively simple management structure – a general manager, two assistant general managers with responsibility for administration and branches respectively, six administrative functions (card service, personnel, operations, marketing, inspection and finance), two regions, through whom all the branches report, and an advance controller, chief planner and company secretary who report directly to the general manager.

A summarized profit and loss account and balance sheet are set out in Figures C9.1 and C9.2 in the appendices to this case.

## The strategic options

Immediately following the acquisition of WEB by CCT, a taskforce comprising representatives of both institutions was set up to consider the mains strategic options. These were considered under the following eight headings:

- Personal banking
- Commercial and corporate banking
- Related services
- Branches and automation
- Human resources
- Marketing and public relations
- Financial strategy and informatioan systems
- Relations with CCT

### Personal banking

WEB's present situation is one where it enjoys a significant share of the personal banking market in its traditional region of the South West and a much smaller, but growing and profitable, share of the Midlands, Welsh and (to a lesser extent) South East regions. Within the South West, account growth fell to virtually zero in the late 1980s: this area is regarded as fully banked and the scope for attracting customers from other banks has proved strictly limited since the general introduction of 'free-if-in-credit' banking. There is, however, a clear need to remain competitive vis-à-vis not only the established retail banks but also the building societies, newly empowered as they are to undertake a wider range of banking business. There is also a need to improve the average level of customer profitability; with the decline of the endowment effect, it is now important to generate more explicit revenues from the sale of both banking and non-banking products. Much has already been achieved in this regard, notably through the development of WEB's mortgage business, but it is mindful of the pressures that its traditionally high rate of profitability in the personal banking market is now under. It is also mindful of the difficulties of matching its larger national rivals in advertising and marketing expenditure. While anxious to safeguard its strong franchise in the South West, WEB needs to decide at the same time the basis on which it should seek to compete outside this region – in particular whether it should seek to focus on a specific group of customers or products in future or adopt a more broadly based policy.

*Commercial and corporate banking*

WEB's commercial (small business) banking developed as a natural adjunct to its core personal banking business, and its market share characteristics are not dissimilar. On the positive side it has a reputation for supportiveness and quick decision-making which has stood it in good stead vis-à-vis the major clearers. On the negative side, there is a tendency for its more successful business customers to reach a stage where they feel they have 'outgrown' WEB and need to bank with a 'real' clearer. WEB has recently devoted significantly increased revenues – both human and financial – to this part of its activities and has been rewarded by strong growth in the credit balances on its business accounts and in corporate lending volumes. Its loan portfolio is a well-balanced one and, so far at any rate, its loan loss experience has been better than average. It has recently successfully launched a business Visa card. In the past it has undoubtedly faced credibility problems as a corporate bank, but its ownership by CCT could well help to overcome these. At the same time, it needs to consider the implications of a rapidly developing corporate business for the rest of its activities, its network and organizational structure.

*Related services*

WEB has already diversified to some extent from core banking activities – the most significant feature being the achievement of a substantial £450 m mortgage book. Instalment credit, vehicle rental and leasing activities have also grown in importance and it has recently moved into the new fields of insurance broking and venture capital. Its related services strategy is reflected in the fact that, unlike most of the large clearers, it has chosen to 'polarize' as an independent intermediary rather than a company representative under the Financial Services Act – a decision it recognizes it may now need to revisit. It is concerned, however, about the competitive viability of the strategy. The venture capital offshoot has been established at a somewhat unpropitious time and WEB lacks any meaningful investment banking capability. (Fortunately, however, it has not invested in estate agencies or stockbrokers.) In considering whether or not to expand its existing portfolio of related businesses, it also has to consider which of them should be developed under WEB's name and which under CCT's.

*Branches and automation*

WEB's strategy has latterly been to expand gradually (at a rate of six branches a year or so) in areas not too far removed from its home base. The main constraints on its expansion have been ones less of finance than of the availability of suitable premises approved for banking use – and, to a lesser extent, the availability of appropriate staff. In addition to opening new branches, WEB has recognized the need to devote increasing attention to the state of its existing network, given the emphasis that many of its competitors have latterly placed on revivifying their premises. It recognizes that it needs to generate more profit from its existing branch network, while its acquisition by CCT now raises the question of whether it should continue or alter its existing policy of branch expansion.

WEB operates Unisys-based systems – something of an embarrassment now that it is owned by a company which is almost entirely IBM-dependent. WEB sees its automation strategy as strongly complementing its branch strategy, and the average volume of transaction on its 250 ATMs is among the highest of any bank or building society in the country. Its attitude towards ATM reciprocity is somewhat ambivalent. As a small bank it would see value in allowing its customers access to a larger, more evenly spread ATM network; but it is reluctant to see its own machines subjected to even higher usage than at present. It is currently considering membership of the Link reciprocal ATM network.

*Human resources*

WEB employs over 6,500 staff, of whom just over 10 per cent are managerial and of whom just over 85 per cent work in the branches. The remaining head office staff worked principally in operations, advances, card services, personnel and inspection. The bank has latterly been recruiting some 600–700 new staff each year, of whom some 12 per cent are A-level school leavers or graduates destined for management. It has its own training college. BIFU is the recognized trade union and industrial relations have been generally good. Rates of pay are broadly in line with the major clearers, with profit sharing and (for managerial staff) an increasing performance-related element. There is a non-contributory pension fund. On the positive side, the bank's staff have a reputation for being loyal and hard-working which is envied by the other banks, and the good industrial relations record partly reflects the relatively small size and friendly ambience of the bank. By contrast, the bank has not been able to offer such varied and attractive careers as its larger competitors and the calibre of its management, on paper at any rate, is somewhat lack-lustre. There is concern about the ability of the existing management and staff to adapt to a significantly more competitive and market-focused environment and a recognition of the need for more explicit and forward-looking recruitment, training, development, succession and remuneration policies.

*Marketing and public relations*

Generally, WEB lacks a pro-active marketing policy that reflects it size and distinctive market position. It has only recently developed a formal marketing and PR department, and this is still less than thirty strong. It has not regarded product development as an area of particular emphasis and has tended to follow rather than lead. It has not adopted explicit policies of market segmentation. Its one major marketing initiative was to abolish bank charges for personal customers in credit ahead of the major clearers, but it was not alone in this. Its overall approach to pricing policy is to be neither the dearest nor the cheapest bank in the region.

Within its core region, its image is a strong one – certainly amongst personal customers. It is regarded as a friendly place to do business, and committed to fair dealing. As already mentioned, it has something of a credibility problem amongst actual and potential business customers, although this has not prevented it from expanding that part of its business significantly. It now faces the challenge of how best to preserve the strengths and address the weaknesses of its public image now that it is a member of a wider group.

*Financial strategy and information systems*

WEB's financial position and record has been set out fully in the Appendices. Profit growth has been more than healthy and it has consistently bettered its own forecasts. Partly because of the essentially retail complexion of its business, most of the key performance indicators are better than its main competitors. It has been particularly successful in controlling costs, which have fallen noticeably as a percentage of operating income. It has, however, greatly increased its reliance in both absolute and relative terms on the wholesale deposit markets as its lending has expanded. Its loan loss record has been good. In the absence of significant large corporate or LDC debt exposure, its write-offs over the past five years have averaged less than 0.5 per cent of end-year lending balances. Its capital ratios are well above the Basle Committee minima. There are no special tax characteristics.

On the basis of present strategies, further strong profit growth is expected in 1990 and beyond, though probably at a decelerating rate, resulting in some reduction in the return earned on shareholders' funds, as these are augmented by retentions. The level of dividend cover is also expected to ease slightly, from three and a half to three times. (The exceptional payment in 1989 was made for technical reasons to the previous shareholders and offset by a subscription of new share capital.)

Internal reporting systems have been traditionally geared to the needs for statutory accounting and supervisory returns. With the increasing emphasis on product/customer profitability, however, there is now an acknowledged need to improve the amount, accuracy and timeliness of management information.

*Relations with CCT*

WEB has traditionally operated at arms-length from its shareholders: they have not been required to subscribe new capital for many years, have benefited from an increasing flow of dividend income, and have accordingly been happy to allow the bank's management its head. CCT's style is bound to be more intrusive. As a single shareholder it will be in a position to exert more influence; while as a bank it will be accustomed to the strict limitations to delegated authority customary within a banking group in respect of such matters as lending limits and capital investment.

Aside from questions of control, CCT is clearly interested in WEB for more than just its dividend payments. It sees WEB now as an integral part of its European network and will wish to explore the scope for synergy in respect of new products, customer relationships, systems development and so forth. In particular, it will wish to see whether it makes sense to use WEB as the vehicle for a wider range of UK activities. However, it is aware of the need not to antagonize WEB's existing management and customers by adopting too heavy-handed an approach. The challenge is to find ways in which CCT can enhance the value of the business it has acquired without 'killing the goose that lays the golden eggs'.

**Questions**

1 In the light of the foregoing assessment of WEB's position in each of the eight areas considered, make recommendations in respect of the bank's

overall strategy as a member of the CCT group. All the major issues considered in the assessment need to be addressed in those recommendations, in particular:

(a) The market segments (size and type of customer, nature of product, geographical area) on which WEB should concentrate in future.
(b) How it can safeguard its existing franchise in the South West.
(c) The basis on which it should seek to compete outside the South West.
(d) The relationship between its core and ancillary services.
(e) Whether it should alter its branch, ATM and computing strategies.
(f) How far its human resources constrain its strategic development, and the steps it might take to ease the constraints.
(g) How best to segment its markets.
(h) How it can overcome its image and credibility problems, particularly in corporate banking.
(i) The financial objectives which CCT should set for WEB.
(j) How it can meet its strategic challenge without impairing its financial strength.
(k) How much delegated authority CCT should afford WEB management.
(l) How any benefits of synergy between CCT and WEB can be identified and exploited.

## Further reading

Clarke, P.D., Edward, P.M., Gardner, P.F. and Molyneux, P. (1988) The genesis of strategic marketing control in British retail banking. *International Journal of Bank Marketing*, **6**(2), 5–19

Ennew, C. T., Watkins, T, and Wright, M. (1990) *Marketing Financial Services*. Heinemann, Oxford

Lewis, B.R. (1990) Bank Marketing. In Ennew, Watkins and Wright (1990)

McIver, C. and Naylor, G. (1987) *Marketing Financial Services*, Chartered Institute of Bankers, London

Marsh, J.R. (1988) *Managing Financial Services Marketing*, Pitman, London

# Appendices to Case 9

| | Notes | 1989 (£'000) | 1988 (£'000) |
|---|---|---|---|
| Interest receivable | | 625,800 | 402,467 |
| Interest payable | | 394,546 | 199,092 |
| Net interest income | | 231,254 | 203,375 |
| Other operating income | | 85,122 | 68,220 |
| Operating income | | 316,376 | 271,595 |
| Operating expenses | 1 | 158,813 | 132,134 |
| Trading profit (before bad and doubtful debts) | | 157,563 | 139,461 |
| Charge for bad and doubtful debts | | 21,806 | 18,955 |
| Trading profit | | 135,757 | 120,506 |
| Taxation | 2 | 50,876 | 43,870 |
| Profit after taxation | | 84,881 | 76,636 |
| Minority interests | | 52 | (900) |
| Profit attributable to shareholders of bank | | 84,933 | 75,736 |
| Dividends | 11 | 357,360 | 21,600 |
| (Deficit)/Retained profits | | (272,427) | 54,136 |

**Figure C9.1**   Consolidated profit and loss account, year ended 31 December 1989

| | Notes | 1989 (£'000) | 1988 (£'000) |
|---|---|---|---|
| Assets: | | | |
| Liquid assets | 3 | 947,148 | 765,858 |
| Items in the course of collection | | 78,080 | 62,975 |
| Certificates of deposit | | 282,367 | 128,972 |
| Short-term placing | | 142,080 | 218,160 |
| British government securities | | 48,748 | 76,188 |
| Advances and other accounts | 4 | 3,223,651 | 2,445,768 |
| | | 4,722,074 | 3,697,921 |
| Trade investments | | 2,140 | 1,910 |
| Fixed assets | 5 | 142,836 | 122,725 |
| | | 4,867,050 | 3,822,556 |
| Liabilities and shareholders' funds: | | | |
| Current, deposit and other accounts | 6 | 4,379,129 | 3,397,573 |
| Other liabilities | 7 | 59,954 | 56,792 |
| | | 4,439,083 | 3,545,365 |
| Deferred taxation | 8 | 7,004 | 7,748 |
| Loan capital | 9 | 120,000 | – |
| Minority interests | | 147 | 200 |
| Shareholders' Funds: | | | |
| Issued share capital | 10 | 285,000 | 72,000 |
| Reserves | 11 | 15,816 | 288,243 |
| | | 300,816 | 360,243 |
| | | 4,867,050 | 3,822,556 |

**Figure C9.2**   Consolidated balance sheet, year ended 31 December 1989

## Notes on accounts, year ended 31 December 1989

| 1 Operating expenses | 1989 (£'000) | 1988 (£'000) |
|---|---|---|
| Operating expenses comprise: | | |
| Staff | 94,103 | 76,257 |
| Premises and equipment | 25,621 | 22,302 |
| Other | 39,089 | 33,575 |
| | 158,813 | 132,134 |

In 1989 the bank employed 6,647 members of staff of whom 681 were managerial

| 2 Taxation | 1989 (£'000) | 1988 (£'000) |
|---|---|---|
| The charge for taxation comprises: | | |
| Corporation Tax @ 35 per cent | 51,364 | 47,103 |
| Deferred taxation | (744) | (3,451) |
| Associated company | 256 | 218 |
| | 50,876 | 43,870 |

| 3 Liquid assets | 1989 (£'000) | 1988 (£'000) |
|---|---|---|
| Liquid assets comprise: | | |
| Cash in hand and balances with other banks | 89,513 | 86,238 |
| Money at call and short notice | 757,237 | 679,620 |
| Bills discounted | 100,398 | – |
| | 947,148 | 765,858 |

| 4 Advances and other accounts | 1989 (£'000) | 1988 (£'000) |
|---|---|---|
| Advances and other accounts comprise: | | |
| Advances to customers | 2,908,465 | 2,209,813 |
| Hire purchase agreements | 203,597 | 154,411 |
| Finance and operating loans | 111,589 | 81,544 |
| | 3,223,651 | 2,445,768 |

In 1989 the bank advanced £1,920 m to business customers of which £1,620 m was for business overdrafts. Lending to personal customers was £988 m of which £450 m was for home loans, £430 m was for personal instalment finance and £108 m for personal overdrafts. Approximately 87 per cent of new overdraft business is to business customers.

| 5 Fixed assets | 1989 (£'000) | 1988 (£'000) |
|---|---|---|
| Book values of fixed assets comprised: | | |
| Freehold premises: | 110,338 | 92,940 |
| Leasehold premises: | 16,632 | 13,692 |
| Computer, machinery and vehicles | 15,866 | 16,093 |
| | 142,836 | 122,725 |

The bank owns 338 properties, most of which are branches. The total book value of the properties is £126 m, which represents a valuation on an existing use basis.

In total the bank has 230 freehold premises and 108 leasehold. The bank's current policy is to acquire freeholds where possible.

### 6 Current, deposit and other accounts

Wholesale deposits represented 41.8 per cent of total funding at £1,830 m. Current accounts represented 29.1 per cent of total funding at £1,270 m. Savings and interest bearing accounts 22.7 per cent at £994,000 and term accounts 6.4 per cent at £280,000.

### 7 Other liabilities

Other liabilities included taxation payable within the next 12 months at £48,554 and dividends payable at £11,400.

### 8 Deferred taxation

Full provision has been made for the potential liability for deferred taxation.

|  | 1989 (£'000) | 1988 (£'000) |
|---|---|---|
| Short-term timing differences | 14 | 2,056 |
| Capital allowances on bad assets | 6,990 | 5,692 |
|  | 7,004 | 7,748 |

### 9 Loan capital

Loan capital comprises Subordinated Loan Notes 2004, subordinated to the claims of depositors and other creditors. Interest is payable at a rate of 0.375 per cent over LIBOR.

### 10 Share capital

On 17 November 1989 the authorized share capital was increased to £324,000,000 and a further 213,000,000 shares of £1 each were subsequently issued at par for cash.

### 11 Reserves

|  | £'000 |
|---|---|
| 1 January 1989 | 288,243 |
| Profit for the year | 84,933 |
| Dividends | (357,360) |
|  | 15,816 |

### 12 Summarized earnings record

|  | 1984 (£m) | 1985 (£m) | 1986 (£m) | 1987 (£m) | 1988 (£m) | 1989 (£m) |
|---|---|---|---|---|---|---|
| Trading profit | 41.3 | 53.6 | 78.8 | 106.5 | 120.5 | 135.8 |
| Taxation | 14.3 | 20.8 | 29.8 | 39.8 | 43.8 | 50.8 |
| Profit after taxation | 27.0 | 32.8 | 49.0 | 66.7 | 76.7 | 85.0 |

## 13 Summarized balance sheets

| | 1984 (£m) | 1985 (£m) | 1986 (£m) | 1987 (£m) | 1988 (£m) | 1989 (£m) |
|---|---|---|---|---|---|---|
| Liquid assets and UK Govt. securities | 513.7 | 696.5 | 934.9 | 991.7 | 1,252.2 | 1,498.4 |
| Advances and other accts | 1,237.6 | 1,236.4 | 1,448.5 | 1,761.9 | 2,445.7 | 3,223.6 |
| Fixed assets and trade investments | 86.5 | 92.6 | 98.9 | 105.8 | 124.7 | 144.9 |
| Total assets | 1,837.8 | 2,025.5 | 2,482.3 | 2,859.4 | 3,822.6 | 4,866.9 |
| Less: Liabilities | | | | | | |
| Current deposit and other accounts | 1,578.7 | 1,768.7 | 2,180.3 | 2,498.8 | 3,397.6 | 4,379.1 |
| Other liabilities | 71.9 | 40.3 | 51.1 | 63.8 | 64.7 | 186.9 |
| Total liabilities | 1,650.6 | 1,809.0 | 2,231.4 | 2,562.6 | 3,462.3 | 4,566.0 |
| Shareholders' funds | 187.2 | 216.5 | 250.9 | 296.8 | 360.3 | 300.9 |

## 14 Comparative performance measures

| | Pre-tax return on average shareholders funds (%) | Pre-tax return on average total assets (%) | Operating costs as a % of income† | Net interest margin* (%) | Spread* (%) |
|---|---|---|---|---|---|
| Barclays | 27.0 | 1.45 | 66 | 4.7 | 2.7 |
| Lloyds | 36.2 | 1.96 | 65 | 5.4 | 3.3 |
| Midland | 24.3 | 1.33 | 71 | 4.9 | 3.1 |
| National Westminster | 26.0 | 1.40 | 67 | 5.5 | 3.5 |
| West of England | 36.7 | 3.6 | 49 | 6.5 | 6.2 |

* Figures based on domestic business only.
† Operating expenses exlude bad debt provisions.

# References

Advertising Association (1993). *The Lifestyle Pocket Book*. The Advertising Association in conjunction with NTC Publications, Henley-on-Thames.

Advertising Association (1994a). *The Marketing Pocket Book*. The Advertising Association in conjunction with NTC Publications, Henley-on-Thames.

Advertising Association (1994b). *The Regional Marketing Pocket Book*. The Advertising Association in conjunction with NTC Publications, Henley-on-Thames.

Albrecht, K. and Zemke, R. (1985). *Service America: Doing Business in the New Economy*. Dow Jones-Irwin, Homewood, Illinois.

Ansoff, I. (1965). *Corporate Strategy*, McGraw-Hill, New York.

Arora, R., Tamer Cavusgil, S. and Nevin, J.R. (1985). Evaluation of financial institutions by bank versus savings and loan customers: An analysis of factor congruency. *International Journal of Bank Marketing*, **3**(3), 47–55.

Association of British Insurers (1994). *Insurance Statistics Yearbook 1983–1993*. Association of British Insurers, London.

Babakus, E. and Boller, G.W. (1992). An empirical assessment of the SERVQUAL scale. *Journal of Business Research*, **24**, 253–268.

Baker, K. and Fletcher, R. (1987). OUTLOOK – a generalized lifestyle system. *Admap*, March, 23–28.

Baker, M.J. (1983). *Market Development*, Penguin, Harmondsworth.

Baker, M.J. (1992). *Marketing Strategy and Management*, 2nd edn. Macmillan, London.

Baker, M.J. (1993). Bank marketing – myth or reality. *International Journal of Bank Marketing*, **11**(6), 5–11.

Ballarín, E. (1986). *Commercial Banks Amid the Financial Revolution*. Ballinger, Massachusetts.

Balmer, J.M.T. and Wilkinson, A. (1991). Building societies: Change, strategy and corporate identity. *Journal of General Management*, **17**(2), 20–33.

Bank of England (1989). *The Single European Market: Survey of Financial Institutions*. Bank of England, London.

Bank of England (1993). Cross-border alliances in banking and financial services in the single market. *Quarterly Bulletin* **33**(3), August.

Bank for International Settlements (1992). *Annual Report*, BIS, Basle.

Banks, R. (1990). Money management for the mature, their needs and the services competing to meet them. *Admap*, March, 26–29.

Barksdale, H.C. and Harris, C.E. (1982). Portfolio analysis and the product life cycle. *Long Range Planning*, **15**(6), 74–83.

Barnes, P.A. (1985). UK building societies – a study of the gains from merger. *Journal of Business Finance and Accounting*, **12**(1).

Barro, R.J. and Romer, P.M. (1987). Ski-lift pricing with applications to labour and other markets, *American Economic Review*, **77**(5).

Bateson, J.E.G. (1977). Do we need service marketing. In (Eiglier, P., Langeard, E., Lovelock, C.H., Bateson, J.E.G. and Young, R.F. Marketing Consumer Services: New Insights, *Marketing Science Institute Report No. 77–115*.

Beane, T.P. and Ennis, D.M. (1987). Market segmentation: A review. *European Journal of Marketing*, **21**(5), 20–42.

Belton, E.F. (1989). The distribution war. *Canadian Insurance*, **94**(11), October, 16, 24.

Benink, H. and Llewellyn, D.T. (1995). Financial fragility: a case study of the UK and Scandinavia, in *Competitiveness of Financial Institutions and Centres in Europe*, (Fair, D. and Raymond, R. eds), Kluwer, Dordrecht.

Berry, L.L. (1980). Services marketing is different. *Business*, **30**(3), May/June, 24–29.

Berry, L.L. (1981). The employee as customer. *Journal of Retail Banking*, **3**(1), 33–40.

Berry, L.L., Parasuraman, A. and Zeithaml, V.A. (1988). The service–quality puzzle. *Business Horizons*, July–August, 35–43.

Berry, L.L., Zeithaml, V.A. and Parasuraman, A. (1985). Quality counts in services too. *Business Horizons*, **28**(3), 44–52.

Berry, L.L., Zeithaml, V.A. and Parasuraman, A. (1990). Five imperatives for improving service quality. *Sloan Management Review*, **31**(4), Summer, 29–38.

Betts, E. (1994). Understanding the financial consumer. In *Retailing of Financial Services*, (McGoldrick, P.J. and Greenland, S.) McGraw-Hill, Maidenhead.

Betts, E. and Yorke, D. (1994). Direct marketing: Its 'excesses' and 'expertness'. In *Marketing: Unity in Diversity* (J. Bell et al., eds. pp. 101–110), Proceedings of the Marketing Education Group Conference, Coleraine.

Binks, M.R. and Ennew, C.T. (1991). Bank finance to small businesses. In *Bolton Twenty Years On*. (Curran, J. ed), 40 pp.

Binks, M.R., Ennew, C.T. and Reed, G.V. (1990). The single market: Finance for small and medium-sized businesses. *International Journal of Bank Marketing*, **8**(3), 24–28.

Binks, M.R., Ennew, C.T. and Reed, G.V. (1992). Information asymmetries and the provision of finance to small firms. *International Small Business Journal*, **11**(1), 35–46.

Bitner, M.J. (1990). Evaluating service encounters: The effects of physical surroundings and employee responses. *Journal of Marketing*, **54** (2), April, 69–82.

Bitner, M.J. (1992). Servicescapes: The impact of physical surroundings on customers and employees. *Journal of Marketing*, **56**, April, 57–71.

Bitner, M.J., Booms, B.M. and Tetreault, M.S. (1990). The service encounter: Diagnosing favourable and unfavourable incidents. *Journal of Marketing*, **54**(1), 71–84.

Booms, B.H. and Bitner, M.J. (1981) Marketing strategies and organisation for service firms. In *Marketing of Services*. (Donnelly, J. and George, W.R., eds) 47–51. American Marketing Association, Chicago.

Booms, B.H. and Nyquist, J.L. (1981). Analysing the customer/firm communication component of the services marketing mix. In *The Marketing of Services*. (Donnelly, J.H. and George, W.R., eds), 172–177. AMA Proceedings, Chicago.

Booz, Allen and Hamilton (1982). *New Product Management for the 1980s*. Booz, Allen and Hamilton Inc., New York.

Bourke, K.J. (1992). Implementing a marketing action programme for AIB Group, Long Range Planning, **25**(6), 30–39.

Bowen, D.E. and Schneider, B. (1988). Services marketing and management: Implications for organizational behaviour. *Research in Organizational Behaviour*, **10**, 43–80.

Bowles, T. (1985). Does classifying people by lifestyle really help the advertiser? *Admap*, May, 36–40.

Boyd, H.W. Jr. and Walker, O.C. Jr. (1990). *Marketing Management: A Strategic Approach*, Irwin, Homewood, Illinois.

Boyd, W.L., Leonard, M. and White, C. (1994). Customer preferences for financial services: An analysis. *International Journal of Bank Marketing*, **12**(1), 9–15.

Brantley, R.L. (1989). Banking products appear to sell well in grocery stores. *Savings Institutions*, **110**(6), June, 85.

Brown, S.J. and Sibley, D.S. (1986). *The Theory of Public Utility Pricing*, Cambridge University Press, New York.

Brown, T.J., Churchill, G.A. and Peter, J.P. (1993). Improving the measurement of service quality. *Journal of Retailing*, **69**(1), Spring, 127–139.

Buck, S. (1990). Turning an old problem into a new opportunity. *Admap*, March, 20–22.

Burton, D. (1994). *Financial Services and the Consumer*. Routledge, London.

Buswell, D. (1983). Measuring the quality of in-branch customer service. *International Journal of Bank Marketing*, **1**(1), 26–41.

Carey, T.P.A. (1989). Strategy formulation by banks. *International Journal of Bank Marketing*, **7**(3).

Carmen, J.M. (1990). Consumer perceptions of service quality: An assessment of the SERVQUAL dimensions. *Journal of Retailing*, **66**(1), 33–56.

Caron, J.K. (1987). Upgrading delivery systems for success in a changing market. *Bottomline*, **4**(3), March, 27–28.

Carter, R.L. (ed.) (1990). *Personal Financial Management*. Kluwer Publishing, London.

Carter, R.L. Chiplin, B. and Lewis, M.K. (1986). *Personal Financial Markets*, Philip Allan, Oxford.

Carter, R.L. and Falush, P. (1994). *The London Insurance Market: Issues and Responses*. London Insurance and Reinsurance Market Association, London.

Carter, R.L. et al. (1989). *Insurance Industry Statistics 1990*, Croner, London.

Central Statistical Office (1988). *Social Trends*, 18. HMSO, London.

Central Statistical Office (1994a). *Family Spending*. Central Statistical Office, HMSO, London.

Central Statistical Office (1994b). *Social Trends*, 24. HMSO, London.

Chan, A.K.K. and Ma, V.S.M. (1990). Corporate banking behaviour: A survey in Hong Kong. *International Journal of Bank Marketing*, **8**(2), 25–31.

Chan, R.Y.-K. (1993). Banking services for young intellectuals. *International Journal of Bank Marketing*, **11**(5), 33–40.

Chandler, G.D., Goodrich, J.W. and White, D.E. (1984). Developing winning distribution strategies. *Bankers Magazine* (US), **167**(6), November/December, 30–40.

Channon, D.F. (1986). *Bank Strategic Management and Marketing*, John Wiley, New York.

Channon, D.F. (1988). *Global Banking Strategy*, Wiley & Sons, New York

Cheese, J. (1994). Quoted in Nicholas, R. (1994), Why are banks so bad at marketing? *Marketing*, 1 September, 15.

Chéron, E.J., McTavish, R. and Perrien, J. (1989). Segmentation of bank commercial markets. *International Journal of Bank Marketing*, **7**(6), 25–30.

Chiplin, B. (1986). Information technology and personal financial services. In (Carter et al., eds.).

Chiplin, B. and Wright, M. (1987). *The Logic of Mergers*, IEA Hobart Paper 107, London.

Choraphas, D.N. (1988). *Electronic Funds Transfer*, Butterworths, UK.

Christopher, M., Payne, A.F.T. and Ballantyne, D. (1991). *Relationship Marketing: Bring Quality, Customer Service and Marketing Together*, Butterworth-Heinemann, Oxford.

Christopher, M. and Yallop, R. (1990). Audit your customer service quality. *Physical Distribution and Logistics Management*, **9**(5), 4–9.

Churchill, G.A. Ford, N.M. and Walker, O.C. (1974). Measuring job satisfaction of industrial salesmen. *Journal of Marketing*, **11**, August, 254–260.

Churchill, G.A. Ford, N.M. and Walker, O.C. (1979). Personal characteristics of salespeople and the attractiveness of alternative rewards. *Journal of Business Research*, **7**, April, 25–49.

Clarke, P.D. Edward, P.M., Gardner, P.F. and Molyneux, P. (1988). The genesis of strategic marketing control in British retail banking. *International Journal of Bank Marketing*, **6**(2), 5-19.

Clucas, Sir K. (1992). Report on the feasibility of a new retail SRO. SIB, London.

Collins, B. and Payne, A. (1991). Internal marketing: A new perspective for HRM. *European Management Journal*, **9**(3), 261–270.

Consumers Association (1994). Bank service. *Which*, December, 14–17.

Cornish, P. and Denny, M. (1989). Demographics are dead – long live demographics. *Journal of the Market Research Society*, **31**(3), 363–373.

Cowell, D. (1984). *The Marketing of Services*. Heinemann, Oxford.

Cowen, T. and Glaiser, A. (1991). Ski-lift pricing with applications to labour and other markets: comment, *American Economic Review*, **81** (2).

Cron, W.L. (1984). Industrial salesperson development: A career stages perspective. *Journal of Marketing*, **48**, Fall, 41–52.

Czepiel, J.A., Solomon, M.R. and Surprenant, C.F. eds. (1985). *The Service Encounter: Managing Employee/Customer Interaction in Service Businesses*, Lexington Books, Lexington, Massachusetts.

Davis, E. and Smales, C. (1989). The integration of European financial services. In *1992: Myths and Realities* (Davis, E. et al., eds.), Centre for Business Strategy.

Davison, H., Watkins, T. and Wright, M. (1989). Developing new personal financial products – some evidence of the role of market research. *International Journal of Bank Marketing*, **7**(1), 8–15.

de Brentani, R. (1993). The new product process in financial services: Strategy for success. *International Journal of Bank Marketing*, **11**(3), 15–22.

Devlin, J. (1995). Technology and innovation in retail banking distribution. *International Journal of Bank Marketing*, **13** (forthcoming).

Devlin, J.F. and Ennew, C.T. (1993). Regulating the distribution of savings and investment products: Retrospect and prospect. *International Journal of Bank Marketing*, **11**(7), 3–10.

Devlin, J. Ennew, C.T. and Mirza, M. (1995). Organisational positioning in financial services retailing. *Journal of Marketing Management*, **11** (forthcoming).

Diacon, S.R. (ed.) (1990). *A Guide to Insurance Management*, Macmillan Press, London.

Diacon, S.R. and Carter, R.L. (1992). *Success in Insurance*, 3rd edn. John Murray, London.

Diacon, S.R. and Ennew, C.T. (1995). Ethical issues in insurance marketing in the UK. *European Journal of Marketing*, **29** (forthcoming).

Doherty, N.A. and Smith, C.W. (1993). Corporate insurance strategy: The case of British Petroleum. *Journal of Applied Corporate Finance*, **6**(3), 4–15.

Donnelly, J.H. (1976). Marketing intermediaries in channels of distribution for services. *Journal of Marketing*, **40**(1), 55–57.

Donnelly, J.H., Berry, L.L. and Thompson, T.W. (1985). *Marketing Financial Services*. Dow Jones-Irwin, Homewood, Illinois.

Dowling, G.R. (1993). Developing your company image into a corporate asset. *Long Range Planning*, **26**(2), 100–109.

Doyle, S.X. and Shapiro, B.P. (1980). What counts most in motivating your salesforce? *Harvard Business Review*, May–June, 133–140.

Drake, L. (1989). *The Building Society Industry in Transition*, Macmillan, London.

Draper, P. (1989). *The Investment Trust Industry*, Avebury, Aldershot.

Dyer, N. and Watkins, T. (eds.) (1988). *Insurance Marketing*, 2nd edn. Kluwer, London.

Easingwood, C. and Arnott, D. (1991). Management of financial services marketing: Issues and perceptions. *International Journal of Bank Marketing*, **9**(6), 3–12.

Edgett, S. (1993). Developing new financial services within building societies. *International Journal of Bank Marketing*, **11**(3), 35–43.

Edgett, S. and Parkinson, S. (1993). Marketing for service industries – a review. *Service Industries Journal*, **13**,(3), 19–39.

Edgett, S. and Thwaites, D. (1990). The influence of environmental change on the marketing practices of building societies. *European Journal of Marketing*, **24**(12), 35–47.

Edvardsson, B., Gustavsson, B.O. and Riddle, D.I. (1989). *An Expanded Model of the Service Encounter with Emphasis on Cultural Context*. Research Report 89:4, CTF Services Research Centre, University of Karlstad, Sweden.

Edwards, P. (1992). Foreign banks and the UK middle corporate market. *International Journal of Bank Marketing*, **10** (5), 26–31.

Edwards, P. and Turnbull, P. (1994). Finance for small and medium sized enterprises: information and the income gearing challenge. *International Journal of Bank Marketing*, **12**(6), 3–9.

Eigler, P. and Langeard, E. (1977). *A new approach to service marketing*. In *Marketing Consumer Services Report 77–115*, 31–58. (Eigler, P., Langeard, E., Lovelock, C.H., Bateson, J.E.G). Marketing Science Institute.

Elton, E.J. and Gruber, M.J. (1987). *Modern Portfolio Theory and Investment Analysis*, 3rd edn., Wiley, New York.

Engel, J.F., Blackwell, R.D. and Miniard, P.W. (1991). *Consumer Behaviour*, 6th edn. The Dryden Press, USA.

Ennew, C.T., Watkins, T. and Wright, M. (1993). *Cases in Marketing Financial Services*. Butterworth-Heinemann, Oxford.

Ennew, C.T. (1992). Consumer attitudes to independent financial advice. *International Journal of Bank Marketing*, **10**(5), 13–18.

Ennew, C.T. and Binks, M.R. (1995a). The provision of finance to small business: Does the banking relationship constrain performance. *Journal of Small Business Finance*, **5** (forthcoming).

Ennew, C.T. and Binks, M.R. (1995b). Participation in the banking relationship and the impact on perceived quality. *International Journal of Bank Marketing*, **13** (forthcoming).

Ennew, C.T., MacGregor, A. and Diacon, S. (1994). Ethical issues in the marketing of savings and investment products in the UK. *Business Ethics: A European Review*, **3**(2), 123–129.

Ennew, C.T., Watkins, T. and Wright, M. (1989). Personal financial services: marketing strategy determination. *International Journal of Bank Marketing*, **7**(5), 3–8.

Ennew, C.T., Watkins, T. and Wright, M. (1990). *Marketing Financial Services*. Heinemann, Oxford.

Ennew, C.T. and Wright, D.M. (1990a). Building societies in transition: Strategy in a new market environment. *Managerial Finance*, **16**(5), 14–25.

Ennew, C.T. and Wright, M. (1990b). Retail banks and organisational change: Evidence from the UK. *International Journal of Bank Marketing*, **8**(1), 4–9.

Ennew, C.T., Wright, M. and Thwaites, D. (1993). Strategic marketing in financial services: Retrospect and prospect. *International Journal of Bank Marketing*, **11**(6), 12–18.

Ennew, C.T., Wright, M. and Watkins, T. (1990). The new competition in financial services. *Long Range Planning*, **23**(6), 80–90.

Ennew, C.T., Wong, P. and Wright, M. (1992). Organisational structures and the boundaries of the firm: Acquisition and divestment in financial services. *Service Industries Journal*, **12**(4), 478–498.

Fama, E. (1991). Efficient capital markets: II. *Journal of Finance*, **46** (5), 1575–1618.

Faulhaber, G.R. and Panzar, J.L. (1987). *Optimal two-part tarifs with self-selection*, Bell Laboratories Economic Discussion Paper No. 74.

Faust, W.H. (1990). The branch as a retail outlet. *Bankers Magazine* (US), **173**(1), January–February, 30–35.

File, K.M. and Prince, R.A. (1991). Sociographic segmentation: The SME market and financial services. *International Journal of Bank Marketing*, **9**(3), 3–8.

File, K.M. and Prince, R.A. (1992). Emerging critical success factors in marketing to the smaller business: issues and trends from the US market. *International Journal of Bank Marketing*, **10**(5), 19–25.

*Financial Times* (1993). November, p. 1.

*Financial Times* (1994a). 26 January, p. 21.

*Financial Times* (1994b). 28 February, p. 8.

*Financial Times* (1994c). 7 July, p. 22.

*Financial Times* (1994d). 11 July, p. 8.

Firth, L.P. and Lindsay, D. (1989). *Direct Marketing in the UK Financial Services Industry*, Kingston Business School, London.

Fletcher, K. and Wright, G. (1994). Organisational strategic and technical barriers to successful implementation of database marketing. In *Marketing: Unity in Diversity* (J. Bell et al., eds.), 362–371. Proceedings of the Marketing Education Group Conference, Coleraine.

Ford, D. (1980). The development of buyer–seller relationships in industrial markets. *European Journal of Marketing*, **14**(5/6), 339–353.

Ford, D. (1990). Introduction: IMP and the interaction approach. In *Understanding Business Markets: Interaction, Relationships and Networks* (Ford, D., ed.), Academic Press, London.

Ford, N.M., Walker, O.C. and Churchill, G.A. (1985). Differences in the attractiveness of alternative rewards: Additional evidence. *Journal of Business Research*, **13**, April, 123–128.

Foxall, G.R. (1991). Consumer behaviour. In *The Marketing Book* (Baker, M.J., ed.), 2nd edn. Butterworth-Heinemann, Oxford.

Frank, R.E., Massy, W.F. and Wind, Y. (1972): *Market Segmentation*. Prentice-Hall, Englewood Cliffs, New Jersey.

Friars, E.M., Gregor, W.T. and Reid, M.L. (1985). Distribution: The new competitive weapon. *Bankers Magazine* (US), **168**(3), May/June, 45–52.

Furlong, C.B. and Brent Ritchie, J.R.B. (1986). Consumer concept testing of personal financial services. *International Journal of Bank Marketing*, **4**(1), 3–18.

Gabbott, M. and Hogg, G. (1994). Consumer behaviour and services: A review. *Journal of Marketing Management*, **10**, 311–324.

Gabrielsen, G.O.S. (1993). *An Intra-Organisational Approach Towards the Implementation of Service Quality Management in Norwegian Banking*. Unpublished MSc Thesis, Manchester School of Management.

Gavaghan, K. (1994). Quoted in Nicholas, R. (1994). Why are banks so bad at marketing? *Marketing*, 1 September, p. 15.

George, W.R. and Myers, T.A. (1981). Life underwriters' perceptions of differences in selling goods and services. *CLU Journal*, April,      pp. 44–49.

Glaister, K.W. and Thwaites, D. (1992). International collaborative agreements in the financial services sector. In *Marketing in the New Europe and Beyond* (Whitelock et al., ed.), Proceedings of the 1992 Marketing Education Group Conference.

Goodman, J.A., Marra, T. and Brigham, L. (1986). Customer service: costly nuisance or low cost profit strategy? *Journal of Retail Banking*, **8**(3), 7–16.

Greenland, S.J. (1994). The branch environment. In McGoldrick and Greenland (eds.)

Gravelle, H. (1994). Remunerating information providers: Commission versus fees in life insurance. *Journal of Risk and Insurance*, **61**, 425–457.

Gronroos, C. (1978). A service-orientated approach to marketing of services. *European Journal of Marketing*, **12**(8), 588–601.

Gronroos, C. (1981). Internal marketing – an integral part of marketing theory. In *Marketing of Services* (Donnelly, J.H. and George, W.R.,) eds., 236–238, American Marketing Association, Chicago.

Gronroos, C. (1984a). A service quality model and its marketing implications. *European Journal of Marketing*, **18**(4), 36–44.

Gronroos, C. (1984b). *Strategic Management and Marketing in the Service Sector*. Chartwell-Bratt, UK.

Gronroos, C. (1985). Internal marketing: Theory and practice. In *Services Marketing in a Changing Environment* (Bloch, T.M., Upah, G.D. and Zeithaml, V.A., eds.), pp. 41–47, American Marketing Association, Chicago.

Gronroos, C. (1987). *Developing the Service Offering – A Source of Competitive Advantage*. September, Swedish School of Economics and Business Administration, Helsinki, Finland.

Gronroos, C. (1988). Service quality: The six criteria of good perceived service quality. *Review of Business*, **9**(3), Winter, 10–13.

Gronroos, C. (1990). Relationship approach to marketing in services contexts: The marketing and organizational behaviour interface. *Journal of Business Research*, **20**, 3–11.

Guirdham, M. (1987). How to market unit trusts: A consumer behaviour model. *Marketing Intelligence and Planning*, **2**, 15–19.

Gummesson, E. and Gronroos, C. (1987). *Quality of Products and Services: A Tentative Synthesis Between Two Models*. Research Report 87:3, Services Research Centre, University of Karlstad, Sweden.

Guy, J.R.F. (1978). The performance of the British investment trust industry. *Journal of Finance*, **33**(2), 443–455.

Gwin, J.M. and Lindgren, J.H. (1982). Bank market segmentation: Methods and strategies. *Journal of Retail Banking*, **IV**(4), Winter, 8–13.

Hackman, J.R. and Oldham, G.R. (1980). *Work Redesign*. Addison-Wesley, Reading, Massachusetts.

Haiss, P.R. (1992). The twin challenges to Austrian banking: The environment and the east. *Long Range Planning*, **25**(4), 47–53.

Hakansson, H. (1982). An interaction approach. In *International Marketing and Purchasing of Industrial Goods* (Hakansson, H. ed.), John Wiley, Chichester.

Haley, R.I. (1968). Benefit segmentation: A decision-oriented research tool. *Journal of Marketing*, **32**, July, 30–35.

Hall, M.J.B. (1989). *Handbook of Banking Regulation and Supervision*, Woodhead-Faulkner, Cambridge.

Hamel, G. and Prahalad, C.K. (1991). Corporate imagination and expeditionary marketing. *Harvard Business Review*, July–August, 81–92.

Hammond, C. (1981). Running a profitable branch network. *Bankers Magazine*, **225** (July), 15–16.

Harness, D. and McKay, S. (1994). Product elimination strategies of the financial services sector. In *Marketing: Unity in Diversity* (J. Bell et al., eds.) 455–464. Proceedings of the Marketing Education Group Conference, Coleraine.

Harrison, T.S. (1994). Mapping customer segments for personal financial services. *International Journal of Bank Marketing*, **12**(8), 17–25.

Hart, C.W.L. (1988). The power of unconditional service guarantees. *Harvard Business Review*, July/August, 54–62.

Hart, C.W.L., Heskett, J.L. and Sasser, W.E. (1990). The profitable art of service recovery. *Harvard Business Review*, **90**(4), July–August, 148–156.

Hastings, B., Kiely, J. and Watkins, T. (1988). Sales force motivation using travel incentives: Some empirical evidence. *Journal of Personal Selling and Sales Management*, **8**(2), 43–51.

Hastings, G. (1984). Sponsorship works differently from advertising. *International Journal of Advertising*, **3**, 171–176.

Head, V. (1981). *Sponsorship – The Newest Marketing Skill*. Woodhead-Faulkner, Cambridge.

Heimer, C. (1985). Allocating information costs in a negotiated information order: Interorganisational constraints on decision making in Norwegian oil insurance, *Administrative Science Quarterly*, **30**, 395–417.

Higgins, B. (1977). Interest payments and demand deposits: historical evolution and the current controversy, Federal Reserve Bank of Kansas City, *Monthly Review*, July 1977, 3–11.

Hill, D.J. and Gandhi, N. (1992). Services advertising: A framework to its effectiveness. *The Journal of Services Marketing*, **6**(4), 63–76.

Hisrich, R.D. and Peters, M.P. (1974). Selecting the superior segmentation correlate. *Journal of Marketing*, **38** (July), 60–63.

HMSO (1994). *Social Trends*, 24, Central Statistical Office.

Hooley, G.J. and Mann, S.J. (1988). The adoption of marketing by financial institutions in the UK. *Service Industries Journal*, **8**(4), 488–500.

Horovitz, J. (1990). *Winning Ways: Achieving Zero Defect Service*. Productivity Press, Cambridge, Massachusetts.

Howard, J.A. and Sheth, J.N. (1969). *The Theory of Buying Behaviour*, John Wiley, New York.

Howcroft, J.B., (1992) Increased marketing orientation: UK branch networks. *International Journal of Bank Marketing*, **9**(1), 2–9.

Howcroft, J.B. and Lavis, J. (1986). A strategic perspective on delivery systems in UK retail banking. *Service Industries Journal*, **6**(2), 144–158.

Howcroft, J.B. and Lavis, J. (1987). Image in retail banking. *International Journal of Bank Marketing*, **4**(4), 3–13.

Howcroft, J.B. and Lavis, J. (1989). Pricing in retail banking. *International Journal of Bank Marketing*, **4**(4), 3–13.

Hughes, J. (1994). The financial environment. In *Retailing of Financial Services* (McGoldrick, P.J. and Greenland, S.), McGraw-Hill, Maidenhead.

Ingham, H. and Thompson, S. (1994). Wholly owned vs collaborative ventures for diversifying financial services. *Strategic Management Journal*, **15**, 325–334.

Jain, A.K., Pinson, C., and Malhotra, N.K. (1987). Customer loyalty as a construct in the marketing of bank services. *International Journal of Bank Marketing*, **5**(3), 49–72.

Jensen, M. (1991). The politics of corporate finance. *Journal of Applied Corporate Finance*, **4**, 13–33.

Johne, A. (1993). Insurance product development: Managing the changes. *International Journal of Bank Marketing*, **11**(3), 5–14.

Johne, A. and Vermaak, L. (1991). Head office involvement in financial product development. *International Journal of Bank Marketing*, **11**(3), 28–34.

Johne, A.F. and Harborne, P. (1985). How large commercial banks manage product innovation. *International Journal of Bank Marketing*, **3**(1).

Johnson, P. (1990a). Economic trends in population – last 25 years, next 10 years. *Admap*, March, 14–16.

Johnson, P. (1990b). Our ageing population – the implications for business and government. *Long Range Planning*, **23**(2), 55–62.

Johnston, R., Silvestro, R., Fitzgerald, L. and Voss, C. (1990). Developing the determinants of service quality. In *Marketing, Operations and Human Resources Insights into Services* (Langeard, E. and Eiglier, P., eds.), pp. 373–400. 1st International Research Seminar on Services Management, IAE, Aix-en-Provence.

Jones, C.S. (1985). An empirical study of the role of management accounting systems following takeover or merger. *Accounting, Organisations and Society*, **10**, 177–200.

Jones, M. and Dearsley, T. (1989). Understanding sponsorship. In *How to Increase the Efficiency of Marketing in a Changing Europe*, p. 257, Esomar, Turin.

Jones, P. (ed.) (1989). *Management in Service Industries*, Pitman Publishing, London.

Joseph, C. (1994). Quoted in Nicholas, R. (1994). Why are banks so bad at marketing? *Marketing*, 1 September, 15.

Joseph, L. and Yorke, D. (1989). Know your game plan: Market segmentation in the personal financial services sector. *Quarterly Review of Marketing*, Autumn, 8–13.

Joy, A., Kim, C. and Laroche, M. (1991). Ethnicity as a factor influencing use of financial services. *International Journal of Bank Marketing*, **9**(4), 10–16.

Kamakura, W.A., Ramaswami, S.N. and Srivastava, R.K. (1991). Applying latent trait analysis in the evaluation of prospects for cross-selling of financial services. *International Journal of Research in Marketing*, **8** 329–349.

Kaynak, E. and Yucelt, U. (1984). A cross-cultural study of credit card usage behaviours: Canadian and American credit card users contrasted. *International Journal of Bank Marketing*, **2**(2), 45–57.

Kimball, R.C. (1990). Relationship versus product in retail banking. *Journal of Retail Banking*, **12**(1), Spring, 13–25.

Kimball, R.C. and Gregor, W.T. (1989). Emerging distribution strategies in US retail banking. *Journal of Retail Banking*, **11**(4), Winter, 4–16.

Kirk, Y. (1994). Promotion and advertising. In *Retailing of Financial Services* (P.J. McGoldrick and S.J. Greenland, eds.), pp. 240–265, McGraw-Hill, Maidenhead.

Knights, D., Sturdy, A. and Morgan, G. (1994). The consumer rules: An examination of rhetoric and reality of marketing in financial services. *European Journal of Marketing*, **28**(3), 42–54.

Kotler, P. (1994). *Marketing Management: Analysis, Planning and Control*, 8th edn. Prentice-Hall, New Jersey.

Koula, S. (1992). *Service Quality and Internal Marketing in the Hellenic Bank in Cyprus*. Unpublished M.Sc. Dissertation, Manchester School of Management.

Kreitzman, L. (1994). Quantifying the 'Third Age'. *Admap*, July/August, 19–22.

Large, A. (1993). Financial services regulation: Making the two tier system work. SIB, London.

Laroche, M. and Manning, T. (1984). Consumer brand selection and categorisation processes: A study of bank choice. *International Journal of Bank Marketing*, **2**(3), 3–21.

Laroche, M., Rosenblatt, J.A. and Manning, T. (1986). Services used and factors considered important in selecting a bank: An investigation across diverse demographic segments. *International Journal of Bank Marketing*, **4**(1), 35–55.

Larsson, L. (1990). Service encounter evaluation: Different perspectives. In *Marketing, Operations and Human Resources Insights into Services*. (Langeard, E. and Eiglier, P., eds.), 426–449. 1st International Research Seminar in Service Management, IAE, Aix-en-Provence.

Lavidge, R.J. and Steiner, G.A. (1961). A model for predictive measurements of advertising effectiveness. *Journal of Marketing*, October, 61.

Leach, C. (1987). How conventional demographics distort marketing realities. *Admap*, May, 41–45.

LeBlanc, G. and Nguyen, N. (1988). Customers' perceptions of service quality in financial institutions. *International Journal of Bank Marketing*, **6**(4), 7–18.

Lehtinen, U. and Lehtinen, J.R. (1982). *Service Quality: A Study of Quality Dimensions*. Working Paper, Service Management Institute, Helsinki, Finland.

Lehtinen, U. and Lehtinen, J.R. (1991). Two approaches to service quality dimensions. *The Service Industries Journal*, **11**(3), 287–303.

Leonard, M. and Spencer, A. (1991). The importance of image as a competitive strategy: An exploratory study in commercial banks. *International Journal of Bank Marketing*, **9**(4), 25–29.

Levitt, T. (1960). Marketing myopia. *Harvard Business Review*, July/August, 26–00.

Levitt, T. (1980). Marketing success through differentiation – of anything. *Harvard Business Review*, January/February.

Lewis, A. (1949). *Overhead Costs: Some Essays in Economic Analysis*, Urwin University Books, London.

Lewis, B. and Smith, A.M. (1989). Customer care in financial service organisations. *International Journal of Bank Marketing*, **7**(5), 13–22.

Lewis, B.R. (1982a). An investigation into school savings schemes and school banks. *European Journal of Marketing*, **16**(3), 73–82.

Lewis, B.R. (1982b). Student accounts – a profitable segment? *European Journal of Marketing*, **16**(3), 63–72.

Lewis, B.R. (1982c). The personal account sector. *European Journal of Marketing*, **16**(3), 37–53.

Lewis, B.R. (1982d). Weekly, cash-paid workers: Attitudes and behaviour with regard to banks and other financial institutions. *European Journal of Marketing*, **16**(3), 92–101.

Lewis, B.R. (1989). *Customer Care in the Service Sector: The Employees' Perspective*. Financial Services Research Centre, Manchester School of Management.

Lewis, B.R. (1991). Service quality: An international comparison of bank customers' expectations and perceptions. *Journal of Marketing Management*, **7**(1), 47–62.

Lewis, B.R. (1993). Service quality measurement. *Marketing Intelligence and Planning*, **11**(4), 4–12.

Lewis, B.R. and Bingham, G.H. (1991). The youth market for financial services. *International Journal of Bank Marketing*, **9**(2), 3–11.

Lewis, B.R. and Entwistle, T.W. (1990). Managing the service encounter: A focus on the employee. *International Journal of Service Industry Management*, **1**(3), 41–52.

Lewis, B.R. and Mitchell, V.W. (1990). Defining and measuring the quality of customer service. *Marketing Intelligence and Planning*, **8**(6), 11–17.

Lewis, B.R., Orledge, J. and Mitchell, V. (1994). Service quality: Students' assessments of banks and building societies. *International Journal of Bank Marketing*, in print.

Lewis, M.K. (1986). Financial services in the US. In Carter et al. (1986).

Lewis, M.K. and Chiplin, B. (1986). Characteristics of markets for personal financial services. In *Personal Financial Markets* (Carter, R.L., Chiplin, B. and Lewis, M.K., eds.), Phillip Allan, Oxford.

Llewellyn, D.T. (1990). In *The Future of Financial Systems and Services* (Gardener, E.P.M., ed.) Macmillan Press, London.

Llewellyn, D.T. (1991). Structural Change in the British Financial Systems, in *Surveys in Monetary Economics*, (Green, C. and Llewellyn, D.T. eds), **2**, Macmillan, London.

Llewellyn, D.T. (1992), The British Financial System, in Kaufman, G, (ed), *Banking Structures in Major Countries*, Kluwer, Boston.

Llewellyn, D.T. (1995). The regulation of retail investment services, *Economic Affairs*, February.

Llewellyn, D.T. and Drake, L. (1988). A convergence of regulation, *CBSI Journal*, September.

Llewellyn, D.T. and Drake, L. (1993). Economics of bank charges for personal customers, Research Monograph No. 9, Loughborough University Banking Centre.

Llewellyn, D.T. and Holmes, M.J. (1991). In defence of mutality: A redress to an emerging conventional wisdom. *Annals of Public and Cooperative Economics*, **62**(3), 319–354.

Lovelock, C.H. (1981). Why marketing management needs to be different for services? In *The Marketing of Services* (Donnelly, J.H. and George, W.R., eds.), 5–9. AMA Proceedings, Chicago.

Lyall, K. (1983). *Investment trust companies, 1971–80*. Unpublished PhD Thesis, University of Edinburgh.

Magrath, A.J. (1986). When marketing services, 4Ps are not enough. *Business Horizons*, **29**(3), 44–50.

*Marketing* (1989). Financial marketing, Special Report, 33–41.

Marsh, J.R. (1988). *Managing Financial Services Marketing*. Pitman, London.

Marshall, D. (1993). Does sponsorship always talk the same language? In *Sponsorship Europe*, pp. 23–25, Esomar, Monte Carlo.

Martenson, R. (1985). Consumer choice selection in retail bank selection. *International Journal of Bank Marketing*, **3**(2), 64–74.

Mason, J.B. (1993). The art of service recovery. *Arthur Andersen Retailing Issues Letter*, **5**(1), January, Texas A & M University.

Matthews, H.L. and Slocum, J.W. (1969). Social class and commercial bank credit card usage. *Journal of Marketing*, **33**, January, 71–78.

Mayers, D. and Smith, C.W. (1982). On the corporate demand for insurance. *Journal of Business*, **55**(2), 281–296.

McGoldrick, P.J. and Greenland, S.J. (1994). *Retailing of Financial Services*, McGraw-Hill, Maidenhead.

McIver, C. and Naylor, G. (1986). *Marketing Financial Services*. Chartered Institute of Bankers, London.

McKechnie, S. (1992). Consumer buying behaviour in financial services: An overview. *International Journal of Bank Marketing*, **10**(5), 4–12.

McKechnie, S.A. and Ennew, C.T. (1993). Environmentalism and the banks: A stakeholder perspective. Paper presented to the 2nd SIMRU Conference, Cardiff, March.

Meenaghan, T. (1991). The role of sponsorship in the marketing communication mix. *International Journal of Advertising*, **10**, 35–47.

Meidan, A. (1983). Distribution of bank services and branch location. *International Journal of Physical Distribution and Materials Management* (UK), **13**(3), 5–17.

Meidan, A. (1984). *Bank Marketing Management*, Macmillan, London.

Meidan, A. and Moutinho, L. (1988). Bank customers' perceptions and loyalty: An attitudinal research. *European Marketing Academy Proceedings*, 472–493.

Miles, R.H. and Perreault, (1976). Organisational role conflict: Its antecedents and consequences. *Organisational Behaviour and Human Performance*, **17**, October, 19–44.

Mintel (1991). *Sponsorship*, Special Report, Mintel International Group Limited, London.

Mintel (1993a). *Corporate Image*, Special Report, Mintel International Group Limited, reported in *Marketing Business*, February 1994, 5.

Mintel (1993b). *PFI1*, Mintel International Group Limited, reported in Nicholas, R., 1994, Why are banks so bad at marketing? *Marketing*, September, 14–15.

Mitchell, J. and Wiesner, H. (1992). *Savings and Investments: Consumer Issues*, Office of Fair Trading Occasional Paper, London.

Mohammed-Salleh, A. and Easingwood, C. (1993). Why European financial institutions do not test market new consumer products. *International Journal of Bank Marketing*, **11**(3), 23–27.

Monopolies and Mergers Commission (1989). *Credit Card Services: A Report on the Supply of Credit Cards in the UK*. Cmnd 718. HMSO, London.

Morgan, G. (1993). Branch networks and insurance selling. *International Journal of Bank Marketing*, **11**(5), 27–32.

Morgan, G. (1994). Problems of integration and differentiation in the management of bancassurance. *Service Industries Journal*, **14**(2), 153–169.

Morgan, N. and Piercy, N. (1990). Marketing in financial services organisations: Policy and practice. In *Managing and Marketing Services in the 1990s*, (Teare, R., Moutinho, L. and Morgan, N., eds.), Cassell, London.

Morgan, N.A. (1991). *Marketing Professional Services*. Heinemann, Oxford.

Mottura, P. and Munari, L. (1990). Competition and competitive strategies of Italian banks. *International Journal of Bank Marketing*, **8**(3), 17–23.

Murray, K.B. (1991). A test of services marketing theory: Consumer information acquisition activities. *Journal of Marketing*, **55**, January, 10–25.

Newman, K. (1984). *Financial and Marketing Communications*. Holt Reinhardt and Winston, London.

Nicholas, R. (1994). Why are banks so bad at marketing? *Marketing*, 1 September, 14–15.

Nicholas, T. (1985). Strategic management of technology in competition in world banking. International Banking Summer School, *Institute of Bankers*.

Nicosia, F.N. (1966). *Consumer Decision Processes*. Prentice-Hall, Englewood Cliffs, New Jersey.

OECD (1989). *Competition in Banking*, OECD, Paris.

O'Shaughnessy, J. (1988). *Competitive Marketing: A Strategic Approach*. Unwin Hyman, Boston.

Office of Fair Trading (1987). *Study of Insurance Intermediaries' Costs – Report of a Survey*, London.

Office of Fair Trading (1993). *The Marketing and Sale of Investment Linked Insurance Products*. Report by the Director General of OFT to the Chancellor of the Exchequer.

Onkvist, S. and Shaw, J.J. (1989). Service marketing: Image branding and competition. *Business Horizons*, **32**(1), 13–18.

Palmer, A. (1994). *Principles of Services Marketing*. McGraw-Hill, Maidenhead.

Palmer, A. and Bejou, D. (1994). Buyer–seller relationships: A conceptual model and empirical investigation. *Journal of Marketing Management*, **10**(6), 495–512.

Parasuraman, A., Berry, L.L. and Zeithaml, V.A. (1990). Guidelines for conducting service quality research. *Marketing Research*, December, 34–44.

Parasuraman, A., Berry, L.L. and Zeithaml, V.A. (1991a). Refinement and re-assessment of the SERVQUAL scale. *Journal of Retailing*, **67**(4), Winter, 420–450.

Parasuraman, A., Berry, L.L. and Zeithaml, V.A. (1991b). Understanding customer expectations of service. *Sloan Management Review*, **32**(3), 39–48.

Parasuraman, A., Zeithaml, V.A. and Berry, L.L. (1985). A conceptual model of service quality and its implications for future research. *Journal of Marketing*, **49**, Fall, 41–50.

Parasuraman, A., Zeithaml, V.A. and Berry, L.L. (1988). SERVQUAL: A multiple item scale for measuring consumer perceptions of service quality. *Journal of Retailing*, **64**(1), Spring, 14–40.

Parasuraman, A., Zeithaml, V.A. and Berry, L.L. (1993). More on improving service quality. *Journal of Retailing*, **69**(1), 140–147.

Peattie, S. and Peattie, K. (1994). Promoting financial services with glittering prizes. *International Journal of Bank Marketing*, **12**(6), 19–29.

Personal Investment Authority (1994). *Prospectus*. PIA, London.

Piercy, N. and Giles, W. (1989). Making SWOT analysis work. *Marketing Intelligence and Planning*, **7**, 5–7.

Piercy, N. and Morgan, N.A. (1991). Internal marketing – the missing half of the marketing programme. *Long Range Planning*, **24**(2), 83–93.

Piercy, N. and Peattie, K.J. (1988). Matching marketing strategies to corporate culture: The parcel and the wall. *Journal of General Management*, **13**(4), 33–44.

Porter, M.E. (1980). *Competitive Strategy*. Free Press, New York.

Porter, M.E. (1985). *Competitive Advantage*. Free Press, New York.

Reichheld, F.F. (1993). Loyalty-based management. *Harvard Business Review*, March–April, 64–73.

Reichheld, F.F. and Sasser, W.E. (1990). Zero defections: Quality comes to services. *Harvard Business Review*, **68**(5), September/October, 105–111.

Richards, A. (1994). Insurances and Strategy Goes Astray, *Marketing*, 20 January, 18–19.

Rider, B., Abrams, C. and Ferran, E. (1989). *Guide to The Financial Services Act 1986*, CCH Editions Ltd.

Ries, A. and Trout, J. (1986). *Positioning: The Battle for Your Mind*. McGraw-Hill, New York.

Roach, C. (1989). Segmentation of the small business market on the basis of banking requirements. *International Journal of Bank Marketing*, **7**(2), 10–16.

Robbie, K. and Murray, G. (1992). Consumer behaviour and institutional strategy in a maturing market: Venture capital and buy-ins in the UK. *International Journal of Marketing* (forthcoming).

Robbie, K. and Wright, M. (1988). *Personal Financial Services*. Euromonitor, London.

Robinson, P.J. and Faris, C.W. (1967). *Industrial Buying Creative Marketing*. Allyn & Bacon, Boston.

Robson, J. (1989). Unpublished research on building society marketing strategies, Plymouth Business School.

Rothwell, M. and Jowett, P. (1988). *Rivalry in Retail Financial Services*. Macmillan, Basingstoke.

Rust, R.T. and Oliver, R.L. (1994). *Service Quality: New Directions in Theory and Practice*. Sage, California.

Sanderson, S.M. and Luffman, G.A. (1988). Strategic planning and environmental analysis. *European Journal of Marketing*, **22**(2), 14–30.

Sasser, W.E. and Arbeit, S.P. (1976). Selling jobs in the service sector. *Business Horizons*, **19**, 61–65.

Saunders, J. and Watters, R. (1993). Branding financial services. *International Journal of Bank Marketing*, **11**(6), 32–38.

Scheuing, E.E. and Johnson, E.M. (1989). New product development and management in financial institutions. *International Journal of Bank Marketing*, **7**(2), 17–22.

Schlesinger, L.A. and Heskett, J.L. (1991a). Breaking the cycle of failures in services. *Sloan Management Review*, **32**(3), Spring, 17–28.

Schlesinger, L.A. and Heskett, J.L. (1991b). The service-driven company. *Harvard Business Review*, **69**(5), September/October, 71–81.

Schnaars, S. (1991). *Marketing Strategy: A Customer Driven Approach*, Free Press, New York.

Shanklin, W.L. and Kuzma, J.R. (1992). Buying that sporting image. *Marketing Management*, Spring, 59–67.

Shapiro, B.P. and Bonoma, T.V. (1984). How to segment industrial markets. *Harvard Business Review*, May–June, 104–110.

Sheth, J.N. (1973). A model of industrial buyer behaviour. *Journal of Marketing*, **37**(4), October, 50–56.

Shostack, G.L. (1977). Breaking free from product marketing. *Journal of Marketing*, **41**(2), April, 73–80.

Shostack, G.L. (1982). How to design a service. *European Journal of Marketing*, **16**(1), 49–63.

Shostack, G.L. (1987). Service positioning through structural change. *Journal of Marketing*, **51**, 34–43.

Shultz II, C.J. and Prince, R.A. (1994). Selling financial services to the affluent. *International Journal of Bank Marketing*, **12**(3), 9–16.

Silman, R. and Poustie, R. (1994). What they eat, buy, read and watch. *Admap*, July/August, 25–28.

Silvestro, R., Fitzgerald, L., Johnson, R. and Voss, C. (1992). Towards a classification of service processes. *International Journal of Service Industry Management*, **3**(3), 62–75.

Silvestro, R. and Johnson, R. (1990). *The Determinants of Service Quality – Hygiene and Enhancing Factors*. Warwick Business School, Warwick.

Simmonds, D. (1988). Direct marketing – direct mail. In (Dyer and Watkins, eds.).

Sleight, S. (1989). *Sponsorship: What It Is and How To Use It*. McGraw-Hill, Cambridge.

Smith, A.M. (1989). Service quality: Relationships between banks and their small business clients. *International Journal of Bank Marketing*, **7**(5), 28–36.

Smith, A.M. (1990). Quality aspects of services marketing. *Marketing Intelligence and Planning*, **8**(6), 25–32.

Smith, A.M. (1992). The consumers' evaluation of service quality: Some methodological issues. In *Marketing in the New Europe and Beyond*, (J. Whitelock, ed.), 633–648. MEG, proceedings of the 1992 Annual Conference, University of Salford.

Smith, A.M. and Lewis, B.R. (1988). *Customer Care in the Service Sector: The Suppliers' Perspective*. Financial Services Research Centre, Manchester School of Management.

Smith, A.M. and Lewis, B.R. (1989). Customer care in financial service organisations. *International Journal of Bank Marketing*, **7**(5), 13–22.

Speed, R. and Smith, G. (1992). Retail financial services segmentation. *Service Industries Journal*, **12**(3), July, 368–383.

Speed, R. and Smith, G. (1993). Customers, strategy and performance. *International Journal of Bank Marketing*, **11**(5), 3–11.

Stanley, T.O., Ford, J.K. and Richards, S.K. (1985). Segmentation of bank customers by age. *International Journal of Bank Marketing*, **3**(3), 56–63.

Stevenson, B.D. (1989). *Marketing Financial Services to Corporate Clients*. Woodhead Faulkner, Cambridge.

Stevenson, B.D. and Kiely, J. (1991). Success in selling: The current challenge in retail banking. *International Journal of Bank Marketing*, **9**(2), 32–38.

Stewart, K. (1991). Corporate identity: A strategic marketing issue. *International Journal of Bank Marketing*, **9**(1), 32–39.

Stonham, P. (1994). HSBC/Midland Bank takeover, Part 1: Strategy, tactics and logic. *European Management Journal*, **12**(1), 39–48.

Storey, C.D. and Easingwood, C.J. (1993). Key factors of successful new financial services. In *Emerging Issues in Marketing* (Davies, M. et al., eds), 914–923. Proceedings of the 1993 Marketing Education Group Conference, **2**

Sturdy, A. and Morgan, G. (1993). Segmenting the market: A review of marketing trends in French retail banking. *International Journal of Bank Marketing*, **11**(7), 11–19.

Swiss Reinsurance Company (1994). World insurance in 1992: Accelerating worldwide growth. *Sigma* (3).

Teas, R.K. (1981). An empirical test of models of salespersons' job expectancy and instrumentality perceptions. *Journal of Marketing Research*, **14**, May, 209–226.

Teas, R.K., Dorsch, M.J. and McAlexander, J.H. (1988). Measuring commercial bank customers' attitudes towards the quality of the bank services marketing relationship. *Journal of Professional Services Marketing*, **4**(1), 75–95.

Thomas, D.R.E. (1978). Strategy is different in service businesses. *Harvard Business Review*, **56**, July/August, 158–165.

Thomas, M. (1980). Market segmentation. *Quarterly Review of Marketing*, **6**(1), Autumn, 25–28.

Thompson, R.S. and Wright, M. (1988). *Internal Organisation, Efficiency and Profit*. Philip Allan, Oxford.

Thurman, C. (1992). Corporate banking: Services and relationships. *International Journal of Bank Marketing*, **10**(2), 10–16.

Thwaites, D. (1989). The impact of environmental change on the evolution of the UK building societies. *Service Industries Journal*, **9**(1), 40–60.

Thwaites, D. (1991). Forces at work: The market for personal financial services. *International Journal of Bank Marketing*, **9**(6), 30–36.

Thwaites, D. (1994). Corporate sponsorship by the financial services industry. *Journal of Marketing Management* (forthcoming).

Thwaites, D. and Lee, S.C.I. (1994). Direct marketing in the financial services industry. *Journal of Marketing Management*, **10**, 377–390.

Thwaites, D. and Lynch, J.E. (1992). Adoption of the marketing concept by UK building societies. *Service Industries Journal*, **12**(4), 437–462.

Tillinghast (1993). *The Insurance Pocket Book*. In conjunction with NTC Publications, Henley-on-Thames.

Tuck, M. (1976) *How Do We Choose?* Methuen & Co. Ltd, London.

Turnbull, P.W. (1982a). The purchasing of international financial services by medium- and large-sized UK companies with European subsidiaries. *European Journal of Marketing*, **16**(3), 111–121.

Turnbull, P.W. (1982b). The role of the branch bank manager in the marketing of bank services. *European Journal of Marketing*, **16**(3), 31–36.

Turnbull, P.W. (1982c). The use of foreign banks by British companies. *European Journal of Marketing*, **16**(3), 133–145.

Turnbull, P.W. (1983). Corporate attitudes towards bank services. *International Journal of Bank Marketing*, **1**(1), 53–66.

Turnbull, P.W. (1991). Organizational Buying Behaviour. In *The Marketing Book*, 2nd edn (Baker, M.J., ed.), Butterworth-Heinemann, Oxford.

Turnbull, P.W. and Gibbs, M.L. (1987). Marketing bank services to corporate customers: The importance of relationships. *International Journal of Bank Marketing*, **5**(1), 19–26.

Turnbull, P.W. and Gibbs, M.L. (1989). The selection of banks and banking services among corporate customers in South Africa. *International Journal of Bank Marketing*, **7**(5), 36–39.

Turnbull, P.W. and Moustakatos, T. (1995). Marketing and investment banking: Practical and theoretical challenges. *International Journal of Bank Marketing*, **13** (forthcoming).

Tyagi, P.K. (1982). Perceived organisational climate and the process of salesperson motivation. *Journal of Marketing Research*, **19**, May, 240–254.

Tynan, C.A. and Drayton, J. (1987). Market segmentation. *Journal of Marketing Management*, **2**(3), 301–335.

UNIC (1994). *Insurance Company Performance 1994: A Statistical Summary of the Top 200 UK Insurers*. University of Nottingham Insurance Centre, Nottingham.

*Unit Trust Year Book* (1994). Financial Times Business Information.

Vittas, D. and Frazer, P. (1982). The Retail Banking Revolution. Lafferty, London.

Walker, O.C., Churchill, G.A. and Ford, N.M. (1977). Motivation and performance in industrial selling: Present knowledge and needed research. *Journal of Marketing Research*, **14**, May, 156–168.

Ward, K. (1989). *Financial Aspects of Marketing*, Butterworth-Heinemann, Oxford.

Watkins, T. and Wright, M. (1986). *Marketing Financial Services*. Butterworth-Heinemann, Oxford.

Watson, I. (1986). Managing the relationships with corporate clients. *International Journal of Bank Marketing*, **4**(1), 19–34.

Webster, Jr., F.E. and Wind, Y. (1972). A general model of understanding organizational buying behaviour. *Journal of Marketing*, **36**, April, 12–19.

Wells, W.D. and Gubar, G. (1966). The life cycle concept in marketing research. *Journal of Marketing Research*, **3**, November, 355–363.

Whitesell, W.C. (1992). Deposit banks and the market for payments media, *Journal of Money, Credit and Banking*, **24**(4), 483–498.

Whitmore, A. (1988). Market analysis. In (Dyer and Watkins, eds.)

Whittle, J. and Handel, W. (1987). Pricing strategies for competitive banks, *Bankers' Magazine*, October, 45–50.

Wiesner, H. and Mitchell, J. (1992). *Savings and Investments, Consumer Issues*. OFT, London.

Wilcox, R. and Rosen, D. (1988). Marketing Financial Services. In *Financial Services* (Coler, M. and Ratner, E.), New York Institute of Finance.

Wilkie, W.L. and Cohen, J.B. (1977). *An Overview of Market Segmentation: Behavioural Concepts and Research Approaches*. Working Paper, Marketing Science Institute, Cambridge, Massachusetts.

Wills, G. (1985). Dividing and conquering: Strategies for segmentation. *International Journal of Bank Marketing*, **3**(4), 36–45.

Wind, Y. (1978). Issues and advances in segmentation research. *Journal of Marketing Research*, **15**, August, 317–337.

Winer, L. and Schiff, J.S. (1980). Industrial salespeople's views on motivation. *Industrial Marketing Management*, **9**, 319–323.

Witcher, B., Craigen, J.G., Culligan, D. and Harvey, A. (1991). The links between objectives and function in organisational sponsorship. *International Journal of Advertising*, **10**, 13–33.

Worthington, S. (1986). Retailer credit cards and direct marketing – a question of synergy. *Journal of Marketing Management*, **2**(2), 125–311.

Worthington, S. (1988). Credit cards in the United Kingdom – where the power lies in the battle between the banks and the retailers. *Journal of Marketing Management*, **4**(1), 61–70.

Worthington, S. (1993). The trailblazer card. In *Cases in Marketing Financial Services*, 240–243, Butterworth-Heinemann, Oxford.

Worthington, S. (1994a). Car groups gamble on playing the right card. *The Financial Times*, 13 January, 11.

Worthington, S. (1994b). Marks and Spencer financial services – where do they go from here? In *Cases in Retail Management*, 293–300, Pitman, London.

Worthington, S. (1994c). Metal cars and plastic cards – what is the connection? In *Marketing: Unity in Diversity* (J. Bell et al., eds.) 1048–1056. Proceedings of the Marketing Education Group Conference, Coleraine.

Worthington, S. and Horne, S. (1992). Affinity credit cards in the United Kingdom – card issuer strategies and affinity group aspirations. *International Journal of Bank Marketing*, **10**(7), 3–10.

Worthington, S. and Horne, S. (1993). Charity affinity credit cards – marketing synergy for both card issuers and charities? *Journal of Marketing Management*, **9**(3), 301–313.

Wragg, D. (1992). PR for banks and building societies: Is there a difference? *CBSI Journal*, **46** (214), 18–19.

Wright, M. and Ennew, C.T. (1990). The single European market: Its impact on strategic bank marketing. *International Journal of Bank Marketing*, **8**(3), 5–10.

Yorke, D.A. (1990). Interactive perceptions of suppliers and corporate clients in the marketing of professional services: A comparison of accounting and legal services in UK, Canada and Sweden. *Journal of Marketing Management*, **5**(3), 307–323.

Yorke, D.A. and Hayes, A. (1982). Working females as a market segment for bank services. *European Journal of Marketing*, **16**(3), 14–22.

Yuspeh, S. and Fein, G. (1982). Can segments be born again? *Journal of Advertising Research*, **22**(3), June/July, 13–22.

Zeithaml, V. (1981). How consumer evaluation processes differ between goods and services. In *The Marketing of Services* (Donnelly, J.H. and George, W.R., eds.), pp. 186–190, AMA Proceedings, Chicago.

Zeithaml, V.A., Berry, L.L. and Parasuraman, A. (1988). Communication and control processes in the delivery of service quality. *Journal of Marketing*, **52**, April, 35–48.

Zeithaml, V.A., Parasuraman, A. and Berry, L.L. (1985). Problems and strategies in services marketing. *Journal of Marketing*, **49**, Spring, 33–46.

Ziff, R. (1971). Psychographics for market segmentation. *Journal of Advertising Research*, **11**(2), April, 3–9.

# Index

Abbey Life, 11
Abbey National, 212
  and Friends' Provident, 12
  plc status, 18, 264
Access, 93, 296
ACORN (A Classification of Residential
    Neighbourhoods) system, 53–4
Acquisitions, 29
Advertising:
  banks, 230
  industry specific, 116, 122–5
  off-the-page, 130–31
  SIB rules, 16–17
Affinity Credit Card, 295
Age and life cycle (market segment base) 48–50
AIB Group, 213
AIDA (Awareness, Interest, Desire, Action)
    process, 39
Alliance and Leicester BS, 264, 267
  sales promotion, 129
  status, 12
Allied Dunbar, 14
Allied Irish Banks, 340–4
  identity, 128
American Express, 294
Annualized Percentage Rate (APR), 299
Ansoffs Product/Market opportunity matrix, 77–9
Association of Futures Brokers and Dealers
    (AFBD), 7, 9
Association of Investment Trusts (AITC), 283
Automatic teller machines (ATMs), 26–7, 182–3,
    227, 228

Bank of America, credit card, 296
Bank of England, lead regulator, 5
Bank of Scotland, sales promotion, 129
Banking Act 1987, 5
Banking Directive, EU, 25
Banking services, 148–50
  costs and revenue, 150–51
  financial intermediation pricing, 151–5
  interest margin, 151–5
  pricing, 156–7
Banks:
  distribution systems, 227–30
  diversification, 218
  employees role, 234
  environmental analysis, 214–15
  growth strategies, 215

  internal analysis, 215
  marketing, 212–13, 216–17
  pricing strategy, 225–7
  product development, 217, 223–5
  promotions, 230–33
Barclaycard, 296, 303
  Ford, 301
Barclays Bank, 11, 212
  Barclayloan, 94
  sales promotion, 129
  sponsorship, 134, 135
  *see also* Barclaycard
Barings, 290
'Best advice' rules, 12–13, 288–9
  *see also* Fiduciary responsibility
'Big Bang', *see* Stock Exchange, rulebook reforms
Black Horse Life, 11
Borders Investment Managers, 357–63
Boston Consulting Group (BCG) matrix, 73–4
Bradford and Bingley BS, 263
Branch networks, 178–82
Branding, 93–4, 105–6, 224
Building societies, 56
  cinema advertising, 274
  competitive strategies, 263
  cost leadership strategy, 266
  differentiation strategy, 263–4
  focus strategy, 265
  interest rate cartel, 5
  marketing mix, 270–7
  merger options, 268–9
  press advertising, 274
  public relations, 275
  rationalization, 269–70
  TV advertising, 274
Building Societies Act 1962, 17
Building Societies Act 1986, 262
  credit cards, 153
  differentiation, 264
  market competition, 4
  plc status, 18
  range of services, 17
  review proposals, 18–19
Building Societies Commission, 17
Building Society Association, 262
Buyer–seller interface, 40, 45

Capital Movements Directive, EU, 23
Catholic BS, 83

Cheltenham and Gloucester BS, 12
    focus strategy, 265
    and Guardian BS, 29
    and Lloyds Bank, 19, 21, 29, 212, 220, 268
'Churning' practice, 13
Cinema advertising, building societies, 274
City of London, 4
Clucas, Sir Kenneth, 8, 9, 14
Clydesdale Bank, 212
Co-branded cards, 3
Co-operative Bank, ethical and environmental
        orientation, 84
Codes of Practice, 208
Collective investments, France, 334–9
Commercial Union, sales promotion, 129
Commission disclosure rules, 14–15
Commission payment schemes, 188–9
Communication process, 113–17
    alternative channels, 120
Compensation reserves, 14
Competition:
    between firms, 66
    changes in, 1, 3, 4
    from substitutes, 66
    legislation, 20–1
    monitoring, 100
    unit and investment trusts, 287
Competitive positioning/advantage, 79–83
    building society strategy, 263–70
    cost leadership, 82
    differentiation leadership, 82
    focus/nicheing, 83
Consumer buying behaviour, 39–40
    bargaining power, 65
    financial services, 41–5
    interaction model, 40–1, 44, 45
    needs, 67, 99–100
    see also Market segmentation
Consumer credit, 297–300
Core (or generic) element, 97–8
Corporate customers, 57–8, 222–3, 226
Corporate electronic banking, 229–30
Corporate identity/image, 94–5, 127–8
Corporate plan, see Marketing plan
Corporation needs, insurance, 244–6
'Corset', see Supplementary Special Deposit Scheme
Cost control, 93
Cost leadership strategy, 82
    building societies, 266–70
County Unit Trust, 11
Coutts Bank, 64
Credit Agricole, 64, 221
Credit cards, 228, 294–6
    competition, 3, 20
    current market, 297–301
    future developments, 304–5
    history, 296–7
    new entrants, 301–2

    relationship building, 302–4
    see also under specific names
Credit Lyonnais, 219
Cross subsidies, 161–3
Customer care/service, 194–5
    external, 195–7
    measurement, 199–200, 201–2
    quality dimensions, 197–8
    research findings, 202–204
    training programmes, 205, 206
Customer expectations, 199, 200, 201
Customer needs, insurance, 242
Customers:
    dissatisfied, 209–10
    external, 195–204
    internal, 204–7
    targeting, 185

Databases, construction and use, 27
Debit cards, 184, 227–8, 295
Decision-making process, 39–40
Delivery channels, see Distribution channels
Demographic segments, market, 220
Demographic trends, 33–5, 47–8
Department of Health and Social Security (DHSS),
        personal pension schemes, 23
Department of Trade and Industry (DTI), 7
Deregulation process, 4, 174
Design message, 119
Differential advantage, 81–3
Differential pricing, 13
Differentiation, 218
    building societies strategy, 263–5
Differentiation focus, 83, 218
Differentiation leadership, 82
Diners Club, 294
Direct Line, telemarketing, 186
Direct mail, 184–5
Direct regulation, 5–6
Direct response advertising, 185–6
Direct selling, 90–1, 126–7, 129–31, 186–91, 232
    banks, 230–1
    building societies, 275
Disneyworld pricing, 164–7
Distribution channels, 92, 196
    changes in, 176–8
    developments, 178
    strategic choice, 175–6
    unit trusts, 291–2
Diversification strategy, 3–4, 29–30, 79, 84
    banks, 218–20
    building societies, 266–7
Divestment strategies, 218
Dominion Insurance, 307–33

Early surrender, 13
Eastern European threats, 84
Ecology BS, 83

Efficient Market Hypothesis, 286
EFTPOB (electronic funds transfer at place of
    banking), 26
EFTPOL (electronic funds transfer at place of
    living), 26, 27
EFTPOS (electronic funds transfer at place of sale),
    26, 27, 183–4, 227–8
'Electronic purses', see Smart cards
Employees:
    bank, 234
    commitment to, 194
    and customer care, 197
    research findings, 207–8
    rewards/benefits, 206
Entry threat, 65
Environmentalism challenge, 84, 214–15
Equities, investments, 2
Estate agency networks, 29–30, 30–1, 179–80
Ethical responsibility/standards, 85
European Union, regulatory procedures, 23–5
Exchange controls, 23
Expansion process, 84
Explicit pricing, banking services, 159, 163–4
External customers, see Customers, external

Fiduciary responsibility, services, 38, 88, 141
Financial ACORN, 54
Financial Intermediaries, Managers and Brokers
    Regulatory Association (FIMBRA) 7–8
Financial intermediation, 150, 151–5
Financial Services Act, 1986 (FSA) 4–5, 17
    advertising rules, 16, 125, 130
    best advice rule, 12
    costs, 16
    disclosure rules, 14–15, 130
    independent intermediary, 1
    mis-selling practices, 12–14
    polarization rule, 11–12, 264
    recognized professional bodies, 9
Financial services firms, changing boundaries,
    27–31
FinPin geodemographic system, 53–4
First Direct:
    competitive advantage, 62, 80, 186
    consumer needs, 99
    Visa Card, 225
Fixed charge pricing, see Disneyworld pricing
Focus strategy, building societies, 265
Free banking, 162
Free trade principle, 23–5
French savings banks, 30
Friends' Provident, 12

Gender (market segment base) 51–2, 52
General Accident, sponsorship, 134
General Electric (GE) Business Screen, 73
General Motors, credit card, 301, 303
Geodemographic market segment bases, 53–4

Globalization, 25–6
Gold Credit Card, 295
Government policy and legislation, 100
'Greenfield site' outlets, 29, 30
Guarantees, see Service guarantees
Guardian BS, and Cheltenham and Gloucester BS,
    29

Halifax BS, 12
    branding, 106
    Maxim, 94
    merger proposal, 18, 29, 212, 264
    public relations, 127, 263
Hambro Countryside, 218
'Hard disclosure' rule, 15
Harmonization of standards, 25
Heterogeneity, of services, 87, 92, 98, 124
Home banking, 228–9
Hong Kong and Shanghai Banking Corporation:
    branding, 106
    electronic banking, 229–30
    First Direct Visa Card, 225
    Midland acquisition, 21, 212, 219
Household Finance Corporation (HFC) 301
Hub and spoke branching, 180–1

Implicit interest charge, 154–5
Implicit pricing, banking services, 157, 159–63
Independent financial advice/representatives,
    11–12
Information flow, two-way, 38–9
Information sources, 66–7
Information technology (IT) links, 26–7, 182–4, 197
Inseparability, of services, 38, 87, 92, 98, 124
Insurance:
    advice service, 241
    corporation needs, 244–6
    customer needs, 242
    definition, 239–40
    individual needs, 243
    investment service, 241
    market overview, 246–50
    marketing mix, 251–8
    organizational work, 241
    product life cycle, 258–61
    risk transfer role, 240
    role in financial services, 237–8
Insurance Companies Act 1982, 7
Insurance Ombudsman Bureau, 13
Intangibility, of services, 36, 38, 87, 92, 98, 103, 124
Interaction model (decision-making process) 40–1,
    44, 45
Interest-free deposits, 155
Internal customers, see Customers, internal
Internal marketing, 204
Investment banking, 233
Investment Management Regulatory Organization
    (IMRO) 6–7, 8, 10

Investment service, insurance, 241
Investment trusts, see Unit and investment trusts
Investors Compensation Scheme, 10

Joint Credit Card Company (JCCC) 296
Joint ventures, 27, 29, 30, 31

Key/satellite branch policy, 181

Lead regulator approach, 5
Leaflet inserts, 130
Leeds Permanent BS:
    focus strategy, 265
    merger proposal, 18, 29, 212, 264
    public relations, 127
    status, 12
Life assurance business, 288
Life Assurance and Unit Trust Regulatory
        Association (LAUTRO), 7
    commission agreement, 14–15
    complaints, 13
    differential pricing, 13
Life cycle, see Product life cycle
Line stretching, product, 107
Lloyds Bank, 11, 212
    advertising, 119
    and Cheltenham and Gloucester BS, 19, 21, 29,
        212, 220, 268
    and professional introducers, 345–8
Local Education Authority (LEA), grant payments,
    48
London Clearing Banks (LCBs), 174

Magazine articles, 232
Mailing lists, 185
Market analysis, 215
Market development strategy, 78
    banks, 217
Market penetration strategy, 78
    banks, 216–17
Market segmentation, 46–7
    banks, 220–2
    corporate, 57–8
    financial services usage, 56
    multivariate bases, 53–7
    personal, 47–8
    traditional univariate bases, 48–52
Market specific strategy, 71
Marketing audit, 214–15
Marketing mix, 71, 86–9
    4Ps, 86, 88
    building societies, 270–7
    insurance companies, 251–8
    people, 88–9, 90–2
    physical evidence, 93–4
    processes, 92–3
Marketing plan, 62–71
    objectives, 70

Marketing strategy, 61–2, 70–1, 78, 98–9, 216–17
    banks, 220
    challenges, 83–5
    implementing, 71–2
    techniques, 72
Marks and Spencer:
    store cards, 295
    unit trusts, 292
MasterCard, 295, 296
Maximum Commissions Agreement, 15
Merchant Service Charge (MSC), 294
Merger options, building societies, 268–9
Midland Bank, 11, 212
    branding, 94, 105
    competitive advantage, 81
    psychographic approach, 55
    take-over, 21, 212, 219
    see also First Direct
Minitel network, 229
Mis-selling practices, 13–14
Mission statement, 63–4
Mondex card, 13, 296
Monopolies and Mergers Commission (MMC):
    credit card rates, 20
    mergers, 20
    small business lending, 21
Mortgage Credit Directive, EU, 25
Mortgage product, securitized, 3
Munich Reinsurance, 364–6

National Australian Bank, 212
National and Provincial BS, 264
National Westminster Bank, 1, 212
    alternative accounts, 103
    competitive advantage, 80
    independent advice role, 11
Nationwide Anglia BS, branding, 105
Nationwide BS:
    diversification, 267
    estate agency business, 180, 218
New product development (NPD) 108–12
Nicheing strategy, 83
Non-Life Insurance Services Directive, EU, 24

Office of Fair Trading (OFT):
    commission rates ruling, 14–15
    mergers, 20
Organizational changes, 28–9
Overselling, see Mis-selling
Own Funds Directive, EU, 24

'Passport principle' 24
Pay-later cards, see Credit cards
Pay-now cards, see Debit cards
Pension transfers, 13–14
People, importance in services marketing, 88–9,
        90–2, 277
Perishability, of services, 38

Personal assets/liabilities, 2–3
Personal equity plans (PEPs) 21, 284–5
Personal Investment Authority (PIA) 6, 8, 9–11, 14
Personal pension plans, 22
Personal selling, *see* Direct selling
PEST (political, economic, social and technological) analysis, 64
Physical evidence, importance of, 93–5
Portfolio performance, 286
Positioning, *see* Competitive positioning
Pre-paid cards, 295
Press advertising, building societies, 274
Preston and Lancaster Building Society, 354–6
Price discrimination, *see* Differential pricing
Pricing process, 84, 92–3, 145–6, 163–4
    bank services, 148–57, 225–7
    building societies, 272–4
    consumer choices, 171–2
    Disneyworld style, 164–7
    insurance, 253–4
    international experience, 172
    risks, 146–7
    single transactions charge, 167
    two-part tariff, 167–71
Processes, importance of, 92–3
Product, building societies, 271–2
Product attributes, 102–6
Product development strategy, 78
    banks, 217
Product launching, 111–12
Product life cycle, 74–7
    insurance, 258–61
Product modification/development, 106–8
Product portfolio analysis, 72–7, 224
Product range strategy, 101–8, 195
Product strategy, 99–100
Product/Market opportunity matrix, 77–9
Promotion:
    budget for, 21
    building societies, 274–5
    unit and investment trusts, 282–4
Promotion mix, 117–22, 121, 245–6
Promotional activities, 116–22
    *see also under specific types of activity*
Prudential Insurance Company, 10
4Ps (product, price, promotion and place) framework, 86, 88
Psychographic market segment bases, 54–7
Public relations (PR), 127–8
    banks, 231–2
    building societies, 275

Quality standards, 84, 92, 104–5, 234

Rationalization strategy, building societies, 269–70
Recognized Investment Exchange (RIE), 8
Recognized Professional Bodies (RPBs), 5, 9
Regional Bank of Northern England, 349–53

Regulation process, 4
Regulatory changes, 3–4, 9–11
Relationship banking, 105, 154, 175, 226, 232–3
Relationship building, credit cards, 302–4
Restructuring process, 84
Retail financial services, specific characteristics, 139–45
Retraining programmes, 28
Risk transfer role, insurance, 240
Royal Bank of Scotland, sponsorship, 135–6

Sales force, 186–8
    motivation, 126–7, 190–1
    registration, 7
    remuneration, 188–90
    training and support, 126–7, 191
    *see also* Direct selling
Sales promotion, 128–9
Scottish Amicable, 119
Scottish Banks, 11
Screening process, new products, 110
Securities, unit trust, 281–2
Securities Association, The (TSA) 6, 8, 9
Securities and Futures Authority (SFA) 9, 10
Securities and Investment Board (SIB) 5–6, 7
    advertising rules, 16
    commission disclosure, 15
    differential pricing, 13
    regulations for trusts, 288
Self-Regulating Organizations (SROs) 5, 6–9
    advertising rules, 16
Self-regulation, 5, 14
Service product, 96–9
Service recovery process, 209–10
Services:
    building societies, 271–2
    delivery, 208–10
    guarantees, 208–9
    marketing characteristics, 36–8
    quality specifications, 199
SERVQUAL scales, 200, 201–2, 203
Single fixed charge pricing, *see* Disneyworld pricing
Single Market, 23–5
Single transactions charge pricing, 167
Situational analysis:
    marketing strategy, 64–70
    promotion mix, 117–18
Small and medium-sized enterprises (SMEs), 58
Smart cards, 27, 184, 227, 295
Social class and income (market segment base), 51–2
Social Security Act 1986, pension schemes, 22
Socio-economic trends, 33–5
'Soft disclosure' rule, 14
Solvency Ratio Directive, EU, 24
Sponsorship, 132–6, 231
State Earnings Related Pension Scheme (SERPS), 22

*658.809368 ME*

Stock Exchange:
    monitoring role, 8
    rulebook reforms, 4
Store cards, 3, 20, 295
STP (Segmentation, Targeting and Positioning)
    process, 70
Strategic marketing, *see* Marketing strategy
Strategic plan, *see* Marketing plan
Supplementary Special Deposit Scheme, 4
Suppliers, bargaining power, 65
SWOT (Strengths, Weaknesses, Opportunities,
    Threats) analysis, 67–70

Taxation, effect on pricing, 161
Technology, *see* Information Technology
Telemarketing, 186
Third Life Assurance Directive, EU, 24
Tied representatives, 11–12
Training programmes, 28, 205
Transparency, need for, 141
Travel and Entertainment (T & E) cards, 294
Treasury:
    Building Societies review, 19
    commission disclosure rules, 15
Trustee Savings Bank (TSB) 11, 212
    competitive advantage, 81
    mission statement, 63–4
    youth market segment, 48

TSA, *see* Securities Association, The
TV advertising, building societies, 274
Two-part tariff pricing, 167–71

Undertakings for Collective Investments in
    Transferable Securities (UCITS), 24
Unit and investment trusts, 2, 279–87
    market, 287–9
    marketing schemes, 284
    new directions, 289–93
    performance comparisons, 286–7
    product differentiation, 282–4
    profitability, 285–6
    promotion, 282–4
    regulations, 288–9
    remuneration, 285–6

Visa, 295, 296

West of England Bank, 367–77
West of England BS, focus strategy, 265
Williams' and Glyns' Bank, 212
Woolwich BS, 12

Yorkshire Bank, 212

Zoning policy, branch layout, 180